Balancing Life

A Memoir

NICHOLAS HELBURN
December 20, 1918 – June 11, 2011

Balancing Life

A Memoir

Nicholas Helburn

NICHOLAS HELBURN

with Suzanne Helburn

All that we know about those we have loved and lost
is that they would wish us to remember them
with a more intensified realization of their reality.
What is essential does not die but clarifies.
The highest tribute to the dead is not grief but gratitude.

—Thorton Wilder

Mashalla: allow God to look down and admire you

Soft eyes in indigo dye
workboots and wheelbarrow
to work, to build,
a garden for the children
to play and eat
indigo eye.
mashalla.

World walker, with a map
knows the hills, and the tongue
another nation's
rips, riches, and revolutions
inspire loving attention.
map walker.
mashalla.

Voice attune to a drum
gruff, gracious, gravel voice
a wise beat
in the symphony of reason.
instrumental voice.
mashalla.

— Dana Logan, Nick's granddaughter

*This poem was read at the Rocky Mountain Peace Center
2002 Peacemaker of the Year Award ceremony.*

PREFACE

Many of us go through our last years more or less alone, either literally alone or in the company of someone significantly younger. In either case sharing the experience of someone who has done it self-consciously or is actually doing it may be useful. Furthermore it gives me a sense of usefulness that I need (and have always needed).

Some younger people would like to know what is in store for them. While the experience is going to be different for every individual, there may be enough similarity to make it worthwhile. If not, stop reading right now and throw the book away or give it to someone else who might find it useful or give it to a second hand book store and take the cost off your income tax as a charitable gift. Uncle Sam will squander most of it on war preparations.

The most important thing is to be grateful for all the things you have been able to do, to contribute, to have had the opportunity to do. Not to grieve the loss of ability to do them now. Enjoy the previous accomplishments. Don't get depressed over your weakness now. It might have been worse.

Every thing goes slower. How much slower? Practice picking up the pace. Stop and rest if you need to. Take a "brain rest" every morning, a nap every afternoon, another brain rest whenever you feel tired.

—Nick Helburn

Contents

Introduction

Nick began his memoir at the suggestion of our friend Joan Block five years ago or so at a time when intellectually he was at loose ends, adapting to his reduced physical energy and prowess and searching for some intellectual project. He did not really work at it systematically, but he did a pretty thorough job of remembering and recording the first fifty years and some periods since. He moved from writing long hand to writing on the computer, to dictating onto a tape. In 2010, a couple months before the accident that crippled him, Liz McCutcheon started to help Nick finish the project and they continued working together in the fall of 2010. He recorded on tape with her help. At some point that fall Liz and Nick realized diminishing returns had set in, and they finished through a series of questions and answers that Liz calls his legacy.

I'm so grateful to have Part I of this memoir covering the time when I did not know Nick except through the stories he told of his early life. (I now know more about this period, because I finally went through the voluminous correspondence he preserved from those early years. Unfortunately, I don't think that Nick took advantage of them, so his memoir is mainly from memory—actually, quite a good memory.) But we lived together for another forty-three years and I want some written record of those years. Fortunately, Nick wrote beautifully and was a letter writer extraordinaire. He came from a family of letter writers. He wrote to his father sporadically until Willard died in 1950 and continuously to his Mother for the whole of her long life. I also have Nick's and my letters during our courtship that tell a quite powerful story. Finally, his writings about politics, ethics, peace, geography reveal a lot about his concerns and passions.

In Part I of this volume Nick speaks mainly in a formal voice, sometimes verging on the academic. It is him remembering his past. He doesn't pay much attention to the deeply personal. While he writes in detail about certain important events and about his career, there is less about his private life, and even less about emotions, passions, ideals.

In Part II I fill in some holes in the memoir to tell more of Nick's last forty-three years of life after I entered it. Luckily, this was possible because I have Nick's letters and essays written at the time; some are newsy and playful, often they are revealingly self reflective. They describe daily life while he was living it, causes that he championed, ideals that he tried to live by, poetry he wrote. Through them we hear Nick as we remember him, expressing his thoughts, feelings, and aesthetics in the voice we remember. I provide background and context, sometimes try to answer for myself questions I wish I had asked him. Since this is Nick's memoir I mainly confine my role to filling in aspects of his (our) life that Nick wrote about at the time. I do include one section on his earlier life related to parental influences, because they are so revealing yet seem to have remained a concern to Nick himself, even at the end of his life.

Part III gives a bit more chronology. Nick wrote our annual letters to friends and many of these are charmingly Nick. They also give some sense of our life together over time. Fortunately or unfortunately, depending on your patience, they don't cover every year by any means. One of the constants in Nick's life as an adult, and one I shared, was over commitment. Living a high-intensity life meant that Nick didn't get around to the annual letters every year. One plus in including these letters is Nick's descriptions of some of our more memorable trips. We loved traveling together; we were all alone, for one thing, but also, they gave vent to Nick's imagination and love of place.

The appendices include some of Nick's writing that add to this portrait. For instance, in Part I Nick's comments on our experience living in community on Nelson Road are mainly philosophic, so the appendix on the community gives more detail based on his earlier writing. "The Wildness Continuum" appeared in *The Professional Geographer* and is an original contribution to thinking about planning. "Second Thoughts" includes a series of three minute broadcasts on KGNU where Nick thinks out loud about important political and ethical themes. In the two essays included Nick offers some history and insight that still seem relevant today. Don't miss his poetry; I'm sure he wrote much more, but this is all I could find.

— Suzanne Helburn

PART I

MEMOIR

Margaret and Willard Helburn with Nick in 1919
Photograph by Clarence White

Family Background

Father And His Family

My father's family came from southern Germany, established themselves in New York City, and was in the leather business. There was restricted employment for Jews in Germany, and one opportunity was to go from farm to farm collecting the hides of animals that had died and then processing the hides. That was no longer the case, but the tradition of being in the leather business was in the family, so it was quite natural that Grandpa Helburn would be qualified to start a leather business.

By the time I was conscious, my father had taken over and formed the Helburn Thompson Company. It might still exist, but probably not. The tannery business has quite a bit of turnover, and there are more than enough factories to satisfy the demand. In the middle of the Depression, my father left the Helburn Thompson Company and started his own business as Willard Helburn, Inc. He had a good deal of expertise in the buying of sheepskins, so he could take advantage of that. He established a successful business. By that time, the family had already been in Massachusetts for quite a while.

Grandpa Helburn's brother Hugo got into the chemical business in New York. He operated alone, and it was not a very large business, but one which provided a handsome life for him and his wife and their daughter. They were rather isolated from me, or at least I never got to know them well. My most vivid memory is of a trip to downtown New York from the Bronx, I with Uncle Hugo's chauffeur driving the Cadillac. I don't know how many of the family were in the back of the Cadillac, but certainly Uncle Hugo and his wife. It was a proper limousine with fold-down seats in the middle. The chauffeur drove very professionally. Everybody else was talking. I was about fourteen, so I was observant of the fact that the chauffer could follow the lights for so long and then turn and take advantage of the side street in order to catch the lights on the other avenue.

It was my grandfather and his parental family that moved from Germany to New York City, and somewhere in his maturity my father moved to Massachusetts. I don't know whether my grandfather established a separate residence or not, but my grandfather lived with us for quite a while and was a steady influence in the family. I don't know that my grandmother had ever had any roots in New England. She was apparently a very able woman and a leading intellectual of the time. She died before I was born.

We have a portrait of my grandfather in the hall. He was reasonably plump in stature, very quiet and reserved, and was never a real companion. He never played with us; he was beyond that. He wore a shirt with a well-starched collar that was tipped up at the ends, and my image of him is in a wing-backed chair sitting diagonally next to the fireplace, enjoying the warmth. He didn't come down for breakfast, but he was with us for lunch and dinner. I don't know how much he added to the conversation, because at that period, I was still fairly young and not particularly conscious of adult conversation.

By the time I knew him, he was quite a reserved old man. In my image of him, he's dressed in quite proper morning clothes. I don't know which meaning of mo(u)rning to use. He wore almost exactly the same clothes that you would wear to a funeral. He never made a scene about missing his wife. Evidently, he did very deeply and quite honestly, but he didn't bring it out in family affairs.

I suppose I was in my teens when he passed away. I had no emotional attachment. There was not a period of mourning for me. In fact, I don't remember any period of mourning by anybody. But he had had a full-time nurse for maybe a year as he got older and was less able to differentiate approved behavior from disapproved. There were a few instances, for example, of coming on to the nurse.

My father's first name was Julian, but he had it changed formally to just his middle name Willard Helburn. That's the way he was known in my memory. Julian was associated with being Jewish, and while my father was not really erasing that connection, he was erasing the obvious part of it. Willard Helburn was more acceptable.

My father's sister, Theresa Helburn, was a prominent person in the theater business. She became a producer, and with Lawrence and Armina Langner, started the Theater Guild. Members subscribed to the season and took their chances on what the Guild produced, mostly avant garde. The business was not very profitable in the twenties, but with the success of *Oklahoma!*, my aunt could blossom out and do things and became better known. She became fairly well off financially as a result. She was married to Oliver Opdycke.

Father's education was not unusual except it was top of the line. He went to Harvard and did well there. He graduated cum laude. He had a very wide-ranging vocabulary, and he never gave up using it.

He did not want to go into the leather business. He expected to be a journalist. He got a job as a reporter and submitted daily accounts. I don't know which newspaper he worked on, but it was just at the time of the San Francisco earthquake, and he reported on that first hand. Apparently all the landscapes he reported on made an impression on him. I think he particularly loved the dry interior of Washington and Oregon. He was well traveled by the time he settled into his career. I think he did well in the newspaper business, but he didn't last long.

He didn't stay in journalism because his father talked him out of it. It was quite common for a young man to go into his father's business. Father followed the path of least resistance. There must have been some disagreement, but it may have been rather hidden because, in general, Father was quite respectful. There's something that makes me hesitant about calling him dutiful, but that was the case. He was apparently in sympathy with adopting his parents' values. I can't say that with any certainty, and it may have been difficult for him.

I think he regretted it. He was always interested in the linguistic meanings of a word. That would have been a characteristic. He loved the more erudite companionship of journalists.

I think father did well in the leather industry. In his last years, he went to New Zealand to buy skins. They had a monthly auction, and it was better to represent a single firm than to represent buyers for multiple customers. He also gave the sheep farmers advice, advice that they were happy to follow. He must have earned their respect in some way, how I'm not sure. It may have been just that he understood the business and could encourage them in keeping their sheepskins of good quality. New Zealand had the best quality sheep skins on the market. They had a different population of insects so there was a different set of wounds that stood out in the tanning process. Father took advantage of that in respect to where the hides came from.

My father was thoughtful and a cultured adult, so no one questioned his sincerity, even my brother Peter who was always questioning authority whenever he could.

Mother And Her Family

My mother's parents were long-time New Englanders. The origins are lost in the archives somewhere. Frank Mason—Mason was my mother's maiden name—was a banker by the time I knew him. He was pretty well accepted in middle and upper class Boston society. He was an outdoorsman and helped to establish the Appalachian Mountain Club in New England. What part he played in the Mountain Club, I don't know, but I know he developed the summer camp known as the Cold River Camp in New Hampshire at Evans Notch. We as a family went up there occasionally in the summertime. He also founded the first Boy's Club, which grew into quite a movement, emphasizing healthy use of leisure time for disadvantaged youth.

My grandfather lived in New England, mostly in Salem and Marblehead. In a later period, he lived in Charlestown, in suburban Boston.

I don't know whether Charlestown is a suburb or not, but if it is, it was an inner suburb. The early part of his life I don't have any image of, but when we came along, he was already retired. As a vice president of the Shawmut National Bank, I suppose he did what vice presidents do. His wife was a second wife. His first wife, my grandmother, had died much earlier. My mother was very close to her mother, and apparently Grandmother Mason was quite a personality, an intellectual. The second wife was less distinguished. She came into the family when my mother was twelve or thirteen. My mother (Margaret Helburn) had a younger sister, Dorothy, who was ten years her junior. After their mother died, for a year or two my mother did the female part of the family and took care of her sister. She very much resented the stepmother, so we were never very close to her.

As a competent young girl and presumably energetic, Margaret was a substitute mother for Dorothy. The father didn't take up that role very well, so Margaret stepped into it. This must have generated a sense of "this is my family." She was, I want to say miffed, but it was a more profound sense than that, at having the maternal role taken away from her. She must have been fairly headstrong and difficult to deal with. I don't remember any specific stories about that.

We didn't live with this grandfather, but we saw quite a bit of him. My parents were active in the Appalachian Mountain Club, and while he was already retired from that, he had been prominent in the club. He was a fairly stiff figure in my memory. I never saw him in a relaxed way. For instance, we never went camping with him. We did go to the Cold River camp, but only a few times while we were pretty young. Most of our exposure to the mountains came after Frank Mason was already too old to enjoy that kind of thing.

He, and presumably his first wife, certainly raised their older daughter with a fair amount of independence and nonconformity to the modes of middle class Boston. I would differentiate between his daughter Margaret, my mother, and his second daughter Dorothy. Dorothy was much more a good Bostonian. She married a man named Carl Fuller, and they had a very proper household in Belmont. We would occasionally go to dinner there. So we knew the Fuller family and we got along well, but there was no intimacy. The daughters had the same mother, but Dorothy was only two when their mother died, so she was much more influenced by the stepmother. My mother was presumably an independent spirit, even at twelve when Grandpa Mason remarried, and lived on the fringes of polite society with little respect for the normal modes of that group of fairly rigid Bostonians. She did, however, maintain some of the snobbery.

My mother came from a long line of New England people without any Jewish admixture, quite independent of the Jewish, or of any, religious mode. She would take us to a Christian Easter ceremony occasionally because there were nice slides and we could observe these illustrations of

Biblical life. That was the extent of our religious training. Religious holidays were not celebrated in any way by us. It was a decidedly secular upbringing. Father classified himself as an atheist. Mother would be thought of as an agnostic.

Mother went to Simmons College, which was a women's college. I don't know what her major was, but she finished the four years and was awarded a degree. A woman finishing a four-year degree was unusual in those days. Mother wasn't a person to be proud of it, but she undoubtedly was. I'm not sure of the sequence but I think Mother did work before she was married. She knew how to drive and chauffeured the Filene family around (of the Filenes Department Store). I suppose she enjoyed the second look people gave when they saw a female driving. I don't know if she wore a uniform or not.

My mother's nickname as a grandmother was Guppy, a corruption of Mother or Grandmother. I don't know how you get from Margaret to Guppy, but that's the way corruptions grow.

Mother And Father Together

I suppose Mother was in her middle twenties when my parents married, and Father was five years older. He was already part of the Helburn Thompson Company at that point. My parents probably met on an Appalachian Mountain Club activity, but I'm not absolutely sure of that. The mountain experience was important in their life. For instance, Father planned their honeymoon as a surprise. It started with two one-way tickets to Lowell, at which point he ran off to buy tickets to Manchester, New Hampshire. He bought tickets to successive towns ending up in North Conway, where they stayed at the equivalent of a bed and breakfast and spent their honeymoon skiing and snowshoeing.

Margaret and Willard reflected their passion for mountaineering to us children. We were introduced to rock climbing and camping quite early. We had a different approach to holidays: camping trips. Father made fun of cooking half of the day and recovering from eating the other half.

The Bemis Crew was a group of at least half a dozen men and women, a sub-set of the Appalachian Mountain Club. My parents were part of the Bemis Crew. It was an informal group. They never had a membership or anything like that. I have no idea about where the name came from. It wasn't common in those days to dress like men and go off in male recreation. Apparently, Mother didn't mind the uniqueness, and probably enjoyed it.

I don't know how long my parents were free of children and just a duo. My older brother Steven was four years older than I, so he was born in 1914. He was a very able guy. The second child was Peter. He established his place in the family as a dissident, as a person who did not relate easily to middle class Bostonian manners. I was the third child, and I was the accommodating child. Much later I ran across a box of condolence letters that my mother had received from friends, because clearly Mother had hoped for a girl at that time and she got another boy. It was a very sad occasion in the sense that she really wanted a girl. The girl came when Peg was born two years later. She was named Margaret and known as Peggy in the family circles.

I should add at this point that Mother, in the process of childbirth, lost part of her hearing at my birth and another increment of deafness occurred when Peg was born. All of our memories were of Mother using a hearing aid and having a problem with deafness. She never completely lost her hearing, except for the last few months of her life, but it was a nuisance that she had to rely upon the hearing aid. She mastered the skill of lip reading.

Brother Peter and Nick at Carlisle, the family retreat outside of Cambridge
Photograph by Clarence White

CHILDHOOD

The story begins with me in my crib. I was left there with the kerosene lamp slightly maladjusted so that it had too high a flame and caused a serious case of pollution. It put soot to the whole room, including onto baby Nicholas. The soot was apparently not damaging, so it was just a case of considerable effort to clean up the room and make it all respectable again. It was apparently a very vivid incident for those conscious of it, those who were able to tell the story again and again to the children.

The place was Salem, Massachusetts. We started out there, but I have no memories of Salem as a place where we lived. There was a major fire in Salem that burned a good deal of the city, including our house.* I don't know how much, but enough that it made the national press as the "Salem fire." This was a major disaster for Salem and wiped out a good fraction of the history that was preserved in individual houses. I don't know that the museum was affected. Much of the early clipper ship history of Massachusetts was associated with Salem rather than Boston. We have a few antiques from that period, but not many, and most of it was accumulated later. My parents said that the fire was a real boon to their marriage because the impedimenta, as it's known in Roman history—the accumulated baggage of previous generations—was wiped out and they could start fresh.

I was not privy to the discussions that occurred then, but I understand the family moved to Cambridge as a result of the fire and set up a new household there. The choice to settle in Cambridge rather than Salem was a decision by the family to move to a city that had an unusual school. I do not know that Salem schools were particularly bad, but it was unusual for a family to be located a long way from the father's work place, which was in Peabody, close to Salem. In our case, my parents didn't move the work place, because Father's work was in Peabody and Salem, and many other people were involved. The choice to live near the school reflects something of the values that the family had. Father went through a rather difficult period of commuting, for there were no real through routes from anywhere to anywhere at that time.

---

*There was a large fire in Salem in 1914, but that was before Nick was born. It is possible that the family memory has combined this large fire with one that destroyed the family home when Nick was a baby. –Editor

I was the third child, and so I just fit in and took things as they came, without much emotion. Peter was always on the outs with my parents and always objecting to the manners of the middle class. Steve was always accepting and excelling in what was expected of him. Peg was the baby of the family and was the darling of the parents. She had to conform like the rest of us did, but she was able to bear it without shame or restraint. It was a funny sort of relationship. Funny in the sense that she could break off whatever it was and change the mood. Her relationship to the parents was quite different than the three boys, or at least it seemed so to us. We didn't want to interfere, but likewise we couldn't use the same tricks to maintain a relationship with our parents.

We had a couple working for us for almost as long as I can remember. Tom and Kisti Johnson were established as the butler and cook of the household, and were very much family friends. Even after my folks could not afford the luxury of having Tom and Kisti always there, we still saw a lot of them. They became part of the household of the Marshalls, who lived across the street. He was President of the Polaroid Corporation. We continued to be friends with Tom and Kisti after they left our employ. Aunt Dorothy was married to Carlton Fuller, the Polaroid treasurer. During the Depression, my brother Peter went up and spent a couple of summers in New Hampshire on the chicken farm that Tom established while still working for the Marshalls.

My father was fairly reserved and had a life that included the family, but included a lot of other relationships as well. Margaret and Willard had agreed on an open marriage. It had quite an influence on us. I think that monogamy was not part of what we were instructed in or what we thought was proper. Father's relationship with other females was a subject of some dining room humor, but never intruded on the family itself. My parents were very loyal to each other, even though they did not disapprove of outside relationships. Some of it was associated with the mountain trips, and we knew a few of the people that Mother must have had affairs with, but we didn't associate it with any intimacy. I didn't realize how different it was until several years after I was married when I found that I was expected to be monogamous.

Mother was a considerable innovator and spent at least two summers climbing in the Alps that I can remember, and she probably spent more before I was born. It was not customary for women to do much climbing, but she and Miriam Underhill took great pleasure in climbing and doing a lot of things that were not considered ladylike by the people who could afford to take the summer off.

She would boast to her male friends or family that she climbed Mont Blanc under circumstances that they could not reproduce. It turns out that she was pregnant with Peg when she climbed Mont Blanc. She had quite a long relationship with the guide, of whom she was fairly fond. Father didn't go abroad; he stayed with the responsibilities of the leather business. For some of the trips he was along, but there were a number of them where he was not. We have a photograph of Mother and her guide in their mountain clothes from Chamonix. She kept that on her bureau or her desk until the time she died. It must have brought up memories that she felt very close to.

On those trips, she took the children with her, at least me and Peter. There was a summer camp we went to later, but in my infancy I was turned over to a nurse maid most of the time who took care of me while Mother was on the mountain. It turned out that I was ready for language and learned the language of the nursemaid, which was French. I spoke French and understood French before I understood English. The knowledge soon faded, and I learned English as we got back to Cambridge and took up residence with other English-speaking people.

One of the things that stands out in the myths of the family is one time when Mother came back from climbing the Alps and was lecturing to the Women's Club of Boston. She arranged for me to do a *cour de rappel* down two spiral flights with the rope wrapped around the top pillars that supported the banisters. I was dressed in the proper mountaineering clothing and illustrated the *cour de rappel*, the independent descent from the top of whatever you were climbing. I remember it more from the stories about it than the actual experience.

Our house at 38 Francis Avenue (right across from the Harvard Theological School) looked like a square box with a rounded roof. There was nothing fancy about it. It had seven bedrooms. We boys occupied the third floor along with a live-in Harvard student. I didn't have a room of my own until well along. I shared a room with my oldest brother. He got me to put on the "wrong" socks every time I put my shoes on. I got used to that and built it into the time it took to get dressed since I had to change my socks after putting on my shoes.

My closet was my favorite place, because it was mine. My brothers and sisters could not get in there. I would go in and hide often. There were lots of things to hide in back of.

My siblings and I got along fairly well. In the course of rough-housing, we divided up into teams, with Steve and me as one team and Peter and Peggy as the opposing team in pillow fights and so on. There wasn't any active enmity, but that pairing up was a significant part of the childhood experience. Steve was not quite as big as Peter, and in high school Peter learned blacksmithing skills and was more of a hunk than Steve. Steve was the natural athlete in the family, and until he got polio at seventeen, he was very active.

The piano was an important instrument in the house. Father played very easily. He could take a tune and make up an accompaniment for it. We all took music lessons, and none of us used the ability to play as adults. I took lessons because I had to. I took piano lessons for two years and violin lessons for another five years. The violin lessons came to naught also. I think a lot of upper middle class kids took piano lessons and didn't follow the education with performance.

Our favorite thing was our pile of blocks. These were real blocks, not toy blocks. They were made of Norway pine, the same stuff that builders use. We had quite a few blocks. There were pieces of steel pipe that went through each block, so we could put several pieces of block on one pipe. We built forts. We could build anything. We didn't have to worry about reproducing any strange shapes. The blocks were all rectangular and all easily stored. The smell of Norway pine always takes me back to childhood. It may not be accessible to you, but it was powerful for us. The blocks were part of my parents' efforts to create a rich environment for us. They wanted us to play games that simulated reality.

The most favorite game was a hide-and-seek game. The house was great for playing hide-and-seek. It could take quite a long time because we did it all over the house. In a space that large, you could hide quite a bit. It was lots of fun. The hiding place I got the most fun out of was the attic. No one thought about the attic. Pretty much you could account for space in a hall, because there it was.

We liked to collect lots of things. Four-leaf clovers were the favorite thing. We preserved them on white paper, maybe with lines. We had a place for almost everything. We had to think hard to find an item that was not collectible by us.

Charles Lindbergh, of course, was the hero of the day. He was my hero too. He fit the image of a hero without any question. A hero should be ten feet tall. I must have had other heroes. They were all rulers of one kind or another. When you pick a hero, you pick somebody with quite an entourage.

When I was young, I enjoyed organized sports. I participated in football and baseball and soccer. I came up through grade school with a very conventional sport experience, except the school added more things to it, such as second-grade Olympic games.

My favorite book was a thick account of the Spanish and Portuguese explorers. This was during my explorer stage. I paid quite a bit of attention to that. I was fascinated with Cortez at one stage. I don't know why it was him. Why should one stand out from another? They were all military figures. As an adult, I look back on it as some wasted time. We didn't identify that they were killing off the population of South America, and we wouldn't have been admiring of them if we had known.

Birthdays were usually celebrated with a party. That meant at least four parties a year, five if we had a tutor staying there. The day before a birthday we tried to collect the blocks to tidy up. Everybody at that time would have chicken and peas and mashed potatoes. I said, "Do we have to have that?" Mother said, "No, you can have anything you want." So I said, "I'd like to have halibut with egg sauce and cut up fruit." That was pretty radical.

We enjoyed Christmas very much and put a fair amount of energy into it, both in making our own Christmas holiday fun and in activities for making the group experience good. My parents had quite a bit to do with that and allowed us a good deal of freedom. They also gave some stimulus to making it a constructive experience. Christmas was something we really looked forward to. Getting something for nothing was part of it.

Listening to the radio was not an active thing with the family the way it was in other families. We went to movies, but it was not the regular Saturday afternoon experience that some youngsters describe. We certainly knew what was showing and had favorite actresses and actors. My favorite actor was Clark Gable, and my favorite actress was Myrna Loy.

I don't remember what I wanted to be. I suppose I went through the usual ambitions of fireman, postman, etc. Those don't seem to be particularly familiar looking back. By the time I was about eighteen, I knew I didn't want to work in the leather business. My exposure to the leather business was gradual over three successive summers. It took me awhile to pick up the drudgery of day after day in the same role, but I eventually learned. I think my work was carefully designed so I would pick up the negative. My father didn't like what he was doing, and he didn't want me to do it either.

We went through some tough times during the Depression when Father started the new business. The firm was not doing well, and Father felt that there were entirely too many uncles and cousins on the Thompson side to resurrect it. He broke off in a dispute over the relatives, and it was a fairly difficult time. We children were protected from the difficulties, but Father borrowed money from relatives to establish the new company. My aunt Theresa Helburn had some cash by then that could be used in that direction.

We lived in Cambridge, in a very established neighborhood. Our granddaughter, Dana, went to Harvard Divinity School and was surprised that the family's household had been just across the street on Francis Avenue. Compared to our modest middle class existence, it was fancy. The house was and still is pretty close to the Somerville boundary. Part of my early childhood experience was protecting us or our belongings from the tough guys in Somerville. Somerville must have changed a good deal, but in those days it was a real slum.

We had a sign on the bicycle shed saying, "High Explosives." Fights with gangs were real and often enough that we were conscious of them. Not every month, but two or three times a year, I would get involved. I had a grade-school girlfriend that lived up the street, and when I went to visit her I had clean and proper clothes on, but occasionally they would get roughed up by the gang. I soon learned to insist on it being a one-to-one relationship that we fought it out rather than taking on the whole group. They recognized this as a fair operation also. I certainly didn't want to do it. I wouldn't have initiated it, but when forced to, I rose to the occasion.

That house was sold somewhere in the bottom of the Depression, and we moved to an apartment in Cambridge on the other side of Harvard Square, on the proper side. My folks had a housewarming for the flat, the invitation of which was on a postcard saying, "We fix flats." It turned out that most people threw the invitation away without reading it, so not very many people came to that housewarming. That's the kind of thing that my parents were fairly famous for.

Despite moving to a smaller place, I don't think there were more than a few months that we didn't have a maid of some kind to take care of the drudgery of the housework. My mother started a flower business. She and Father surveyed the businesses that she might have established, and the flower business was an obvious one where there was a lot of overhead associated with the need to have enough flowers at the end of Saturday to still provide a choice to the last customer despite the fact the flowers were fading by the time the weekend finished and the florist restocked. Mother started a florist subscription service called The Flower Club. She went into the flower market very early in the morning and bought a little of this and a little of that, depending on what was a good buy. If some things were a glut on the market, she would then concentrate on those. She had a group of customers, "subscribers," who had joined the club. They paid 75 cents a week to have flowers delivered or $1.50 for two deliveries a week. Mother mixed up a bouquet of flowers, which were not available in the grocery store at that time the way they are now, and delivered them.

Mother's business made enough income to pay for somebody to do the cleaning and some of the cooking. Mother escaped the drudgery of housework by this procedure and provided employment for me when I had my driver's license. Mostly the job gave me the use of the car for a date after it was no longer needed in the delivery process. There was a freedom and an ability to call on my girlfriend at a time in a teenager's life when driving makes a major difference.

I did notice the Depression in a visual way. When I was about sixteen, I wanted to get a job for the summer, but jobs were not abundant, especially for an inexperienced youngster. Peter by that time had established enough relationships with the lower classes to be conscious of the union movement, and he oriented me to it in terms of not taking a strike-breaking job.

Peter finished his high school education at Rindge Technical High School and had learned wrought iron work. He worked in that for a while. He didn't ever go to college, which was something of an apostasy as far as the family was concerned. In the process of learning iron work, he developed a specialty in safecracking tools, so he had an association that was entirely independent of the family for a while there. He continued to live at home until he finished high school, but work with these customers was not recognized in the family, certainly not publicized. I don't know that he ever got close enough to safecracking to be in danger of being arrested. He would more likely be arrested for his union activities. He was a loyal union member. He gradually separated himself from the middle class family in the process of finishing high school and not going to college. His first job was in the ornamental iron business, and we still have a couple of the results of that period. He was a very imaginative artist and did some beautiful things. Gradually the family got together with him and he did things for the family, but he was never with the family much.

Most of the recreation that I remember was outdoors, like mountain climbing. We were introduced to rock climbing pretty young because just north of metropolitan Boston is a field of glacial erratics. There you can get all of the skills of rock climbing without getting very far off the ground. We were introduced to that very well.

As we matured the family developed a pattern of spending the summer either in an ocean side resort or up in the mountains. We never went to a resort as usually defined, but rented a cottage in the location which was chosen. I remember when we got older; there was some discussion of where we should spend the summer, so the children were somewhat in on the decision even if they did not cast the deciding vote. The location on the ocean was a place called Barn House on Martha's Vineyard. We didn't spend all the summers at Barn House, but every other summer we went there.

An ocean vacation place was the site of my earliest memories. We did not have a location at Barn House, but chose a spot on the mainland side of Cape Cod, probably Hyannis. The driveway had been added to the house very recently and had not really packed down. The car was parked in the driveway as usual. I was interested in cars and hoping to drive, so I got in the car when I was not being watched closely and sat in the driver's seat turning the steering wheel one direction and the other. It must have loosened the gravel somehow, and pretty soon I had turned it enough so that the car slid twenty feet down the embankment and came to rest against the trees with me still in it. I was found, the car was righted, and I never drove again until under supervision at probably age fifteen. I got my license on my sixteenth birthday and was suddenly a free-ranging teenager instead of being confined to my bicycle. The early car incident was dramatic enough so that it was fixed deep into my memory although I was only four years old.

The most common early memories occurred in summertime vacation periods at Barn House. Barn House was a cooperative summer facility, with fifteen cottages. When we went, we occupied three cottages. There was a common barn owned by the whole group, and we had meals together, so it was a kind of commune in the sense that everybody had a common work program and the common space. Usually a cook was hired for the summer, and we would share meals and clean up.

There was always a place to relax with a book. There were group migrations to the beach, which was maybe a quarter of a mile away through a grassy pasture and some brush, and past a little space behind the dunes. We had to be careful of the poison ivy, but otherwise it was relatively free of hazards. It was a nice long beach, with good-sized waves of three or four feet. The waves would break toward the shore, and then run out. There was not very good swimming, unless you were a really good swimmer. You could not go out beyond the surf, but it was a wonderful place to enjoy the waves and to build castles on the wet part of the beach. You would leave them, and they would be gone by the time you came back again.

The routine at this camp was to go down to the beach. The march with the family on the trail brought us to the edge of a high cliff with constructed wooden steps leading down to the beach itself. We learned to do some body surfing there. We would get out where the waves broke and stay on the front of the wave and ride it out until we came to a stop. The wave would carry us up the beach a while, then recede, and we would get up and shake the sand out of our swimming suits and go back and try again. That thrill of riding the wave stayed with me for a long time.

We had lots of generational games and experiences. We went back as an adult family with my second wife, Suzie, and I can remember the caution associated with clearing the poison ivy off the ground. Everybody did chores, and we did our share. When we got back from clearing the ground, Suzie found a small tick. The tick was removed, but the bite had transmitted Lyme disease. She had the classic symptoms of concentric inflammation and non-inflammation. The doctor called in all of the staff to show the symptoms, because it wasn't that common to find the classic evidence of the tick bite and the Lyme disease in Boulder, Colorado.

Near Barn House was the town of Menemsha. I suspect Menemsha was the active fishing port for the island. We could go there and buy fresh lobsters and many varieties of fish, so that part of the shopping was nearby. There was a grocery store somewhere up or down the island. I was never part of that, although I was in on the selection of the lobsters quite often. There was a pond at Menemsha, and that was where I learned to sail. It was pretty much the only time that I sailed, a little cat boat on the pond. It was quite simple and safe. We would go there, with a car full of kids and maybe a parent or two, and we would have a pleasant time for the afternoon.

The trips to the other end of the island were not as frequent, but that is where the ferry came to dock at Vineyard Haven or Oak Buff. We would load the car on the ferry (with a reservation), and that would take us to Woods Hole where we could drive to wherever we were going. The pattern was to take the ferry with the car and the family and drive down to the

Barn House where we spent our time. Occasionally we would come back up for an appointment of one kind or another or to pick up a person who was coming with no car. There was no public transportation on the island.

The upper end of the island had two rather different neighborhoods. One was the Vineyard Haven and Edgartown, two communities that were very much upper middle class, even upper class. Then there was the Oak Buff neighborhood that started as a resort for black people and continued the tradition as an interracial resort, so it was definitely more lower class than the rest of the island. There was still a resort effect in the sense that there were accommodations, places for rent for a week or less. There was also a sort of resort there, with a roller coaster, a merry go round, and entertainments of that sort. Occasionally the children would have an expedition there and take advantage of the active recreation that was available.

My parents were not actually members of the Barn House cooperative, but were welcomed as intellectuals, perfectly free to bring the children and have a month or three weeks stay at this place on Martha's Vineyard Island. I think there were vestiges of discrimination against Jews there. Much later, one of the children took a membership and had the responsibility to take a segment of the maintenance and carry it out. That was my sister's oldest child, known as Eric when he was young and Glen when he approached manhood.

Barn House was clearly organized not as a children's place, but a family place for relaxation and adult behavior for most of the people. Children were well tolerated, even welcomed, and the families were pretty easy in making the resort available to everyone, even Jews.

The other place that the family went, on an every-other-year basis, was to the mountains of southern New Hampshire or south-central New Hampshire. There was no single place that we went. The Appalachian Mountain Club ran Cold River Camp, and that was a common destination. Lots of wilderness or semi-wilderness skills were learned during the summers in the mountains. My father and mother were early outdoor recreation enthusiasts, and we learned to hike and climb and even ski in the mountains to the north of Boston.

My best friend was Billy Hinton. He later went to Cornell, majored in Agriculture, and was one of the few Westerners to participate with the Communist takeover in China. We did almost everything as kids. We played with model automobiles and little play toys. We went to school and did all the things that you do in school and some more besides. Schooling was a very rich experience, but we didn't really recognize it as such. It was carefully designed to catch our interest.

One thing I wanted to do when I grew up was be an explorer. I had considerable interest in the unknown and wanted to widen my experience. The period from 1400 to 1600 in the European experience was very dramatic for me. My parents encouraged the exploration of it. That lasted quite awhile. I don't know that Billy ever wanted to be an explorer, but he certainly had no objection to exploring together. We reinforced one another in that.

Billy didn't live near us. His father was dead, and his mother taught at Shady Hill School, so they didn't have much money. He had a semi-rural experience, whereas mine was straight urban. We came through it with different attitudes. His family lived at the edge of the city to accommodate his mother's income.

I was nine years old when Carmelita Hinton, Billy's mother, included me as a member of their family for a trip out to the Rockies along with Billy and his two sisters, Jean and Joan. She had reserved a cabin in Glacier Park away from the tourists. I remember one of many hikes that involved quite a bit of shale that broke off and moved slowly down the mountain. I triggered quite a large rock on this unstable surface, and it went rolling down the hill. Billy was down below, ahead of us on the descent, and we were able to yell at him that it was coming. He ducked under a place and the rock went over him. That was a sufficiently powerful experience, that the rock bounced free of him, to stick in my memory.

I remember also working with a hatchet, a short-handled axe, cutting firewood. I missed the log and cut my knee. Perhaps you can still see the scar, which was tended in the normal way, with first aid. I was okay until we came to the end of the vacation and I got the first real bath I'd had for quite a long while. That was enough to infect the wound. By the time we got to Duluth, I think it was, where the car was stored in the garage, it was pretty well infected. Driving from Duluth to Cambridge, I was in the back seat with hot wet compresses on it to encourage the recovery of the wound. My whole knee area turned jelly-like and almost white. We stopped in five or six places to have a doctor look at the knee, but they said to continue the hot wet compresses. This was before the days of antibiotics. When we got to Cambridge, it was better and I didn't need the hot wet treatment any more.

Also on that trip, was a very memorable first night in Glacier Park. Glacier Park was designed at that point for horseback travel, and the cabins were far apart. We had to go by foot to our cabin, but on that first day we never made our destination. When dark came, we decided we had to spend the night out. We cut fir branches and made a lean-to shelter and laid our sleeping bags out on the fir branches. We kept a fire going most of the night. We had the Hinton dog and he was awake the whole night guarding us from the horrors. We never were visited by a bear. In the middle of the night, a ranger came to find us and found that we were all right. The next day we did the second half of the trail and got to the camp. The dog lay on his back with all four feet in the air. They were really tired and maybe sore. We were relatively in good shape.

The next summer, our family went to the Rockies, but we went to the Canadian Rockies on the Canadian Pacific Railroad. We stayed in the fancy Empress Hotel in Montreal getting ready for the trip, and we were entertained by Mr. Bernheim. He was a friend of the family and had been quite wealthy before the Depression. He is reputed to have said the only thing he really regretted about his life so far was that he hadn't had a yacht when he was prosperous. It was a luxurious hotel, and my sister is reputed to have said, looking at the menu and deciding about dinner, that she'd like to have some olives, but they were seventy-five cents! That seemed like a lot of money for olives.

The trip west on the railroad was eventful in the sense that the four of us could roam the train easily. There was another family with two or three kids, and we struck up very close relationships with them. They were an English family, and we were sure these friendships would last forever. When we got back to headquarters, to Cambridge, we established an England fund and contributed a fair amount of spare cash to it. I don't know how that cash was distributed or used, but it must have had four or five dollars in it, contributed in increments of twenty-five cents or less.

When we got off the train in the Rockies, the family split up, with Mother and Peggy going by some faster conveyance to the camp. My brother Peter and I were allowed to approach the camp by horseback. We had a night camping out in between. I think we were part of a pack train carrying supplies to the camp. I had the sense of being very grown up at ten years old to be allowed to go on a camping expedition with my brother and no other familiar adults. The camp was about twenty miles south of Banff. It is now a famous resort area, Mount Assiniboine. It has a very dramatic, sharp peak reminiscent of the Matterhorn in the Alps. It's known as a Matterhorn. Later I learned in geomorphology class that it had become a common name applied to the sharp peaks in glacial areas.

The camp was on the lake with a wonderful view of the mountain. My older brother, who must have been fourteen at the time, was part of the group that went to climb the mountain. The younger children were left in camp. We did do a number smaller hikes. My brother Peter was a fairly active fisherman, and he caught trout in the streams. One day we left our shoes to go wading in the stream while Peter fished. When we got ready to leave at the end of the afternoon, he couldn't find his shoes. He was quite clear about where he took them off and put them down. They weren't there. We spent half an hour looking, and finally my sister admitted that she might have kicked them. The story stayed in the family archives for generations.

The trip back was by train again to Montreal, and then back to Boston and Cambridge. Those two summer vacations were memorable.

Many things were different when I was young than they are today. I'm reminded of Kenneth Boulding saying that in his lifetime all of the important inventions had been created. His lifetime was a little earlier than mine, but not much. By 1918, when I came into the world, automobile transportation had not developed fully, but certainly it was developing as I matured, and in my adolescence, it was pretty much there. There was automobile transportation and delivery trucks and so on.

There were some differences. We chased the ice man when I was young. He had a horse-drawn vehicle and we'd jump on the tailgate of the wagon and chip a little bit of ice. That was an exciting adventure. In the household, of course, there was an icebox rather than a refrigerator. Milk was delivered by horse and wagon. I don't even remember if there were any other things that were more primitive. Family life was quite different from conventional life, but I think that's more a reflection of the post-Victorian attitudes of my parents rather than any general sense of children being isolated.

We had a telephone, and a telegraph was accessible. There was no television, of course, so our leisure was probably quite different from today. A lot of our play was games that we as the four children and guests could play. We did things like charades that could be played by both adults and children together. I don't know how many families play charades now. I doubt if very many do. Our radio was clear, and we listened to some radio as recreation. Amos and Andy were there on the radio. I don't remember it being very attractive, other than Sunday afternoon concerts that the family listened to, probably from the New York Philharmonic. That was a regular feature of the week. Otherwise, the radio didn't make much of an impact on the family.

We ate dinner as a family. Thursday was the maid's day off, so we had dinner every other Thursday with the Coolidges at our house. On the intervening Thursdays we went to their house. The families were quite intimate in that regard. I don't know that the friendships were closer than contemporary families would have with families that their children went to school with. Grandmother Coolidge endowed the Coolidge Quartet and commissioned important chamber works.

The vacations were a little different from what we would do now. To travel by train was different than a lot of present-day travel, not that the trains were different from the contemporary trains, but rather, the use of the automobile was much less prevalent for long-distance travel. The two vacations that took me out to the Rockies were planned by the parents rather than by a travel agency, and long-distance communications were fairly simple on a telephone. There was certainly no interstate highway system, so that long-distance travel by automobile was hazardous in the sense that you didn't always know which town was coming up at the end of the road. Things were similar to today in cities, but as you got into the rural areas, transportation was much less sure.

One difference was the use of the kerosene lamp. One Christmas vacation I went with my friend Herbert Green to New Hampshire to a place that his parents had. I remember sitting around the dining room table with a big kerosene lamp in the middle of the table and being impressed by the rural technology at the time. The electricity was not yet distributed in the rural areas, so that was quite a contrast.

I'm confident that my mother had a greater influence on me than anybody else, but the specifics I don't know. When I learned not to steal from the five- and ten-cent store, it was Mother who took me back to the store to the manager. I apologized and went through the humbling experience of having to admit that I had violated the norms of the society. My father was away some of the time on business, so Mother was the only adult figure there.

I had the most interest in my mother and what she could teach me. The others in my youth didn't ever reach that level of trust or interest. My mother taught me almost everything, including cooking. She didn't teach me anything in the way of boy's sports, but I'm sure she had an influence on the second grade Olympics choices.

I remember one time I was reciting to her my amazement that I could carry out more adult leadership roles than many of my classmates. I had a certain sense of adult-like leadership. I remember Mother saying, "Well, shouldn't you expect it? After all, you've had these privileges along the way." That was when I realized that it was planned rather than accidental. If I could say something to my mother now, I would say, "Thank you for providing such a rich environment for my experiences." It was a youth that almost anyone would appreciate. I don't know how many adults can say that about their family. I would think not very many. She was a special lady.

I had a closer relationship with my mother than my father. I don't know what the background of that was, whether there was an emotional moment or it just accidentally happened. It certainly was a much stronger bond. She was around more, even though she wasn't around more than was expected. She just happened to be there.

At one point I accused my parents of not showing any emotion, of not giving the four kids a sense of their affection. They responded that that was intentional, that they didn't want to create a dependence on them, so they tended to back off the intimacy. I accepted that, and I probably reproduced it in my own family quite a bit. At least I was not emotionally dependent upon them as I went to Exeter and later to the University of Chicago. Knowing what I know now, I think they did the right thing. They created me. In the sense that it was personality-forming, I'm pretty much satisfied with the personality they helped to create.

I learned quite a bit from my siblings. My two older brothers set an example which I'm sure had an influence on me. A few things I remember from being told as an adult. I can remember the problem of tying my shoes and selecting my socks. For some time I was encouraged to think that I had to know which foot the sock fit in, like you do for shoes. I shared that room with Steve, so he must have had quite a bit of influence. There was not as much influence by my brother Peter, and very little by my sister Peg.

Another influence of the younger period was the graduate student from Harvard who lived with us. We always had one. He was always a male, and so there was always an influence there in terms of the mechanics of growing up and the discipline that was expected.

One of the lessons I learned as a child was the responsibility to do chores. In the summer when we went down to Chilmark on Martha's Vineyard, the children would do the dishes from the meals. There was a fairly strong tradition of this being the children's responsibility. In our own regular family life, there were chores to be done, mostly picking up the room and making the bed. Tom and Kisti took care of the meals and the kitchen.

There were punishments for misbehaving. My brother Peter and I were once punished by having to have the next meal separate from the family. We were limited to just milk and bread and jam. So we feasted on milk and bread and jam and thought it was a pretty good way of enduring "punishment."

Shady Hill School

I was a dreamy kid. By all odds, the most significant thing for me was schooling. I didn't do much in the way of self improvement. I was in school six or seven hours a day and it couldn't help but have an influence on me. Early memories are of Shady Hill School. I did my assignments, but I was never a really strong student. The routine things were let go mostly.*

One of the profound influences on my life was the elementary school I attended, Shady Hill. My parents were part of a group reacting against the prevailing educational philosophy or attitude. The curriculum was influenced by both John Dewey and Rudolf Steiner and evolved independently. It was the philosophy that we should be exposed to as much nature as possible.

The school was famous for having started out as an open-air school. They were definitely opposed to the overheated classrooms of the public schools, and there was plenty of ventilation. It may be apocryphal, but it could be said that the students of Shady Hill learned to write with their mittens on. We learned to print rather than use flowing longhand, and that was part of the problem, because most of us began connecting our printing together. That doesn't fit very well with what people expect. I never got the opportunity to make a good impression by having good handwriting.

In the nine grades that Shady Hill provided were wonderful teachers. They were imaginative and put things in a way in which the young people

---

*Nick used to talk about how his interest in girls appeared at an early age. He "sold" Ellen Madison for five cents to take up with Ester Schell. —Suzie

could really get into. In second grade we were taught by Carmelita Hinton. We concentrated on Greek civilization and learned some of the art forms. We stenciled our own tunics, produced the Olympic Games during recess, and learned to throw the javelin and the discus. We were really caught up in the whole thing. We didn't study the Greek philosophers or the language, but we pretty much studied everything else. Greek contributions to math were included as part of history as well as math.

In second grade the class did shop as an activity. We were each handed a stack of wood vaguely resembling a boat that we were supposed finish. We had to dig out the interior. I was clumsy enough that I put the chisel through the bottom. That didn't seem like a boat. After the second try, the teachers said, "We'll give you a different opportunity." I was able to build a tray that could carry stuff for guests. I did pretty well on that. I was able to handle a nail. I maybe even used the glue. The tray stayed in the family, and we still have it.

In third grade we focused on Roman civilization, although no one was thrown to the lions. In the fourth grade, Mr. McCarthy was our teacher. He led us through the expansion of Europe, and I was really caught up in that. We discussed the circumnavigation of Africa and the exploration of the Congo. We learned about the conquest of the Americas by Cortez, with an emphasis on the ruthlessness of the Spanish conquistadors. We learned about the individual explorers and conquerors, and I had an image of Balboa sighting the Pacific Ocean for the first time. That class went all the way to modern times.

I remember doing a paper on Andre, the French balloon explorer whose expedition to the Arctic never came back. His remains were found later, and I could connect with that very vividly. I used several sources and put together a five-page report of Andre and his balloon explorations. I was in college when the remains of the expedition were discovered. This may have influenced my choice of geography as a career. I have very clear memories of my parents giving to me illustrations of the clouds being rolled back as Europe became aware of the rest of the world. It was very much a European-centric view. No attention was given to the displacement and extinction of the aboriginal population. Columbus was a hero. Only in adulthood did I learn of the die-offs and the enslavement and oppression of the native populations. It was to be expected that the Conquistadors overcame the Inca and Aztec empires.

The fifth and sixth grades have faded. Somewhere after that I memorized a poem for a presentation to the school assembly. When I rehearsed it, for fun I lisped, "I stood tiptoe upon a hill. The air was cooling and so very still." The teacher almost had a heart attack.

The math program was pretty rigorous, and I enjoyed it. I still have a very vivid memory of Miss Idget, a large woman in all directions, who taught us fractions. She would draw a line on the blackboard and say, "this line means divide." She would make the line four or five times in the same place with enough emphasis that I would remember it. I still remember it now as an emphatic point of beginning arithmetic.

Ms. Putnam was a teacher who made a powerful impression on me. She kept looking for "self-starters" as individuals who thought on their own. I took an interest in the problems which she posed. She led us on a series of explorations which ended up as concepts which were learned thoroughly. For instance, in the fall of the year, she waited for a chilly day when we were dressed in warm woolens and took us on a field trip. This was part of our study of plant reproduction and the dispersion of seeds. We left the classroom and crossed the athletic fields out into the more or less wild brush that grew in that area. We spent most of the morning finding seeds in different locations, and when we came back we noted that our clothing was covered with seeds, so we added the attachment to clothing as one of the ways that plants dispersed their seeds.

In addition to the dandelions that we could see, the wind carrying the seeds, the seeds that fell in the water, and the seeds that were picked up by birds and dropped in random fashion over the landscape, we were part of the seed dispersion process ourselves. The seeds would stick to us and be carried to some other place where we would pull them out of our clothing and leave them. We were obviously agents of seed dispersion, and the message was learned thoroughly. The edibility of seeds and their ability to pass through the digestive system was emphasized, and we were happy to be part of the process of eating fruit and thereby passing the seeds on to the sewer system.

This piece of inquiry was my model forty years later when developing the High School Geography Project. We were able to set up experiences that ended up capturing students' imagination, because the participative aspect of the learning exercises was obvious to me as a quality education experience. The problem was that it required a freedom of imagination on the part of the teacher, and he or she must be free to put the students in harm's way and allow the variations in classroom procedures that would carry them out. The variation from the normal classroom requires a self-imposed discipline and doesn't fit with much of the present normal classroom situation.

When I got to teaching in college, I remembered the various ways that the teachers involved us in the subject so that we were participating in the educational process rather than just listening and memorizing. I remembered specific teachers and incidents, and with some of the stuff on the planetary movements that give rise to the seasons, I could use almost the same strategies that they had used. I was teaching in college the stuff that I had learned in eighth and ninth grade. Somewhere I began to formulate the fact that it was participatory teaching, and it resulted in much better learning than the straight didactic approach that I knew from a couple of years in Cambridge High and Latin. When I was director of the High School Geography Project, I knew what good teaching was, and I could encourage the people who wrote the various units to explore all the possible teaching strategies.

Nick (top row, far left) with his ninth grade class at Shady Hill School

TEEN YEARS

My sophomore year of high school was at Exeter Academy in New Hampshire. I was happy to go there, but I didn't do very much. Being on my own was great. I don't think I had any problem in adjusting to living away from home. The one class that I remember most was Algebra. I was able to do the class quite well, so I was offered the opportunity to sit in on an advanced class. It was a presentation of some of the pioneering work in the fourth dimension. I don't remember much about the fourth dimension, but I remember it as being quite a stimulating class, one that introduced concepts to me that I otherwise would have missed.

The other experience that was memorable was in the dormitory where fellow students and I had set up a still in my closet. The still was there to extract the alcohol from a brew that had been mixed up. It must have contained molasses and some other things. One day it exploded. Nobody was hurt in the explosion, but it created quite a mess in the closet and in the room. We spent most of the day cleaning up the mess, washing the walls and generally trying to pretend that nothing had happened. I don't remember anybody getting into trouble over the explosion and the still, but it was quite a job to try and cover-up the fact that there had been a still in the closet. We didn't want the proctor to find out about it.

That year I got a B and three Cs, and that wasn't enough to maintain what scholarship I had. My parents said, "Until you're ready to buckle down and really pay attention, there is no point in our supporting a private school." I was diagnosed as still drifting, still dreaming. And I was trying to head for Harvard. While being a resident of Cambridge gave me a certain advantage and assured a discount on tuition, it was not a blank check. I needed to bring up my grades. I came back to Cambridge and enrolled in Cambridge High and Latin school, which was something of a comedown for me. Most of my friends from Shady Hill had gone to prep school; there were no immediate friends in Cambridge High and Latin. The curriculum was traditional, and while the standards were pretty good, it was not a feather in my cap.

The mandatory American history class at Cambridge High and Latin was the outstanding memory of the two years that I spent there. The mayor of Cambridge was a bachelor, so his sister was the first lady of Cambridge.

She was also the history teacher assigned to take us through the whole course of American history. She would come into the class every morning after we were already there and, raising her voice a little bit, would say, "And who is going to lead the salute to the flag this morning?" This was a chore that was rotated around the class, so whoever's turn it was would stand up and lead the salute. Well, one day she came in as usual and was about to do it when I whispered to the person in front of me, "And who's going to lead the salute to the flag this morning?" She overheard me and must have observed closely. She was pretty upset about this and did nothing at the time. But she had it in for me for the rest of the semester. Even if I got ninety-five percent on the examination, she would somehow figure that I had answered a question wrong or omitted something from the list of significant items that the exam called for. She had me tagged for a D or an F for the final grade. That would have put a real crimp into my college expectations, so I had to work hard to exceed the standards of the course in order to get a passing grade. When I took the College Board examinations, I did very well in American history.

The German teacher at Cambridge High and Latin was an older woman. She seemed pretty old to me, but was probably fifty or sixty. She had graying hair and was a little bit overweight. She convinced me that I should go on to become a Foreign Service officer, or at least that I had a real interest in international affairs and should follow out that interest and develop a career that was related to international affairs. This was the first time that I had that kind of influence, and it seemed profound.

The most significant thing was the study hall that I was assigned to. It was a large room with sixty or seventy students. The back of the room was used for a study hall during that period for students who didn't have any other class. We were supposed to be using the time for preparation for our other classes. The course at the front of the room was a course in geography on the commercial side of the curriculum. College-bound students and students who were going to be secretaries had different curricula. The teacher was a secretarial teacher, accustomed to teaching shorthand or typing, and had no interest in geography. Students were assigned a certain number of pages in the book.

The class was strictly memorizing the names of the countries and their major products. It might have served a function in the commercial curriculum, because the students learned to spell the names of the countries and might have known the principle exports and imports. But it seemed so much drudgery for the students to learn the number of bushels of wheat that were produced in Kansas or the pounds of butter that were produced in Wisconsin. The process of memorizing it, at least well enough to get by the next day, seemed pointless to me. I suffered through at least a whole semester of commercial geography where I was not involved, but could sense the boredom of the students. That was a negative influence for me. I was offended by the uselessness of it, and I kept thinking there must be a better way of teaching this. That form of thinking was present, and it stayed with me. I continued to be aware of teaching strategies and classroom procedures in part because of this strong negative reaction.

I took the preparation for the College Boards very seriously. Mother got up at 5:30 and would get me up. I would prepare for school in the hour or two that lay between then and breakfast. The memory of sitting there studying while mother fixed her own breakfast and took off for the Flower Club purchasing is still with me. I was enrolled in a tutoring school. It was a profit-making operation in Cambridge that guaranteed, or almost guaranteed, that you would pass the College Board examinations with a high enough score. This I did. The business of preparing for these special classes was pretty demanding, especially when added to whatever home-work was given by the teachers at Cambridge High and Latin. Most of the semester, I was up early, studying for these examinations.

I learned to drive some time during my teen years. First I drove a jeep around the pasture that the Hintons had access to and where I helped bring in the hay. That prepared me pretty well. The jeep was part of the equipment of the family, ours or the Hintons. It was perfectly normal to learn to sit in the front left seat and drive whatever car there was. By the time I was old enough to drive a car, I had a lot of experience turning left and right, finding the place where the others in the pasture could throw the bales of hay, finding a way back to the barn, and generally making good use out of the time. We were often playing at doing the things that needed to be done to become adults. That rubbed off in wanting to be useful and the discrimination against idle, useless activity. It's not that we didn't do idle, useless activities, but it was a negative thing when picking recreation.

I got my driver's license on my sixteenth birthday. I got permission to use the family car when I was sixteen, too. The first car I owned was a 1932 Ford. My father picked it out for me as a good buy. I was perfectly happy with his choice. It was a sedan, with nothing romantic or exceptional about it. Having a car at my disposal was very important as a teenager. It was a chance to get away from adult supervision. I don't know that the adults looked at it that way, but I always thought it was the primary function.

My first date was a high school date. It must have been similar to the experience of others. My first dates were with a girl from a lower socio-economic class. I guess I did know that there was a class difference there. It wasn't an influence on my choice. I found her attractive; otherwise I wouldn't have wasted time. I was embarrassed in that I knew that the social differences were there, but they were not strong enough to make me change my choice of partner and activity.

Apparently I was a dreamy kid. I enjoyed the music of the day and I had a girlfriend, and we saw quite a bit of each other. I wasn't very serious about a life of the mind, so my parents provided me with alternative employment. I delivered flowers for my mother who had come out of child-rearing ready to do something with her life.

My girlfriend at the time that I was finishing high school was Natalie Pierce. We had a two-year affair that kept me pretty well occupied. I was more faithful to Natalie than I was in my first marriage. We ran around with a small heterogeneous group of fellow students. I can't remember the sociology of how we found each other, but our group was from about sixteen years old (me) to an eleven-year-old who participated fully in the sex play of the group. Our loyalties were fairly strong individually, but not necessarily to the group.

Our afternoons when we got out of school by three o'clock were often started as a group. We would do I don't know what by way of play, but when the game was underway, we would break-up into pairs and proceed privately to the main purpose of the afternoon, which was a full range of sex. I practiced a consistent pattern of withdrawal before ejaculation. We seemed to have an infinite appetite for this sort of thing and repeated it day after day with little variation.

I remember at one time, Natalie belonged to a youth group in the Unitarian church, so for a while I was a Unitarian. I would pretend that I was at the library, as far as the family was concerned, but often I was at the rehearsals for the play being organized by the Unitarian youth pastor. I thought I was pretty secretive about the whole thing, but when we came to perform our play, there was my sister and my mother in the front row of the audience. The subject of my activities was never discussed at home. As far as I can remember, it was always a private matter and never received any public attention. Why this conspiracy was never spoken out loud, I really don't know. Added to the privacy and apparent conspiracy was the fact that Natalie was never included in the family affairs. It was strictly a private affair. We avoided carefully the inclusion of the topic in any family discussion or arrangement. This was by mutual consent, or at least reluctant consent on the part of my parents. I'm sure they would have been more than happy to include advice on this topic if I had been open to it.

During the summers starting when I was fifteen or sixteen, my father found me jobs in a leather business. The leather industry was overbuilt, and I worked in one of the small tanneries that did the tanning and dyeing of the skins. This was after the skins had been graded once and tanned and needed to be dried before they could be dyed. After they were dyed, they needed to be graded a second time and sold.

The mechanism for drying the skins was a moving rack, consisting of steam pipes and a moving series of bars on an endless belt. There were steam pipes above that and big fans that blew the air over the steam pipes and the skins. The skins had to be attached to little hooks on the bars that kept moving away from me. I would take the skins one by one from the saw horse and hook them onto the bars. It certainly wasn't demanding work and required no judgment, but it was an essential part of the tanning process. As they got to the other end the skins were pretty well dried, and I had to be there to take them off the drying rack and put them on the saw horse. Then they were ready to go down to the basement to the coloring vats. If they were colored already and this was the final drying, they could be transferred to the graders and trimmed. The temperature there was over a hundred degrees since it was summer. At the end of the shift, I was glad to be out of the intense heat of the drying room and into the relative cool of Peabody summer temperatures.

The second summer I worked in a pickle cellar of a different tannery (there were plenty of them to go around in Peabody and Salem). In the pickle cellar, you accept sheepskins from a railroad or a trailer truck pulled up beside the tannery. The skins were wrapped in packages of a dozen and were folded maybe five times into a bundle and had been preserved in salt and water. I don't think there was anything but salt and water in the preservation process, but they were fresh from the wool puller, which was a factory that was entirely separate. The tractor trailer would be driven up to a door in the pickle cellar. There would be six or more of us lined up and the skins would be thrown down to the first guy. He would pass them on like a bucket brigade, and the last guy would stack them up on wooden pallets and move them in. The stacks were about five feet high and could be moved by a forklift to make room for the next packet to be unloaded. Stacks of raw skins were moved to the graders who graded the skins, sorting them according to the quality, and restacked the skins one by one on the wheeled sawhorses. Then they were ready to go to the tanning room.

Because the temperature of the pickle cellar was the same as the outside temperature, the large doors were wide open, and we didn't have a problem of perspiring all day. Instead, we worked stripped to the waist with aprons on and couldn't help but absorb large quantities of lanolin through our skin. The skins were direct from the wool puller and contained all of the natural lanolin, or "sheep grease." We were soaked from the waist up with what was an ingredient in hand lotions and body lotions sold in commercial establishments. But unprocessed lanolin smells very much like raw wool or sheep and is a very pervasive smell. The body absorbs a certain amount of this in the pores of the skin, and after working in it for awhile, you don't notice much of the odor. However, as you get out in to the wider world, you carry the pickle odor with you. The normal thing was to take a bath right away to wash it off, but all you can do is wash off the first layer. You cannot get the odor out of the pores of your skin. As you got out of the bath you were reasonably free of any odor, but as soon as you started to dance or began to perspire, you smelled almost as bad as you did in the pickle cellar.

It was a touch-and-go situation as to whether you should go to the Polish dances, which was the common recreation in the area, or whether you should stay home. There were quite a number of the Poles that worked in pickle cellars around the town, and the odor of the sheep skins was not an uncommon phenomenon. I was welcome even with the sheep grease smell. I danced the foxtrot that I had learned at the dancing school I attended as part of my upper middle class upbringing. I don't remember building any enduring relationship from these dances. I had a girlfriend from Cambridge who had a summer job waiting on tables in a resort hotel in Marblehead. She would have a day off and I would go visit her, but I can't remember what transportation I used. I would see her pretty much once a week as our schedules meshed.

The second summer I lived with a family who worshipped in the orthodox Jewish temple. They depended on me to light the fire on Saturday morning and turn on the electric stove. Apparently, the room lights were not sufficiently associated with work to be a taboo as far as the orthodox religion was concerned. However, the cook stove was a different matter. They could not start the cooking until somebody of non-orthodox persuasion would be willing to turn on the stove.

The diet was definitely controlled by their religion. There was one set of dishes for milktik, and another set of dishes for fleshtik. Likewise, pots and pans were segregated according to which class of foods they were preparing. I learned to follow the mandates of the religion and keep the fleshtik separate from the milktik.

During the second summer I had planned to learn to type on my own with a keyboard diagram and a course of study to master the touch system. The problem was that one needed to use the typewriter to communicate, and before you had mastered the system, you fell back into the old patterns of typing. Even though I very much wanted to be able to use the touch system, my motivation was not strong enough to resist the temptations of the hunt and peck system. I have regretted the failure to master that skill for seventy years or so.

Steve and Polio

One of the problems of the time was the recurring polio explosion, which occurred every fall. Some years it was much worse than others, but it was a constant reminder. Class was no guarantee of independence from the epidemic. The family was consumed by problems of how to get away from the polio epidemic in the fall of the year. One year, and it must have been before I had my license, when I was maybe thirteen, the family took advantage of the Coolidge's second home in western Massachusetts in the

Berkshire Mountains. The Coolidges had an estate there, and we were invited to occupy it during the early fall. There must have been five or six families, the Hintons, the Madisons, the Coolidges, and the Helburns. The children were fully compatible. We were all in the age range of elementary school and attending Shady Hill.

We would receive instruction during the morning hours from the parents, all of whom were well-educated. The fathers would commute from Cambridge, coming out on the train from Boston to Pittsfield and joining the family for the weekend. It was one of the high points of my childhood, for we had very imaginative parents, and they kept us occupied during the whole time. Their own instruction was apparently very good. In the afternoons, we played with little supervision. I don't remember the indoor games at all, although there must have been some rainy afternoons when we were confined. I do remember vividly playing with our toy automobiles in the sandy banks along the driveway, and especially games like hide-and-seek, which ranged over a good deal of the estate. Sometimes the game would end when the first child was found by whoever was "it," and sometimes it was the whole group. We waited until the last child was found by the person who was "it," and the remainder of the group, one by one, would be squeezed into whatever space was available, a tool shed or some spot that was not obvious to the non-participant.

It was during one of these polio epidemics that my brother Steve came down with the dread disease. He was in Exeter in Southern New Hampshire. My mother went up to confirm the diagnosis and bring him back to Massachusetts General Hospital. The urgency of the situation was such that they got a police escort from Exeter to Boston. Steve kidded later that it was almost worth the paralysis to have the police escort roar through the towns with a siren blaring.

At that time, the vaccine for polio was just discovered and was being used experimentally. There was no excess supply. Usually two injections of the serum was the maximum, but in Steve's case permission was given to see if they could stop it by using more serum. On the fourth injection, they stopped the disease within a few fractions of an inch of his heart. He was completely paralyzed, but he survived. He was in an iron lung for a while, but not long. After the disease was no longer active, he began a long period of convalescence. There was considerable debate about the best technique for recovery from the disease. He was following a routine that had been developed with some promise of absolute quiet for as much as a whole year. He was immobilized in a half cast and had to lie quietly on his back for twenty-four hours a day. There was a brief period when he could be massaged and exercised, but the theory was that the muscles would regain use by this complete rest for as much time as it took. This went on for at least six months.

Fortunately, the house on Fresh Pond Lane had a room on the ground floor that was not committed to any other use and could be occupied by Steve and his medicines and his attendant. It was very convenient from that standpoint. A ramp was built suitable for a wheelchair. He could be wheeled out to the street and lifted into the automobile at that point. The situation was not ideal, but it certainly worked pretty well for the couple of years while he was regaining the use of his upper body. He never did really regain the use of his legs, although he learned to use full crutches and full braces with the crutches, and could get around a little bit with those. But the braces were very clumsy. He was never really mobile in the sense of being able to walk.

Steve did master the wheelchair and developed very strong muscles in the upper body, so that when we wrestled there was no question that he could throw me and hold me down, even though he had no use of his legs. In the time that he was recuperating, he finished high school and entered Harvard College. He went through his first year being carried into the classroom lectures and carried out again. He drove a car that was especially equipped. In those days, there were no automatic gearshifts, so he had a car that was equipped with a hand-operated clutch. He could throw the clutch in with his left hand while he changed gears with his right hand. He became very skillful in driving this vehicle. He kept it with him all through college and graduated from Harvard with a degree in Political Science with honors.

He found a job with the United States Government in the National Resources Planning Board. He later married and had a successful four years before he died of complications from the polio, which apparently affected the liver and kidneys and gave him high blood pressure and terrible headaches. They didn't last too long, for he was admitted to the experimental work in the Lilly Clinic at Indianapolis. In the experiments, they controlled the high blood pressure, but the side effects were pretty serious. He only lasted for about a year in the clinic and died of the complications of the medicines.

It was a tragic time for the family, for we all admired his guts, his courage in staying with the procedure, his adaptation to having the disease, and his energy in living out that part of it. He even had a good career during that time, and must have had two years or three years of very happy marriage before he died. His widow Mary was accepted into the family. My father gave Mary away when she remarried a year or so later. Even though Steve and I were very close, I do not remember the grieving process, and I somehow have put the grieving about the polio into my subconscious. I do remember that at the time of his death, I was around twenty-three and feeling a change in my own maturation. I felt that I had to live both for him and for myself. It gave me a maturity that I don't think I had until that time. That's when I really buckled down and began serious preparation for my career. By that time, I was married also, and the two factors contributed to my readiness to avoid some of the distractions of youth and get on with my studies. I was then in the first year of my doctoral work at Wisconsin. I did not really relax from that until the Doctor's degree was conferred five years later.

Pinkham Notch 1938

College

Harvard

When I got to the College Board examinations, I did show off my prowess reasonably well, and was admitted to Harvard as a freshman the following year. I was admitted to Harvard partly because I was a Cambridge boy; I don't know if I would have gone in that direction otherwise. I didn't have a plan for my life at this point. I just went to Harvard and coasted along, with no particular energy involved. I spent a fair amount of time in a friend's dorm room listening to phonograph records and exchanging matters of taste with him. It was a kind of lackadaisical period. In the course of the next couple of years, I did form a general plan that I wanted to go into the diplomatic service. I thought geography was a pretty good preparation for that. I later realized that in the diplomatic service one doesn't decide what to do until one is a fairly high official.

The ability to communicate was much more important than the ability to analyze the situation. Languages, and especially facility in English, were the crucial thing on the Foreign Service exam. By the time I realized that, I was fairly well along in college. I think I was a junior, so my feeling of being at sea, the sense of not knowing what to do, was fairly strong.

At Harvard I had the example of my brother Steve in terms of academic affairs. One part of leadership dealt with the course selection. The freshman geography class was team-taught by two professors, Whittlesey and Kemp, who lived together and were reputed to be gay. They taught a very good course, *Orientation to the Cultures of the World.* I did quite well in the class, and it was the most interesting class I took. The course included quite a lot of slides that the geographers had taken. It had enough graphics so that it was fully comprehensible to me, as against some other abstract courses. It was the only B I got freshman year. I knew the professors because they came to the house when Steve was studying with them.

Whittlesey was one of the first generation of geographers from the University of Chicago, and an illustrious scholar. He published fairly widely. Kemp had never finished his PhD. He was known in the field, but actually both of them were excellent lecturers. I found it quite useful, in spite of some derisive comments from my father. He considered geography a miscellaneous collection of useless facts.

The course was well illustrated and was really quite memorable. Images of the Far East particularly stay with me, as well as a few of the phrases that we used, such as the mention of how cold it could be in a Shanghai hotel. The location of a cannery in British Columbia adjacent to the bar was an example of good location in terms of efficiency because it was the only bar allowed for 10,000 residents. The guy who had the license had established on the mainland a very steep deep water location where ships could come in, but there was very difficult terrain for housing and commercial operations. That was interpreted as a mislocation, but in terms of the labor force, this was the place where workers would live, because it was close to the cannery. The better site from the standpoint of canning fish would obviously be on the island offshore a little bit, which was relatively flat and accommodating, but the access to beverages was limited by the need to cross a small channel to where the license to sell beer and other intoxicating beverages was. Mr. Kemp was lecturing here about the location of activities and pointed out that the red light district was very well marked in this community. He described it as three blocks up the steep terrain and right at the corner. Our attention was captured in this way. We had quite a clear image of the cultures of the world from the two lecturers. This class influenced my choice of profession.

Despite my interest in these two courses, freshman year at Harvard was very so-so. I was very dreamy. I earned a B in geography and Cs in my other subjects. This was not an acceptable record as far as the scholarship committee was concerned. I finished the year ineligible for a scholarship. This was a pretty serious thing as far as my parents were concerned. Father had finished with honors at Harvard in Literature, and I was supposed to do at least as well.

I decided that if I couldn't do better than that in my grades, I should go off and learn something of the way of the world so that I would be more serious about my studying and find a career that would support me in the manner in which I was accustomed. The alternative to going on in college was to put me in care of the Appalachian Mountain Club.

Appalachian Mountain Club

Our family outdoors activities led to employment for me. The Appalachian Mountain Club ran a series of huts in the White Mountains of New Hampshire accessible only by foot trails. To man the huts in the summer, they employed otherwise unemployed high school students. The trail crew made sure the trails were passable.

We hut men were sort of second-class in that the trail crew had the prestige of being skilled in wilderness techniques. But the hut man was the next tier in terms of ranking, and we maintained the huts, providing food and a place to sleep for hikers of all sorts. The huts were simple, providing only bunks and blankets for people. If you wanted sheets, you had to bring them yourself and take them away.

The food was fairly simple, as you might expect, because it was cooked by teenagers. Furthermore, we had to supplement the food that was there with fresh food that we carried in our backpacks three or four miles from the road. We would meet the truck at the road and carry up the fresh meat, butter, and things like that twice a week. As we went down, we took an order for the next truck delivery. The load would vary from a negligible weight to as much as eighty pounds. That was quite a struggle for us, but we rose to the challenge and carried up the food. If necessary, we could leave some at the road head and go back. I don't remember ever leaving part of the weekly order at the road head. You increased the load as necessary and carried it up.

My tour of duty included two summers at the Zealand Falls Hut, and most of the path to it was gentle because it had been a railroad grade when the lumbering took place. The vegetation was thoroughly recovered from the initial logging which supplied the eastern cities with lumber for all sorts of purposes. The archeological remains of the harvesting of the logs were still there, mostly in the form of the railroad bed from the earlier exploitation. Other evidence of the railroad completely disappeared. They had clear cut the whole area, it was now second growth. The trail was four miles, so it was a sizable hike with a big load.

Fortunately, the staples to last the summer were brought by mule at the beginning of the season, so we did not have to carry the non-perishables except as we ran out. I spent two summers working at the Zealand Falls Hut, and it was an important experience for me in the sense of independent living and decision-making. There were two of us, and my partner played the trumpet. I took a recorder flute with me, and we would sometimes practice when there was no one around, or even when there was. The recorder flute was known as a blockflurter. The song that I particularly remember was a folk song called "Tell Me Why." We learned to play that as a duet in a reasonably good manner. The sense of belonging to an "in" group of hutmen with the obvious distinction from the "out" group, which was the tourists and hikers we served, was very clear.

The chance of practicing my authority in that role was very good. I must have learned a great deal about managing the food and cooking and cleaning up. We were recreation directors. We oriented the people who used the hut to the trails around, how long they would take for a particular hike, and how severe the climbs were. We generally were the local authorities on everything. In addition to the two resident males, there were guests who came through, including females. That interaction was an important part of the maturation of the teenagers. There was quite a bit of rivalry between the crews who maintained the huts. The communication was mostly by word of mouth, by a tourist who came through. We could get a message to the Lake of the Clouds hut or one of the huts in the other direction by asking hikers to tell the nearby crews the news from our hut. Creating the rivalry to produce the best meal or the cleanest hut must have been carefully planned by the management.

Pinkham Notch was open all year round and served the budding ski industry. This is where I worked for the eight or nine months between the first summer at the Zealand Falls Hut and the following year, when I went out to take it over again. Pinkham Notch served the Appalachian Mountain Club and visitors throughout the year. As such, it was quite a different establishment. At Pinkham Notch we did all the food preparation under the direction of a full-time cook and kept the two bunk houses clean. We did a lot of skiing and some guiding to accompany visitors to outlying spots.

University of Chicago

After a year and a summer break, I resumed my studies. I decided to abandon Harvard and go out to the University of Chicago. The decision not to go on at Harvard was fairly important for me because, working behind the desk at Pinkham Notch, I had had to deal with the college boys for various things. The attitudes of the Harvard students who came through for the spring skiing was really quite offensive. They assumed that Jesus went to Harvard, and therefore they could do no wrong. They left a feeling that Harvard was somehow superior to any other school, and they had picked-up this superiority. It was more important what your grandfather could do than what you could do, and there was a clear consciousness of whether you were upper class or just ordinary. Ordinary included the scholarship students. That ran counter to the sense of equality that I had been brought up with, and I didn't want to be put in the category of being a "Hahvahd man."

My geography course in that first year at Harvard included something of the morphology of Chicago. I took the train without any hesitation and made the transfer to Chicago at New Haven in Hartford, to the Illinois Central. I got off at 57th Street and carried my suitcase over to the dorm that had been assigned and started on a new chapter. It did seem like a new chapter to me being completely away from home in a new school. I treated it as a starting over and paid attention to my studies. I spent a fair amount of time over coffee at the International House, but I didn't drift along or dream away the time.

Chicago at that time was an institution that took itself seriously. Its mission was clearly to pioneer in education, as well as in many areas of research. I was involved in the educational side, and I took it seriously. The university was divided into a college for undergraduates and the rest of the university. The college had set up a series of survey courses for incoming freshman. As a transfer student, I was given credit for the physical sciences and the humanities, but I still had the biology survey to take. It was an outstanding course. We met three times a week for lectures and had a small discussion group once a week. The discussion leaders were younger instructors who took seriously their responsibility to try and help these youngsters into scientific inquiry. My instructor was Joe Schwab, whom I later ran across as a major figure in curriculum reform. At that time, Joe was able to interest us in the inquiry into the nature of life and living things. The lectures were of comparable quality by major figures in their field. The one who reached me most seriously was an elderly professor with just a little bit of a Danish accent, Anton Carlson. He had a beautiful set of lectures. I'm sure they were repetitive in the sense that there were the same experiments from the podium for each year, but they seemed fresh and vital to me.

At Chicago, Burton-Judson Hall where I lived was right across the midway from the main campus. There must have been 150 or 200 students there. I think they were all male students at that time. I waited on tables at Burton-Judson. I think we earned at least the meal that we waited on, and I learned to carry a tray full of meals. It was an innocuous way to earn my board. You did see a lot of the residents, but there was not enough recognition to fix in one's memory.

Most of my social life revolved around the International House, which was one of the places for intellectual conversation. There was a restaurant there where you could get your meals. In between mealtimes, there was usually an active conversation, or maybe several active conversations, going on over coffee. You could almost always find a congenial group, sit down, and gradually join the conversation.

At one of those sessions, there was a dark-haired girl that I came to know named Tess Loth. She was actively engaged in the conversation. I sat down and was a little self-absorbed in my tobacco and pipe and getting it lit and tamping it down and making something of a show of being a sophisticated Easterner. Later it developed that Tess and I struck up a very close friendship, and before the year was over she and I had gotten married. I was sleeping with her, and I suppose that created some tension with the not-marrying condition.

The campus is on the south side of Chicago. You could take the Illinois Central commuter trains the five or six miles to the middle of Chicago and downtown. We took advantage of that from time to time. I was something of a jazz aficionado. I would take Tess down to The Three Deuces, and I would drink and be absorbed in the music. We would be at a nearby restaurant or bar where the musicians would gather after hours and play in various pick-up bands. A lot of the players were engaged elsewhere and then came for after-hours music and conversation. I suspect that we would normally catch the Illinois Central, or IC as it was familiarly known, back to campus before midnight.

Maybe once a semester, there was a dance. Tess and I would be asked to do our little performance at the midpoint, when everybody was sitting around. We would do a take-off on all of the styles of dancing that were prevalent. We would start out with the chaperones dancing formally, only touching parts of the arms that were appropriate and doing a very modest fox trot. One, two, slide and step, one, two, slide and step. Moving on to various styles, each one exaggerated in its own way, and ending-up with the jitterbug, which I never learned to do properly, but we made a pretty fair imitation of it with knees bent and lots of whirling around.

I opposed the war, World War II that is. We participated with the Young Communists on campus to oppose the war as long as the Stalin/Hitler pact was viable. We really worked at it for a while. Tess was employed part time in the "Keep America Out of War" congress, which later became "Keep Roosevelt Out of War." The United States was preparing for participation, and there wasn't anything that could be done. But we didn't realize that, so we were active.

Tess had some time on her hands, as I was busy with course work trying to finish up quickly. When Hitler invaded Poland and then went on into Russia, overnight the Communist group on campus changed course. They were for the war, while we continued to be against the war in spite of everything. The various groups that we participated in included the Quakers, and they never changed course the way the Communists did. I went to Meeting. There was a fair amount of dislike about the idea of the United States going to war, even though that part of the history of the United States has been erased. Tess worked in the various activities, while I joined in very enthusiastically and felt that we were really doing good work.

Montana State

When I was a senior at the University of Chicago, and a Geography major, I met a visiting professor from Montana, Roland Renne, who taught a course in agricultural economics. I enjoyed the course and did well in it. I enjoyed the connection with Renne and his family. Obviously, he didn't bring his family with him to Chicago. He was "batching" it there. He had some respect for us, and we for him, so we invited him to our apartment. He offered me a graduate assistantship for a Master's degree in agricultural economics. That took me out to Montana after graduating from Chicago, and it was the beginning of a career-forming experience as a graduate student. Tess had graduated as well. She was taking graduate courses in history, but dropped out to accompany me. Montana State was a small college at that time.

Once we got settled in Bozeman, Montana, we had to find an apartment. It was the upstairs of a very modest house owned by a Norwegian couple. I don't know how Norwegian they were, whether they were first or second generation. He had been a railroad engineer. He was distinguished for me by a very large nose that was full of blackheads. The blackheads were so prominent in his nose that I could hardly keep from squeezing them. The couple was nice and left us pretty much alone.

We settled in with a group of graduate students and faculty members surrounding an English professor, whose name I have completely forgotten. He was interested in folk songs and folk tales. The graduate students were not in agricultural economics, but in something related to English. There was a young woman, a graduate student, who published a small book of poetry while we were there. It was a very informal, friendly group. We gathered on weekends and sang and played the guitar. I don't remember what we did about eating or drinking, but we had a very pleasant relationship that lasted throughout the year.

The other fraction of our leisure was learning something of the semi-rural lifestyle that Roland and Polly Renne practiced. They had about eighty acres, where they cut the hay and raised some beef and chickens. They had a rather diversified farm, with a garden where they raised their own vegetables and canned fruits and vegetables for the winter. It seemed like a very sensible mode of life. We learned as much of it as we could. That mode of life interfered somewhat with our social life, but we enjoyed it that way, and we learned as much as we could, participating in their subsistence farming. After the war, when we came back to Bozeman, we had five acres and practiced that simpler lifestyle.

On the faculty, there was a Carl Kraenzel, who was perhaps closest to me in an academic way. His specialty was the adaptation of culture to the environment. This was very easy for a geographer to accept. His concern for cultures that were adapted to the variability of rainfall, and all of the other things that derived from that, was a continuing interest of mine for much of my professional life. He had published, or was publishing then, a fairly significant volume entitled *Wanted: A Culture for the Great Plains.*

Enrolling in Kraenzel's rural sociology class changed my life. Carl's mission was to try to explain the special role of the farmers in Eastern Montana and the Great Plains, and to explain the fact that they were in unique circumstances with the insecurity that derives from not being able to count on the crop from one year to the next. The rainfall in the mid-plains was low enough that if it fell much below the average, practically no crop was produced. There were various adaptations to this, but none of them adequate. The best alternative was to plant half the acreage in any one year and let the other half lie fallow so that the moisture would be preserved. The following year, you would plant the area that had been fallow and let the acreage that had been planted lie fallow.

The pattern worked pretty well. Kraenzel argued that there needed to be other cultural adjustments to help the farmers in this high-risk environment. He pointed out that most of the economic institutions in agricultural communities were based upon an annual, rather than a biannual, cycle, so that it was difficult to pay the hospital or the mortgage on an every-other-year basis. His work was encapsulated in his book. I swallowed the theme and was an enthusiastic advocate.

My Master's thesis research involved a reclamation project and changing the land use in three counties in the northern part of the state—Blayne, Phillips and Valley counties that were semi-arid with some irrigated land. The project involved removing families from dry-land farms that were not big enough to support the families onto smaller irrigated acreages. The intent of the fellowship was to go up there and review the accounts of the Bureau of Reclamation to make sure that they were not spending money frivolously. There was a great deal of criticism of the director of the project. Critics of Depression-era government projects wanted to get the goods on him if they could. But I was not about to straighten out their accounts, and furthermore, what the director had done seemed to me sensible, and I worked out a rationale for it.

The title of my thesis was *A Dynamically Mature Landscape for the Great Plains*. The idea was that people who farmed might live in town or in an adjacent irrigated area, and produce a diversified mix of profitable enterprises. They could go out to their farm and practice the specialized agriculture of the area, which of course was the dry-land farming of wheat. They would leave half the acreage unplanted, giving the soil a year of rest while the other half of the farm was producing wheat. Theoretically, the land that was not producing wheat was kept cultivated and clear, so that weeds did not use up the moisture that soaked in. When the next year started, the soil had enough moisture stored in it that it would produce a crop. The system was quite well developed, and I think that most everybody thought it was a proper land-use pattern.

The land-use pattern I advocated was similar to that used, with the settlements concentrated on the rather limited irrigated land. The dry land farmers would live in town or on the irrigated land, doing a bit of gardening and other farming.

I was also supposed to produce something as a result of my $400 fellowship. There was a resettlement activity going on in Blayne, Phillips, and Valley counties on the irrigated area of the Milk River. The Roosevelt administration programs were very popular in some quarters, but they were the object of a good deal of ridicule and resentment on the part of others. This project was under the direction of a very active man. The criticism of it was focused on some of the activities in which the project participated. There were farms that were entirely too small to maintain themselves with a summer fallow every other year. Those were being bought out by the resettlement administration, and the farmers were resettled in the irrigated areas and in the towns nearby. I suppose a number of them moved to larger cities, but the abandonment of a lot of the farms was characteristic and was a function of the settlement pattern based on 320 acres per person, which was entirely too small for a summer fallow every other year operation. Now this was understood and not subject to criticism. It was a pattern of trying to make the irrigated areas more attractive.

Among other things, the resettlement administration had invested in a swimming pool immediately adjacent to the town of Malta, which was one of the areas to which the farm families were being settled. This "extravagant" investment of the administration funds in the recreational activity drew the ire of the more conservative people who didn't feel it was appropriate to make urban town or small town living more attractive. They didn't feel that that was what the money should be used for. They didn't have any other suggestions, but they latched onto that as an extravagance of the project. I was supposed to go up and do an accounting of the investments of the expenditures of that project.

I was not equipped, not by any means competent, to evaluate the amounts invested in recreational activities. Tess and I went up and analyzed the areas. In order to justify the activities, I had to design what a proper settlement pattern would be in that area if one were going to substitute one settlement pattern for another. I had to know what we were moving away from and what we were moving toward. I was selling the state an idea of a better settlement pattern. I had to describe it and referred to it as a dynamically mature landscape. Things that contributed to such a landscape were adjustments that were positive and therefore appropriate. Gradually this idea became the dominant theme in my Master's thesis, and I composed a fairly elaborate thesis in that direction. I don't think that this was anticipated by the authorities who approved the thesis topic and paid for the research, but that's the way it developed.

Tess and I spent several weeks, usually a week at a time, up on the high line interviewing farmers in the valleys, and I produced a thesis on this general theme. Just like today, the critics of the Farm Security Administration policy made jokes about the extravagance of the pattern of purchase. One that stands out: the way you could tell the difference between a rich farmer and poor farmer was that the poor farmer was one who had to wash his own Cadillac.

University of Wisconsin

I didn't have anything lined up for the next year. I hoped to go on to graduate school and get my Doctorate, and decided that I would do the Doctorate in Geography. I wanted to be able to come back to Montana State as a geographer. It was unlikely that I would be able to come back as an agricultural economist, the field of my Master's degree.

There is a constant stream of students coming back to the place where they did their earlier work, because they know people on the faculty, and the faculty knows them. There's a natural tendency to come back to the home department. Cornell, for instance, when Roland Renne was offered the head of the Agricultural Economics Department found that twenty of the twenty-one faculty members were graduates of a Cornell department. That is a fearsome situation in which the department becomes more and more ingrown.

I applied and was accepted at the University of Wisconsin and was awarded a research assistantship. I think this was around 1941, just before Pearl Harbor. By this time, the draft law had been passed, and people were being drafted for service in the army and getting ready to go to war. My conscription was modified by my intent to be a conscientious objector. I think the draft board in Bozeman was happy to postpone my call up until absolutely necessary. They did not want to have a conscientious objector on their books. I was given a deferment on the basis that I was married and that I was a student, and I continued to be able to study.

The University of Wisconsin did not have many applications, needless to say, because most of the geographers were being drafted or going into some sort of intelligence work. It seemed like many of them went to the Office of Strategic Services (OSS), which was the antecedent of the CIA. Geography was pretty good preparation for knowing what's on the other side of the hill when you can't be there, or there's nobody there to let you know what the circumstances are. I think our class was only four people and maybe five the second year when we were joined by a Brazilian, Jorge Zarar. He had a law degree, as well as a baccalaureate degree, and was going to bring back to Brazil some of the expertise that the Americans had. We had a very good relationship with Jorge and with some other people who were in the department.

There was a German who had not been happy in Germany and had escaped. There were some Mormon graduate students in a different department, who, for some reason, were not drafted. It was a very congenial group of students and some faculty. At the time, rationing had developed in the United States. With a Navy pretty much committed to taking war materials to Britain and to Russia, the United States was facing shortages in both coffee and sugar. We adapted to it by trading a pound of sugar to the Mormons for two pounds of coffee, which they didn't use, and then trading a pound of coffee to the Germans for two pounds of sugar, which they didn't need. We ended-up with plenty of both for our lifestyle. Each of the others came out better as far as they were concerned. The joys of barter!

The rationing of meat and of gasoline had a somewhat different effect. The meat we got along without pretty well, but the gasoline prevented doing any fieldwork on an extensive basis. The ration of gasoline was not enough to cover a large territory or anything like the fieldwork that was customary in geography. Doing a project strictly from statistics was less well developed, and there didn't seem to be any statistics that could lend themselves to manipulation of a significant geographic area. I chose a topic on the development of the urban fringe, so I could study that from a succession of maps from the 1910s up to the present. You could map the successive land use expansion as the city grew and expanded, and some combination of the two could be mapped and explained on the basis of certain barriers at certain facilities.

Each tenth day of the month came, and there was no notice from the draft board, so I would start again to collect the data and interpret the succession of maps. When the second summer arrived, I had passed my prelims and presented the work I had done, and the professors rejected the topic as being inadequate. I was disappointed. It seemed impossible to find another topic that could be done on a bicycle or as a pedestrian, so I abandoned the Doctorate for the time being.

Indianapolis

We contacted the American Friends Service Committee (AFSC) to see what kind of volunteer opportunities they might have. They suggested a year-round work camp that was going in Indianapolis. By way of background, there had been serious race riots the previous summer, and the AFSC thought that Indianapolis might be the next city in which race riots broke out. The Indianapolis work camp was established in order that there be a few whites that the residents of the ghetto could relate to, and perhaps that would keep the riots from occurring.

In the Indianapolis black ghetto, as in most Northern cities, the only whites present were rent collectors, prostitutes, pimps, and a few derelicts. Having even a handful of whites with good intentions and a respectable situation would seem to allay any fears. There was practically no communication between the white population and the blacks in the ghetto. We thought that was a worthwhile operation, so we packed up our belongings and put them into the Buick and drove to Indianapolis. It turned out that the group was congenial, and we were accepted into it very easily.

The work was chipping the mortar off used bricks. There had been a brick factory in the area, which had been torn down. The bricks were still lying around. A black settlement house was nearby, and they felt they could build a facility there using the bricks, but the bricks had to be cleaned in order to be re-used. It was slow work, and we were happy to do anything constructive that might help the situation.

The operation of the settlement house was under the direction of Cleo Blackburn, who is one of the most admirable people that I have ever been acquainted with. He was full of energy and probably was slightly manic, but he had a profound sense of good will and mission. He was a minister in one of the churches, as well as the director of the settlement house. Many people would come by and stop and chat with us and ask us what we were doing and why. We were not entirely isolated. We would describe to them that the bricks could be used, but the old mortar had to be cleaned off before they could be used in new construction.

The remains of the building included an enormous room covered so that it was in from the weather, but empty. One of the things in this room was a concrete stand on which some machine had been placed. It had to be taken out, I remember, using the jackhammer to chip away the concrete. The jackhammer noise was increased a couple-fold by the empty room in which we worked. I think my present modest deafness might be from that time, because the echoing back and forth of that noise was enormous. We didn't have any ear muffs to decrease the noise.

We lived in a modest house, provided by the settlement. I think Tess and I had a room, but shared the bathroom and kitchen. Spending every day in the company of people with whom you live and work, and with whom you are quite intimately involved, is very powerful. It represents a much more intense experience than with people you only see once a week. This living situation was sufficient and reasonably private. But there was one aspect that was rather unpleasant. It was impossible to get rid of the bed bugs for more than a week or two. In order to do it, even for that period of time, we had to fumigate the whole house with some sulfurous compound that killed the bed bugs. Then, when they were killed, we remade the beds, and started living again. We had a week or two of relative undisturbed sleep, but after that, we would find that there were bed bugs that had either survived or perhaps moved into the house. They would irritate the body. The bites were a constant source of itching.

We were isolated pretty much from the black community around us. But we got to know our black neighbors, and they would drop in and visit for half an hour or an hour. We began to realize that we could associate with them as friends and enjoy them again and again. Gradually they became sufficiently familiar that when they would drop in, we would think of them as friends and neighbors first, and only secondarily would we think of them as black people. The first sensation of racism in that context is to associate the person with the social relations around wherever you are. First you think of these people as blacks who happen to live nearby, and only gradually begin to treat them as whole persons that you've come to know and associate with. It took at least a couple of months before this transfer effect began to feel normal. I was surprised at how long it took. I had always assumed that I had very little race prejudice, and here it was showing-up in the most intimate way.

The circumstances of our lives were enough different that we were glad to escape the work-camp atmosphere once in a while. Most probably we called friends of our families who lived in Indianapolis and were happy to associate with us, although they didn't come by to the work camp to see the neighborhood. They played bridge, and that was the occasion for going to their house, perhaps as often as once a month for the five months that we were there. We would get cleaned up, as clean as we could be, and put on our "respectable clothes" for an evening of bridge. It felt quite relaxing to be in the presence of white society for even that one evening.

We never exchanged meals with our neighbors, but we did have them over for conversation. We did attend church services in the black community, but we felt quite out of place there. We were definitely outsiders, and there seemed to be no way to become insiders.

Nick geared up for smoke jumping in 1944

Conscientious Objector

One of the strangest things that ever happened to me was the award of conscientious objector status. It was a major concern, because the alternative would have been jail. I didn't know what to expect of my reaction to jail. It might have been okay and it might have been very difficult. Given the experiences of others that I knew about, being a conscientious objector was the best alternative. The others all had significant negative aspects. It was quite a relief when the letter arrived that I had been granted the 4E classification.

The letter arrived without any stimulus from me while we were in Indianapolis. I could breathe much more deeply and look forward to several months of quiet acceptance of that categorization. That meant that I wouldn't go to jail if I kept my nose clean, and I would find my place during the war. From then on I was pretty well set, or so it seemed to me. It seemed quite a relief to know I had that much leeway.

It's hard to know if I would have decided to go to jail if forced to decide. I'm just as glad not to have had to make that decision. Some of my colleagues thought that if they hadn't come up against that decision, it wasn't a complete test of their conviction. But it wasn't much of a test for me. The 4E classification meant that I accepted the legitimacy of the draft.

The fact that the classification came without seemingly any initiative on my part, was the strange thing about the process. I had to submit evidence of religious training and belief to get the 4E classification. That was difficult because I had no formal religious training, and little informal training, even though I was doing work with the Quakers at the time. It was the fact that I was willing to do that work that seemed to have swayed the draft board. I didn't think I had made a convincing case. I guess the draft board could understand someone not being willing to face the prospect of the draft, but they couldn't understand the willingness to forgo lucrative opportunities. The members of the draft board were sufficiently materialistic that they couldn't understand choosing an unrewarded choice. Ten dollars an hour looked too good to them.

I have often speculated that it was the luckiest experience in my life. Was there something in my sincerity that shone through all the various interpretations of my application? I couldn't put my finger on that something.

The draft had a fairly defined role for conscientious objectors. It wasn't like similar cases in World War I where individuals chose not to put on the uniform. They were much more coerced into a statement of objection. Some of them just refused to put on the uniform. It's fairly clear that they were going to spend the rest of the war in the brig. I had it fairly easy in that sense.

Other people also heaved a sigh of relief when I got the 4E classification. My parents were not in agreement with my position, but it was easier to accept the 4E than the other classifications. One was a 4F classification that would be shared with others who were considered insane. It wasn't that I was afraid of being considered insane, it was that I wasn't considered normal somehow.

The 4E classification meant that the government accepted my sincerity, but I was still under the draft. I still had to serve, just not in uniform. I underwent the physical exam as if I were going to be a private. It was the only overt experience with the draft that I had. There were other people who ran across a fair amount of heckling, but I didn't. The physical exam was the only place. The sergeant at some point asked, "What if we all took that position?" Our answer was, "that's what we would like."

It was about Christmas 1943 that I was re-classified 4E and sent a notice to report to Gatlinburg, Tennessee, as a draftee. The bus ride was notable by the fact that I could sit in the back of the bus and pretend that I was a black person, and I did indeed do that. When I took out cigarettes, I passed them around to the other blacks who were sitting around and declined a cigarette offered to me by a white person. I'm not sure what their attitudes were, but it was clear that there was a tension in the back of the bus. I was accepted perfectly well by the black passengers, but there was continuing wonderment among the white passengers. We stayed that way until Gatlinburg. We changed buses somewhere, and I resumed my normal white character.

Tess and I had no sense of what the Gatlinburg camp would be like and assumed that she was not welcome there, I think rightly so. She could have stayed in Knoxville, but I could not see her regularly. We sent her back to Cambridge where she could live with my parents and work in whatever. The whatever turned out to be a settlement, where she worked with the young people, and was somewhat surprised that they interpreted the Girl Scout symbol as a reflection of the Trinity, instead of a completely independent code relief. The priests and the nuns in the Catholic surroundings were clearly saying that the three leaves were associated with the Trinity, for the Father, the Son, and the Holy Ghost.

I settled in to the camp life reasonably well. The facilities were a former civilian CCC camp. This was the headquarters for all of the park facilities in Great Smokies National Park. With the war, the whole CCC program was dissolved. Many CCC workers went into the Army more or less directly.

We filled the vacuum they left. We were to work on the maintenance and facilities of the Great Smokies National Park. Since that time, Gatlinburg has flourished as the gateway town to the west of the park, and now bears no resemblance to the rather primitive situation that we experienced.

The local foremen were ready to make disparaging remarks about us, but we let the insults roll off our backs. We were among friends, because the Quakers were providing the administration of the day-to-day living circumstances, and we only had to deal with the foremen during the work hours.

My first assignment was on the rock quarry. That part of the world has no natural gravel the way the Midwest and New England have. The gravel for the roads had to be broken up from the underlying granite. The granite would be exposed by dynamiting a section of the bedrock. Some of that could go right into the rock crusher, but the big pieces could not be handled by the mechanical rock crusher, so the campers had to break the bigger pieces down to perhaps a foot in diameter. Then they could be pushed into the rock crusher which would break them down to gravel size that could be used on the roads. This was the bottom level of the work situation.

I came down with a psychosomatic cold almost immediately, and after spending a few days in the infirmary, I was strong enough to go back and do my work. The sense of having a ball and chain around one's ankle was entirely vivid. I looked forward to moving into some other work assignment. With good behavior and regular appearance, I was transferred to the trail crew. We maintained the trails and the telephone lines and bridges, which had been built by the CCC boys before our assignment. I learned to climb trees and poles with the spurs that are standard equipment. The trail clearing was a matter of using an ax and saw to put aside the trees that had fallen down across the trail.

A major part of the work was replacing bridges that had been built ten to fifteen years before. The logs and the planks were beginning to decay and were therefore no longer serviceable. We would cut down chestnut trees that had died from the chestnut blight. They served as stringers, the longish poles that lay underneath the bridge and supported the planks. We cut them and snaked them to where the new bridge was being built. We smoothed off the round side of the log to a flat surface at least a few inches wide and pulled them across into place. I don't remember much of the technical side of snaking the trunks of the chestnut trees into the bridge site and getting them across. What I remember particularly was nailing the planks onto the logs.

I had limited forestry skills from my experience with the family in the White Mountains, but I learned fairly fast. I could handle the ax and smooth off the rounded surface of the stringers with the adz, a sort of ax turned ninety degrees on the handle so that you swing it like a pick in a pick-and-ax operation. The oak planks were delivered by truck to the site.

They were probably eight or ten feet long, depending on the nature of the bridge, and three inches thick. They were cut from the nearby woods. They were prepared commercially outside of the camp and delivered to the bridge site.

When the stringers were smoothed off, we took a plank from the pile, put it into place, and nailed it on. You nail a three-inch thick oak plank onto the stringer with a ten-penny spike. A spike is about a foot long and maybe a half inch thick. Your instrument for doing this is a double-jack, a sledgehammer with a full-length handle. To hit the ten-penny spike from a standing position, and have it go directly through the oak and chestnut, is a skill that requires a good deal of practice. I mastered it, finally, so that I only missed once or twice hitting it squarely enough so that the weight of the sledge hammer drove it in through the very resistant oak plank and chestnut stringer. In doing so, I earned some admiration from the foreman, who had nothing but disparaging remarks to say about a new and green workman. The one that I remember best is when we were getting the chestnut logs over to the bridge site, and he said, "Now, be careful of those smaller shrubs and trees. The Park Service values them a good deal more than it values you!" I don't know if that was true, but it gave us a sense of our own inferiority in the eyes of the local population.

At the end of an eight-hour shift on the trail crew, with an hour for lunch, we would all climb into the flatbed truck and be driven back to camp. Camp was a series of five or six long buildings. They were barrack-like accommodations. On one floor we had our bunks, and there were forty to fifty men in the room, with a washroom and toilet outside. The cooking facilities were in another similar building, and the headquarters, camp offices and so on in another building. The camp was a fairly self-sufficient operation, with the necessities supplied by the forest service. The maintenance and operation of the camp was left to the staff of the American Friends Service Committee and whatever traditions and obligations they wanted to give the campers. The infirmary was one end of one of the buildings. Meals were served in the same building as the cooking.

Campers got along as best we could. We were not paid. My memory is that we were given $2.50 every month, but it might have been every week, for spending money. We got along on that with whatever family support each individual camper could provide. Our days were filled from eight to five with a regular work schedule. The work was organized and supervised by the Forest Service, except for the general maintenance. Campers were responsible for the normal meals and other necessities which came along. It was a fairly economical commitment by the American Friends Service Committee to provide supervision of the camp. There were Mennonite service committees and Brethren service committees that operated similar camps. The AFSC had several camps they supervised. The campers were assigned to camps of their own religious persuasion, and then all of the others were divided up among the Friends, the Brethren and the Mennonites. There was an amazing mix of persuasions among the campers, all the way from the fundamentalist Mennonites and Brethren to non-believers. There were not many non-believers, but some.

The day then was divided between work, sleep and meals, with several hours of leisure time in between. The leisure was used in several ways. Much of it was in conversation with other campers about the work and the administration of the camp. There was also a small library where one could go and read. For many of the campers, the period under the draft was an interruption of their college careers, so there was a fair amount of studying to do on their own if they could arrange it. Since I was most of the way through my Doctorate, and had some experience teaching, I could offer a geography course. One or two campers volunteered for it. We acquired a textbook and an atlas and proceeded to do an introductory course. I think there was only one student who finished it, and he got credit from a nearby Quaker school.

The other leisure was used mostly talking to other campers about whatever topic there was for the day, usually some complaints about the work schedule and the Forest Service, or about the administration of the camp. There was surrounding us a magnificent wilderness. Most of the campers did not explore it, but some of us did. The individual hikes from the camp were easy to find. Trails were well maintained, and you could get a very good sense of the natural life of the Great Smokies on your own. We didn't know the names of the plants, but you could begin to recognize the common plants of the region. Likewise the animals, except there were not many animals in view.

On one hike when I was on my way back to camp, I spotted a mountain lion or a lynx up on a branch above the tree quietly watching the trail. What he thought of this biped invading his territory, I don't know, but he didn't move. And I didn't move for a while. Then I proceeded slowly down the trail, which met a switchback, and he was out of sight behind me, and I didn't see anymore of him. On the weekends, if you had the energy, you could go off in any direction. Gatlinburg was the closest town, and it was a mile and a half or two miles away. The populace of the town was not sympathetic with the conscientious objector position, perhaps because of feeling guilt that they were not making a contribution to the war effort themselves. There were very few attractions in the town, and we didn't mix much with the local population.

Within camp, there was a reading room and there was the studying. I don't remember any music, but there must have been an opportunity to practice. I'm sure some of the campers did. In the evening, the conversation would often go on in the dining area. The camp administration left bread and butter and peanut butter and jam out for people who had evening appetites. Gradually a group formed that would stay up after the generators had been turned off to talk. Gradually this was institutionalized and called "The After-Ten Club," since that was the regular time for turning off the generators.

We continued our conversation by the light of gasoline lamps. Sometimes the conversation would be focused on some common topic, usually a gripe that the campers had, and that would go on informally for a while. As the conversation focused the problem was isolated. We had few alternatives. We could protest or we could suggest a different way of doing things. Both had to be channeled through the camp management for we had no access to the Park Service. The natural tendency of the group was to protest, to let off steam, and to express our frustration. This was facilitated by a camper with a long red beard. He was both articulate and confrontational. He had emerged as an informal leader of the group. I found that I could wait until he had whipped up an adequate emotion, and then come in with a constructive course of action. The discussion would shift to how to bring about the change? Who would make the appeal? And to whom? My red-bearded colleague soon realized the advantage of this dual strategy. We worked together without ever discussing it.

After several months in a base camp such as Gatlinburg, there were options available for which one could volunteer. Each was a job difficult to fill because the military had shrunk the available labor force: prison guards, mental hospital attendants, subjects for medical experiments, and parachute firefighters. This last alternative appealed to me, partly for the excitement and partly because it would get me back to Montana. I applied and was accepted. In a couple of months I said goodbye to the Great Smokies and was on my way to the Rockies. I left Tess in Cambridge for a couple of months until I finished the training and it was clear that we could live together in Missoula, the headquarters of the Forest Service's Aerial Fire Control.

Meanwhile a couple of hundred of us new recruits went through rigorous physical training both in calisthenics in camp and in the woods, building trails and maintaining telephone lines. A couple more practice jumps and we were ready for the real thing. My turn came early one morning after a lightning storm. Two of us put on our heavy canvas suits and checked that we had our fifty-foot ropes in the right leg pocket of the suit. In case we landed in the branches of a tree we could thread the rope through four buckles of the harness and detach ourselves from two shoulder buckles and let ourselves down to the ground, similar to rappelling from a cliff in rock climbing. With everything in order we took off: the pilot, the spotter, and the two jumpers. Using the detailed topographic map, the spotter went over with us the location of the fire, where we would probably jump (a small meadow near the fire), the nearest trail where we could leave our gear after we had put out the fire, and the route to the road head where we would be picked up by the ranger.

We flew west northwest across the panhandle of Idaho into the northwest corner of Washington. There, about six miles south of the Canadian border, we could see a tiny bit of smoke coming up from the dense forest. There was plenty of smoke around for the Canadians did not fight forest fire unless it threatened something more valuable than mere forest. The plane circled around looking for an open space in the forest. On a ridge about half a mile from the tiny smoke was a small meadow. The spotter dropped a tiny weight with its own parachute, about the size of a bandana, when the plane was just over the meadow. This would tell us how far the wind would carry us as we descended. My partner clipped his static line on the cable above the door and knelt down, one foot on the step outside. The spotter tapped him one the shoulder. Out he went. The static came taut pulling the cover off the carefully folded chute. It blossomed out round and white against dark green forest below.

The plane circled while I went through the same sequence. Clip the static line to the cable, kneel in the door, and put one foot on the step outside. When I felt the tap on the shoulder I stepped out into the wild blue yonder. Before I had time to think about it, I felt the opening shock of the parachute. The parachute straightened me into a vertical position, and I was floating gently a thousand feet above the ground.

I floated gently down to the meadow and landed normally. The plane circled around again and dropped the two backpacks that contained all we would need for a couple days. They landed near by. The plane flew off toward Missoula; we were on our own. We shouldered the backpacks and headed off to find the fire. It was already dusk, and the fire was not going anywhere. Everything was moist from the afternoon rain. We put a couple shovels of dirt on the smoldering coals, found a level spot to lay out our sleeping bags, ate our K-ration, and sacked out.

In the morning, we were wakened by a rustling in the brush above our heads. We had no idea what caused the rustling. We grabbed our Pulaski tools and started to get out of our bags when a white faced cow pushed through the brush and we relaxed. We checked the ashes we had left the night before. They were cool. We fixed our K-ration breakfast, packed up, and walked down hill to the trail. We left our gear, consulted the map, and decided we needed to go left on the trail to our rendezvous with the ranger who took us back to base camp. First jump successfully accomplished!

From here on the story seems less exciting. I do remember a few incidents where the landing with the parachute was not quite normal. In one case I came down and saw a fearful collection of rocks, not so much the rocks themselves as the spaces between them. It seemed as though there was too much chance of breaking an ankle in the available spaces. As I got closer to the ground, I realized the rocks were much bigger than they appeared. I could see one that was twelve or fifteen feet in diameter, big enough to land on, so I steered the parachute in that direction and sure enough, there was plenty of room to touch down, roll over, all on the same slab of rock. We wore enough clothes on the jump so that the rolling was cushioned. I could stand up, unhook myself from the parachute, and walk over to the meadow with no problem.

In another case I was drifting toward the trees and could not steer myself to the open meadow. I landed in the trees, and the parachute hung up on one of them, so I was dangling twenty or thirty feet from the ground. I had to thread the rope through four buckles on the harness and then lift myself with one hand while I unsnapped the harness from the lines of the parachute. Then I could unbuckle the parachute by lifting myself with one hand and unbuckling with the other. I descended safely to the ground very much like a *cour de rappel*. I extracted myself from the harness and proceeded to find my tools, leaving the parachute in the tree. Later we climbed the tree and cut off the limbs to let the parachute fall to the ground. I think that was my only tree landing.

The fires that we fought were called forest fires, but were more accurately described as ground fires in the forest. We would start near the top of the fire where it was spreading most rapidly up hill. Only after we had dug a trench wide enough to contain the fire would we go to close off the spreading sides of the burning area. Frequently we needed to go back and check places where our trench was inadequate. Once the fire was contained, one could relax a little and go put out the hot spots, places where stumps had started to burn. Mostly, these fires were small enough so that two jumpers were adequate. We never jumped alone.

Rarely did we face the prospect of a fire crowning out, where the whole tree would get hot enough to explode. The needles would burn explosively making a sound that was really scary. If there were no other trees near the explosion, that was all there was to it, but if the adjacent trees caught the fire, the fire was crowning out and there was nothing to do but maintain your distance or evacuate. We were not equipped to create a fire line in a closely packed stand. This is why they used aerial control, to stop the fire before it got out of control.

At sundown the ambient temperature dropped rapidly. The fire itself would slow down and we could and would take a break. One of us would go back and make sure that the ground fire was really contained and the remaining hotspots would not spread. The fire was then considered controlled. We could deal with meals and sleeping arrangements. We would come back to the fire in the morning until we were sure that the whole area was cool. We would actually run our hands through the ashes and if there was anything that felt hot we would mix the ashes with dirt. Then we would break camp, gather up the parachute and the tools, and take them to the trail where they could be picked up by the ranger's mule train.

We would walk to the designated rendezvous and wait. If there was any chance that the wait would be a long one, we had to carry our sleeping bags and K-rations with us. Mostly, the rendezvous was close enough so that there was no problem, but occasionally there were several miles of wilderness before we reached the road head. On one of these I learned an important topographic lesson. Walking up to the road head at the divide, one was tempted to identify several headwalls, cirque-like amphitheatres. The glacial valley is not a smooth descent, but step-like so that one identifies the false headwall as the final ridge, only to be disappointed that there is another one beyond it.

Most of the jumps were in the drainages that flowed into the Clark's Fork River, but sometimes we were in the drainages beyond. In that case we would be brought from the rendezvous to the nearest airfield where we could be picked up and taken home. In a busy fire season it might be the next day before a plane was free to pick us up. We could shower and shave, put on more-or-less respectable clothes, and tour the town. The town would have a bar or two. On one occasion Dexter McBride and I spent most of an evening trying to inveigle a barmaid to join us, but without success.

I jumped fires two seasons, 1944 and 1945. By the end of 1945 there were able-bodied veterans who took over, and our camp was disbanded. All in all we jumped for fifteen fires and seven training jumps. During the winter of 1944-45 we were dispersed to various useful jobs with the Forest Service.

Most of the nonfire season I worked in the Office of Timber Management under the direction of a particularly broadminded civil servant, Axel Lindh. He had me doing historical statistical analysis of the timber harvest for the whole northern region. It became obvious that the system of competitive bidding left many communities unsure of their future. The problem Axel was interested in was how to organize the timber harvest so that it could be fair to all the communities but still provide an economic support to them and the lumber companies. This work was a precursor to my later doctoral dissertation.

There were several weeks at the beginning of the summer when the fire season had not yet begun. The whole preparation for the fire season, including our retraining, took place before the fires started. The Forest Service used us in these weeks to build fences, roads, and telephone lines. My favorite job was cutting down the lodge pole pines and skinning them for fence rails. We made a competition out of how many we could fell and skin. We could fell and skin as many as fifty an hour from dense stands. You had to sharpen both your abilities and your axe. I've enjoyed these skills for another fifty years.

Sometime during the first fire season Tess drove from Cambridge to Missoula. She had a friend with her who had never been west before and who was sure there must be some use for sagebrush. She went back to

Boston without ever finding a use for sagebrush. Tess and I rented a little house close to campus. We developed rather close relations with five or six families from the smoke jumper unit. We held Quaker meeting in our living room. Tess found a job in the winter teaching sixth grade in Stevensville, a town thirty miles to the south. The members of the surrounding community were conscious of Tess's relationship to the conscientious objectors, but she suffered no overt discrimination.

At one point we felt our isolation from the important circumstances of the war. It was Halloween. We had some sort of celebration. I said, "Supposing we had a job pasting black cats on to orange wrapped noise makers. Would we feel more involved?"

My assignment ended somewhere in the fall of 1945, but we stayed on in Missoula because Tess was trying to get pregnant. I was still under the control of the Selective Service Administration, but they treated our situation as a medical problem. I continued to work with Axel Lindh in the timber management office.

After the first of the year, the Selective Service Administration brought this "vacation" to an end and assigned me to the San Dimas Hydrologic Experiment Station in southern California, east of Los Angeles. Most of the men were working in physical labor jobs on trails and picnic grounds. Because of my education and experience, I went to work in the office recording rainfall.

The war with Japan was finally concluded, and six months after the treaty was signed was the end of the Quaker obligation to run the camps. They turned over the camps to the Selective Service Administration. The new management had no experience with conscientious objectors and tried to tighten regulations. When they asked us to sign out and sign in when we left the camp, somehow the ink for the signatures always got spilled. We refused to go along with the tighter regulations. Finally, they threatened to transfer two of the men to an isolated camp in Oregon. We interpreted this as a punishment and organized a strike. By this time, six months after VJ day, we could see no point in our "incarceration" and remaining under the control of Selective Service. We were anxious to return to our peacetime occupations or education. Eighty of our 120 men refused to work in spite of the threat of five years in jail or $5,000 fine or both.

In lieu of our assigned work we conjured up worthwhile activities, especially packing food to send to Europe to relieve the suffering there. The Post Office had a stringent limit on the size of packages they would handle, maybe as little as five pounds. We shopped for nonperishables we could fit into the limited space. We did this partly for public relations purposes. We understood that the strike would be interpreted to the general public as slacking off unless we substituted public service. We raised money for the project through sympathetic members of the public, mostly from members of the peace community. Gradually, we became sophisticated fundraisers!

Somehow we were notified that we would be arrested if we did not return to our assigned jobs. The group assembled and discussed options. Of the 120 men in the camp, the same eighty of us agreed to continue the strike. We were all arrested and now our antagonist became the District Attorney.

We were in jail just a weekend, but I already had a bad cold which turned into pneumonia with incarceration. They put me in the jail hospital, but I was by this time hallucinating. Mother showed up and took responsibility for me by moving me to the Huntington Hotel. She had to buy me some decent clothes so that I could come down to the dining room.

After the group was arrested they set us free to go back to camp to continue our packaging of food. Essentially, we organized our own community and provided our own services. The Selective Service Administration left us in the camp unsupervised. At every stage of the conflict we had one or more meetings of the whole group and all decisions were made by consensus. We held together by sheer loyalty. Any man could leave at will.

The Selective Service Administration was between a rock and a hard place. If they dismissed us from service, it would set a precedent. The whole system would collapse. The Selective Service Administration wanted to maintain their procedures for letting the conscientious objectors free at the same rate as the members of the armed services.

The District Attorney didn't want a conviction of eighty conscientious objectors who were doing useful work. On the one hand he was responsible to the government. On the other hand, he didn't want to appear to be responsible for our conviction. Pro bono lawyers represented us to the District Attorney. This confrontation dragged on for six months. Finally, about twenty men were found guilty and given suspended sentences. They dropped charges against the rest of us, and we were free to pick up our civilian lives.

During much of these six months I hitch-hiked back and forth to Bozeman, Montana, to be with Tess who was having a difficult pregnancy, ending in a miscarriage.

Teaching at Montana State

Bozeman Years

Sourdough Road

After the war, I was in Montana. When I left the camp that we were in, Tess was trying to hold a pregnancy and having a lot of difficulty. I arrived in Bozeman, and we set up housekeeping together there. I've forgotten where we lived the first stage, maybe we mooched off the Rennes. We took a small apartment and decided that we wanted to build a house and start a subsistence operation imitating the Rennes. We looked for land to buy, and at the edge of the built-up area, we found a five-acre plot that was just about right. It was on a creek, one of the headwaters of the Missouri River, called Sourdough Creek. Somehow the sourdough title keeps entering into it: Sourdough Road, Sourdough Creek. If it keeps cropping up, it's a fairly important creek. It was about two miles from town and about the same distance from the university.

We bought the five acres, having looked it over and finding it to our liking. So then how to build a house? We had exhausted anything we could invest in buying the property. Tess and I were anxious to get started on the house and took advantage of a lot of experience in living in other houses, including a temporary house on campus where we were living currently that was built for officers during the war. It was a minimal house, and very efficient. We copied a number of things, especially the lighting and the condensed kitchen from that design. Of course, it was not appropriate that a former conscientious objector occupied one of these; it was a lot better than the rest of the veteran housing. But we were in line like the others and our experience made us eligible.

We met a very competent and intelligent carpenter, who had worked a lot with logs, and we wanted to build a log cabin. Bozeman is very well situated to get round logs that are suitable for this. We had heard about radiant heating and were ready to experiment with that. The experiment was not something you could abandon easily, but we had every reason to believe that it would work. We borrowed, I think, $1,000 from Aunt Terry. With that and the land purchased in our own name, we could borrow the $5,000 needed to build the cabin.

We recognized that our initial structure was probably not one that we could live in permanently, and that we would expect to build a more spacious house. The house that we first built was about the size of a small apartment, I want to say 700 square feet, but I'm not sure that's right. It was mostly one big room with a small kitchen off it. The rest of the east side of the house was a dressing closet and a crib room and bathroom. It served us very well for a while, several years, actually. We thought in the end we would probably build a larger house and have that small one for a graduate student or another family. That's the way it worked out.

Bozeman is in a peculiar location, just behind the front range of the Rockies, and something of an outlier. It is a little to the east of the Continental Divide, so unpleasant weather comes in the form of an east wind. With a large Canadian air mass to the east, you have cold wind from the east, whereas the major circulation is from the west. It was appropriate with our location and the topography to put the house below the road a little bit and dug into the west-facing slope to protect us from the uncomfortable east wind. The house served us very well as a place to get started.

We finally adopted a child from a couple who had dreams of medical school and didn't want to start their family. He was a difficult infant. He sort of came to us without us having any experience in parenting. We didn't think you needed experience, but this baby was colicky. We moved into the cabin a few months after Steve had joined us. From there on my circle of dependents for which I had a particular loyalty and responsibility was expanded from two to three. That was a fairly serious responsibility. We had a curtain across the end of the main room that could separate the bedroom function from the rest of the room. We enjoyed that.

We needed to keep Steve from drowning in Sourdough Creek when we needed an hour or two in the vegetable garden. At two years old, he had outgrown his playpen. How to keep him safe? A chicken wire enclosure was an obvious possibility. It was built, but not very sturdily. The second or third day he was enclosed we found him with his shoes off climbing the fence using his toes through the fencing. I think he was still within the enclosure, but we never tried using it again.

We tried a tether tied to a harness. He never learned to get out of the harness or to untie the rope, but for some reason, we had to abandon that solution. We must have learned to keep an eye on him. One time when he roamed loose, a neighbor driving by slowed down and pointed excitedly. There was little Steve on the roof of the chicken coop! I had kept a ladder leaning up against the building. It wasn't a very big building, only eight feet from roof to ground. We thanked the motorist. I climbed up and brought him down.

It turned out that Steve was allergic to cow's milk, but not to goat's milk. Goats have milk with very small fat globules, so it's much more easily digested. We were buying goat's milk that was canned in the Los Angeles area and fairly expensive. But it solved the colic problem, and Steve matured as a very normal and fairly adventurous youngster.

We began producing our own goat's milk. Mostly we had Alpine goats; they were all white, and no billy. We would take the nannies to other subsistence farmers to get them bred. There was no artificial insemination for goats at that time. We built a barn with the plans for the goats, so it included a place to take the milk and cool it off quickly. We had the state dairy inspector check the goat's milk. It wasn't necessary that we had an inspection, but we found that we were producing milk with a bacteria count that was way below the norm. We continued the procedure, which was to put the milk through a filter at the very beginning and have it sitting in cold water. It cooled down quickly. That was the answer to the question of the bacteria count.

We found two or three other families that had similar problems with their children and needed goat's milk. We got to delivering three or four quarts of milk every other day and kept that up for a couple of years. We kidded that the title of our dairy enterprise on Sourdough Road was not a particularly attractive title, and if we added the goat dairy name to it, it would be even less attractive in a culture that had a lot of cattle ranching in its traditions.

We also had chickens, but no other animals. We had a large garden, and it had to be irrigated, but the slope that we had was a little too steep for a ditch or flood irrigation, so it was mostly sprinklers. The garden was quite successful, and we adapted our diet and our cooking to the subsistence pattern. We mostly ate the vegetables that we had, certainly during the summer, and ate from the freezer for a significant part of the cold season. Of course, we had the milk and butter, and that represents quite a large part of the total food situation. We did have to buy meat, but we had old chickens and young goats, and they filled in a good deal.

The subsistence lifestyle was sufficiently clear that it was very much part of our son's life. When one of the grandfathers died, Steven asked from the dining room table, "When are we gonna eat Grandpa?" That has been with us as a family joke for a long time.

The initial work of developing a subsistence lifestyle is more time-consuming than just to keep it going. I would dash home at five o'clock from the office, pull on coveralls, go down to milk the goats, and bring the cool milk up to the house. The goats would be fed while they were being milked. I think we had three nannies milking at the most, but with three, we could cover the low periods pretty well. I would then take off my coveralls and eat supper and then go on until dark at least with the various chores that needed to be done. For instance, there were a couple of meanders within the property, parts of the Sourdough Creek meandering around. We learned to cut willow branches and tie them up to place them in strategic positions in lieu of rip-rap to keep the ground from eroding where the meanders made a sharp current. That was quite successful, but it involved a fair amount of cutting and tying and burying the bundles of willow in places where the erosion was threatening and extending the protected area so that they didn't get undermined by the stream. These cuttings eventually turned into a nice open semi-circle surrounded by willows.

We did eventually build a bigger house about five years after the cabin—the small house came to be described as "the cabin"—was completed, when Steve's tricycle outgrew it. There was a visiting architect by the name of Richard Neutra. He was a very convincing sort of person. He made a good deal of fun out of the pattern of urban expansion that was happening then, and still happens in the individual family on a lot. He described it as "the ranch houses with seven feet of ranch on one side and seven feet of ranch on the other." We knew that we didn't want to be part of that, and we had the means to have a different subsistence kind of life.

We asked Neutra if he would be interested in designing a house for us. We should have perhaps introduced ourselves as being very fussy about the practicality of a design, because he was not used to people with as much experience in building houses as we had. Most customers sit back and let the architect design the house and then move in and make the best of it. We wanted to be a part of the design team; we were not about to invest as much money as one puts into a house without being part of the design team.

The house site that we wanted was on a piece of fairly level ground. We wanted a one-story house, which we were up front about. Tess could see out of either eye, but not both at the same time, so she had relatively little depth perception and clearly a one-story dwelling was to be desired. Taking everything into account, Neutra designed a very beautiful one-story house with a log and glass structure. It had a single sloping roof, which is much more efficient than a gabled roof, because the plane surface of the roof tends to hold together the sides. The situation with the house below the road and adjacent to the driveway meant that the house could have a sod roof. There was one building in town that had a sod roof, so we knew it could be done. Neutra took this into account, and we had a lovely overall design.

On the inside, things were not as convenient. We finally concluded that the interior design had been delegated to the newest apprentice in the architectural firm. We couldn't get answers to a lot of our concerns. Our concerns were probably much more detailed than he was accustomed to, and certainly more detailed than the apprentice to whom the project had been delegated could handle. We got increasingly frustrated with the business of accepting the plans and suggesting modifications and not hearing back anything that seemed to answer our questions. This being our first project with an architect, we didn't have much compunction in breaking off the relationship. We paid our bill and went on with the design and preparations on our own.

One of the elements was a roof design that extended the roof out over the western edge of the house quite a ways. It was of course a fairly heavy roof, since it had to carry a snow load as well as the wet sod. The architect had thought that, like California, you could buy heavy timbers easily to support the extension of the roof. We couldn't find those timbers in any lumber yard nearby, and the cost of shipment from California was exorbitant, because it was less than a carload lot of dimension lumber. We checked around and found that we could get the structural strength that we needed with steel I-beams. We suggested that that was a better solution, and Neutra accepted that solution.

The steel beam didn't give the decorative effect of the heavy timbers, but it saved us several thousand dollars that would be involved in having a wood structure. The steel was to be concealed by the ceiling, whatever the ceiling would be. We broke ground for the new house four and a half years after we built the other house. We used the same log contractor, Wally Dightman, and his son. The two worked together very well, and the house began to take shape. It followed the architect's design as a shell, and we moved things around on the inside somewhat. We had a big fireplace in the living room. In order to preserve the effect of the grass growing all the way around the house, we had a half-partition on the north side with glass from there up, so that we had a view to the north as well as the west and the south. The east side was built into the hill below Sourdough Road.

We started building the house well before we had enough resources to pay the whole cost. We borrowed some money in the construction period, and then we sort of ran out of money when we hired a cabinetmaker to complete the kitchen as we designed it. We had specified that we would like birch plywood finish for the kitchen area, and we ran out of money as we paid off the cost of the design and the kitchen. There were two different work levels, a work level for cooking and cutting and a different lower level, two or three inches lower, for mixing. The whole stove area was stainless steel. The oven was separate from the top of the stove. It wasn't the conventional stove that you can get in a hardware store. These were all modifications that we had come up with in thinking about how a kitchen is really used. The east side was built into the hill below Sourdough Road.

We did finally end up with a dining room adjacent to the kitchen, really a part of the entryway into the house. There really wasn't any dining room, we just widened out that hall and ate there with a narrow table against the wall, the other side of which was the kitchen. Having run out of money, we didn't hire any more help to complete the interior. We bought a table saw which had the capacity to be turned into a lathe or a drill press and set that up in the utility room. Every night we would sweep up the sawdust before we went to bed. The interior took us most of five years to complete, but we did other things meanwhile.

We lived in the little house for about a year, and then we lived in the incomplete big house, for four years before it was finally done. The most arduous task was the ceiling of the great room. We used tongue-and-groove plywood in eighteen-inch-wide pieces to make a tight ceiling that matched the woodwork with the paneling of the walls. The wooden ceiling and the walls would make a dark room if it weren't for the brightness provided by all the windows. Fitting the tongue-and-groove panels of the ceiling to the rough stonework of the fireplace was quite an arduous task. I would be up on the platform built between two sawhorses marking in the exact shape of the stonework for the end of panel. I would drop down and saw out the shape with a little coping saw. But since you can't match it exactly, there was always a little change needed to bring the ceiling panels right up against the stone. Again and again, over I suppose most of the year, we worked on this problem. The panels of plywood would be handed up to me by Tess and then handed back to her with the adjustment, always a little change in angle so that we never got the thing quite the way it should be. But when we ended up, we had a smooth transition from the plywood to the stonework.

We had a real satisfaction when the house was complete. We had chosen the materials for the rest of the interior and used some materials that were not widely available at the beginning. For instance, there was an opportunity to use the wood from sawmills that couldn't be used for lumber and was usually shredded, almost like shredded wheat. It could be mixed with cement to create wall panels that would go up adjacent to one another with a batten in between. I brought it back from Missoula, over two hundred miles away, in the same trailer that we used to cut firewood. I almost came to an end coming down a hill very close to Missoula. I did not recognize that I had to really slow down, because braking with a trailer causes it to swerve such that it could easily have tipped over with the jeep pulling it. But we got through.

We adopted our second son almost at the end of the construction. We were offered the opportunity to take two unrelated children by the welfare office, and we thought that would be fine. It turned out that the older boy, Victor, was somewhat retarded, not significantly in terms of schooling, but it probably would become significant. The younger child, Peter, was a very attractive youngster. Both of the boys had somewhat darker skins than most of the population of Montana. They both had had difficult childhoods thus far, ending up in foster homes. They were very pleased to have a regular home. But the somewhat suppressed rivalry between Peter and Victor began to show up, and at one point, we found Victor suggesting to Peter that he put his hands in front of the saw.

At that point, I closed off the acceptance of the two children. We had to give one of them back to the welfare agency after most of a year in our care. We chose to keep Peter and give back Victor. They found a home for

Victor in eastern Montana that already had a teenage girl who could accept this youngster and mother him as a younger sibling. We assume that Victor moved into a good situation.

We never discussed the failure to accept Victor with Peter. I think Steve was probably aware of the kind of decision we had to make, but Peter was still only two and a half years old. It never occurred to us that this might be a serious subject for discussion with a younger child. Whether that left a scar on his personality, I have no idea. His whole childhood was normal. He was a very attractive child, so much so that in the checkout line, he would speak to the cashier and say, "Aren't you going to say something about my big brown eyes?" He was accustomed to being complimented that way. That again stayed with us as a family story.

It wasn't until high school that problems began to show up. How much of it was the result of a misfit between his adolescence and Tess's personality, we can't judge. It ended up with the divorce separating the family. Peter stayed with me and went through a variety of schools, but he didn't like school, although he did seem to like high school in Kalamazoo where I moved with Suzie and Sherry after Suzie and I married. He took the GED exams and came through very well, but the last two years after the divorce were touch and go as to how he would complete his formal education.

Steve was seven years older than Peter, so by the time these struggles between Tess and Peter surfaced, he was away at boarding school. Steve was obviously quite talented in a variety of ways, and we wanted to make the most of it and thought that a boarding school was the best bet. We enrolled him at Westtown, a Quaker Boarding School outside of Philadelphia. We didn't realize that his sense would be that he was rejected from the parental home and that boarding school was a convenient way to get rid of him. We didn't have any inkling of that until almost the end. In his senior year, Steve bought a car from one of the workers at the school, and that was strictly against the rules, so he was sent back home. I had to go and retrieve the car and bring it home. Steve outgrew his interest in mechanics fairly soon after that. I can't remember if Steve finished high school in Montana. I think he took the GED and sailed through. After several jobs in Montana, Steve went to Florida and enrolled in a deep sea diving course and made a living retrieving golf balls from golf courses.

Getting a PhD

I was teaching at Montana State while working on my dissertation. I had made a couple of false starts on the dissertation that were pretty much dependent upon where I was at the time I made them. While I was still parachuting, for instance, I thought the Bitterroot Valley would make an interesting case study in geography. The drainage that came into the Bitterroot River was a kind of ready-made piece of evidence of regionalization.

I don't think I got very far, but I did collect a few maps and think seriously about the evidence. There was an employee of one of the federal agencies who tried to get the agencies sufficiently sensitive to the valley, so that he could get them cooperating. He never did get that far, but it was part of the proposed dissertation. I never submitted a draft to my committee about this, but I did think about it. I had my pilot's license by that point, so I could fly over the area and sort of pull it together. I didn't have a full license to take passengers, but I had my permit to solo, and I enjoyed doing it. That was about all that I did with the flying myself.

The first false start was the draft that was done before I left Madison using maps. The draft that I submitted was turned down because I needed a bigger subject.

At Montana State we were on a quarter system, so I could take two quarters off after a certain period of time, and that gave me half a year of free time to do what one does during a sabbatical. It replaced the more typical system of a sabbatical every seven years. When I had built up seven quarters of teaching, I planned to start on the dissertation seriously.

The two previous subjects were not really far enough along, so I decided to pick a new topic. Talking around to different people, the most important question I found led to a study of the location of sawmills and the problem of sustaining a community when you have to give free access to sawmills competing for stumpage. It included the problem of who's going to cut the trees down, the transportation to a sawmill, and then the sawmill itself. It turned out to be a clear example of a weight-losing industry, one where it's more expensive to transport the raw materials than it is to transport the finished product. A lot of the tree gets thrown away in the process of making lumber out of it.

The question I decided to tackle for the dissertation was how to control the choice of stumpage (raw material), who harvested it, and the relationship of that harvesting to the sawmill. I already knew quite a bit about the process from my apprenticeship with the U.S. Forest Service, because I had written two or three short pieces for Axel Lindh, the head of the timber management division. I laid out the research and started collecting data about the location of sawmills. The study area was western Montana, west of Glacier National Park and north of the big lake there. There were a lot of sawmills.

Most of the sawmills were pretty small and were referred to as "gypo" outfits. They were a single saw with a carriage that would carry the piece that was being sawed, moving back and forth. That carriage has a ratchet that the operator used to move the log in one inch to saw off the next inch. The whole thing was mounted on a single platform, so that when the nearby trees had been cut, the sawmill could be moved over to cut the next batch of trees. It was a fairly small area that you could cut at once. You can't invest too much in the accuracy of the saw, and the saw makes a fairly wide cut, maybe a quarter of an inch for a circular saw that's big enough to get through the log. The result is a fairly uneven piece of wood and lots of sawdust. It certainly is not set up in a careful engineering way. After the gypo cut, the rest of the process is quite carefully engineered. The important question was how much lumber you can get out of a given chunk of wood. You've already thrown away the sawdust of that first cut, and since the circular saw makes a wide cut, there is a good deal of sawdust.

The squared-off log cut by the gypo sawmill is transported by truck to a more central location where there's a larger and more permanent mill. It was a facility that required a lot of investment. In this case, the largest mill was adjacent to Missoula, and it was a great big establishment. They had a pond they could dump the logs into to wash them. They had to do that because the logs had been skidded by tractor to the point where they were picked up, so they had lots of gravel and dirt and gunk in them. If you had spent quite a bit of investment in the band saw, you couldn't afford to chew up the band saw with gravel. The logs were brought up and the first cuts were made. The band saw was as fine as possible, maybe an eighth of an inch, or a little bit narrower than that, so you don't lose as much of the log to sawdust as the gypo mill.

But there was the problem of how much timber the mill could get close to. It was much more expensive to transport the round logs, and all the sawdust that's involved, than it was to transport the lumber resulting from it. The big mill adjacent to the city of Missoula was well located, because several different drainages come together close to that point, so it was mostly downhill truck transport to the mill. Some of the logs were hauled there as round logs, but it's pretty difficult to keep a load on the truck when it's all wobbly because it is round. The choice of location is important, as is the duration of the supply of raw material. Since it was growing in the forest, you can't be close to a whole lot of lumber, the way a smelter can be close to quite a bit of ore. The Missoula location was good because you could go up several different valleys from there and you had access to all of the downhill transportation.

My dissertation asked how the lumber industry fit the theoretical adjustment expected of a weight-losing industry with a fairly widely distributed raw material. The answer is that you get as close as you can with the engineering of the manufacturing process. The gypo mill, cutting railroad ties and logs that will be made into lumber, can be very close to the raw material, but it can't do a very fine job of manufacturing. The big mill in Missoula or several intermediate locations are possible. I was asking how much engineering goes into making these intermediate locations possible, and how long do they stay in place. Because if they're close to the raw material, they exhaust the supply fairly quickly, and if they're distant, as the mill near Missoula was, they can be thought of as permanent.

There are examples of each accommodation in any given region. The Forest Service insists on a competitive bid process so that all of the sawmills can compete for the supply of lumber, or even two or three different stages to get up to the final product that's marketable in the industry. It was a simple example, but it had not been studied, so my dissertation was really a final check on that hypothesis. How to keep the bidding process competitive yet still provide a situation where the mill can have some permanence is a question that plagues the whole sawmill industry.

I was going to go off on a parallel between the sawmill location problem and the retail grocery, where again, the grocery store wants to be close to the consumers, but how close can you get and still avoid the extra costs of providing access? You have the corner grocery, which is really close, and you have the large market and the supermarket. They get further and further from the furthest customers.

I had done a good deal of the fieldwork before my dissertation committee was alerted to it. A lot of studies like this were done with a descriptive character rather than an analytical character. As I went from gypo to gypo and the intermediate sawmills and so on, I was collecting data on whether there was a roof over the sawmill or not and other information that was extraneous to the central problem. I must have wasted three or four months collecting this descriptive data that wasn't needed for theoretical work.

I submitted the chapter that had all of this descriptive material to my thesis advisor, and he suggested that I throw away about three-quarters of it, or maybe four-fifths, and concentrate on the analytical work. That was difficult to do, because I had invested so much in collecting the data, but it did make sense. From there on I concentrated on the analytical problem.

The thesis pretty well fell into place. I finished the bulk of the data collection in the six months that I had off. Then there was a lot of paring down and throwing away and starting over, so it was three years in process before I finally submitted the draft to the examining committee. They reviewed it and found it acceptable. I took my orals in the first part of 1950.

Professor

I was starting out on my first experience of professional teaching at Montana State, because being a graduate student is a little different. All the teaching I had done was as a graduate assistant, and I had never had the full responsibility for a course. I had completed my comprehensives at the University of Wisconsin, but had not finished my thesis.

Teaching seemed fearsome to do all by myself, and I was pretty frightened when I met the first geology class. I had to teach both geography and geology at that point, since I had had some minimal training in geology.

There was quite a pent-up demand for these courses, at least for the geology course, so there were 120-some students in the first group.

I faced the audience and started to lecture, and once I got into it, it was pretty simple. I shouldn't say simple, but it followed the experience I had as a student, because I could imitate the memories that I had of previous professors. The class was fairly respectful and nobody made fun of me, so I moved on through a course in geology that seemed reasonable.

The geography courses were a good deal more relaxed. I had one in general geography and one that was oriented to business school students, economic geography. I found that I could do quite well with the general geography. I stumbled on and somehow got the idea of teaching from an atlas rather than from a text. The text material was mostly covered in mimeographed material that was handed out regularly, while the atlas provided the source material. It became a series of exercises, based upon the enormous wealth of reference that the atlas gave.

So I had a start on the courses that I was going to teach, and I knew from experience on the other side of the podium that I could make it, and I didn't need to have any stage fright. There were some concerns about my teaching at first because many of the students had been soldiers in the war, and I had been a conscientious objector.

It turned out that there was some jealousy mixed in with the prejudice. I didn't have any feeling from most of my students that they objected to the conscientious-objector experience, but some faculty members didn't like the idea of me as a conscientious objector taking a position on the faculty. It was three or four people maybe out of more than a hundred faculty members.

I was not as circumspect as I might have been. There was another former smoke jumper on the faculty in the engineering school, and the two of us were fairly close, although he was older than me and more conventional. There were also some students that shared the same ideals, or at least joined us in our concern. We got into a fair amount of trouble when the state legislature was considering passing laws to restrict the freedom of the Hutterites. The Hutterites are a group of Christians that held the pacifist position. Most of them had been German and were offered a haven by Catherine the Great, I think, in southern Russia, since she was in need of good farmers, and peasants raised in that medieval system. When they came to the U.S. or Canada, they kept fairly close family and neighborhood relations and were quite distinctive as they settled in Montana.

The expansion of the Hutterite settlements was quite a threat to their neighbors. Their communal system seemed to work very well, so they bought more land and more land. The general populace could see no end to the success of the Hutterites. There were several attempts to disadvantage them. There were discussions about whether they could own land or not and whether they had full citizenship.

The colleague in the engineering school, the two students, and I wrote a letter saying that if we took the Constitution seriously, these attempts to rein in the Hutterites were illegal. This created quite a firestorm. There was an editor of the county newspaper, a weekly, who was definitely on the other side of the fence. He kept bringing it up and asserting that we were not properly patriotic. Renne, who was then president of the college, stood by us without questioning it. There was no fighting back on his part, because there was definitely an expectation that this was within the realm of respectable academic freedom.

I convinced the administration of Montana State that I needed a second person in the department. I had the authorization to hire a geologist, since I could cover the geography, and he would cover the geology. When I went back to Madison to defend my PhD thesis, I asked the head of the department of geology if he had anybody who would be interested in taking on such an appointment, where he had the whole field to cover. The chairman of the geology department said, "I just might have the right person for you," and had me interview Charles Bradley. He had finished his undergraduate work, was working for his doctorate, and had a business as a photographer in Madison, but was really looking for a different career. His alternatives seemed to be Waco, Texas, and Bozeman, Montana. He didn't have any question about where he wanted to be. We hit it off very well, and I recommended him for the open position. He came in the fall of 1951. We had a very good relationship and worked well together.

Eventually I got authorization to hire a second geographer, and later authorization to hire two more geologists. Charlie was tagged for the deanship of Arts and Sciences, so we had in the department three geologists and two geographers. It has developed into a department of Earth Sciences that is particularly well suited for the academic analysis of environmental problems. I think we probably got a climatologist in there, but it was after I had moved on to the High School Geography Project.

There was one point early in my career where I might have gone in a different direction. I was offered a very good job with the U.S. government. The Department of Interior is responsible for a lot of resources and their proper use. When the Department of Interior deals with an area, it tends to set up minerals in one compartment and water in another compartment and so on. The treatment of an area is quite fractured. They wanted to have a coordinated management, and so scouted around for people who knew something about everything but not much about any one thing. When they contacted me, I was in the field collecting sawmill data for my dissertation. It came as something of a surprise that they wanted me. They offered me a job at the GS-15 level, which was enough to live on.

I had a few friends at Interior, and I had done some work for one of the agencies. They thought I had great judgment. They explained the job and where it would lead. It sounded quite appealing, but I was just getting started on an academic career. I had a push-and-pull reaction. I wasn't home so I couldn't consult with Tess. I was in the third attempt to get back to my dissertation and get that part of my career over. I didn't want to interrupt that. It was good fun, for one thing, and it was interesting to see the reaction of the people, the "gypos" to an academic exercise.

I think I turned the Department of Interior down flat. I thanked them for their interest, and they went back to their personnel files. The offer was sweet enough so that it didn't go by me completely, but I didn't want to interrupt this third attempt at my dissertation.

I should mention here that while I was living on Sourdough Road and working on my professional life, I also had a number of sexual affairs. These affairs were not only an important part of my life; they were also an important concern in the division between my life as a generous and well-meaning person and the actual nature of my life. When you take the whole ball of wax, I don't really feel badly about the affairs, but as you look more closely at my life, they stand out in sort of contrast to the whole thing. They stand out more as a significant element to which we normally only devote footnote space.

I tended to look at any activity in terms of whether it provided me with an opportunity to seduce someone. When, for instance, I became active in the Association of American Geographers, I thought in terms of whether or not it got me out of the narrow confines of Bozeman and whether I could use some of the time away from Bozeman for sexual advantage. The only explanation that I can offer is over-active testosterone.

It was important to me that I continued to be attractive to women well beyond the expectation of going to bed with them. I doubted my attractiveness, but that doubt was fairly easily satisfied or eliminated. I have some regrets about this part of my life, but it's hard to imagine my life without it. I have regrets, but I don't know that I would like me any better, or like my life any better, if I didn't have them.

During almost every relationship with someone of the female gender, I was constantly thinking about the possibility of a sexual relationship. At some point, I would push that part of the relationship aside so that I could deal with the other parts of the relationship. That mostly happened when it was clear that the other party was not interested.

I pretended to treat those relationships as ones which gave the woman the status of being equal in freedom. Some women were open to being treated as objects of my affection and other women were not. The women who were not interested sexually were equally valued for their work. I recognized at the time that it was a difficult problem to treat both types of women equally.

I had both long-term affairs and one-night seductions. The seductions didn't seem to diminish the importance of the long-term affairs. The seductions were unfaithful both to the marriage and to the long-term affairs.

One of the important long-term affairs was with Deborah (not her real name) in Bozeman. The affair started unexpectedly. I didn't even realize the intensity of the relationship that was going to develop. I leaned over and kissed her once when we were together, and the response was so positive on her part. Deborah said, "You are the only other person beside my husband who ever kissed me." That came as a "Wow." From that developed a long-term and very intense relationship that lasted several years.

I think anybody would want Deborah in their life, even if not sexually. She was very kind and she had a refreshing attitude. Her view of the world was different from not only Tess, but from almost everybody else.

We took field trips that Deborah and I organized for students at Montana State for students to help on the Indian reservation. The Indian reservation was 150 miles away. The trips were rarely less than a long weekend. They provided an opportunity for Deborah and me to be together. The trips started under the auspices of the American Friends Service Committee.

I think Deborah knew about my other seductions during our relationship, but I'm not sure. I don't think that Deborah and I ever talked about leaving our spouses to be together. We probably thought about it, but we didn't bring it up to the surface. The affair ended with my marriage to Suzie.

Turkey

The Ford Foundation announced a program for training in overseas area studies, designed with people who could speak Arabic and live in Arabic countries. They were looking for Americans who would be conversant with the culture and be specialists in the regional areas of the world. The ignorance on the part of educated Americans in this aspect of foreign affairs was obvious when the State Department asked the Ford Foundation to get a program started. They announced the program to start in the fall of 1951, but the fellowships were available starting in the summer. It was March or April when they made the first announcements.

We had in Montana a group of specialists in agriculture, who were in Turkey already, but one was home on leave. He was going to coach me on the local situation, so I could write a prospective research program on the same theme I had used in my Master's Degree, the cultural adaptation to a semi-arid environment. I had a good source for the local conditions. I put in an application for such a fellowship for the following year.

Why was I interested in this opportunity? The question might be posed in the negative. Why wouldn't any geographer be interested in an overseas fellowship? The sense of wanting to know intimately what you were studying is perfectly natural. That's the way I felt about, not specifically Turkey, but any of the semi-arid areas that I might have studied. After getting my PhD, I tried to keep in touch with overseas opportunities. I may have run across this opportunity in that routine activity. Tess agreed with me that it was an exciting opportunity.

I won the fellowship, so from June on I knew what I was going to do for the following year. We studied Turkish and boned up on the area that we had chosen which was Central Anatolia. The application successfully passed through the screening and we were off to Turkey before the fall was over. We had organized ourselves to camp out, since the $8,000 the fellowship could pay was marginal. We turned in our 4X4 Jeep for a new Jeep pickup and found a carpenter who could build a van body on the back of it. So we had a truck that we could use to travel through the countryside in Turkey and interview farmers and find out how they were adjusting to the environment that they had to work with. The environment was surprisingly like the environment of the Great Plains. We got hold of detailed maps of the area and converted some assets that would not payoff until retirement into ready cash. We must have had close to the amount of the fellowship in resources of our own. We thought we were in good shape to support a year's fieldwork in Central Turkey.

Steve was five, so we knew that he could adapt to the camping experience and built him into our plans. There doesn't seem time between when he was an infant and the time we left for him to have gotten that old. But he was five going on six when we left with a pickup full of the things that we would need camping out in Central Anatolia.

At that time, ocean transport was the only transport available, so we reserved a place for the truck and the three of us on the American Export Line ship that went regularly from New York to the Mediterranean. It happens that we scheduled it so that we arrived in Istanbul, Turkey, on the night of the celebration of the independence of Turkey.

We got off the ship in Istanbul to discover that there were no hotel rooms because the people were celebrating the anniversary of the Republic of Turkey. Turkey came into being when Ataturk took control of the country. Prior to World War I, Turkey lived for several centuries under Ottoman Empire control. The people probably had no particular interest in changing that and likely had little idea of what the alternatives were. After 400 years of living under the moderate rule of an inherited despotism, whatever sense of possible new opportunities or new freedoms might be gone. The big wide world beyond Turkish boundaries was reserved for the upper class.

There was a strong bureaucracy, built in part upon an artificial class that is hard to visualize for Americans. The Ottomans had the pattern of going through the Balkans, picking up youngsters and training them as Janissaries. They were pretty much brainwashed of their own ambitions and taught to accommodate to those of the nation that captured them. They were raised in the expectation of being the ruling elite in Turkey, and they could forget whatever they had in their origins.

Of course, we were completely unprepared for urban living and had no reservations in Istanbul. Fortunately, we had made friends on the boat with a Turkish student, and he took us under his wing. We circulated through all the first-class and second-class and third-class hotels before finally ended up in a place. It was more of a bawdy house than a hotel, but it did at least provide us with a room where we could spread out and sleep, and we could move the following day.

We stayed in Istanbul for about a week. We knew that our research area was in Anatolia, a rural area across the Bosporus, but we had to go through Istanbul to get there. Our time in Istanbul gave us a feel for how much we could do on our own and how much we were dependent on an interpreter. We needed three months in study and practice in order to feel more or less competent on our own. We thought of it as a distinct period. We had left the U.S. and the English-speaking area and were now sink or swim in finding our way in Turkish culture. We were still in the preparatory period getting ready to do the research.

We took an apartment in Ankara, which is fairly well inland and not part of the Mediterranean culture. That meant that it was fully Turkish, and celebrated that fact. We did a lot of language lessons. We did not attend school. Our lessons were strictly one to one.

We got to know some of the Turkish people while in Ankara, but didn't form close friendships. The people who were automatically close were the agricultural advisors or the technical aid people who were attempting to show the Turkish farmers how to do better with their resources. They would not say that they were working with the Helburn family, but they were the automatic friendships, the automatic contacts.

We did go to wedding celebrations and other events in the community. The celebrations were pretty well segregated so that men danced with men and women danced with women. The food was sufficiently homogeneous so that it all fit together. There was a modest amount of alcohol consumed in the form of raki or wine. Does that sound like a choice? I had an appetite that was catholic, so I would drink anything.

After the closeness and tightness of Istanbul, Ankara was refreshingly open and modern and easy to live in. While we were there, I was preparing to do the research. I left Tess and Steve there in the apartment while I went off on my own to develop an interview schedule. I wanted to be able to compare one village with another in a fairly readily statistical way.

The research was designed to look at the way that the culture of Anatolia was adapted to the physical environment. If you think of culture as human beings adapting to a natural system, we were trying to look at the way in which Turkish culture adapted to the semi-arid, upland, isolated natural environment. How did they change it and how did they use it? How many cattle did they graze and how much grain farming was there?

Anatolia itself is not very extensive. It is a clearly delimited peninsula that sticks out between the Black Sea on the north and the Mediterranean Sea on the south as far as the Bosporus. That's not an insignificant area — you can identify it on a world map. It's a big enough region that it sticks out there, but it's not a big region like the Siberian steppes.

Steve and Tess stayed in Ankara during the preparation for the research, but when the time came for us to do the actual interviews, they traveled with me. We would drive into a village completely unannounced. There was a friendly reception. The villagers didn't have a lot of international visitors. The fact that we were interested in how they did things was a little unusual to them. They were more accustomed to people trying to find out how they responded to the tax system. When we expressed interest in their agriculture, they would say, "One year there's lots of rain and things go well. Other years it's not so generous and the crops are limited. One year the wheat is like this and one year the wheat is like this. One year everybody is rich". By this time we were ready to answer, "One year everybody is poor."

The men who gathered around for the interview were probably the leaders of the village. They were quite interested in making their knowledge of the village system available to the world. Each interview took about three hours. It was formal, because we clearly wanted some comparability. We had an interview form that we kept in front of us as we were interviewing and filled out answers as we went.

There was not a whole lot of variation between villages. There were some that had better agricultural land than others, and they adapted by having more generous agricultural allotments. That sounds as though they were government sponsored things, which was not the case. They had access to larger agricultural land. Others had less agricultural land and more grazing, so they had larger flocks. The herds were mostly sheep, with very little in the way of cattle.

During my interviews with the men, Tess was introduced as far as possible to the domestic culture of that village. For the most part, the villages were connected to the whole economy as a consumer rather than as a producer. They didn't have a lot to sell to nearby villages or to the general market. Their participation in the broader economy was quite limited. There was a subsistence economy that was very real. She could describe that.

We tried to be separate from the village culture after dark. We stopped our interviews at five or six in the afternoon and picked a place that seemed remote. But if you hadn't been there before, sometimes it seemed pretty close. We didn't do much interviewing after dark. This was based on some intention of avoidance of the tuberculosis that was widespread in the villages. There must have been other diseases that we didn't have names for. The other purpose was maintaining a degree of American diet and getting some rest from the pretty intense interviewing process.

We were in the villages roughly from Christmas to May. I've forgotten the number of villages we visited, but it was quite a few. The villages were quite open. The people who ruled over these villages assumed we were getting a picture of the area that was distorted in the villages' favor, that we couldn't help but get a one-sided view. That was all right with us because that would be the image that the villagers wanted to project to the rest of the world. If it wasn't accurate, at least it was biased always in the direction of the villagers.

There was no interference from the government whatsoever. They were aware that we were not prying into things that they were worried about, like the Kurdish minority and the Turkish majority. Sensitive areas were clearly not what we were interested in.

There were a couple of interesting incidents during our travels. The first was an ill-fated venture. We were in the east-central part of Anatolia in December, and it was very cold. We were venturing over the mountains and into the southeast corner of the area. It was an area that I had not visited. It was outside of the mainstream of the research because we figured we had enough information about the general area.

We started out with the truck and all our possessions, and ran into worse and worse conditions from an expeditionary standpoint. There was a somewhat decreased quality of the roads, as well as an increase in ice and snow. Finally we got to a town that a Turkish official told us was the end of navigation; we couldn't go any further. It wasn't that we were forbidden, but rather that there was no road maintenance and no expectation that anyone would go over the mountains beyond this town. It was a moderately important town.

We accepted the hospitality of one of the local officials who offered it. They were pleased to have guests and we were pleased to have hosts. One afternoon, our hosts noted that we had better transportation over their not-very-good road system than anything they had. They said, "Let's go fishing," that being apparently a favorite activity for a December afternoon. We said, "Sure." I don't know if there was an actual hierarchy of people who could be invited in such a situation, but about twenty men loaded in the back of our truck.

Off we went into an area that was just an agricultural field. The truck made its way along and got to a convenient spot where we stopped. There was no motorized traffic moving in that area. The men got out of the truck and walked across the field to a stream that was flowing through the pasture. We followed as we could. The men stopped at the stream, and a few of them took off their trousers and rolled up their undergarments to wade out into the stream.

Suddenly there was a blast. It was not an extraordinarily loud blast, but it was certainly unexpected. Someone had thrown some dynamite into the stream, which is not unheard of in that part of the world. In fact, it is a fairly common form of fishing. The partially disrobed men out in the stream threw the stunned fish to those of us on shore. The word for trout is *allabelek*. The belek refers to fish, and this is God's fish. This is, in all parts of the world that I'm familiar with, a respectful title for the fish. Everyone prefers trout to almost anything.

We gathered up all the fish that we could identify. Some of them got away, but we had a good load. We loaded back into the truck and returned to the village. We were pleased with ourselves. We had no sense of there being an unfair advantage of human beings over the lower vertebrates. That was one of the ways in which our presence was noted and rewarded.

On the way out of that village as we returned to the rest of Turkey, we got stuck while fording a little stream. The local farmers, without any organization, were going to help us out. Since we were high-centered, they tried to hook up a couple teams of oxen to pull us out, but that didn't work. The only solution was to rebuild the road underneath us. Rock by rock, they created enough surface for us to get traction and drive on. It was quite an engineering feat to rebuild the road right there. It now seems quite strange to me to do it that way, but given the circumstances, it was the convenient solution. It took several hours.

Another memorable visit was to Kayseri. The term Kayseri is derived from *kayser*, or ruler or emperor. At one time this was clearly the dominating city in Turkey, and it still was a very important metropolitan area. I say that without meaning to exaggerate the importance, but to acknowledge that this was a capital city even though now it is just a run-of-the-mill regional capital. It had been an important city for agriculture and livestock production.

We included the region in our research. We had no reason to leave it out, but we had a good reason to include it, because some American missionaries had their headquarters in a suburb of Kayseri. It was a place where we could accept hospitality, and we were happy to do that. Furthermore, the senior person in that mission was a doctor. He was an elderly guy, all of fifty or sixty. As a thirty-year-old, I was respectful of his seniority.

The doctor regularly made horseback trips into the villages surrounding Kayseri. He invited me along one time. I loaded up for a three-day expedition into the hinterland. That job wasn't too complex, because life was pretty simple. We took horses that were part of the local livestock and rode off. There was not a special infection or reason to go in this area, but doctors' visits were rare and always welcome.

A doctor is always welcome, and there are always sick people to see. I was a sort of special guest. We spent the night in the home of a man who was referred to as "Doctor Sali." The "Doctor" was an informal title. Sali had been in the medical section of the army and administered drugs to his community. Informally he was the agent that accepted the drugs from the city and actually administered them. He was a key person in the village.

The missionary doctor and I accepted the hospitality of Doctor Sali and his family without special remuneration. I think Doctor Sali gained enough out of the relationship to make it worthwhile. Doctor Sali's house was no bigger than the usual village home. The village was set against the hill, and a number of the rooms of dwellings were caves. The home had facilities for livestock downstairs and for humans upstairs. That was not an unusual pattern at all. In fact, that was more common than any other form of habitation. It is quite easy to get started and slowly build onto whatever came before.

When Suzie and I went back forty years later, we didn't meet Doctor Sali, who had died just a few years before, but there was a memory of the incident of my prior visit. It made an impression. The village had been at least a day's journey from Kayseri when I first went there. When I returned, it had a big road that led there, so it was suburban rather than an outlier. It was quite changed. The village had become a city in its own right. That was a special incident, a special experience in our exploration of village life.

During Suzie's and my trip in 1993 with our friends the Feldmans, Kayseri was part of several side trips, another was to take advantage of a hot springs. We went there and found that it was well organized. Strangers were put up in a separate building, independent of the springs themselves, but served with piped hot water. The healing qualities of the thermal water were piped into individual bathtubs, so we were quite separate from anybody else. We did not, could not, participate in the common bathing, which is what we were really looking forward to enjoying. They automatically siphoned us off.

After we finished the interviews, we went back to Ankara to close up whatever investment we had made in living there. We spent a good deal of time going from one government office to another to sell our Jeep, which was clearly adapted to the terrain, but not a bit adapted to the bureaucracy. The Turkish nation wasn't interested in setting aside the rules about vehicle importation for us. We were pretty much involved in trying to untie the knots that the bureaucracy had. It felt like day after day of finding our way through this maze. We did finally get permission to sell the Jeep to a government agency that was focused on the fish and livestock part of the harvest.

We set a date to leave, got our airplane reservations, and picked out a route to return. We flew to Beirut and returned on the same steamship line that we used to get to Turkey.

We published a piece of research results in Turkish and English, illustrated by almost as much space in maps as in prose, showing the concentration of irrigation and concentration of various adaptations before we left. One of the agencies that glommed on to us was the central statistical agency for the country. They were really interested in the data we had and the way it fit their data. In general it was a good fit. We made it available in graphic form. It was free as far as they were concerned. It was nice to have a publication in print that showed the research.

We should realize that Steve wasn't part of research on the comparative statistics. At six years old, he was interested in other things. When we got back to Ankara for a few days, he and I would explore the parks and swings and recreational facilities. As far as the Turkish villagers were concerned, he looked like a ten-year-old child. He was much bigger and relatively more sturdy than the Turkish children his age, if not any better coordinated. The kids couldn't help but treat him that way. In the street soccer games they played, he was observed to be a large but clumsy member of the team. That wasn't an easy role for him. He had to make his own adjustment to that. That was the only school Steve had for that year. We didn't try to enroll him or enforce the American curriculum. He was free to expand his world as he found it.

I had no trouble adapting to a different culture. This was a part of a career ladder that I was making for myself, so I didn't have any problem in that direction. If I had a problem, I was not aware of it. I was fully occupied in trying to understand the intellectual problems that we had. Tess, on the other hand, was somewhat isolated from that by language. She didn't put as much effort into learning the language as I did. She could have been useful in identifying the Kurdish villages as against the Turkish ones. While the men all spoke Turkish easily, the women who had not been drafted, and therefore had limited experience outside the village, were confined to Kurdish. We couldn't tell which type of village we were in. It was very real to the Turks, but they all talked Turkish to us.

We took the steamship back and took a deep breath of European/ American culture. Then we went back to our house on Sourdough Road.

Chairman of the Geography Deparment at the University of Colorado
(and McGovern supporter)

BOULDER YEARS

High School Geography Project

The High School Geography Project (HSGP) eventually took me to Boulder. It started with Bill Pattison from California State at Northridge as the director. He was quite a philosophic guy. The steering committee didn't think he was tough enough to kick the various people involved in the shins and get the thing going. They had the money promised from the National Science Foundation, but they needed a new director. Gilbert White was the chairman of the committee, and whether he had gotten clearance to hire me before that, I don't know. There were meetings of the Association of American Geographers in Columbus, Ohio, at the time and when I came down one morning in my hotel, Gilbert was in the lobby and said, "I have a concern for thee." I could tell it was a serious concern. He described where the project was, what they were looking for, and that the obvious person was me. They needed someone who had administrative experience on his own, along with some research reputation, and was ready to take on this fairly difficult administrative role.

I asked Gilbert whether he was ready to stay with the project, and he agreed that he was. I accepted at that point the appointment as director of the project. That was in the spring of 1964, and the appointment to the project was going to be in the fall, so there was a fair amount of time in between. The International Geographical Union was meeting in London in late summer, and I planned to go to that a little bit ahead to go to Switzerland and climb with a bunch of kids who had visited in Bozeman. The steering committee thought I ought to visit with Bill Pattison, the previous director, and get a feel for what was expected.

I had to cancel the climbing trip to Switzerland, but decided to explore a little of Ireland and Scotland before the meeting in London. I flew off to Ireland from Boston, arriving at Shannon Airport. From there I was going to figure out how to get to London. I took a train from Shannon to Marysville, Ireland. I got off the train at Marysville and carried my suitcase up to the hotel. After I checked in, I went down to the bar and introduced myself and had a couple of drinks. I mentioned that I was a Quaker, and they said, "There are Quakers in the village next to us." I arranged to borrow the town clerk's bicycle and rode off in the direction of this village.

I noticed a man working in the fields, so I parked the bicycle and went over and talked to him.

His command of English was about as good as my Irish brogue. I could just barely understand him, which was kind of a shock. He was digging peat in the field and setting the blocks of peat out to dry from their swampy condition so they would be available for selling as a fuel. Not a very good fuel, but one that was at least inexpensive.

I had my camera with me and took pictures and enjoyed getting the feel for central Ireland. Much later Suzie and I developed some friendships in southern France and among other phrases that they used was that it was *"France profonde."* Had I had that expression in mind, I could have said that this was "Ireland *profonde*."

I got to the village that was designated, and it turned out that the Quakers were upper-class people of English origin who had moved to Ireland, presumably in order to take advantage of the social structure there and the availability of land. I was not much interested in the English exploitation of the Irish. I returned on the bicycle, and that was pretty much the extent of my explorations there. I moved on by train to Dublin and then north to Belfast and then across the channel to Glasgow and then down to England, with a stop in Norwich, England. It was a little experience in English history to make that side trip to central Ireland.

In England I went to the Geographical Union meetings. I didn't have any special role there. We had another field trip right after the meetings which took us to Poland, and we had a whole circuit of cities that we went to as part of the field trip. Polish geographers came with us on this trip. I developed a friendship with a man named Kostrowitsky. He used classification systems and farming. We maintained a correspondence for quite awhile. Then I came back to the States and took on my responsibilities as director of the HSGP.

The project started and had its first year in Bozeman, and we kidded that it was only geographers that would set up a national project with Bozeman as its headquarters. It was understood that the location was probably temporary, but it allowed us to get our feet on the ground and get the project going. The project started in Bozeman using a variant of the procedure that they had used in the biology project, which was to get teachers and scholars together for a very intense writing experience, with teams that included both teachers and university professors. It seemed to me that an intense writing experience like that was no way to get thoughtful curriculum materials developed, so we chose a different strategy. Our strategy was to pick a scholar, a university person, who was respected for their specialty in a particular area and have him or her get help to reorient to the style of high school and develop the materials. We had arranged for Arthur Getis and his wife, who was a former teacher, to write the first unit on urban geography. The title of our year-long course was to be

"Geography in an Urban Age," so it was appropriate that Arthur develop the first unit. It worked very well.

We moved to Boulder after the first year. My leave of absence from duties at Montana State was limited to two years, so I had to resign my appointment—my tenured appointment, no less—after the first year on the High School Geography Project. It also developed that the HSGP was becoming a national operation. We had people starting to write units, with a good deal of autonomy, everywhere from New Jersey to San Diego, so we wanted to be closer to a big airport. We chose Boulder because there were a couple of other high school curriculum projects here, a biology project and an earth science project. The National Science Foundation could combine their visits to the several projects.

The material developed needed to be tested, so we went to the Educational Testing Service and hired a member of their staff to work with Arthur and his wife. We allocated something like $60,000 to develop this set of materials and turn it over to us at the central office. This writing strategy worked quite well. The unit authors, as they were called, had the autonomy and no interference from the central office. They developed materials in their own way. I urged them to use as wide a range of teaching strategies, materials, and classroom procedures as they could imagine. They did indeed develop material that was not the standard textbook and lecture, but rather experimental techniques, novel techniques, techniques that were not foreign to the high schools, but were definitely not orthodox.

In the second year of the project, we were able to pick several teams. There was one at Ohio State that developed a second unit on cities, focusing on the interrelationship of one city and another. Another team did a unit on manufacturing and the location of manufacturing. A team from the University of Kansas did a unit on agriculture. There was a unit on water resources done be a group from Illinois. This was the pattern that we developed, and it seemed to be progressing as the year went on. The Getises pioneered a nice, wide-ranging choice of strategies, and so what we had was a series of nine or ten different teams, each working with their own teachers, evaluators, and fellow academics. They were connected to the Boulder office by correspondence and phone, but given a lot of leeway to choose the way they wanted to develop the materials.

I was involved in the project for five years. There was the year in Bozeman and then four more in Boulder. When we brought the various units back from the writing teams, we gave them a trial in high schools that were nearby. We took the same evaluator who worked on the urban geography unit and hired him directly. He had an assistant, Bob Richburg, who was a graduate student at University of Colorado, to help him with the evaluation. He went through the unit authors' evaluation, and then a second evaluation that we organized. From there, it was a matter of throwing away the things that the students or teachers couldn't handle or that were boring, and modifying the materials that really "swung."

The materials varied all the way from the most boring to the most exciting stuff that you could imagine. Pulling them together was a difficult and complex job, as was merging the several units into a single course. This was done in the central office, and in the course of that we hired a staff. We had people all the way from the secretarial staff, who had some experience with high school, to editors to specialists in their subfield of geography.

One of the central figures in this was another geographer, Don Patton, who kind of pulled the manuscript from these disparate units together. There were a lot of materials that didn't work, and we definitely threw away those materials. We focused on the materials that caught the enthusiasm of the students and of the teachers, because without the teachers being really interested, the students wouldn't be interested. It was the reaction of the students that we were really after.

Once we completed the testing we were expecting to have the material picked up by a publisher and marketed as a year-long course in geography. Macmillan was selected as the publisher, and they put an editor in the team who worked very closely with the evaluators. We developed even the artwork to go with the subject. We picked a local artist who had the skills in abstracting the subject matter that we liked very much, and she worked out very well doing an introductory sketch to each unit.

Macmillan did publish the course, but never got their labor force to sell it. They already had a high school textbook in geography, and as far as their sales force was concerned, it was a lot easier to sell than this much more expensive thing with slides and filmstrips and recordings and models. The worst decision that we made was to put the urban unit in first. It had a map with an overlay of transparent materials that students could use to actually build a city. The narrative that went along with it was that it was Portsville, and it was modeled after the growth and site of Seattle, Washington. We had an underlying map of the Puget Sound.

We questioned whether we should start with as expensive a thing as the Portsville activity, where there would be six copies of the map and the overlay and the right number of little things to go on top of it. Our decision was based on the fact that this may be the first time that the students ever had a chance to build a city on their own. There were a lot of readings to go with it that followed the history of "Portsville." The students came up with a variety of buildings and neighborhoods and so on. They were able very quickly to get into the sense of building the city, and it became their city. The class was divided into teams of five or six students, each team working independently on the same problem. They became pretty possessive of their model and really got into it. It was a very successful activity, involving two weeks of class time, and it was their own. We didn't want to give that up. We knew that once they got into that, they could begin to feel that they were in a different kind of geography class.

It was different from the conventional, "Read pages 35 to 40 and answer questions 5, 6, and 9." It was so different, but it was expensive. It was also fairly complex in the sense that the teacher would need to get all the materials out and have them available to the students for the period of the growth of Portsville, and then put it all away somewhere where it would be available for next year. That put extra demands on the teacher, and of course extra demands on the salesman who handled it. We didn't do much training of the salespersons. We did have training sessions for the teachers, and they were almost uniformly in favor of it. They liked it, at least as long as the project staff could store it and get it out. We thought it was crucial to the project, but it was certainly an enormous drag on the sales force. That's why we had to finally consider it a mistake to start with that.

The project wasn't going to last forever. We tested the materials once with the unit authors and maybe three times from the project office. We had a couple of years to refine the material and to edit it and re-edit it and edit it again until we thought we had it pretty well acceptable to the teachers. I could see the end of the project coming, and Gilbert White said it is very difficult to organize a perpetual revolution. It was enough to develop one set and let it go and dissolve the project, which we did. There was a year of evaluation and publishing details after I left and accepted an appointment at Western Michigan University.

It was a tough decision to give up a tenured position to do the HSGP, but it was so exciting to develop new materials and have a fairly generous staff. There were maybe thirty people working in the project office. That was so exciting that I went ahead and resigned the tenured job at Bozeman. I was confident that in the profession there was a widespread acceptance that this was going to be significant. I thought that we had plenty of reason to expect that there would be a job at the end of the tunnel.

During the High School Geography Project I had an intense relationship outside my marriage with someone involved in the project. This was when I was living in Boulder, while Tess was still in Bozeman. Joan (not her real name) pretty much took the whole focus of my sexual activity for almost three years. Despite that, I continued a sexual relationship with Deborah. Joan and I broke up when she went off to a university to work on a doctorate. She disappeared from my life, and the last I heard (many years ago), she was not well.

Divorce

Tess and I looked at various residential areas in Boulder, but none of them looked attractive—or at least none of the ones that interested most people. The urban and suburban landscapes didn't strike us. We finally agreed on a place up in the mountains. I don't know whether Tess was in on the decision to buy the plot of land or not. She certainly was disparaging of the areas around Boulder that fit our expectations as far as having a larger piece of property. Tess stayed in Bozeman while we constructed a house.

We bought a property of about three or four acres at the very top of a mountain subdivision, but just outside the subdivision itself. The property had been used as a quarry, so the most prominent feature was a cliff where the rock had been removed. It looked obvious to me that we could drive on the driveway that the quarries had used and build a house where the quarry had been.

We hired an architect, Roger Easton, to do the house for us. We expected to spend about $30,000 and ended up spending about $90,000. Roger (the architect) came up with a design, a really lovely design. You felt as though the house was pinned to the quarry wall. The bedroom used the quarry wall as the head of the bed. The house looked out to the east in the most dramatic fashion. It was a very simple house, but quite expensive to build. Even the redwood matched so that you could go from inside to outside without changing the match of the wood. That was really quite extravagant.

Tess was in Bozeman, and I don't think she came down to look at the plans. I don't think we sent the plans up to her enough so that she could really get the feel of it. It was a very beautiful house, but it was probably almost the opposite of what Tess needed. She needed a one-story house with no stairs because of her lack of depth perception. She never reacted against the stairs in that design, even though there were a couple of places where you had to take a couple of steps up or down. I don't know why I was so obtuse in the design, except that every time a decision came up, the sensible thing and beautiful thing was to repeat the angle and incorporate the original quarry into the contemporary design.

During the experience in building the house in Montana, seven years of working out the details of lighting and finishes, I had learned enough about domestic architecture. I used that knowledge to design the interior of this house. Everything from the indirect lighting in the bedroom to the finish of the floors was part of the way I approached that house.

The beginning of the end of the marriage with Tess was when I left for Boulder, leaving Peter with Tess. Tess stayed behind in Bozeman because Peter was in school, but she didn't really want to move. Tess did move into the Tall Timbers house when it was finished, and we lived together in it for a couple of years with Peter. We had the two St. Bernards who were my mountain companions. Tess had nothing really.

The tsunami of a divorce came pretty soon after Tess came from Bozeman to Boulder. Peter was with us while Tess and I were in the Tall Timbers house. He used all the empty bottles from the consumption of alcoholic beverages to decorate his room, and it was a pretty significant bunch of bottles. Of course he was doing it to demonstrate how much we were drinking, and we got the message. But we didn't stop drinking. Peter went to live with Jim and Nita Nickerson, old friends from Bozeman, who had moved to Mankato. A trip down the Grand Canyon brought things to a head, and I even had a small heart attack driving home.

I finally gave up my extreme loyalty to the marriage and said there wasn't anything I could do about it. That literally meant that there wasn't anything I was willing to do about it. I moved into an apartment in town. It must have been a fairly small one, because I didn't buy much in the way of a second collection of furniture. Tess stayed in Boulder until it was clear that this was the end of the marriage. Then she moved to Fort Dodge, Iowa, where her father was living. He was a fairly prominent lawyer. He never forgave me for giving up on the marriage.

Peter went to a boarding school in Switzerland for 1968 to 1969. The dysfunctional family created behavioral problems, and this was a way of diminishing them. The whole thing gets mixed up in my mind as to when I went to Europe to see how Peter was doing at school. The European schools for American kids specialize in troubled kids. They're pretty much accustomed to the kinds of problems we had. I went over once for a short time in March to be with Peter; there wasn't very much snow, and it was terrible skiing. Tess and I broke up in September just before he left, so he was living with me in the apartment at the time of the breakup.

I continued to live in my apartment in Boulder. The Tall Timbers house was beautiful enough that I didn't want to sell it, but with time it became obvious that I couldn't use it. We gave the St. Bernards to people who would take good care of them.

David Loth

David Loth is Tess's uncle. David was a trained journalist, and quite successful. The main part of his life, he worked half time for the *New York Herald Tribune* as the nighttime cable editor for half a year. The other half he took off and researched a book of some kind. He wrote some thirty books. He was a very fluent writer and wonderful raconteur.

We knew David and his wife Helen from fairly well back. David entered the High School Geography Project when we needed a writer. We got to a point where we were close to finished. We had the body of the work done, but one part needed rewriting. David was called in and did the job better than we could have expected.

We were in what seemed like the last stages of completion of the units' preparation to turn them over to the McMillan Company. We needed one more unit, on urban geography. It was on a part of geography that you don't usually think of, because it's the "other end." The unit involved waste management; this was before "waste management" was a common idiom in American language, and I took a major role in writing the unit.

In this unit, the class is faced with the problems of an urban area having to get rid of all its garbage. It's easy enough to think of how you reached to the mountains for clean water, but there is the problem of how you dispose of the water after you have dirtied it. Each student in the class was given a topic: one focuses on used water; another on sewage, a third on unusable automobiles.

The students were in committees, as if they were consultants brought in by the city. Each student researched one topic individually, then they came together to make recommendations to the city. Each student was quite confident because they have distinct mission, but they find that their problems overlap. The solid waste committee finds that it can't do this job the way they thought it would be best handled because it impinges on airborne waste. When the students realize that their problem impinges on the solutions that other committees have, they have to deal with the whole problem. It is really a beautiful unit.

David worked with me to write the unit, based on a report that had been released within the last year. It was a matter of only two or three months when he had it all written up. David came to Boulder and lived here while he worked on this assignment.

Earlier Helen, David's wife, had worked in public relations for the people who make Angostura Bitters. She knew the whole alcohol industry and was a very sharp, talented, urbane woman. Helen was instrumental in trying to protect Peter during the divorce. After David's work on the High School Geography Project, the Loths moved back East. However, several years later, toward the end of our commune experience, they moved back to be near Peter, whom they dearly loved, and us. They became part of our family. In fact, the day we helped them move into their apartment, Peter, Sherry, and Hal, Sherry's first husband, were there. Helen sat back, smiled, and commented, "Isn't this a lovely family, all wine and no blood." Several years later Helen was very important to Suzie and me in bringing our relationship with Peter back together. There is no need to give details, but it involved finances over starting a local music club called the Blue Note.

Peter started that venture with his inheritance. Tess's mother was quite wealthy in her own right, and Tess left Peter quite a lot of money when she died. He used it to establish the night club that didn't survive, although I tried to be supportive and Suzie and I enjoyed many nights there.

It was a terrible time for us, because instead of being pretty well off for our dotage, we were suddenly not very well off. It caused some hard feelings, but Peter was too much a part of our lives. We had to make peace with it, and Helen was instrumental in that. She helped us to look at it in the past tense. She said we weren't going to change it, so we had to live with it.

Suzie

Suzanne Wiggins was a new name for me. She and I were in the same business, creating high school curriculum, but in different subjects. I had a National Science Foundation grant and she and her colleague John Sperling had an Office of Education grant. They were working in the field of Economics and were not well financed in comparison to us. I was given a grant that had been in existence for awhile. They were in the early stages of starting a program, but with less advice from their profession and more discretion in how to handle that.

We were at the point where we knew we were going to produce innovative materials with the High School Geography Project. We knew that teachers in general would not change their behavior just because somebody wanted them to, so we organized a teacher training session in Ann Arbor, Michigan. Bill Stevens was part of our project. He had also played quite a large part in Suzie's project and had known her from this previous context. He asked me if it was okay to bring in someone from the outside. I answered that of course it was fine. He offered Suzie a chance to be in on the conference. I guess she was the only real outsider in the operation.

I had heard Suzie's name, but I had no image of her. I was quite impressed after the first day with how sharp and attentive she was. That night I called her up and offered to meet her downstairs in the bar. Of course, my intentions were honorable, but nobody else knew that. She declined my offer of a drink that night. She was a young thirty-six and I was an elderly forty-eight. I didn't see the age difference as reason to stop the personal side of things. That seemed to be the end of it. We went our separate ways, the ways our projects took us. Where she sat in my memory, I'm not sure; where women do. She didn't assume my intentions were honorable, and she processed that information on her own.

The long weekend conference was quite successfully carried out. Our consultant who organized the conference continued to help us. Suzie moved to Boulder from Berkeley in September 1968 on sabbatical to teach in the Experienced Teachers Fellowship Program created by the Social Science Education Consortium. The first week in town Bill Stevens told her that my wife was leaving town and that we were getting a divorce. He asked if he should let me know she was in town. I was just recovering from a heart attack, and Peter was leaving town to go to school in Switzerland. I was living in the apartment in town and the Tall Timbers house was empty.

Suzie took my divorce proceedings into account as she organized herself. We had a series of dates and seductions. It's hard for me to know which was which. I wasn't single for very long. Single didn't suit me very well. I must have dated some other women, but I took Suzie into account in a different way from other prospective wives.* We were married August 1969.

---

* Nick didn't get this part of his story quite right. See Part II. —Suzie

I'm very glad I made the decision about Suzie, a powerful woman and a positive influence on me, keeping me honest and humble, gregarious and gentle. But one of the factors of my choice was Peter's reaction. He was sixteen and smart-alecky. Suzie and Peter got along well by any standards. They were both strong personalities. Neither of them was so strong that it blocked out the affection. I'm sure they went head to head on occasion, but I don't remember that. Suzie had a child as well, Sherry, who was fourteen when we married and she lived with us as we created our family.

Kalamazoo

Despite my expectation that there would be jobs for me after the High School Geography Project, I found that wasn't the case. While the project was respected by the profession, I was discriminated against because I had been involved in a high school project. If it had been a university project that would have perhaps been more acceptable. Secondary schools don't provide for the prestige that we associate with the university. It ended up being a bit of an impediment for my career.

If I had it to do over again, I think I would still accept the job with the HSGP. Given what I had to look forward to in a continuing professorship, I would take the chance of finding a department that would hire me. In terms of adoption of the materials, the project was a failure. In terms of modifying the way geography is taught, it was at least a semi-success. There were enough people who were touched by it so that the high schools were stimulated to find better ways of teaching, not uniformly around the nation, but enough to breathe some life into the material. The place where it had the biggest influence was probably college geography, because enough collegiate people from a variety of institutions were involved and got caught up in the idea of imaginative curriculum materials that college geography has never been the same. It's gone on, the waves of influence from this pebble tossed into the big lake of educational materials.

By the time I left the project I was fifty, so I still had twenty years of useful service. But it was almost as though I had taken a leave of absence from geography and gone off on a different tangent, and now I wanted to come back and join, presumably, a prestigious department, and they didn't want a faculty member tagged as working in the secondary school area. I looked throughout the Bay Area, because Suzie was on the faculty at San Jose State, and the normal thing would have been for her to go back there and me to be somewhere close by in a university position. It turned out there was no university position in the Bay Area that I fit into.

I finally, in late December, got a job at Western Michigan University. Our associate director, George Vuicich, had come from Western Michigan University, and he went back to an appointment there. They were retiring their department chair the following year and I would fit the bill to replace him. Also, they thought they could become a leader in geography education with me and George in the department. They did, and still are known for that, but without me. They hired a very able young geographer named Joseph Stoltman, who has become an international leader in the field, and has done very well. I was expected to play that role.

Suzie, Peter, Sherry, and I moved to Kalamazoo, Michigan. It shocked the neighbors that we stayed there before we were married. Suzie and I went there in the summer where we fell in love with the big, roomy 1910 house that we bought. The neighbors were really disappointed when we moved in as a married couple and there wasn't anything to gossip about. Sherry had refused to go to "nowheresville" as she called Kalamazoo until we agreed to take along her best friend from Berkeley, Lesli Dalaba.* The two of them distained any friendships until Suzie described the situation to an acquaintance in the neighborhood who took the girls to her house containing several eligible boys.

I thought I had settled in at Western Michigan, but it was a terribly depressing year. It's awfully cloudy in Kalamazoo, and that was depressing. I moved from an executive position with a staff of about thirty to a university appointment where I was pretty much alone except for George. The return to a simple professorship was quite a shock. I had learned a lot about good teaching and felt that I should do it, but I was all alone; no assistant, no evaluation, and no editor. The easy thing for me to do was to fall back on lecturing. The first semester I couldn't do anything but straight teaching. The second semester was a little better. I was able to corral a couple of students from the previous semester into helping with more complex and satisfying teaching strategies.

Suzie found a job in the business school. They were amazed to have a woman on their faculty, and a Marxist at that!

But the sun stayed hidden behind the almost continuous cloud cover. My continued depression remained. Suzie and I found a pond and enclosing park only a block or two from our house. It made a convenient destination for a walk or bicycle ride with Gladstone. Gladstone was a young and lively whippet, a present from the new Ms. Wiggins. Gladstone would jog along beside us until he would spot a squirrel a block or two away. He would suddenly become a four-legged arrow flying toward its target, only to find the target a few feet up the safety of the tree. He never tired of the fruitless chase.

The university gave us three weeks off at Christmas. That seemed long enough to schedule a ski trip to Colorado. We reserved space in a motel in Aspen. As soon as the semester ended, we packed the five of us into the station wagon and headed West. Hardly had we started skiing when we had a phone call from Irving Morrissett in Boulder. Could we spare a

---

*Actually, Nick suggested this in a letter to me that spring. —Suzie

couple of days to help write a proposal to the U.S. Office of Education for a grant to collect ephemeral public documents in social studies/social science education, abstract them and send them to Washington so that they would be available to others permanently? We hated to lose two days of skiing, and didn't quite know what abstracting and indexing were. The proposal got written, and I was written in as director of the proposed Eric Clearinghouse for Social Science/Social Studies Education to epic cheers. We returned to Aspen.

As we traversed Loveland Pass, we were passing through some of the most dramatic alpine scenery in the world: cirques of every size, triangular peaks called Matterhorns, deep glacial troughs, steep level walls. I looked over at Suzie, who was buried in a copy of *Newsweek*. I blew up. How can anyone take their eyes off this incredible scenery in favor of a magazine? I had been brought up to revere such mountains. This was a special privilege to have it laid out before you! This was new scenery we had never seen before! Both of my parents would share my humility in the presence of such magnificent landscape.

I was busy laying out routes to climb, avoiding avalanches, looking for continuous snowfields, and determining where one would take your skis off and climb the rest of the way on windblown rock. And there was Suzie, her head buried in a news magazine! For years she made fun of me losing my temper over her disinterest, even neglect, of the sacred scenery. She gave up her reading and watched the scenery. The skiing culminated with one broken leg (Peter's). We returned to Kalamazoo, put Peter on the plane to school in Majorca crutches and all, and started the second semester.

Trip to Africa

Our trip to Africa was often referred to as a second or third or fourth honeymoon. We had had two honeymoons before the marriage, but justified the trip to Africa as the only post-marriage honeymoon. We offered the children the choice to stay home in school or come along with their assignments. They did not hesitate: they would come along.

We met up with Bella and Len Feldman who were living in Uganda. Len had an appointment in math education at Makerari University. Suzie had been friends with them for a long time in Berkeley; she and Len were faculty members at San Jose State. Suzie thought it would be worth the fare to go see Africa through Bella's eyes, so we made plans to join them for about a month. They had two children, Dan and Nina. We got along very well with them.

The trip started in Kalamazoo, of course. We flew from New York to Kampala, the capital of Uganda. I was caught off guard by how long it took to fly across the Sahara Desert. Even though I had taught generations of students, most of the maps we use diminish the size of the lower latitudes. I was not prepared. Even at six hundred miles an hour, it seemed endless—hour after hour of no human habitation, no sign of conventional land-use crossing North Africa from Athens to Uganda.

It was dark by the time we landed. Again, we should have expected it, but the airport was dimly lit and the crowd that pressed around us was uniformly black. They all wanted to help us carry our bags to their cousin, who would drive us to Kampala. We understood that even a moderate tip would seem like a fortune, but we were in the dark. Somehow we chose a porter and a taxi. We breathed again. We were on our way through "darkest Africa." Bella and Len could interpret for us, make sense of the unfamiliar choices.

Bella took us shopping in a large open-air market for a few last minute items. We were shocked by lepers sitting at the entrance. Then we were ready for a major expedition north: eight of us plus two drivers in two station wagons. A couple of things impressed me. One was the effect of disrobed male herders on Suzie and Bella. I had not expected them to be quite so interested in the exposed sexual organs. It was pretty impressive how that drew their attention. As we approached the northern part of Uganda, the dominant mode of making a living, was herding. Gradually we came into an area that was clearly militarized, because we were up on the Sudanese border.

In the park itself, the rangers have authority and control. They control who is there and what you get to see. One of their responsibilities was to control poaching. We did see a lot of wildlife and enjoyed that part of it. Having seen the northern edge of Uganda, we then went south by a different route. That took us through a different landscape again, with gradually increased rainfall as we worked south. My sense is that we went from a dry-land native agricultural area through the park, which was reserved for wildlife and presumably few natives. As we came out of the park to the south, the population was fairly dense, despite the semi-arid character. Quite quickly, within a day's travel, it turned into a humid area that had adequate rainfall for tea plantations, and the wildlife changed accordingly.

We didn't see any hippopotami as we went north. It wasn't until we had turned south that we saw hippos and rhinoceros. We stayed one night at a lovely motel complex near a river. I think this is where hippos came over the porch of the cabin. That's pretty close to Murchison Falls where we took a river cruise and observed crocodile and hippos sharing the river. We returned then to Kampala.

We were stranded for several hours on the trip north. I think it was instructive to us. We got to a stream that was flowing at flood stage, or close to it, so we couldn't go across. There wasn't a bridge, so we had to wait a couple of hours and attracted friendly herders who helped us ford the river. On the way back to Kampala, one car broke down and again we attracted a crowd. The Ugandans were quite unique in their approach to an automobile. They were really interested in how they worked.

There was a village nearby that we visited while we waited. I was invited to join the adults to test locally brewed beer. That was pretty exciting for me. The beer started brewing when they first got up in the morning. By evening it was pretty well aged. It doesn't make much sense in American terms, but it is a form of preserving the nutrition of the grain. It did seem pretty raw to us who were quite accustomed to beer that is three or six months old. We never drank enough of it to get inebriated.

We took the night train to Nairobi from Kampala, but I can't remember the details. We left Bella and Len because they were living in Kampala. We stayed in Nairobi for a short time, and then took the night train off the plateau to Mombassa, which is on the coast. We saw a little bit of the intermediate landscapes, but they all fade in my mind; they all looked like Africa.

The trip on the train was memorable. We ordered curry which was way too hot to handle. Then Sherry ordered kippered herring for breakfast, in spite of Suzie alerting her to the fact that we were in an area where kippers would be dried and nasty. When we woke up the morning, we could smell the kippers cooking. They were impossible to eat.

We didn't see much of Mombasa itself; rather we stayed in a seaside resort on the Indian Ocean that was peaceful. It was very tropical in the sense of being humid and constantly warm. It didn't cool off much at night. The snorkeling was wonderful, and we took lots of shells. We were there three or four days.

We must have gone back from Mombasa to Tanzania, but I don't remember anything about it. We only spent a few days in the capital city. President Nyerere of Tanzania was one of my heroes. He understood that you have to change society in terms of its fundamental values. It was much like our feelings about Mao and Castro. All three understood that capitalist values are way out of whack, that people need to have some appreciation of the collective.

While in Kenya we drove to the Great Rift Valley, north of Nairobi. You go there to see flamingos, but it was the only place we encountered lots of monkeys on the road. The Rift Valley is important in African geography, so even without the flamingos, I would have wanted to go. But the flamingos were there in such numbers on the lake that the whole area seemed to be dominated by pink.

We flew from Kenya to Cairo, Egypt. The tension between Israel and Palestine was at full volume at the time. When we landed, there was tape across the glass windows. We had not explained the Arab/Israeli tension to Peter and Sherry.

Fashion was very short skirts at that time. Sherry wore one of her shorter dresses in spite of our advice, so she was taken aside at the airport. The immigration officers were not accustomed to these fashions, so they took Sherry out of the line and brought her up front where they could feast their eyes on parts of the anatomy that they hadn't seen. Sherry was very frightened by being segregated and observed, but she survived it. The customs officials were no wiser. We passed through as if there hadn't been any problem. Sherry took Suzie's advice a little more seriously the next time the subject of fashion came up.

The trip in Egypt was memorable. There were practically no tourists. All the facilities for tourists were there, but there weren't many takers in June 1970. We were the only source of cash to which the merchants could apply. They were very eager to accommodate us. We were "very welcome." We were "very welcome" to come into their stores. We were not expecting that, and it was quite surprising and a little scary. I don't know that we bought any more than we would have if they had not been threateningly welcoming. It was clear that it was their intent that we knew we were welcome. The term "very welcome" has been in the family vocabulary every since.

We took in a couple of the sights in Cairo with a guide and were stopped by police for taking pictures. Then we flew to Luxor. The temples there were an eye-opening experience. In Luxor we stayed in an old English hotel on the Nile that accommodated us very well. We were impressed by how slack things were when you cut off the source of cash in a tourist facility. When the tourist industry fails, there is practically nothing to take its place.

We had a guide who was very accommodating and arranged for everything. We enjoyed four days of looking at the temples and tombs. Everybody was impressed by the differences in culture and the ways of imperial Egypt, and the degree of difference between common people and aristocracy.

We were also aware of vast differences in present day Egypt. That was as impressive as the difference between King Tut and whoever took care of him. I think Suzie was very impressed by the images of common life and how they were almost like the biblical scenes that she had colored in Sunday school. Here they were winnowing grain by throwing it up in the breezes. The grain fell down and the chaff went somewhere else. Common life had changed very little in 2000 years.

University of Colorado

Our proposal written the previous winter for the new institution, the Educational Resources Information Center (ERIC) for Social Studies was accepted. The center would gather so-called "ephemeral" documents—speeches, monographs, various other things that pertained to elementary and secondary schools—and abstract them and enter them into an archival form where they would be available to serious people. The abstracts could be analyzed by other researchers, and they could take advantage of a wide range of materials that would otherwise be inaccessible to them. That was the ERIC Clearinghouse.

The project actually had a budget and needed staff. Irving called on me to leave Western Michigan and come back to Boulder. He arranged for the Department of Geography at CU to accept me on the faculty even though I wouldn't teach anything, in the first year at least. I resigned my position at Western Michigan before the end of the first year. We brought the family back to Boulder and have been in Boulder ever since.

I became the director of the ERIC Clearinghouse. My job was to guide a wave that was just breaking. I made this metaphor quite explicitly in a talk that summer. As a wave breaks you stay on top of it and then you go into a different mix of sand and water. I was thinking about curriculum reform as a profession and not as a diversion. It turned out to be a very good profession even though the people in it were limited and everybody was looking for ways to be successful.

In my work I kept track of a lot of fugitive documents. I tried to get hold of them and incorporate them into the clearinghouse. It was fairly straight-forward. If somebody gave a speech in Atlanta, I asked for permission to publish it. Usually everybody was happy to have their materials circulated more widely. We collected that kind of document, abstracted it, and put in a database. This was before the age of the internet, so those kinds of documents weren't generally available the way they would be now. I learned about abstracts and citations and God knows what else. We picked people who were abstracters and experienced in picking out a central idea. I think we did our job, but it was quite a different job.

The ERIC Clearinghouse job only lasted for two years. Gradually I returned to normal academic life at CU, with an administrative as well as a teaching position. I became chairman of the Geography Department at a time when it was essential to establish effective leadership. I carried the whole range of responsibilities that the title implies for four years from 1971 through 1975, and then I dropped back to an ordinary professorship; actually, I became director of the graduate program.

I ran the department on an egalitarian mode. We didn't settle for a majority vote: we went on with the discussion to look for complete agreement. I was overt about that. The department was ready to fall apart when I became Chairman. It might very well have become two departments, one of physical geography and one of cultural geography. That would have left American geographers in a weaker position. It was not uncommon for British departments to be split that way, but it was not at all common in America. I interpreted it as not only uncommon, but weaker.

Part of the reason the department might have broken up was because the reputation of some of the individuals was significant. Their reputation grew out of the importance of the subjects included in their professional papers. Two of the geographers in the department were recognized for their individual contributions, and rightly so. The third wasn't recognized so much for his own contributions, as for the energy and significance of some of the professional work he encouraged. He was not only a good professional geographer, but he also had a powerful personality. He was a great person to have on your side.

The pattern of making decisions by consensus was quite an important part of bringing the department together. If they had gone off in their individual directions, we would have had two departments. But we didn't. The department still makes decisions by consensus. It was an important contribution, although it may not have been widely recognized.

I had some experience in trying to bring people together, enough so that it surfaced when an issue came up. I would think in terms of keeping the three professors within the circle. I don't know how many other geographers would have agreed that that was an important thing. They can look back on it and judge it.

I retired when I was seventy and a half years old. That was policy. They didn't make any exception, and I didn't hear of any exceptions. I knew that working as an older professor was not exactly right for me. I had outgrown the place where my reputation carried through to my behavior. I could tell that some of my lectures were extraneous, but I wasn't able with the resources I had to do much about it.

I haven't done much academically since retirement. The retired faculty association doesn't demand much, and I've never spent much effort on it. There are two meetings each year, and I go to them. There are some roles there, but there are none that interested me. I was happy to be passed over as an official of the association.

Association of American Geographers

In 1982, I became the president of the Association of American Geographers (AAG), the principal professional organization for geographers. Being president should make you a notable figure, but I'm not sure that I was. It was a surprise for me because I didn't think of myself as an eminent geographer. It turned out that my nomination was a byproduct of my egalitarian thinking. I had done some favors for the Society of Women Geographers. They were unexcited by the official slate and came up with nominations from outside: me.

To a great extent Reesa Palm was responsible for my nomination. Reesa and her husband, David Greenland, joined the department while or soon after I was department chair. He is a climatologist and she was a cultural geographer. I had been instrumental in hiring them. Reesa remembered that, and when the nominations for President of the AAG were very mediocre, she got the women to nominate me as a write-in candidate.

I think I was in Britain on sabbatical in 1978-79 when I was nominated, working at the London University Institute of Education. I was mostly preoccupied with about ten students who were part of a cohort. They had finished their Geography degrees and now were enrolled in a teacher education operation. We had something like that in America, but not exactly the same. I was unfamiliar enough with the program that I was happy to spend most of the school year going over the teacher education preparations. It was a new experience for me. I didn't know much about the British education system, so I couldn't teach much about it. The students helped me learn quite a bit.

I was halfway through the sabbatical when I was nominated. The nomination didn't push me into eminence; that is, it didn't raise my stature much with British geographers. It did put me in an eminent position for officialdom. It could always be mentioned as a part of my career.

I don't remember much about my accomplishments during my term as President. I made some effort at being egalitarian, but didn't change the culture much. I had a one-year term. There was some recognition of being President-Elect and Past-President, and I carried some official responsibilities that I enjoyed. It was played up some when I was introduced to a group.

Somewhere along the line, perhaps later in my career, I was approached at a meeting of the AAG by two women. One was Bonnie Lloyd, one of the prettiest members of the AAG. The other came from the east coast, perhaps one of the Pennsylvania State Colleges. They wanted to chat, so we took a table in the hotel coffee shop. They were concerned that very few of their gender held office in the AAG. What could they do about it? I was then a member of the AAG council, a group of about a dozen president-elects, President, immediate past president and six or eight regional counselors elected from each AAG regional division. They stated their concern and we discussed what to do. Needless to say, I was agreeable and wanted to help.

It became clear that entry point to the AAG hierarchy was the nominating committee. If they could be sure that there was always at least one woman elected to the nominating committee, she might make sure that at least once in a while a woman would be elected. So it has been ever since. Women have had good representation in the senior ranks of the AAG offices.

Community on Nelson Road (1971-1976)

Soon after we were married Suzie and I participated in an experiment in communal living. We bought a small farm north of Boulder with the intention of starting a "youth collective" for alienated teenagers. That project turned into a "people farm" where somewhat older young people would come to continue their process of growing up. We practiced subsistence agriculture, consensus decision making, and activism for social change, this in addition to our academic pursuits.

Suzie and I looked at society as a whole, saw it was a mess, and looked for an alternative way of dealing with it. We were impressed by how frail the social organization was, or at least seemed to be. We commented in our own discussions on the fact that marriage was supposed to be something significant (it was for us), but in many cases didn't seem significant. A lot of the customs of American life, when you have reason to doubt them, fall away in significance. We had both been divorced, and for these few years, early in our marriage (1971-76), we chose to live differently from most professionals by creating and joining a commune.

It didn't seem that most professionals took advantage of weaving an experiment into their personal lives. We tried to do that. It was almost like saying we were free of the conventions, so we wanted to make the most of it. We tried to define the right life for us. (Grandson Brian says we extended our personal attachment to each other to include the community.) There were some risks that we took in terms of prestige in our professions. I don't know that we would have taken them anyway.

The commune was a very amorphous kind of thing. We didn't know much about what we were doing. Joining the commune was like an astronaut going out into space. We were joining several others in something where we didn't know what was going to happen.

We were not escaping from anything. This was a new adventure. The thing that was different about it is that we had to cut off our roots to some extent as we explored the new soil. Both of us were financially secure, Suzie in her professorship and I in my directorship. Our children were also pretty well set and ready to explore new sorts of relationships.

We didn't have a feeling that the usual American relationship between husband and wife, or parent and child, were the be-all and end-all of life. We thought we could explore a few visions of the "right way." We were open-minded and ready to explore.

The commune did not exist until we created it. We didn't even have a name for it. We didn't know what to tell family and friends we were doing. The group explored all the titles that we could imagine. When I went to the bank with a couple of hundred dollars to establish a bank account, I couldn't give the representative a name for it. I finally came up with "The Community on Nelson Road." It never did get a really definitive name.

By that point we had a piece of property—a 118-acre dilapidated dairy farm ten miles north of Boulder on Nelson Road. There were multiple buildings on the property. There were five buildings that we turned into houses, one of which was the old farmhouse. You occupied a building, and you may have had a sense that you had a right to occupy that building, but that right could be attenuated by a variety of influences.

From the perspective of the others who joined us, it was their commune. In a sense it was joining, and in a sense it was creating the opportunity. It was being responsible for a place to join, a place to fit in. Those involved were not really losing absolute control. They were joining a group of young people. It was not Nick and Suzie laying out a pattern of life and asking them to be part of it, it was more like a few experienced sailors doing something which never had been done before.

Suzie, Sherry, and I had the so-called chicken coop, which was also the commons where we cooked and ate. Other people must have respected our more or less exclusive right to that building. Bobby and Lyle and their two kids occupied the old farmhouse, but not exclusively. There was often another person or couple who shared the building. The other buildings were the west garage, the east garage, and a little house that had been on the property from the beginning. The buildings had varying degrees of exclusiveness and use. There were no buildings started from scratch and built up from the foundation.

Elise Boulding had written or was writing a study of groups living together. I had just finished — if one ever gets finished — relating the idea of a commune to whatever group one applies it to, such as a religious group. We looked at various ashram and experimental living groups.

Building the commune took us into new ground of being part of an organization in which I was not the guru, nor was I part of somebody else's guru group. That was part of the attraction, that it was a social form that did not yet have effective norms and was malleable to our own concerns. I expressed it hundreds of times that we were forming our own community based upon our own ideas. We weren't joining somebody else's already formed community. It isn't very often that you feel that you're stepping off the dock into a rowboat that was still being built.

That would make some people pretty nervous, but I found it exciting. I compared it to marriage as a form of relationship where some aspects are constrained and others open up. I was still a parent and a member of the Quaker worship group. I did, however, have a responsibility to follow whatever norms the community chose to develop. It was a set of situations we had only partly thought through.

Everybody was reassured that they could get out if they needed to. They weren't putting a price on their independence. It was just one aspect of living that we were changing. In the various social knots that one ties in choosing a lifestyle, it didn't seem we were making such a big step. Other people may have thought it was a big step, but we could recognize that it was a modest change in our autonomy. When you woke up and it was your duty to fix breakfast, you fixed it for twenty people instead of four or five.

There were many aspects of living at The Community on Nelson Road that were not experimental. One maintained a marriage as the closest relationship. We also maintained a lot of other relationships. I was still Chairman of the Geography Department, and Suzie was a full professor of Economics. Most everybody still had roots that they had not cut off. Mostly we all maintained a financial connection, a citizenship connection, and so on down the line. Joining the community was not a real wrench in independence.

We did make other relationships in the community. Some of them we entered with our fingers crossed. We weren't becoming a nun or a brother in a religious group. We weren't changing our employment situation. We continued to make a living. It was entirely possible to "do the commune" without tearing the threads in the social network that existed before.

One of the crucial relationships is that of parent to child. There are a lot of different parts of that relationship, and you don't know where it is going to take you. Neither Sherry nor Peter was completely ready to go out on their own. Sherry and Peter were fourteen and sixteen when we married and two years older when we started the commune. Peter was already living away from home in Boulder. There were eight other children. The oldest child was a boy who was maybe nine.

Each adult or near-adult had their own experiences, and therefore were part of the putty that involved other people. New norms and expectations had to be set for all. There were already two or three examples described in books. We would look at these examples and say, "that's for them and not for us." Or we could say, "Yes, we want to be similar in social form and social relationships."

The decision to do the community in the country was a practical matter. Town was well populated with experimental groups of one sort or another. We couldn't find any housing that was appropriate. When the idea of a semi-rural settlement came up, some of us were familiar with living in the country.

Farm work taken seriously is not drudgery. There's a lot of variation in how individual plants accept their condition and what you can do about it. We mixed it up with nudism and other ways of making it a little more exciting. An amusing example was when a group of us were gardening nude, and the engineer in charge of the soil conservation service was there designing a reservoir. He came up to ask which I would prefer of several alternatives. I had to face the fact that I was nude. I was sure they were not accustomed to it. My fellow gardeners seemed to enjoy the fun of it. The engineer must have thought it strange. He took the job in order to design good reservoirs, and here was an oddball. On the whole, the commune was tolerant of odd behavior; I'm not so sure about the general public.

We rotated chores so that everybody had to do everything. We broke down the separation of gender roles and enjoyed the mutuality of that. While nudism was a part of the experiences for at least some of us, I want to make it clear that sharing partners was not something we did. Some people overtly said that this was not going to be part of it; the group was overwhelmingly monogamous.

I don't think there was much outward dissention. We made decisions by consensus. Decisions took place largely independently of the sense of having a ready-made answer. We were pushing the boundaries in many different ways, and not particularly conscious of the impact of one decision on another.

One of the hopes and expectations of the initial group was to create a new and different school for disaffected teens where we would develop a learning community. It would be a youth collective, a community within the community, an experiment that worked itself out with those present. The kids would attend public school but would also participate in community chores and planning, in addition to creating their own rules. We even took in two teenaged boys who did very well with us. But the project was scuttled by the county planning office who wouldn't permit expansion.

We left the community after four years because we could see the direction that it was moving and we didn't want to be part of that set of projects and norms. If you weren't supporting the other members of the community as a community, then you were not really a part of it. If you were, then you were doing things which you wouldn't have done if you were part of the general society. We had to choose between what we wanted and what was best for the group. That was one of the problems. What we thought was best was not the direction the community was going. We wrote a white paper about what we saw as the problems. We gave it to everybody, and they said, "Yes, that's right, but we don't want to change."

Our leaving after four years started the breakup of the community. There were financial adjustments that had to be made. We owned the farm and had paid for most improvements. We went to our lawyer to discuss turning the property over to the community. He said, "You must really like these people an awful lot." We thought that was not completely true. The group had to decide whether or not to buy the farm and chose not to.

We moved into Shady Creek Apartments. Looking back now, it was more like taking a sabbatical from the group. Part of it was the physical separation. Part of it was the sense of sharing. Suzie and I would discuss our response to a thing, and sort of self-consciously say, "This will be our position, but others may take a different position."

We lived in the Shady Creek Apartments while the community dissolution occurred, and then moved back. When we moved back to the farm, we tried to continue the sense of community with the people who rented the other four houses. But the threads that had been pretty tightly spun were now fraying. One of the members, Glenn Browning, had a strong sense of wanting community and stayed on to become manager of the facilities. It fell to him to fix the gate or to observe what needed to be done and get it done.

I'm very glad we had the experience of living in that kind of community. There was the shared intimacy with other people and the understanding—or the attempt to understand—the way in which others reacted to the same situation we were in. I'm glad we did it. It was "the right thing to do" as far as our own values were concerned. I think we're proud of it. We felt like pioneers in a very real sense.

It was a wonderful, emotionally enriching experience. We learned so much about each other and about subsistence farming and about living poor. It was a great people farm in the fact that the hundred or so people who were part of it at one time or another, all ended up stronger and more stable. But it did not free up any time for anything; just the opposite!

Looking back, I'm not sure I would want to do it again. It was quite a stressful situation. I wouldn't want to go through those stresses again. It was stressful from the beginning. It was very complicated. You did your best to fit in somehow. Sometimes you fit and sometimes you didn't fit. We kept doing things that all, or most, of the group felt worthwhile, but we had to give up the youth collective. After that we had no common goal.

After the commune broke up, for seven years we rented out the four other dwellings and tried to maintain some sense of community and sharing. However, the landlord tenant relation interfered to some extent. Suzie often likened the social relations to a feudal fiefdom, and that didn't sit well with our socialist ideals. Trying to continue a group garden, a chicken operation, etc. became trying at times. In 1983 when we decided to create an HOA and sell the houses we were quite clear about making group projects purely voluntary.

We ended up living but not working together. Gradually the farm evolved into a cooperative village, a sort of rural homeowners association. Today's co-housing movement seems like a parallel to what we ended up doing. It offers some of the same support for people who live outside the mainstream.

KGNU

Starting in about 1990, I did a regular commentary on the local radio station KGNU called *Second Thoughts.* I believed that the changes we would like to see in the society depended upon general awareness and public information. The news person for KGNU, an Armenian named David Barsamian, and I had crossed swords a little bit on the matter of Turkish responsibility for the terrible slaughter of Armenians. I had taken the Turkish side, saying that one has to think of Turkey at the time as a society with the enemy built right into the society, so what could they do. He, of course, took the opposite position, that it was as much an Armenian society as it was Turkish. There's plenty to be said for both sides in that argument. It can be argued successfully either way.

We never came to blows about it, and we developed a friendship. I suggested that I was interested in public consciousness, not on this topic, which would rest entirely in his hands, but on other things. He said sure and welcomed me to do some pieces of my own. He said that three minutes was the longest that I should do. I spoke more rapidly then than

I do now, but still three minutes isn't very long. I was proposing to do whatever I did by myself rather than in league with someone else. These were more individual pieces than question and answer.

I practiced up on one that seemed appropriate, and then came several more. The first one was based on a reflection I had as I drove into Boulder from the north. It was a lovely, brilliant Colorado day, the highway was clear, and I had no concerns that I was worried about. The air was quiet. As I drove in, I drove through pristine clear air until I got to the edge of Boulder where you drop into the floodplain. As you look down on the floodplain when you get to the edge of it, it looks hazy. It was a white haze associated with the fireplace smoke and stove smoke that was prevalent at the time. Once you got into the city, you forgot about the smoke. You didn't see it. It was a perfectly good day, but it was not as bright as it had been. I thought to myself, "That's very much like the feelings we have about the nature of the city." You're not aware of the pollution, just as you're not aware of the inequality and oppression that is within the city body politic.

That was my first subject. It stayed with me that you're not aware of the corruption when you're in it. There's nothing that calls your attention to it. When you're outside the society, you're very much aware of it. I watched for similar circumstances, not necessarily about corruption and oppression, but about the sense of being in it or outside of it looking in on it.

I did quite a few drafts for these pieces. I wrote with the idea that they were very compact little essays. Occasionally David allowed me a few seconds over the narrow time slot, not to wander, but to fit the body in there.

I did one every two weeks until I had done five or six of them. Then they stretched out with longer periods in between. They were something David could use when it was convenient to add to the morning broadcast. He had them in reserve. He didn't have to use them that day; he could use them another day. They got further and further apart.

I did this for about thirteen years, until 2003. People have reminded me of them even to the present. In the last couple months, people have said, "We've enjoyed your radio essays and look forward to hearing more." They've had an enduring influence. Why did I stop doing them? Why does the sun come up every morning? I suppose that I ran out of topics and there were other crucial things that needed to be done. I don't think there was any direct negative reaction to them. It's a little bit of the ability of the society to accept the criticism when it's put in this relatively attractive language. I ran out of succinct expressions of criticism.

This was part of an ongoing focus in my life on social injustice. I had been doing this since I was young. The example from my younger days that comes to mind immediately is the conscientious objection. That was very direct and inescapable. The choice of career, where you're dealing with young people and young people's minds was another example. It wasn't quite as direct as the youth ministry in a church, but it reached a wider variety of people.

One youthful example that may not be obvious is the escape from the Eastern establishment. That society was more interested in what your grandfather did than in what you did. The whole class system was based upon remembering the prosperity of your grandfather and forgetting the oppression that helped to create it.

Focusing on social injustice includes those things that don't get done. You could spend your afternoon at the races; you could go up to Blackhawk and gamble away a few hundred dollars. Abstaining from these things is an attempt to be more saintly. Most of us never achieve it. A very few do. Any place along the line that I chose to be constructive rather than destructive, egalitarian rather than taking special privilege, was part of trying to be more saintly. If you accumulate these little decisions through a lifetime, you'll find a considerable difference.

There were a lot of departures from that path too. There was the corruption of the ideal of equality again and again and again. That is true both in the world and in my life. One example is in the treatment of females as against males. The whole process is so unequal, and yet we accept most of it as part of the culture and don't do anything about it. It gets incorporated into the routine.

The examples of where I went against my own ideals I'm not ready to share yet. My unwillingness is a lot of what created the tension and hesitation to do these memoirs. I suppose the one-to-one relationship with women has been a major factor there. There are seductions that I am not proud of. They might still be embarrassing, not only to me, but to the woman on the other side. I hope that the positives outweigh the negatives, but there must be negatives there.

What other kinds of privilege? In the economic sphere, one takes advantage. We take advantage of our whiteness to disadvantage people of color. I don't know how to deal with these injustices any more blatantly than in the *Second Thoughts* essays.

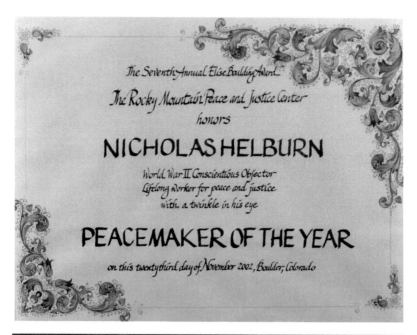

The Seventh Annual Elise Boulding Award

The Rocky Mountain Peace and Justice Center

honors

NICHOLAS HELBURN

World War II Conscientious Objector
Lifelong worker for peace and justice
with a twinkle in his eye

PEACEMAKER OF THE YEAR

on this twentythird day of November 2002, Boulder, Colorado

2001 Peacemaker of the Year Award; with granddaughter Dana at the ceremony

LEGACY*

How did you come to your strongly held beliefs about pacifism?

On the bookshelves in my parent's dining room, where I could see it every day, was a slender volume: *The Economic Consequence of the Peace* by John Maynard Keynes. I never read it, but the principles it espoused were the subject of many adult conversations I was party to. In high school, I was taking American History. I was forming an indelible picture of Wilson's idealism expressed in what would now be called sound bites: "open treaties, openly arrived at," and "a war to end all wars."

I never experienced disillusionment with Woodrow Wilson. It seemed that the Treaty of Versailles was the result of enmity of the French and the British and other allies. The cruelty of the terms imposed on Germany seemed unconscionable in the culture of the 1920s and 1930s. Obviously war engenders hatred, hatred so intense it blinds the victors. They seemed blind to the impossibility of the reparations.

I cannot tell how much I was influenced by a super-patriotic History teacher and a loving German teacher. I came away with a firm conviction that violence engenders more violence, a conviction that I still hold, reinforced by seventy-five years of experience. I have learned to support the conviction by numerous religious teachings. Hitler grew out of the "shame" of the Versailles Conference. I now have the conviction that war cannot solve problems. It just changes the power relations, and it is clumsy and expensive of lives and property.

As you look at your career, of what part are you most proud?

The five years as director of the High School Geography Project is the primary thing that set my career apart from others. During those years I was able to make a real difference. It was the only public recognition that I received. Other things fade in comparison. There were no regrets at the time. There was an association of lower prestige with the involvement in secondary school geography that made a difference when looking for a job when the project came to a close, but nothing dramatic. I had a staff of thirty, which is quite different from an ordinary professorship.

---

* This section is left in question-and-answer format, because the answers don't make much sense independently. –Editor

Were you a good boss?

I hope so. I was able to live up to many of my principles in the hiring and firing of staff. How well my people would agree that I was different I don't know, but it seemed so to me. I had a lot of discretion in the executive role. Not so far as the profession itself was concerned, but certainly on the project.

What else are you proud of?

That's a profound question because almost every decision about the way we live has to be thought of as what we accomplish.

If you could look back over your whole life and change one decision, what decision would you not change?

It would probably be the acceptance of the directorship of the High School Geography Project. It had more influence on my life and on the profession than almost anything else I can think of. I would do it again.

What decision would you change?

There's probably a whole series of minor decisions associated with the choice of profession and other choices that I would change. These are small things that fade from being outstanding: things like who would you hire and why and how much they influenced my life and other people's lives. Our lives are very affected by those who come into them. Those decisions and our influence over those decisions are contributions to the total and represent smaller bits of larger effects.

Who are the people that most affected your life?

I think my mother affected my life more than anyone else. Her sense of what was right and what was not was the strongest influence on me. After that, I choose several professional decisions, like the decision to follow geography rather than other professions. The geography class I took at Harvard had more of an effect than I could have imagined at the time. I often think of how different my life would be if I had chosen something different and thank my lucky stars that I did choose geography.

Has your life been a happy life?

Oh yes. There's no hesitation in answering that question. I hope it's been a constructive life.

If you were to give a young person advice about how to live a good life, what advice would you give?

I don't think there's much question but that it would be to follow one's principles and try to be honest about it.

Do you feel you've done that?

Pretty much. I don't think there have been many aspects of life where I've joined the popular culture.

If your great grandchild were to know only one thing about you, what would you want that great grandchild to know about you?

That great-grandfather was pretty nearly honest in his choices all along the way.

How do you want to be remembered?

I can probably answer the negative more easily than the positive: how do I not want to be remembered? It has never been very important to me how I wanted to be remembered until this situation. I can describe a life that has been fairly open, fairly relaxed, and where casual connections added up to something quite large. If I can be remembered for those things, that's the way it should be. I don't want to feel that I did anything unusual, but rather that the natural consequences of life added up to something quite significant in total.

What's the most interesting thing that you have ever seen?

I enjoy other people and their choices for entertainment and growth. Why did so-and-so choose that?

What's the most interesting place you have ever been?

Uzbekistan. The whole of Central Asia I came upon as an adult, fully developed, without much previous knowledge of it. Tashkent is in Uzbekistan and has a checkered history. Every mountainside was a new experience. We didn't go until I was old enough to know better. Suzie and I had been married forty years.

What is your most treasured possession?

If I can be abstract about it, I suppose it's a critical mind. I don't know that there's anything that comes close to that.

What makes you laugh?

I suppose I laugh at ordinary things that put people in situations they didn't expect. There are all kinds of examples. The ordinary slapstick doesn't last very long. The other sorts of things are more about complex expectations that you have and you don't get. I didn't feel like laughing much about the conscientious objection.

What makes you sad?

The inverse, of course. When somebody acts as though they're acting in good conscience and gets slapped down, whether it's me or somebody else, it makes me sad.

What is your favorite food?

Breakfast. The eggs and bacon combination generally goes down easily. Cereal is the next best thing. There's very little that I turn down when breakfast comes.

What is the coolest thing you've ever done?

Both by my standards and by expectations of those around me, it encompasses behavior you don't expect. Nobody but a goddamn fool would jump out of an airplane 1,000 feet above the surface. After the third jump it gradually became routine. It didn't become routine all at once, but gradually. I did twenty-two jumps. Seven of those were practice jumps and the rest were jumping alongside a fire.

What is your worst fear?

Drudgery.

Describe who you are today?

I have the same name, interests, and capacities that I must have had before. Here I am. The constitution has suffered a real blow with the accident. I'm limited in what I can do. I hope it won't be long before I have a wide variety of abilities. The ability to reach for things is one that I sorely miss. I get myself in situations where I can't reach what I need to carry out what I want to do. I guess every wheel-chair bound person has the same problem. I just seem to have it in spades.

How are you different today than you were thirty years ago?

Thirty years ago I was quite a different person. How would you know the differences? Part of it is that now that I'm not able to pick up and go on a moment's notice or no notice at all.

You were still working thirty years ago?

I had students and responsibilities. I don't know that I changed fundamentally, because one doesn't change in fundamentals very much.

How is your life today different than you thought it would be?

I had no expectation about physical handicap—handicaps, plural. It certainly is different in my capacity to do things. That's where I feel it most.

What are some of the best parts of being the age you are?

People pay respect to you when you're using crutches, more so than when you're just carrying a cane. They give you the right of way. They expect you to have an agenda, and they expect to follow your agenda. People don't have a lot of expectations of you. You are an autonomous person, but you have tastes and biases and obligations that you haven't fulfilled that you expect to fulfill. The world sits waiting for you to ask for what you need.

Is it hard to be in a situation where you ask for what you need?
Yes, quite hard. I'll be glad to get back to "ordinary" living?

What kinds of things give you joy?
When I can surprise people in the sense that they don't expect anything and I come through.

What members of your family are you still in touch with?
My "kid" sister died several months ago. That left me the senior member of my generation. I had to begin to take things on my own responsibility and move on. I couldn't sit down and write an email to Peg asking her to do something. I have had to go on and do it. I've almost always been in a position where I was able to bounce things off others. To take full responsibility seems very strange and dubious.

What do you enjoy doing?
My interactions with other adults are the most fun. Sometimes they're quite surprising. Suzie arranged for a nurse to be on-call for me. I don't know what she expected, but I'm always glad when I can surprise somebody by being more competent than they expect. I've lost two persons in my close relationships in the recent times. One was my sister Peg and the other was my brother Peter. While I didn't see much of Peter, it was a very close relationship. I have valued it highly.

What do you enjoy more today than you used to?
I think it is the social interactions that I'm more aware of, and they are more enjoyable. The other things I sort of expected.

If you could have a conversation with anyone you've ever known, living or dead, who would it be?
A lot of it depends on what you mean by a conversation. If you're going to know Franklin Delano Roosevelt, it would make a difference if you are to know him for an hour or months. I suppose I would have a conversation with Mao Tse Tung. If it were somebody in the family, I would have to say Willard Helburn, my father, because I never got to know him closely. I never had the kind of intimate conversation that I had with Mother. He always had a fair amount of reserve, and probably had more reserve with his children than with anybody else. He died at the end of World War II in 1950.

If you were forty again and could do anything you want for a day, what would you do?
That leaves open a wide set of activities. One set would have to do with personal ability, personal things. There are women that I would like to know better, or would like to have known better.

What things are your priorities now?

I've turned to winding up some things that hadn't been finished, like what we're doing now. I'm trying to make sense out of some of the things that seem cut off. The most important is the relationship with my father. Whether I ever would get close to him is another question. Being close to him was not easy and leaves me less than fully satisfied with the relationship.

What would you ask him if you could?

I would ask him the question about the relationships within the family, and how he took them.

What do you find yourself daydreaming about?

Pretty important things like how I would do if I had the chance to run the German Empire or the Russian Empire. Could I run it any better? It would be nice to know, but I don't have any real reason to think I could run it better. Delusions are things that you can work towards.

What's the most important personal goal that you did meet for yourself?

The most important personal goal was the conduct of the Department of Geography's everyday activity so that I never really felt that I was out there on the fringe and only had one or two supporting members. What I choose to talk about is not necessarily the thing that was important. I want to talk about the relationships with other faculty members. Some that I can be proud of and others that I would rather had ended in a different way. The relationships that I am most proud of have to do with trust and equality. These are the relationships with people that I affected the most. Those weren't always the most powerful relationships that I had. I suppose the ones that I'm happiest about are the ones that ended up with them trusting me or me trusting them.

Grandmother Helburn

Grandfather Helburn

Nick's maternal grandfather, Frank S. Mason, helped to establish the Appalachian Mountain Club in New England.

Nick's aunt, Theresa Helburn, was a theatrical producer and co-founder
of the Theater Guild in New York City.

Margaret Helburn in 1930 on one of her mountain climbing
adventures in Chamonix

Nick's Mother gave this photo of Nick to Susie.
She had written on the back, "About 1920. He was
just as enchanting then as he is now."

Nick swimming at the family retreat at Carlisle

Nick at the time he went to Shady Hill School

At nineteen, Nick carrying supplies to the Zealand Falls
hut where he was hutman for two summers

Nick graduated from the University of Chicago in 1940.

Tess Loth and Nick newly married in 1939

Tess and Nick, with his brother Steve and his wife Mary

Nick, second row second from right, and fellow conscientous objectors
worked at a former CCC camp in Gatlinburg, Tennessee in 1944.

Nick, Tess, Steve and goats at their log cabin on Sourdough Road in Bozeman

Helburn house designed by Richard Neutra in Bozeman, Montana, in 1950
Photograph by John Brittingham

Neutra designed a very beautiful one-story house with a log and
glass structure and a sod roof.

From left, Peter and Steve Helburn, around 1957

The architect Roger Easton designed the Tall Timbers house in the mountains outside Boulder, Colorado, in 1966.

The house used the face of the former quarry as one wall of the bedroom.

Steve and Mary Helburn wedding in Cavite City, Philippines, November 1967

Steve Helburn in 1980, Gulf of Mexico repairing an oil platform.

Peter Helburn at 17 in 1971

Margaret and Willard Helburn in New Zealand after World War II

Margaret Helburn with her children Nick, Peg, and Peter

Nick on his brother Pete's boat in St. Croix, winter 1985-86

Pete and Nick off St. Croix

Nick with his sister Peg near Bodrum, Turkey in 1993

Margaret 'Peg' Helburn Kocher

PART II

SUZIE FILLS IN SOME HOLES

Very little of Part I of this memoir deals with Nick's life after he turned fifty and, importantly, after we met in 1968 and fell in love. He doesn't give much attention to the deeply personal; in Part I we have, at most, half of Nick. I want to give a fuller picture of him in his later years. Of course, in some ways Nick always remained somewhat of a mystery to me; nevertheless, there is much more to him than he recorded. Fortunately, I have his writing describing daily life, beliefs while he was living it, as well as short pieces on his beliefs, politics, concerns during his last forty-three years. They capture the Nicki I knew and love. So this section of the memoir includes some of his correspondence and writing. I will try to fill in some holes in the memoir, provide background and context for Nick's own words, and sometimes try to answer for myself questions I wish I had asked him.

Above, Nick at a conference in 1963; *below,* nature lover on a hike in 1970

THE IDEAL OF LIVING A BALANCED LIFE

I don't think it is completely obvious from Nick's memoir that he was an idealist and that, generally, he tried to live his life by his ideals. He expressed much of this idealism in his "Spiritual Journey" that he read to the Boulder Friends Meeting in 2003.

> I never thought of my journey as spiritual. I never separated moral and intellectual and political from one another… If I have an image of God, it is that sense of goodness in each of us and perhaps in all living things. It is entirely compatible with the Quaker tenet: there is some of God in every person.
>
> As I declared independence from my parental family at about age 20, I committed myself to a balanced life. I knew I had to earn a living but there were other responsibilities to society. I couldn't live entirely in my head. I had to keep my body healthy too. I did not live alone, so I had to pay attention to the family and community I lived in. That sense of balance has stayed with me. A mild stroke 18 months ago changed the weights a little but did not change the commitment. I would still get at least minimal exercise, stay current on current affairs and politically active, and keep my commitment to the small community. (Earning a living no longer makes any demands on my time thanks to retirement annuities and social security.)

Nick's choice of career as an academic and his approach to it illustrate this ideal. He took seriously professorial teaching, research and service responsibilities, but he tried to maintain a balance. He was not ego driven to achieve a national reputation or accumulate a hefty dossier of publications. He worked to improve teaching, the geography department, the university, the geography profession. And he also recognized that tenured professorial status provided cover for his other political activities.

A critical element in a balanced life included a love of and concern for nature. He quotes Aldo Leopold:

> All ethics…rest upon a single premise: that the individual is a member of a community of interdependent parts. (Man's) instincts prompt him to compete for his place in that community, but his ethics prompt him also to cooperate (perhaps in order that there may be a community to compete in).
>
> The Land ethic simply enlarges the boundaries of the community to include soils, waters, plants and animals, or collectively, the land. *(Leopold, 1949)*

Balancing competing ideals has its drawbacks; in his letters Nick reports overwork, inadequate sleep, exhaustion. But it also gave him tremendous satisfaction. In speaking of his life in Montana he writes:

We had achieved the balanced life.

I had a career that I believed in, that dealt with the environment;

We were surrounded by mountains for camping, climbing and skiing;

In addition to the goats, we had a big garden and freezer. We enjoyed a healthy diet prepared largely from food we had produced.

We lived in a beautiful, airy house we had largely built ourselves, with a small house next door we could rent out to graduate students.

We were a stable family in a relatively small city.

We attended a small allowed meeting under the care of the University Meeting in Seattle, whenever we were not off skiing or camping or whatever.

Writing to his mother in December 1959, on hearing news of a family member's death, he comments:

Somehow, now at the height of my productivity I find it hard to be afraid. Any time is O.K. from here on. I've done something. I've lived these last few years and months as intensively as I ever could hope to. I'll enjoy whatever time I get from here on out but I don't see that if I go tonight I'll have missed very much.

One thing I've thought about many times the last few months is that I have very little idea of what to expect as I go from 40 to 50 to 60. What changes in outlook creep up on one? What happens to all these jobs that don't get done now but are postponed until "I get a little leisure"? Are they still there to be a challenge at 65?

Balance for Nick included attention to aesthetics and beauty. In particular he was attuned to natural beauty. My friend Bella Feldman had earlier helped me learn to experience art through her eyes; another friend and talented photographer, Lars Speyer, taught me to see detail and drama in everyday life. Nick introduced me to the beauty of raw nature. We got to know each other through early morning hikes climbing the foothills behind Chautauqua with my whippet Gladstone. I learned to love the broad vistas, the rolling clouds, the details of the forest floor. And in his letters Nick never ceased to comment on his surroundings and their beauty, particularly on the weather. Rain depressed him! The full moon and stars captivated him. He never fails to marvel at the beauty of the night sky or sound depressed by days of rain.

Aesthetics also figured in the details of everyday living. Nick built three lovely homes in his lifetime. In Part I Nick talks about the house he built in Bozeman, Montana, and Tall Timbers in Boulder. In 1983 we built a beautiful house on the Nelson Road farm designed by our son-in-law Jim Logan, and our daughter Sherry and Jim built another one next door.

Nick retired from the university and made a major volunteer commitment to the Rocky Mountain Peace and Justice Center. From time to time he attended the Boulder Meeting. In his "Spiritual Journey" Nick comments about this time:

> Once again we had a balanced life: a comfortable airy house with space for orchard, garden and community playground, at the edge of a metropolis, with a backdrop of mountains and interaction with community at several scales: nuclear and extended family, the hamlet at Nelson Road, many institutions in Boulder and, to a limited extent, in Denver.

Margaret and Willard about 1949

Parental Influences & Family Relations

Nick, his mother (Margaret), and father (Willard) kept up a steady stream of letters and Nick saved them; unfortunately, he didn't go back and read them as part of writing his memoirs. They are impressive; his Mother's letters are intimate, focusing on feelings and relationships; his father's tend toward lectures about appropriate behavior and sparring with Nick over what Willard perceived as infantile idealism in matters political. The letters certainly demonstrate deep caring, evidently from parents that did not show much actual affection.

Nick says without hesitation in the "legacy" statements in Part I that the person who had the most influence on his life was his mother. She taught him what was right and what was not and the importance of leaving the world better than you found it. She was always present during his youth; his father was more remote from the children's daily lives. She considered Nick to have the best temperament in the family and comments in one letter that everyone always says, "Everybody loves Nicky." In a lovely picture of Nick as a three-year old that she sent me soon after our marriage, she scrawled on the back, "About 1920. He was just as enchanting then as he is now. Love MH"

During our courtship, even as a fifty-year-old man, it was important to Nick to "show me off" to his mother and vice versa. He had already filled her in about me as much as he could and sent her my picture (she reacted positively, commenting that I looked upstanding and very much like Mary Bell, Steve's wife of whom she was very fond). I remember fondly our trip to Cambridge to meet her before our marriage. Thoughtfully, she put us in adjoining bedrooms separated by a bathroom! She organized a party, took me to Carlisle, the family country getaway, and fed me a lobster dinner to see how I would approach the beast. I adore lobster and don't mind the mess involved in sucking out the last bit of meat. I passed muster. But she warned me not to wear him out.

I'm pretty sure that Nick's relation with his father was problematic. To the question, "If you could have a conversation with anyone you knew either living or dead, who would it be?" he answered that If it were someone in his family, "it would be Willard Helburn, my father, because I never got to know him closely. I never had the kind of intimate conversations that I had with Mother. He always had a fair amount of reserve." And to the question, "What are your priorities now?" Nick replied, "I've turned to winding up some things that hadn't been finished.... I'm trying to make sense out of some of the things that seem cut off. The most important is the relationship with my father. Whether I ever would get close to him is another question. Being close to him was not easy and leaves me less than fully satisfied with the relationship."

Nick left home permanently after his first year at Harvard, took a year off to work in the White Mountains, then resumed college at Chicago where he met and married Tess Loth. He kept up a correspondence with his father until at least 1944 when his father must have suffered from a mild stroke. Nick's letter from Pinkham Notch explains the decision to his father. It's a powerful letter from a nineteen-year-old. In it he explains the need to get away from the intellectuality and "superiority complex and a scorn for the commonplace" and the absence of evidence of parental love.

March 3, 1938
Pinkham Notch, New Hampshire

Dear Papa
It was very nice to get your letter in addition to Mother's. In it you asked me if I could come down soon. That is near impossible for my time off is from Wed. 8:15 AM to Thur. at 3 PM, every other week, and Tues afternoon on the odd week. This spring, however, I get another week off.

Your story of von Flecker sounds very exciting. You say that The New England territory is difficult. What makes it so? The abundance of leather, the type of manufacturer, or what?

When you write to Pete next tell him that there is a market for good crampons (see diagram). They can sell for as high as 3.50 or 4.00 dollars if they are really good. He should contact Charlie Dudley or Piane at the Dartmouth Co-op in Hanover.

I haven't heard any news of Peg. How is she getting along in Radcliff?

About getting out of the family environment, I agree with you that it is not sheltered in the usual sense of the word, but it is dominated completely by the intellectual side, and runs along smoothly with a slight superiority complex, and a scorn for commonplace and the nonintellectual. I think that it is worth my while to get away from that certain set of prejudices for a space in order to learn how other people think before I am completely unsympathetic. There are certain telling things in the family life which I consider make it sheltered in a sense. For instance, to be called mediocre is to be damned worse than anything else. The adjective, exciting, is used as intellectually and not emotionally exciting. Emotion is frowned on even to the point where parental love is seldom thought of, to say nothing of mentioned, except in signing letters.

These prejudices and opinions are probably the ones I will have when and if I settle down. But I want to have a chance to see and to understand a lot of others before that time comes.

You say that the environment here seems slovenly compared to college. I feel that a fellow here holds more responsibility than the average boy at

Harvard. For here, although nothing is usually said, everybody knows that a poor job is felt, and public opinion carries a lot of weight in a close-knit group like this. On the other hand, in college a bad job is just a slightly lower mark to most fellows, and if you get too high marks you are looked down on anyway.

Your suggestion that I take a year at a western college is a good one. I will write the University of Chicago immediately for literature concerning transfers, requirements, scholarships, and employment bureau.

With lots of love, I remain your most humble and obedient son and servant, Nick

This letter to Nick from Willard dated February 12, 1939, is illustrative of the many letters from father to son. The tone and content might explain Nick's eagerness to get away from the old man. Willard expresses his concern about Nick's slow and possibly disappointing intellectual development, the folly of Nick's idealism, the basis of their political disagreements (often about tactics, not substance).

February 13, 1939

Dear Nick:
Your last letter was a distinct improvement over the last one before that. At least I am sure you are still alive, and that you are writing your own letters. (Nobody else has the originality and charm of spelling that you do.)

The difference you notice in the amount of extra-curricular activity between Harvard and Chicago is mainly you, my boy. At Harvard you always had a place to come home to, with moderately congenial company. You ate at home, slept there, etc., and thus did not hear about what was going on. Now that you are at Chicago, with no place to go but to your rooms, you are on the loose for entertainment, you are palling around with a bigger bunch of friends, and so on, and you do more.

As to the difference in economic status of Harvard and Chicago men, you make me laugh. At the top, in Harvard, you find a small percentage—ten perhaps—of rich boys. The rest are just like the Chicago men: middle class boys with a sprinkling from the really poor. Do you know what percent of Harvard men are on scholarships? One thing that hid the facts from you is that you are essentially a snob. (I say this in all kindness and sympathy. I am one too.) While in theory you admire the lower classes and respect honest virtue at the lower salary levels, you know perfectly well that you feel superior to people who never wear neckties, who never have a tablecloth when they eat, who don't speak anything remotely resembling English, who are ignorant, opinionated and unshaven. You would prefer people of your own background and tastes, like Herby Green or Gordy Day or god knows who, but not muckers. At Harvard you didn't reach down below you and meet the poor boys there: if anything, you reached up, and, meeting some of the rich and aristocratic, you were a little disgusted at their snobbery. Natural result: you said Harvard is a snobby indifferent place (which is not especially true) and my family is intellectually intolerant (which is true, god forgive us), so I am going to get to hell out of here. Unsound reasoning: sound decision.

I might as well tell you now (I was going to save it for you till you got of voting age) that venerating the poor is just as fallacious as venerating the rich. In fact, veneration is a sucker's game all the way through. The only people worth knowing and worthy of respect are people, individuals, not classes. If you have to classify them, I would do it on a basis of intelligence or character (the second is usually the result of the first). I can see you now saying "There are other things besides brains." Well, name three. I can't think of any. Almost everybody has some charm, sweetness, affection, a body you can get used to in time, and a minimum of small talk. The indispensable thing, it seems to me, is intelligence. Am I wrong?

You'll find them all over. Danny Collins has some. He is an uneducated, unprincipled, crooked, sanctimonious politician, the product and slave of an unhappy environment produced by an unfortunate conjunction of poverty and the catholic church, but he has brains: he is an ingenious fellow, and I like him. Dabby Dexter may be an ungainly fellow, Walter Baird may be a moody dreamer, Pedro may be a pigheaded fool, Sprague Coolidge may be a brusque socialist, Groucho may be a selfish bitch, Swede Johnson may be a congenial loafer, but they are all infinitely preferable to a bore. They have a certain amount of intelligence. Any one of them is better than a dozen Mary Walshes—she was so stupid I bet you don't even remember her. The "Faith, now" maid we had.

So don't be undiscriminating, my humble and obedient bro. Carry a salt-celler in your pocket and sprinkle a little on everything you take.

Pedro is teaching at Deveraux Farms, Glen Moor, Penna., a home for feeble-minded mistakes of the rich (as he himself puts it). He also gets up to Phila, for a class or two at night.

With best regards, and with hope that you will tolerate this latest burst of intellectual intolerance.
Helb

In 1960 Nick's mother found Nick's 1938 letter to Willard and asks Nick about the letter and his current reactions. He replied that he had thought about his letter many times and that there were several aspects of it worth commenting on.

February 19, 1960

Dear Moth:
This will be the climax of a wonderful evening. While I brought my briefcase home with me tonight—there was nothing in it that had to be done tomorrow morning. It's the first time in two weeks at least. Furthermore last night I got almost eight hours sleep. So I feel very relaxed.

I read the *New York Times*—or most of it. The last three have gone nonopened. I put Pete and Steve to bed. I listened to a little stereo. I studied the 1st Russian lesson, washed my hair and here I am in front of the fire with your anchor holding a couple of pine logs and some cedar kindling at just the right angle to dry my hair while I write on the card table.

Now to the letter from the White Mts when I was 18. No I don't share that feeling now, though I can remember believing it at the time. It was written sincerely. I'm not sure I can justify my feelings then. At this writing I can assure you that I appreciate the restraint you and father showed. I see all around me the problems of over-devoted parents unable to let their children go in a peaceful way. I even see it in our relationship with Steve—our habitual "paternalism" so often justified only by protective love.

So I'm grateful that you made it easy for me to take my 1st flights from the nest. Only recently have I begun to appreciate the imagination and planning the two of you showed in so many things you did for and with us.

At the time I was maturing fast. I was in a situation where most of my relationships with others were very transitory. Nat Pierce and I still took ourselves very seriously. She had obviously been starved of fundamental affection in her own filial-parental relationship. At that time, I think she was coming back from the University of Idaho pregnant. While I shared no immediate responsibility I certainly felt a deep concern.

Together these things may have piled up to give me a temporary need for more emotional support than I was getting. I had no place to turn but to you.

How's that for a rationalization? I really don't know how much validity there is in it. Do you have a better explanation? Comments?

Willard, ultimately, began to recognize that Nick was growing up, but their letters never achieved the level of man-to-man talk (which they did between Willard and his older son Steve). On the occasion of Nick's twenty-first birthday after a long disquisition about Nick's flawed logic and misplaced idealism Willard wrote, "Well. This isn't a very congratulatory letter to reach you on your coming of age! I hope to see you maturing in your habit of thought and your view of the world, as you have matured this past year in your capacity for work and concentration, and your practical and financial control of your affairs. And so long as you keep yourself modest, tolerant and flexible, time will do the rest." About the same time, in a letter to Tess, who Nick had married earlier in 1939, Willard worries about Nick's idealism and lack of practicality:

If I could get into Nick's mind that the future of the world does not rest exclusively on his shoulders, and that it might possibly be salvaged without his full attention, or may possibly go to hell in spite of him, but that in any case, he cannot expect to go on saving it, except by being able to support himself comfortably in it, he may rearrange the order of importance of his various undertakings. The first job is to lead a healthy life with enough to eat and enough exercise to keep him fit and alert, the second, to rank high enough in his department to be assured of professional encouragement and opportunity, and that doesn't mean B's either. If he can't make a distinguished record as a student, and save the world, he had better let the world take its chances....

A year later in another letter to Tess, Willard says "I came down on Nick like the wolf on the fold a few months ago for calling the Dies Committee hypocrites, not for his opinion but for his manners." Assessing Nick's research he comments, "Nick's best gifts are those of contact and dealing with people. He has no great talents as a pedant." Still later Willard writes, "I always like sense and distrust principles—and true maturity seems to me the process of substituting sense for principles-absolutes-ideals." By the fall of 1940 Dad, evidently relieved with Nick settled in Montana, writes, "It sounds as if you had jumped over adolescence in one leap and gone from boy's work to man's work incontrovertibly."

Nick may always have been a bit deferential with his father. In a letter to Tess in 1944 Willard writes

> ...I am well aware that Nick shows more independence anywhere else than with me, which is perfectly natural. His vigorous and cocky family always impinged on his own slow and quiet development; he felt the need of getting away to Chicago to be out from under the pressure, and his decision was justified. I don't think I shall ever cease to argue with Nick; I love and respect him too much to have his views unchallenged when they seem to me open to criticism, and there may always be more difference between his views and mine than those of the other children, who think more the way I do. (No. I don't think the others accepted my views parrotwise—they're damned independent.) Or there may not—I'm sure it's because Nick, as I've told you, is so much more like what I was at his age than the other children ever were, that I try to stimulate or ease the development that I went through and that, in some directions, I suppose he will. But I judge him, I hope, not by his impression on me, so much as by that on Harry Kelly and Roland Renne and fans, who respect and admire him. And I think as I get older I leave more to time and less to persuasion than I used to—though I have further to go with Nick in that respect than with anyone else.

I don't know about Nick's real feelings for his father. I wonder what he would have felt in those last days had he reviewed these letters. No doubt, Nick's father had a profound influence on his development. Certainly, Willard was intent on knocking some sense into his son's head, reminding him of his privilege, entreating him to approach his adversaries as a gentleman. Nick, by his own inner strength successfully, as the old song goes, accentuated the positive and eliminated the negative fatherly influences. Nick's own child-rearing practice later on may well have been influenced by those of his parents. But Nick emerged from the fatherly advice into a serious, hard working adult, retaining the sweet, enchanting disposition that his mother adored, developing a special tenderness verging on nobility of spirit that his father seems to have lacked, but I am sure would have admired.

What a contrast between father's excessive intellectuality and son's gracious generosity.

Nick also kept up a friendly correspondence with Willard's sister, Teresa Helburn, between 1940 and 1950. Some of these letters are fun since Terry tells of the Theater Guild Productions. April 9, 1943, she writes of being ill. "I got too tired getting our last show on, a musical version of *Green Grow the Lilac*.... But the show was a grand success and one of the loveliest things you've ever seen. You would particularly like it because it has a ballet all its own…with a lot of humor thrown in. Everybody's raving about the show so I'll be modest…. I can tell you it's quite a job to put on a musical these days, particularly one laid in Oklahoma, where all your men are cowboys and farmers as well as singers and dancers, because they're drafted right out from under as soon as they get trained."

Terry was quite close and generous with her niece and nephews, having had no children of her own. In 1950 she loaned Nick and Tess the $1000 they needed to start building the cabin on their Sourdough land. And Nick was a beneficiary in her will when she died in 1959 (that allowed us to buy the Nelson Road farm in 1971). This letter to Terry in 1945 while he was in Missoula with the smoke jumpers is so charming.

January 9th, 1945

Dear Terry:
I am a very excited boy this evening and I want to tell you about it before the thrill fades. I took my first flying lesson this afternoon and it was great fun. I even got compliments from the instructor.

I took a day of furlough today ran some errands got some extra sleep and took my lesson. The airport is only a mile and a half from the house. The runway was spotted with melting snow but it did not interfere with the take off. The Instructor in front, me in back of the little piper cub. The day was very quiet and rather mild. We had a spell of very cold weather in December, but the last week it has been rather warm, above freezing almost every day.

After we were up at about 1000 ft, the instructor gave me the controls. He let me kick the rudder around but explained that gradual rather than jerky movements would get the best results. Then he taught me to bank and turn at the same time and insisted that they be done together. I discovered for myself that the nose tends to drop as you turn, so he told me to hold back on the stick as I turned and banked. He showed me how to climb and the feel of the ship as she starts to stall from too steep a climb. He showed me the glide and how to feel whether I was gliding too steeply or not steeply enough. The toughest job really was to hold the plane in level even flight in a constant direction. The biggest sensation, however was coming out of too steep a glide, otherwise known as a dive. That was the only time that I did not feel that I knew for sure what I was doing. All this in half an hour.

To complete the day, I took Tess out to dinner and to see "Mrs. Parkington." We enjoyed both.

We ran across a review of "Sing Out Sweet Land" in *Time* which said that you missed the boat for the most part. How do the box office receipts hold out? From the ads in the *New Yorker* it looks as if you were doing a lot of work and as though you had a great deal of competition, but I should imagine that the present inflation, combined with the need for escape would result in a real boom in the entertainment business.

Tess is practicing a duet on her flute and I have promised to play it with her. Give our very best to Oliver. Lots of love from us both,
Nick

Above, August 2, 1969, Suzie and Nick's wedding at the Quaker Meeting in Boulder; *below,* Nick and Suzie enjoying a farm party summer 2009

LOVE AND MARRIAGE

Nick and Me and the Path to Committed, Authentic Love

Before telling our story it is important to say something about Nick's views on marriage. In common with his parents, he considered marriage the paramount and permanent emotional commitment. For Willard and Margaret their marriage and family were absolutely central even though they had given each other the freedom to enter into other sexual relations.

In Nick's letters about the family year in Turkey in 1952-53, I found the following hand-printed statement.

> Security lies neither in your
> Possession nor in mine.
> It lies forever between us.
> If we could resist the childish desire
> To grasp it for ourselves alone
> We could live forever in mutual trust.
>   By
>   Nick Helburn

> Lots of people think of marriage as a condition.
> Once you have been married you have achieved that condition.
> But, rather, marriage is a process
> A process that you must continue to work on.

Nick often quoted the first part about security and possession, relating it to conflict resolution in groups. I hadn't realized that they are his own words and that initially he seems to have used them to think about marriage. I have no idea why he included the sheet in his and Tess's personal letters from Turkey and why he was relating security to "possession" in marital relations at this time in his life. It is clear from Nick's correspondence with his mother during his thirty year marriage to Tess that he took the family responsibility very seriously. Countless letters tell of his making breakfast, spending time with the children, and putting them to bed. Tess's and Nick's subsistence lifestyle also speaks to a very family-oriented life.

In November 1968, after filing for divorce, Nick wrote to the Seattle Meeting of Friends to inform them of the impending divorce, and in his letter he describes the difficulty of giving up his commitment to his marriage. But he also summarizes the deep divide that made continuing the marriage impossible for him and damaging to Tess as she had become more and more dependent on him as their problems multiplied. And "I have discovered modes of living quite outside the common experience I shared with Tess." He admits that Tess and he never learned to talk about the really fundamental aspects of their relationship; they were always polite and usually in full control, "but we never mentioned some parts of our lives and we went so far in not hurting the other's feelings that we bottled up how we really felt."

This chapter is about Nick and me, but also about his history of both casual and serious sexual relations with women during his first marriage. Nick is not alone in giving free expression to his sexual desires. His parents modeled an "open" marriage that they discussed at the family dinner table. However, Nick admits a couple times in Part I his quandary about how to discuss his "seductions" and his more serious extramarital relations. He admits they were an important part of his life, emotionally and as a source of recreation. But they were examples of departures from his own ideals which gave a primacy to social justice and equality. He was not proud of his behavior, and his unwillingness to share this part of his life created a tension and hesitancy to write his memoirs. This hesitation and possible tension may also explain the confusion and inaccuracies in recounting the events leading up to and following his divorce and his continuing long-term relation with "Deborah" as well as his vagueness in describing the decision to marry me.

As we approached marriage and got to know each other Nick and I gave ourselves to each other in a kind of unconditional love that lasted his lifetime and which I certainly feel today. This was no small accomplishment, given my fears of abandonment, Nick's emotional commitments at the time, and his long-standing habit of engaging in casual sex. Somehow, Nick unleashed a powerful force within me I had never experienced before. He had to make a very difficult choice between two women he loved, and he had to move beyond his habit of casual sex to true, committed love. I think our journey is quite inspiring. Let me tell the story as I remember it, relying as much as possible on our words at the time.

Our "courtship" lasted eleven months; the first four months in Boulder involved an increasingly intense "affair." Then I returned to Berkeley (actually, Kensington) for almost six months with each of us visiting back and forth until July before our marriage August 2, 1969. I have the many letters Nick wrote me and some crucial ones I wrote him. He was painfully disengaging from another love and introspectively trying to understand what he called his "lack of restraint in matters sexual" because he knew I could not tolerate such behavior and he was beginning to experience something new.

When we came together in September 1968 I had just arrived in Boulder with my daughter Sherry and dog Gladstone on sabbatical leave from San Jose State to lead the practicum for the Experienced Teachers' Fellowship Program sponsored by The National Science Foundation. My bossy therapist back in California, Dr. Stillwell, was suffering from multiple myeloma and was anxious to finish up her work on me after four years. She had informed me that I needed to get married (after nine years as a divorced single mom). In contrast to my usual choices, I needed to marry a "husband." By that she meant a man who likes being married. At my age of thirty-eight, a fifty-year-old widower or recently divorced man would fit the bill. When my friend Bill Stevens got Nick and me together in early September I certainly took notice; Nick matched Stillwell's prescription! His wife had just left town and divorce proceedings were going ahead. Our first date was to the Gold Hill Inn where Nick was well known; the owner Frank Finn had obviously visited with him there many times with other women. We drove back to Boulder with the Ghia top down and headlights off so we could enjoy the full moon! What a charming, gracious, attractive, smart guy; too bad he seemed to drink too much! I got more and more interested and in a couple weeks, after taking me to dinner at a great (now defunct) restaurant in Georgetown, on the way home he took me to his lovely Tall Timbers House and seduced me. Yes, I was just a seduction!! Because he then informed me that he was intending to marry someone else after his divorce was final. His apparent indiscretion was okay because his intended was not possessive and did not live in Boulder.

Quite an announcement! I backed off immediately, but then reconsidered. He was awfully nice and I was going back home to Berkeley in several months. So why not be squired around by him? We reconnected and we quickly became inseparable, starting in the mornings with our hikes. I don't remember the quality of my mothering—I hope it was okay—I was in love and that love was certainly reciprocated, so much so that Nick started looking around the Bay area for a job since he was planning to leave HSGP as the project drew to a close. Son Peter came home at Christmas from his school in Switzerland and we hit it off; Peter was incensed over Nick's marriage plans because the other woman was a very good friend of his mother's. I was pretty sure that Nick and I were moving into new, inspiring depths of mutual love.

In a letter to his mother on New Year's day right after he put Peter on the plane to go back to boarding school Nick reports that Peter

> ...struck it off well with Suzanne Wiggins, a visiting Professor of economics who I have been dating pretty regularly. He liked her and seemed to like the warm relationship between Sue and me. Also when we were in Montana, before Xmas, he behaved himself very differently at [Deborah's]. He got on better with the children and had a long talk with Deborah. It looks to me as though he is ready to...tolerate some competition for my affections—really rather that he can relate to whomever I relate to and can expect to share in the warmth of the relationship.

Right after the new year, possibly before, Nick accepted a professorship at Western Michigan University and in early January after dinner at his apartment he informed me that he was going to Kalamazoo with his intended to look for a house!!!!! I went ballistic and Nick had a hysterical woman on his hands! Who he loved! Although I have a bad temper (increasingly under control as I age) this was not a temper tantrum. I was devastated.

In a letter I wrote Nick January 5, 1969, I announced I was going home as he had suggested but that I was not letting him off the hook.

> If Deborah is such a potent force in your life, then I am nothing to upset that and you should be able to say that straight out. If I have upset things and if you do have qualms, then admit it and work it out—for all our sakes.... Nicki this is so important to me. I love you, I want the best for you and me. I really don't want to be a trinket in your life, something you have enlarged, illuminated, but which is just a beautiful moment.... If we see each other again, it must be with you really meaning that you have a choice to make. If you have no choice, then, sweetheart I need time to adapt to a new friendship which I hope will be profound, everlasting, but in which I am not your loved one.

Nick replied January 9, "The stereo was playing some lovely Barbara Streisand songs and I was putting some very prosaic fish sticks in the oven when the very trite thought—'I wish I could be two persons' popped into mind—and I broke into tears like a baby. I really wish I could." But in a January 7 letter to his mother arranging a visit with her in February he says, "There is some chance I could bring Deborah. I'd like you to meet her and her to meet you."

I had just been dumped, and not for the first time. By thirty-eight years old I was cute, strong and effective, and I easily attracted men. But they had a habit of ditching me when they realized my emotional needs. I am an only child. My father, who adored me, died suddenly when I was five and my mother when I was fourteen. My first husband was a lovely, complicated guy who suffered from serial monogamy, and I persevered through three of his affairs during nine years until I got tired. Lots of abandonment problems wrapped up in a pretty little package. Nick reached deeply into my psyche, and I found profound satisfaction for the first time and I let him know it, also, that I was vulnerable.

Sherry, Gladstone and I left Boulder January 21 by car. Nick drove us to Salt Lake City to reduce the onus of driving back to California in the middle of winter. That last night together in Salt Lake City was quite remarkable and I had a hard time seeing him off back to Boulder by plane the next morning. In Reno I sent him a letter/diary of the trip home, describing the beauty, remarking "The world is a wondrous place and now I see it through Nicki's eyes. Everything will be all right." I end the letter, "This morning I awoke and started to think about the spiritual part of love. It is the awe and wonder in which one holds the beloved—despite or because of the intimate knowledge of the loved one's behavior, of his humanness. The wonder and awe are the framework or viewpoint for coming to know the person one loves. If this attitude is truly part of your make up—you love nature and its mystery—you can love a person and continue to love more and more deeply as both your knowledge of the person and his mystery grow. Nicki we are just beginning to feel this. It is a wonderful awakening but a tragic time to end the exploration, for me at least. I hope you find this so as well...."

Nick responded,

> I got the diary from Reno and cried and cried. I feel just as confused as ever. I don't know how I'll get unconfused but I'll try a number of things and I keep thinking that time will turn something up.

In a long letter a week later—a kind of progress report on my emotions—I tell Nick that "the numbness is beginning to leave me.... I know that life is good.... I am almost back here. In another week I will be all right and engaged in the things to be done here, with the people who are my friends here, with Sherry and her thing. I am surprised at how calm I've been since returning. I think the reason is that I love you profoundly and permanently and this love is a great comfort. I am stable in it and I realize that while you may go away from me I have my own feelings for keeps. (I am crying now, these things are so hard to say and feel, but they are also wonderful). I am not unhappy. I am sad, but not unhappy. You have let me love you and I am so much better and richer (and sadder) for it." I report to Nick, "I mainly want to tell you that, to me you are good and a very special and precious person. I've now seen all of the men with whom I consort around here. They do not have your quality as a person. They have their own which is very nice, but not your special quality of lovingness, good sense, curiosity, savoring of new and old pleasures, a value system which makes you kind, passionate, obstinate, inquiring, none too judgmental, permissive of and delighted by me.... It sounds from your letter that you are having trouble letting me go and if this is so I am heartened by it.... I'm writing because I am beginning to feel the depth of my feelings for you and the importance and beauty of our time together, because I want to free you from any feelings of obligation and thereby free your important feeling towards me...."

The next day I went to see Stillwell who set me straight, and Nick too. I reported our meeting in a letter that night and within two weeks Nick had made up his mind in my favor. Mine is a great, long letter, but this is Nick's memoir, not mine so I'll just summarize. Stillwell was dying so had to cut straight to the quick. When she found out that Nick and Deborah were both Quakers, she told me something like this: "You know, they're a *sect*. They're the only people who can go back and forth between enemy lines in a war. That's because they're *neutral*. *Both sides trust them*. They're the greatest fence sitters in the WORLD! *Of course* Nick can have two love affairs going at once, or a marriage and a love affair that lasted almost half his married life and *of course* he's on the fence now. Also, they're *cagey*." She teased about the spiritual unity that Quakers feel, "You know, they don't talk to each other much, they think the other person already *knows* what they think and *that's* spiritual unity. And *you*, you're so *direct*. You're *always* on one side or the other!"

I wrote to Nick, "The fact that Stillwell was talking of you as a person of another culture does permit me to understand that you can indeed be on both sides, capable of loving us both, on the fence about who to choose, possibly the necessity to choose. Fence sitting (patience?) and cageyness (juggling, hedging bets?) versus partisanship and directness.... You and Deborah seem capable of long-standing uncertainty. Deborah tells you she's not possessive, of course you need to be 'free' to have other love affairs. You both decide, *not* to get married, but to *not* get married until you're sure. Then there's me. For Christ sake, I'm sure after four months! How in hell can I play a waiting game with two pros?... I probably can't play the waiting game so I (we?) lose. Nicky, if I could get in there and play the game right, would this go on for years?" After a couple pages more I end, "I just got a dose of salts from the 'general' and the 'happy lady,' long overdue. Yesterday's letter is true too and describes me. The question now raised is, can a poor little orphan girl from a big spoiled city in the East, find happiness with a rich and handsome Quaker from Montana/Cambridge? I hope so. How about a ski weekend—no analysis, just joy (me being cagey—I'm learning)." I was also sending him E. E. Cummings poems: "i like my body when it is with your body. It is so quite new a thing...."

Nick confides some in his letters to his mother during this period. In a February 3 letter just before flying to Cambridge to see her he writes,

> Sorry about my long silence. Not easy to explain. Maybe we can take enough time this weekend to review it all out loud and you can give me some perspective. I will be alone. Deborah has a conflict here and there are enough uncertainties about the future to make us both hesitant about adding a social commitment to the emotional investments which have already been made.

By March 1, "Finally fell off the fence I was sitting on, on Susan's side."

In his March 13 letter, started over Ireland while flying back from his visit with Peter in Switzerland, he explains his decision.

3/13/69

Dear Mother:
I don't know how far I'll get with this before they bring dinner and show a movie and I fall asleep. I did want to report on Peter whom I found well and reasonably happy. I was surprised and pleased by the apparent depth of his friendships at the school both with students male and female and with faculty....

The other thing I wanted to write was about my ambivalence between Deborah and Sue. I finally climbed off the fence on Sue's side. I'm not sure of all the factors involved but one thing which tipped the scales was a feeling of being more relaxed with Sue most of the time. 10 years ago, I might have considered this a negative rather than a positive, but now I know I have to and want to scale down the intensity of life.

Another was the close parallel of our professional interests—she is a leader in the field of economics education—and the way we reinforce each other in our work.

The fact is clear that in spite of my resolve not to get "hooked" by some infatuation our relationship kept growing during the fall and early winter even while I kept up the same kind of correspondence and contact with Deborah which I had had for several years. So the "sitting on the fence" period now seems to be that long time when I refused, out of loyalty to Deborah, to let the power of Sue's magnetism take over.

No final commitments have been made. Everything is tentative and subject to growth. All is private and confidential until the divorce is final. But I want you to know that I am moving in Sue's direction and that this movement is not trivial or casual, but thought through as well as it can be under the circumstances.

I'll be back in Denver tonight and probably find letters from you. How are your plans for Philly coming? What else is new? I feel as though I had been out of touch for a month. Meanwhile lots of love!
Nick

April 1 he reports moving to a bigger apartment and "Sue will be in Boulder for a visit and life will seem much brighter." Easter afternoon:

Dear Mother, I almost feel domestic and certainly I'm in a state of bliss. Sue has been around since Wednesday and we seem to continue to deepen the rapport which was so evident last fall. A little bit of social life, supper with the Stevens, a little bit of outdoors, we skied at Arapahoe basin Friday. A little bit of Religion—at least we went to meeting this morning. Quite a bit of work. We're up on the very private deck of the new apartment in the sun. Sue is typing on her ECON 12 course for high school seniors....

[About the move to Kalamazoo] The direction we are moving in is toward a big old house in the middle of town with maybe 3 or 4 children living with us. Both Pete and Sheri, Sue's daughter, have close friends who may want to come along. There might be quite a few dishes to wash! We will hope to visit there the middle of the month, job hunting for her, job preparing for me and house hunting for us. All, of course, is contingent on the completion of the divorce.

I got to meet Maggie on a trip back east in early May, loved her combination of strength, femininity and graciousness. By the end of that month I confided in her, "I am really anxious to begin living with Nick, not so much for me, but because I think it is important for Nick to have his life settle down—happily and securely I hope. His full-speed ahead, no-time-out way of pushing himself really worries me and I see less of that when I'm around." At the end of June Nick writes,

I Do feel committed to marry Sue already, and I am happy about that. I don't think I'm acting hastily. If it were Deborah—I would have been building the relationship for 10 years. As it is I have only been building it for 10 months, but it's much stronger than the relationship with Deborah.

One last letter from this period is included here. In addition to plans for the wedding and adjustments to family life Nick describes his hectic pace (and mine). I didn't slow him down much!

7/24/69

Dear Mother,
I don't know how much sense I can make out of the present but I'll try. It's been hectic here and promises to be so for another couple weeks.

Sue is here in Boulder with Peter and me. Arrangements for the wedding proceed fitfully. The affidavit from Friend's Book Store is here being lettered so it can be signed by all those present. Invitations went out some time ago. People ask where we found the poem we composed. Pete's abstractions on the envelopes draw occasional comment. A number of Sue's close friends from California will be with us, also quite a few friends here in Boulder. The Sieburth's, Ilse and Robert, have accepted. A number of distinguished economists and geographers are involved. Gilbert and Anne White (who knew Steve in NRPB days) made the wedding cake, will decorate the meeting house. Kenneth Boulding, President of the American Economic Association, decorated the cake. Irving Morrissett, chairman of the Social Science Education Consortium, will explain the Quaker procedures to those present and unfamiliar with Quaker weddings.

We had our first crisis in the intimate relationships—Peter kicking up a fuss about a co-author who is visiting here and working with Sue. It caused some pain but it also clarified relationships. Pete now knows that it will take some effort and adjustment on his part to fit in to the new "family."

I finished the last "important" work for the project, the creation of an activity on the geography of junk called "Waste Management." I'm really quite proud of it and glad to have made the input though it pushed me all the last 3 months.

I'm off tomorrow for Edmonton where I serve as external examiner for a Ph.D candidate at the University of Alberta, a boy I worked with when I was there in 1962. Then on to Kalamazoo to a teacher education institute. Back here Wednesday the 30th.

Meanwhile Sue is working hard on her project, trying to get the most out of her leisure before a new job in Sept. and also trying to get the most out of John Sperling while he is here….

The house in Kazoo is being remodeled to better serve our needs—especially—a second bath is being put in at the expense of one of the 4 bedrooms. [I mentioned to Maggi in another letter that we were making it into a suite for us, including a study (nursery?) to provide some privacy.] The contractor seems honest and industrious, if not very imaginative. He's a stereotype Dutchman, Neil Opthoff. Southwestern Michigan was heavily infested by Dutch during its early settlement. The cosmopolitan community makes much fun of them. Enough for Now. Much love,
Nick

It turned out that Nick was not above jealousy. He wrote me a letter while on that trip after not being able to reach me by phone one night because I was out somewhere with John. Here's part of it.

7/27? Monday, Holiday Inn of Minneapolis Airport

Dear Suzanne-
I'm not sleeping anyway so I might just as well try to record for you my feelings and confusion. After calling you I tried to go to sleep but the image of you on the mountain with John kept disturbing me—

Under other circumstances I don't know—I might have been able to say to myself—what the hell—she should be free to play around with John if she wants to. Basically I feel that you should be free to—regardless of how you feel about me—If you need and enjoy his company more than the other alternatives—that's what I really want for you.

But as I try to sleep, the image of him answering the phone from bed with you just having said "I'll bet that's Nick" seems so real and so disturbing. It must be partly JEALOUSY, simple disappointment. And of course it's tempered by the fact that probably it's all imagination. Almost everything I know about you says you were not in bed with him, that I'm just resenting the fact that you were not in the stuffy apartment waiting for my phone call.

Then I conjure up the kind of fuss which you would make if I called at 11 o'clock and I was with an ex-girl friend and how it would be impossible for me to convince you with my protestations of innocence—But I don't want to be with anyone else and so it's all irrelevant.

Except what was going through your mind—John was obviously not a working partner according to his story—and so you'd been on a long walk in the moonlight a couple of hours ago—and here I am jealous again and feeling virtuous and really having had a pretty good day considering the pressures on it until your not being home and being with John and my apparently interrupting something—raised all these doubts—which aren't serious anyway—cause there is nothing I can do for you except (1) call you and let you know I love you and (2) keep from messing myself up...I've done both and will continue to. I'm not free of these irrational feelings, however, and that must be why I'm writing them down—whether I show them to you or just tear them up....

Anyway all this was going round in my head Monday night—Tuesday morning. I'd rather not burden you with it—for it's all a function of unreasonable emotions generating on no data. I apologize, feel bad etc. but the confusion is there just the same.

I'm including some of Nick's letters to me from this period, partly because they are so beautiful, also to tell about his daily life, and most important, they trace his soul searching about overcoming his sexual promiscuity that I couldn't handle. Right after he jumped off the fence he went on a planned ski trip to Aspen with another woman that he refers to in the second and again in a later letter. In early March he flew to Switzerland to be with his son Peter who was in boarding school there. He had plenty of time for introspection and I've included a couple letters from this time. I particularly love the March 12 letter from Geneva on his way back to the States in which he rationalizes his sexual adventures by quoting Zorba (in *Never on Sunday*). In the months since Nick's death I realize that, of course, I am attracted to men who love women, the Casanovas of this world; they enjoy us, spending time with us, gently loving us. Nick's love of women, me in particular, was an endearing quality. It's just that I needed committed love and somehow I seemed to sense that Nick could give me that love and security.

11ish Friday night

Just back from seeing Bergman's *Wild Strawberries* and what a combination of emotion! If you've seen it maybe you would have gently steered me away from it. I can't begin to express the confusion within me: the overwhelming desire to express my love for you; the fear of not having expressed it adequately.

Of course it's mixed with all the other emotions of the day and evening. My inability to break through to Angus' hang-up—whatever it is. A tape from Steve and Mary in which Steve is rational and careful and cold and Mary is trying to be warm without being sentimental; a conversation with Tess in which I try to be reassuring without really letting any of the real "me" show through; the nicotine fit so intense I—

That's when your call came and I went on to bed relaxed and happy—

Slept till 7:30. At 6:30 the sky was clear but by 7:30 there was fog. I climbed into jeans and boots and the Ghia and drove to the Flagstaff mountain saddle, found a promising trail. At this level I was in and out of fog and the woods were wet from yesterdays rain, jillions of tiny drops on the needle bunches of the yellow pine. Half an hour and I was on a ridge, an hour and I was within sight of the summit of Green Mountain and in bright sun. From the top the Plains were under a thick cloud blanket but the panorama of mountains from Evans (w. of Denver) to Longs 25 miles North was breathtaking.

A long brunch after a shower and it's noon. Off to the office soon and then on to the cocktail party. I may try a higher climb tomorrow. Love, Nick

P.S. This is all about me but I'm also all tied up in you. Glad your party was gay. Congrats on the job. Good luck on the house. I love to be loved by you. NH

Sat a.m. 1:30

Suzanne Beloved

What a lovely conversation with you. Sorry I couldn't tune to your "stoned" condition. Sorry about my bad news. That it could be a lovely conversation in spite of my bad news speaks (shrieks) to the condition we are in. Our happiness diffuses into every fiber, every minute.

Mostly I thought I ought to send the enclosed to cover your round trip SFO to Denver and return. Now I realize that your fare is probably paid by your Ohio conference. Use it for the next trip, or to take the pressure off somewhere else.

But know that I love you above all else. Work hard and try not to miss the plane Wednesday and bring along your skis and gear if you feel like it and leave it here as you go on.

Good night again. I feel so close and so enraptured!
Nick

3/3/69, on board a plane east on the way to Switzerland to see Pete

Dear Sue:
Your kiss is still fresh on my lips, your presence is deep down within me, secure and happy. The plane is full of skiers back from a holiday. They must be a club of some kind for there is quite a bit of happy rowdy interchange. I'm sitting beside a couple of girls returning from Hawaii. I suspect they've been visiting husbands on leave from Vietnam.

We came back from the end of the runway with some kind of problem and spent half an hour waiting for it to be fixed. People making close connections are uneasy as we finally took off almost an hour late. Otherwise the plane is generally drowsy with the stewardesses serving drinks and a snack.

Tobacco next to me but I'm not tempted. Neither am I concerned about any of the feminine pulchritude present.

It was wonderful to have you present this weekend in person rather than just in spirit. The joy of being together and doing things together was intense. We need many more as we probe each other, learning about and from each other. It's too close for me to have much perspective on it but the ecstatic happiness and the unique response Sunday mornings are rare and precious.

May I hear your reactions and hear what you find when you get back to Kensington and how is Sheri and what does General Stillwell say?

I was right about the girl I'm sitting beside. The one is an Irish girl married to a Marine pilot, anxious for the end of his hitch. Also about the skiers. They are from the Valley Forge area, returning from 10 days at Aspen. A couple of times the whole front of the plane has come down with the giggles.

Descending into Chicago now. Wish I were going toward you rather than away.
Love Nick

3/5/69 11:15 p.m. Newark NJ

Dear Suzie:
It's quiet and peaceful here. The television is turned off after ¾ of an hour of 1st Thursday—a pretty good assemblage of documentaries. The briefcase has been emptied of most of the extraneous stuff and is packaged for mailing back to Boulder. I should be working on the Kent Ohio speech but I'm going to turn in soon. I can already feel the sleep creeping up on me.

But I wanted to share the stress of the meeting and the peacefulness of the late evening with you. And there was a magnificent full moon as we started for the banquet tonight.

It was a short night last night and the desk call brought me to with a jolt. Shower and hotcakes and coffee and an 8:30 pickup. People were registering in the lobby with time to spare before the 1st session. Arnsdorf started it off in a very relaxed, low key way. I was next and Rice after me—Status of the projects—in about 20 minutes each. Coffee and then the elementary and secondary groups broke up. We had about 40 going through site selection, New Orleans and Portsville activities.

At lunch John Mather, head of geography here, talked on geography as a profession. In the afternoon another of our teachers took the H.S. group through the game of farming and one of the tapes. (About half way thru the p.m. I broke down and bummed a cigarette.)

Val served champagne at a reception at his house before returning to the student center for dinner and my "Trojan Curriculum" speech. It went pretty well too. They even opened the session for questions after the speech. We were delivered directly back here and I buckled down to the briefcase after a little TV.

In a sense I feel virtuous—not out carousing around. But in a more important way I just wanted to be quiet and relish the joy of the time we had, and will have, together.

I didn't even pack a flask along so I'm only drinking water. But it is kind of a nice feeling not to feel compelled to go looking for excitement or companionship.

Which reminds me of a comment I was going to make about the weekend, that it was great, just as it was; but normally we should plan to leave some "alone" time in our lives. I don't know how to say it correctly and I'm getting sleepy now.

I'll dream of you.

Love Nick

3/7/69 10:15 Switzerland

Suzie Darling

I guess the big news this evening is that Pete responded favorably to the idea of an old house at the edge of the slum open to all. Not the first time it was mentioned when he had a typical sarcastic "O Great!" kind of a comment, but at supper with art Teacher Luella Ramsay, he described the idea as a kind of groovy idea. Who knows, maybe we could make a home for him too!

It was a funny day. A good long talk with Mr. Semonite, the headmaster, mostly about Pete, his recent apparent readiness to buckle down to his work, his capacities, his stability, his plans.

Then I met his math and English---------- [Nick fell asleep here.] continued Saturday night

That's when I must have fallen asleep. I slept pretty well till 4 a.m. but then was wakeful. I miss you much and you are very much on my mind, Peter's too. I trust we are not romanticizing. We both seem to feel that you add a quality of effervescent joy to life which is very special.

I did meet his teachers. The math teacher is very direct, a solid square sort of guy who makes no apology for it. He seems single minded about his teaching and enjoys the chance to work with students individually. Mr. DeVelder, the English teacher is tall and blond and slender, seems sensitive and appreciative of Peter's talent. He was a little distracted as he was about to leave for Paris to join his wife and their new baby boy—new enough so that she is not free to return to Leysin for a couple weeks. Miss Ramsay was quite a shock to me. In my minds eye I had pictured her as young and cute and the kind of person who might be personally attractive to Pete. Rather she is pear shaped with long slightly unkempt black hair and apparently no concern for her appearance. In the few minutes we had during the morning we talked some about Pete's talent. She feels it is more in decoration than in craftsmanship as illustrated in his tendency toward collages rather than drawing or painting or sculpture.

He brought her along to dinner and we had a very pleasant easy leisurely dinner, much of the conversation relating events at the school during the last few months.

In between I bought a pair of ski boots, changed my reservation to come home Thursday the 13th, took a much needed nap. I felt so lazy and tired I wondered if there were something wrong with me, decided it was only the time change crossing the ocean.

Today we caught the 8 o'clock cog railway down the mountain to Aigle, the 9 a.m. ski special from Geneva to Lausanne to the resorts. It brought us to La Chables where we met a bus for the short climb to Verbiers. (We couldn't find any space in Zermatt and this was 2nd choice and closer). We were here by 11, got registered, rented skis for me, had a leisurely lunch in bright sun on the terrace. When I commented on a perfectly gorgeous blond, he said "I'll tell Sue." A pair of dark glasses for him and we were ready to find the lift.

It must have been 2 o'clock before we were ready to climb into the Gondola for the long ride to the top—2000 ft rise. Pete's 3 week absence from the slopes (because of a cold) and my unfamiliar boots and skis left both of us clumsy on really quite difficult skiing terrain. We tired easily but took our time with bright sun, warm air and the most beautiful scenery you can imagine. Really the views in all directions are breathtaking.

This morning Pete was sullen and difficult but by lunch time he was open and we talked about things which mean something to him and to me. Also at supper. Friends, last year, drugs, the future, you, how his friends feel about you and about me, events at school etc. We are probably closer now than we ever have been.

And I'm about out of paper and all I have to say really is that I love you and miss you and wish you were here and will hurry back to be with you. Say hi to Sheri. Love Nick

3/11 Hotel Farinet Verbier, Suisse

Dear Suzie:

I had planned to write a long and thoughtful letter tonight about how it feels to live in your presence and the ease with which I have made the transition from looking at strange women as possible conquests, to simply admiring them. But Peter and I bought a deck of cards after we came down from the ski hill and I beat him 3 times before he double skunked me the 4th hand—so now it's almost eleven. Further he isn't settled down yet—just finished a shower—so I may be interrupted.

I have been introspectively self-conscious the whole trip. The trick seems simply not to try to make the opportunities: not to strike up the conversations which might lead to something, not to go out after supper to make the rounds of the bars to look for openings. These are habits of fairly long standing and hence the self-consciousness as I change them. But it is clear to me that now I'd rather not be skirt chasing, that I prefer dreaming of you and relishing the times we have had together and prospect of a life together. I want you so much that the game of seducing someone seems trivial, and the prospect of winning seems almost repugnant. This is how it feels after a week away.

I don't think I'm any less interested in sex, certainly not if my nocturnal erections are any measure. It's just that I'm happy to direct these feelings toward you. I keep kicking myself for the Aspen affair, yet on reflection maybe it's well that the issue is raised early before either of us has invested any more in each other than we have. For there is at least a subtle difference in the significance of such a change of habits on my part if it is done while I am more or less unattached.

When I wonder about why it seems easy for me to make the change, I'm sure that I have not adopted a new ethic. I am conscious of the new information that I have, that my fooling around would be so painful to you. (I know it's hard for you to believe that this is new information for me—but charge that up to my innocence or obtuseness or something.) But there seems to be something more, something internal—a quality wanting you so much. Perhaps the last couple of weeks have taught me that skirt chasing is a little juvenile, that there are other satisfactions which mean more to me.

It's hard for me to imagine how this reads on your end—so I'm writing it just the way it comes to me. I hope you'll probe things that seem unclear or unreal.

It's too early for me to have any final perspective on the subject. I'll probably be 70 before I could be absolutely positive, but I did want to give you this interim report.

The skiing has been rough, in spite of almost ideal conditions. The new boots hurt both the feet proper and the ankles. Saturday I took a sharp fall and bruised my hip, but that is all ok except the local bruise, no more pain or stiffness down the leg. This morning I fell downhill and slammed my shoulder into the top of an icy mogul. It's all stiff and there are several positions in which I cannot use my hand and a few into which I cannot raise my arm.

Pete complains that his boot hurts his heel but otherwise does very well. He's pleased with his new ability to handle the moguls. They have been my undoing in both injuries.

I'll be interested in hearing about your progress during your week in the Sierras—and Sheri's too. After the 2nd day feels great, the 3rd feels tired and by the 4th you can't remember why you had so much trouble earlier. I wish we could be with you there. But this has been a good time for Pete and me.

This morning I rolled out earlier than he and got in a good hour and a half on my paper on Geography for the Inner City Curriculum. It has a long way to go and is sort of overdue, but I feel surer of its basic form now. The more I read of what has been written, the more impressed I am with how little is known and understood about the problem.

Off to bed now. I feel very isolated from you, hope there will be news of you in Leysin when I get there tomorrow. Love in large Measure
Nick

P.S. When asked if he has any greetings to send you, Pete says "Yeah, but I'll take a letter to do it." Luv, NH

Leysin Switzerland 3/11/69

Suzie Darling:

I love thee too! What a joy to return here to your letters and be in touch again. (That's the wrong idiom—for touching you is something special.) And to hear from you again is better. I immersed myself in them while Peter patiently read the Berkeley Barb before supper. Then again after supper when he went off to Biology lecture. They enfolded me in a warm euphoric cloud and I slept so soundly for an hour! Now I've delivered his skis and boots to him which he left here at the hotel, I've greeted some of his classmates, met the last of his teachers. He does seem to have warm relationships here. Now I'm free, in the relative quiet of the hotel to try to respond.

I'm not sure I was explicit in my last letter how inadequate I felt words were in communicating what I felt. Much of what I'm trying to say in rational, linear language is really understood (felt) only at a deeper level. Rarely can I put words together which express these more profound feelings. Taken together your letters do get some of this across. Your welcoming note radiates warmth. I interpret your walking the dogs as an extension of our hikes in the early mornings and I revel in that. Your reluctance to phone Stillwell might have been your fear that she would pour a cold pitcher of skepticism on your warm glow. (And I can almost feel the warmth.)

The confusion between freedom and risk is probably unanswerable. But we should remember that while this is a time of honeymoon like ecstasy for us it is also a time of enforced separation. You have reason to question how much emotional investment, professional disruption and financial re-arrangement you can afford. And I still have a divorce to complete with some anxiety, and there is real, if well submerged, stress in the withdrawal from the relationship with Deborah.

Artificial constraints on sexual freedom are not likely to be very effective anyway. But it is important for me to know the costs and for you to have the perspective of my behavior, knowing the costs. If my manliness can only be assured by frequent and varied seductions, then you should not be hooked in a permanent relationship with me. I don't think that is the case. Rather, that getting little assurance in the marriage, I developed patterns of behavior which provided it outside. I'm happy to break these habits with your (expert) help. If I am an inveterate triangle maker—you don't belong in one of my corners. But I don't think I am, for why would I have been so unhappy sitting on the fence trying to give up the long relationship with Deborah for the intense and growing relationship with you.

Your fantasy reflected Friday that it would be fine even if we did not get married is touching—but let's go ahead and make the "love-in" so deep that it lasts a lifetime and infects all those around us with its warmth.

Later you ask if we—one or the other or both—are freaks? And you caricature us both. As usual with both caricatures, there is at least a little bit of truth in back of each. Any two persons who have lived as distinctive lives as you and I have must be different from the models, stereotypes of the society around us. Sure you have more than your share of fear of getting ditched. Standing off and looking at it, anyone should expect you to panic easily. But you are not "unloving." I've no idea what you felt at the time, maybe hatred—

a sort of inverse of love, just as sorrow is the inverse of joy. It certainly was justified and not freakish.

I hope it doesn't happen again, but if it does I think maybe I have the depth of understanding and intensity of love to work it out with you.

So too, as I described above, I have my patterns but they don't represent intrinsic values I hold high and I think you can help me with them. Really I believe the prospect of an unusually rich and rewarding life is very bright for us.

I've read the Wilder quotes a couple of times and want to argue with a few lines, but most of it "speaks to our condition" to use a Quaker phrase. If we have "minds akin" can we have friendship as well as love. Is there anything mutually exclusive about "love by the senses" and "love as education."

Wickedness, like sin and virtue are terms which I have struggled with long and hard. Finally, I have had to reject them as elements in a doctrinaire ethic. But surely carrying anything to its illogical extreme is folly, and this presumably applies to liberty as Cytheris says so eloquently. In the vividness of your love, I welcome your help in "marking out the permissible."

Off to bed now, alone in body but together with you in spirit.

I love thee too.

Nick

Let me interrupt to comment on Nick's reaction to quotes from Thornton Wilder that I had sent him. After reading this letter 43 years later and several months since Nick's death I had a profound need to find the original quotes. Finally, I found them in *The Ides of March*, in a very well worn paperback in our library. The quotes and their context are quite relevant to my current state of grieving and deserve some thought. I've reread this wonderful semi-novel in which Wilder reconstructs the last months of Caesar's life, mainly through letters from the main characters pondering the essential questions of love, power, leadership, friendship. The quotes are from letters from Cytheris, a famous actress greatly admired by Ceasar, to a trusted friend of hers and Caesar's who had become a recluse on Capri. She had been Mark Antony's lover for fifteen years, and had just witnessed him falling under Cleopatra's spell.

In the first reference, Cytheris states: "I come to Capri with a higher recognition of friendship which I could never know with Marc Antony, for friendship flowers from minds akin. Wonderful are its resources, but I am a woman. Only to you, whose wisdom and patience have no end, can I cry out for the last time that friendship – even yours – is and must be second to the love I have lost. It filled my days with radiance as it filled my nights with unbearable sweetness. For fifteen years I have found no reason to ask myself why one lives or why one suffers. I must now learn to live without the loving glances from those eyes on which I have dreamed my life away. (XLI)" Nicki and I found nothing mutually exclusive about love by the senses and love as education. I miss both and I need to learn to live without those loving glances.

The second passage about wickedness and liberty comes from another of Cytheris' letters (LIII) in which she talks of "that mystery, Caesar's marriage" and with love as education. Cytheris comments that "Caesar can only love where he can instruct; the return he asks is progress and enlightenment.... Love as education is one of the great powers of the world, but it hangs on a delicate suspension; it achieves its harmony as seldom as does love by the senses." Having just divorced his second wife Cytheris concludes that Caesar is a bad husband "from an excess of conjugal love;" he failed to reign in his two loves—his wife and Rome." I have only recently come to understand some words that you let fall years ago, that 'wickedness may be the exploration of one's liberty'... and that 'it can be the search for a limit that one can respect.'... can't we say that a great deal of what we call 'wickedness' is the very principle of virtue exploring the laws of its own nature?" While "we are condemned to fashion our own laws... there is great comfort in knowing that those who love you, love you enough to take the responsibility for marking out the permissible."

3/12/69
9:30p.m. in Geneva and just past noon in Berkeley or the Sierras or wherever you are. I've lost track. I've been away too long.

Dear Suzie:
    I mailed a letter this noon in Geneva, hoping it would beat me home. They say the Swiss Postal Service is very efficient, but we haven't done as well with the public sector in the U.S.
    I don't really have much to say except I love you and I miss you and I would have moved my flight up half a day except I didn't want to come in through NYC and I made a mistake tonight—not a very serious one though. As I came in from supper 8:30ish I stopped in the lobby to see what was on the TV. It was England playing Austria in futbal or soccer. It was so exciting I stayed for 45 minutes and didn't get the work done I had promised myself. Sorry about that. You see if it isn't one temptation, it's another.
    It was sort of a restful day. I said good bye to Peter who was a little uneasy about my leaving. Had half an hour to go on with my plans for the inner city paper—this while sipping rich black coffee at the window of the hotel overlooking the deep valley of the upper Rhone through intermittent snowstorms. Caught the 10:23 cog to Aigle and the 9:05 express to Geneva. The clouds lifted as we rounded the long lake (Lac Lemon) which borders the track more or less half of the way. Spectacular mts in and out of the clouds across the lake and on the other side spectacular terracing of orchards and vineyards wherever the land is rolling or steep—generations of hand-labor inputs to get the most out of the more frost free areas.
    Checked in to a second class hotel—Bernina—already almost full because of a major automobile show starting tomorrow, but conveniently adjacent to the RR station and departure location for the airport limousine. Off to shop for presents for you and Sheri, a knife and shoes for me. It was 4 pm by the time I was back. I wondered if I should have late lunch-early

dinner, decided to try a museum. The Ethnography Museum. The Ethnography Museum closed at 5 but the History and Art Museum was open till 6. Took a trolley to within a few blocks and bought some pastries to tide me over.

The display of the upper Neolithic "Lake" villages was good but the reproduction of rooms of a 15th Century palace was the prize. A showing of contemporary woodcuts was mostly beyond me. The geometrical abstractions were attractive but the only ones which moved me were some nightmarish prints—fearsome distortions of the female torso. He must have had a very unsatisfactory sex life. Too goulish (sp?) to want to have around.

I walked back to the hotel, exhausted from standing and looking, through the old city, now the art and antique center. Some beautiful things in the windows, but one would want some time to go back and mull over them before buying. I read some more Ed Psych before falling asleep. Lawrence Kubre's essays: "The Forgotten Man in Education" and "Research in Protecting Preconscious Functions in Education" go a long way in giving the psychological justification for the need for Harvey's Type 4 teachers and for the kind of not-very-verbal, participative activities we have included in the HSGP course.

Dinner alone in a good lower-middle class restaurant next door. A couple of girls in their 20's, obviously travelers by the bags they carried came in and sat across the room. One had a kind of understated, undecorated beauty which made her a real joy to watch. It was no strain to let it go at that. Then the soccer match.

There is one part of the sexual freedom—playing around thing which has come to mind since writing that longish letter from Verbier. It's related to the feeling Zorba the Greek expresses about the widow—"To let a woman like that sleep alone—even one night—is a reflection on the males of the human race." It is a sense that if a woman is attractive, it is only right and proper to let her know and the obvious way to let her know is to kiss her and if she responds....

I suspect that there is a lot of rationalization here, but as I look back on some seductions and attempted seductions I think I was acting as much out of generosity as any drive to conquest or internal sexual urge. It's nice to make people feel wanted. However, it's easy to direct that generosity toward you and let the others fend for themselves. As a rationalization it is no longer valid in the new situation.

So now it's 10:30 and tomorrow is a 31 hour day and I didn't have much to say anyway. I won't mail this until Washington or Denver.
Love Nick

Another thought during the day. My Kent Ohio date the 22nd is followed by one in Washington with NSF the 24th. They want to talk budget.... I expected to go to Cambridge for Sat or Sunday nights and fly down to DC early Monday morning. I am, of course, tempted to ask you to join me in Cambridge and meet Mother Helburn, but I should think through all the variables before I do. I haven't told her much about you and it would probably be kind of a shock. Let's think about it.
Luv, Nick

3/13/69 almost midnight (from Boulder)

Suzie Love:
Home without incident but tired from the long day. 2 nice letters from you. Wish I could have been there to avoid some of the fatigue for you and provide the immediate emotional support—as well as to laugh with you over the comedies and feel your warmth and share the beauty of the black and starry sky. (Or that you could be here enjoying the subtle and primitive harmonies of the madrigals on the stereo.)

Also nice letters from Mother Helburn, Sue March, just divorced from a beautiful geographer at Columbia, Martha Lochner a former editor of mine married to a computer expert in Ann Arbor. You'll enjoy them both. And from Tess an envelope with documents I should have and not even a note.

And from Deborah a couple of long letters sharing some of the pain and progress of readjustment. One I am tempted to save and share with you, but don't know whether you are interested or whether you could easily put yourself in a frame of mind to read them in the spirit in which they were written.

Quite an assemblage of female correspondents. The first three I never slept with and never plan to. The fourth I'm divorcing and you won out over the 5th in as fair a competition as I can imagine. I guess I love them all—though Tess only historically—but I love you so much more it makes all else seem pale.

What I started to write about was to enclose these copies of the snapshots—poor as they were—and to say I'll call before you get this.
Love, Nick

3/21/69 Over Nebraska

Beloved Suzanne:
What a lovely two days! Do you suppose that it was because of equinox? Were these the "rites of spring" we were ushering in? It seems unbelievable that one could project such ecstasy into the future more than a few weeks.

I'm so full of well-being. I could be easy with the fat old couple with whom I was seated in 9-C. The stewardess suggested that the back of the plane was nearly empty so I moved back to share 3 seats with the black girl in the green checked suit. She is going to her parents 50th wedding anniversary in Pennsylvania. The whole world seems full of beauty all because of you.

I went over my speech, word for word, smoothing the few places where I stumbled when I read it to you, replacing a few words for greater emphasis.

Then I wrote Pete and told him of the call to the apt house. I trust he will understand the implications. (moving to a bigger apartment). I also told him some of the interview with Stillwell and the Youngs and Hammers.

Now I'll read and maybe sleep. Many thanks for the lovely time and the chance to meet your lovely friends.
Love, love, LOVE Luv
Nick

PS I don't know if or whether or when you might want to raise the topic with Sheri, but if it would help her transition to Kalamazoo, we might suggest that Lesli come along. You'll know better whether Vivian would stand for it and all the other variables. We could end up with a big family—Peter and Jim, Sheri and Lesli—but I'm sure both Peter and Sheri would be happier with a friend in the "family."

Think about it.

Luv, NH

3/23/69 8989 Memorial Drive, Cambridge Mass

Susan Love,

No reason to write except that I love you and I can't afford to be on the phone with you all the time. It's been a quiet and restful day here. My walk was thru the Harvard Yard and around to see some of the new buildings. Some are indeed spectacular and beautiful. A few, like the graduate school of Education are only spectacular. After talking to you we had sherry with Mother's sister Dorothy Fuller and her husband Carl. He has been a very successful executive in Polaroid until recent retirement and they do many proper things now. But both are very conventional and a little stiff and the Helburn side always makes a little fun of their conformity.

A lovely long nap after lunch. I must have been dreaming of you. I felt so good after it. Then Michael Greenbaum, a possible candidate for a job with us, came by and we talked for most of two hours. He is very thoughtful, has had a Whitehead Fellowship this year to do whatever he wanted to. Before that he had been teaching and then supervising at New Trier H.S. I think he would do very well with us, adding some of recent communications theory to our understanding of materials as we try to design sets of teacher education material.

A couple of stiff games of Quinto after supper and now to bed.

Also talked to Don Patton before lunch and was brought up to date on the editing. Our worst fear now is the paralysis which comes with over fatigue.

It was lovely talking to you as it always is. How you can warm me from that distance, I don't know, but I really don't feel like going out on the town and I'm so happy that you too enjoy the inner sensations of and outer reaction of your being committed.

Hope you got your work done.

Much love Nick

3/29/69 Saturday after 11 p.m. (Boulder)

Suzanne Darling:

I'm trying hard to resist calling you, not till I buy some more stock in the telephone company. But you are such a large part of life, you fill my mind with dreams and plans, my heart with love, my whole being with happiness.

I had not been able to find frozen grapefruit juice in the last two supermarkets I've shopped in. While picking up the cleaning this afternoon, I stopped at Joyces and found it. As I approached a waiting checker, I skipped to the gay music that was playing. She greeted me with "Well, Somebody's happy!"

David and Helen took me to lunch at Magdalena's before I drove them to the Alpersteins for a short visit, leaving them to go on to the airport with the Alpersteins. As I went in Dick Blumenheim spoke to me. He is the guy who sold Bill and Edie their house. He asked "How's it going?" My reply, without thinking, was "Better and Better!" He was caught off guard by my obvious well-being and we chatted a bit. He'll keep the house in mind.

All this in spite of the set back this week about the trial.

Then I've been struggling with the question of whether to try to move into the other apartment before you get here....

And then in the mail were some formal questions from Tess' lawyer, "Interrogatories" to which I must respond in 2 weeks and which involve some research. I resent the time it takes.

But these are minor concerns compared to my basic involvement with you. I even sort of wish I weren't going skiing tomorrow just because it won't be with or even toward you. You can see that I'm pretty badly off.

All in all it was a nice day. I got a lot done and David and Helen are cheery people. And I'm in love and its less than 4 days and you'll be here.
Luv, Nick

4/30/69 6 am

Suzie love:
If I'm not careful you'll be getting no letters and no phone calls either. I was "all business" as I headed east. Read some of a good issue of *Science*, part of a proposal I have to review for NSF—a terrible pretentious thing written in systems rather than English, worked for a couple of hours at the office before checking in at the apt.

Lots of ads and bills but good letter from Peter—mostly full of plans for his return, but he got an A in a history exam. Also a nice note from Mary (Steve's wife) who invites us to the Philippines for our honeymoon. Also a longish letter from Deborah who is making progress in sorting herself out but who has no one else to confide in and uses the letters to think through her deeper feelings....

Off to the mtn now for my early hike. The sun is just up and I love you so much and remember so warmly the relaxed and completely absorbing weekend together. If you occupy me that much after we're married I'll never get anything done—but it'll be nice.
Love Nick

5/16/69 a steady Midwest type rain falling

Suzanne love.
I started getting sleepy—not too long after you called and crawled in to bed (a nice clean bed with a note in it and even the headboard dusted) by 11. I missed you physically but you were very much present in my psyche.

By now I have the laundry running and a cup of tea at my elbow and all the bills and correspondence sorted in front of me....

You sounded happy on the phone with all the people swirling around you. Hope it was a fun evening and that you can get settled toward getting unsettled. I'll try to get in touch with Austin tomorrow and make plans about completing the purchase and the timing of our move....

I'll get on with my bills now but I did want to tell you I love you and it's a wonderful condition to be in.
Love Nick

I think this is the note I left, in which I copied out a paragraph from the last chapter of *Siddhartha* by Herman Hesse. "It tells of two friends meeting after many years and it is very beautiful and I love you. This reminds me of us."

Listen, my friend! I am a sinner and you are a sinner, but someday the sinner will be Brahma again, will someday attain Nirvana, will someday become a Buddha. Now this 'someday' is an illusion; it is only a comparison. The sinner is not on the way to a Buddha-like state; he is not evolving, although our thinking cannot conceive things otherwise. No, the potential Buddha already exists in the sinner; his future is already there. The potential hidden Buddha must be recognized in him, in you, in everybody. The world, Govinda, is not imperfect or slowly evolving along a long path to perfection. No, it is perfect at every moment; every sin already carries grace within it, all small children are potential old men, all sucklings have death within them, all dying people —eternal life. It is not possible for one person to see how far another is on the way; the Buddha exists in the robber and dice player; the robber exists in the Brahmin. During deep meditation it is possible to dispel time, to see simultaneously all the past, present and future, and then everything is good, everything is perfect, everything is Brahmin. Therefore, it seems to me that everything that exists is good—death as well as life, sin as well as holiness, wisdom as well as folly. Everything is necessary, everything needs only my agreement, my assent, my living understanding; then all is well with me and nothing can harm me. I learned though my body and soul that it was necessary to me to sin, that I needed lust, that I had to strive for property and experience nausea and the depth of despair in order to learn not to resist them; in order to learn to love the world, and no longer compare it with some kind of desired imaginary world, some imaginary vision of perfection, but to leave it as it is, to love it and be glad to belong to it. These, Govinda, are some of the thoughts that are in my mind.

5/21/69 1 a.m. from The Shoreham, Washington DC

Suzanne Love:
Let me repeat. I feel so loving and warm and happy and rich living in your presence I can hardly believe it's real.
Good night again
Nick

These letters deal with us, but during these months Nick was also letting go of his long-standing relationship with Deborah. It was not an easy time for him or Deborah. They continued to correspond as Nick tried to provide support. Finally he cut off the correspondence. Perhaps the sweetest tribute to both of us is a poem he wrote Deborah during this period:

Your poem speaks as clearly
     as the crescent moon in a winter black sky.
And I who we thought could lead, find
     my pen paralyzed, my mind awry.

I have no reason to reverse my field
    but still recurs the hopeless wish
    that I might somehow walk both roads.
Impossible dreams that I could at once be two.
For now, what energies survive the project clearly
    flow into making the twosome secure, rich, relaxed, deep.
For what might have been with you,
    all I can do is weep.
And though the sorrow and the tears are real enough,
    they're overbalanced by this new harmonious joy.

Peter came home from Switzerland in June to live with Nick. There occurred a serious bump in the road. It involved a stupid transgression with one of Peter's friends, creating serious reactions from both me and Peter. I, in fact, threatened to call off the marriage set for early August. Trying to explain himself, Nick writes

June 16, 1969

Dear Suzanne

It's been a terrible day—emotionally as bad as any I can remember. Only the routines of work saved it.... But the image of Pete in the orange chair in the corner—depressed and sullen has haunted me all day, as has the sound of your voice angry and insistent. The defenses I try to erect in my rational mind don't do much against these sensations which strike at a much deeper level. Most scary of all to me is the confusion between your forecasting of your behavior and the threat of it.... The sense that you are ready to pull back from the marriage has been profoundly disturbing to me all night and all day. It seems out of proportion to the incident here. But that may be that I don't perceive my responsibility here as others do.

[Nick describes what happened and comments] My sense of proportions must have been way off. It just doesn't seem like a reasonable or sensible thing to do. I wasn't conscious of being drunk or stoned. There was no strong urge and apparently no strong resistance on my part. I left myself open—and I didn't stop. I got hold of Dr. Vercio today and made a Wednesday appointment.... And all day has been one long nicotine fit, but I've hung on and I can feel the "little boy" in me wanting and needing some overt praise, and the man in me saying "Don't be silly—you want to do this for yourself—not for others or for their praise." But every strain is magnified by peevishness of the withdrawal, especially when it's my own foolishness—

I walked in town this morning—and then walked to and from the anti-smoking seminar this evening—about 25 minutes each way. It continues to rain—lightly but almost constantly. No moon or stars for 10 days and hardly more than one hours sunlight.

I haven't had enough aloneness—nor have I thought things thru well enough to write you a poem of my own—maybe in a day or two. Perhaps by tomorrow night I'll be able to compose myself well enough to call you. Not tonight. I'll turn in now—and see if my subconscious can do anything with the confusion here.

Love—lots of it. Too much? I don't see how there could be too much.
Nick

Nick sent Dr. Vercio a long letter in preparation for seeing him to discuss his sexual behavior that would have to change if he chose to marry me.

Sunday, June 22, 1969

Letter to Dr. Vercio

I gather from my limited experience that it is not customary in therapy and counseling to expect homework. Even without any assignment, I've been doing a lot of thinking about what we were talking about last week. It certainly will help me and might help you if I tried to organize some of the thoughts on paper.

What name do we give this topic. Faithlessness doesn't fit at all. Promiscuity isn't right. It is only a part of sexuality. "Fooling around" only fits some of the cases. I guess the most precise title would be "lack of restraint in matters sexual."

In the day dreaming that I have done since our last conversation, I felt there were so many aspects of the subject that I forgot one before I had finished thinking about two others. At my desk this noon, I jotted down nine different perspectives. I'll follow that list though it may change in the course of trying to write about them. (Let me add that I am making a couple of carbons of this to share with Sue and her Therapist.)

One point seemed clear to both of us, that I had no religious or moral objections to extra-marital sex. My concern grows out of what it does to Sue, really out of a conscious and deeply felt preference for a profound relationship with Sue over casual relationships with a number of women. I understand Sue's reaction though I probably have no measure of its intensity, and accept it as a "given" in the present circumstances. She and I have talked about it and the possibility that after n years of comfortable secure married life it may diminish. I really don't expect it to diminish, however, for I think it is only partly rooted in her insecurity and some of it comes from her sense of her sexual competence, her image of herself and her expectations of her image in other peoples eyes.

If my restraint comes from such a rational choice on my part, including the cognitive realization that violations of that restraint will cause pain where I don't want it, how strong is it? Is it strong enough for Sue to count on in her life plans? Does its cognitive character mean that I have to be particularly careful about sex when alcohol or other drugs are likely to diminish the relative power of cognitive and other parts of the controls on behavior?

How can I best alter established habit patterns? It is a fairly well established behavior pattern for me to flirt with attractive women. When I get a response there has been frequently, no good reason not to push the flirtation on to seduction. Any helpful hints will be welcomed.

One of my comments which caught you by surprise was my assertion that I had doubts about my own attractiveness. I don't have any "reason" for this, but self-doubt and wondering if I can prevail certainly has been a part of my thinking in any number of seductions. This is a "first time" phenomenon and does not enter into the psychology of going to bed with someone a second or third time. It may be related to the desire for conquest. It certainly is part of the reinforcement of my sense of masculinity. I do not think of it as competitive against other men. I have never boasted about sexual prowess. I don't think there is any hostility in it usually.

You raised the possibility that these doubts might be related to doubts about my adequacy in other areas. I had never thought of this as a kind of compensation. It doesn't seem reasonable, but may be.

As I think about the subject historically, I'm reminded of the interpretation which I have put on this tendency to get involved more widely than others think proper, that it is a perfectly natural expression of my warmth, my outgoingness, my love. I have never had an adequate distinction between divine and profane love. Loving my neighbor was not difficult for me. Sue has tried to coach me in expressing affection without being seductive, but so far I am not a very apt pupil. Again I can use all the help I can get, for Sue can absorb all the strength I have, both physical and emotional. And I really don't want my life messed up with unnecessary entanglements. On the other hand, repression of genuine affection felt toward other women probably will have some effect. What? How best can I express the affection without causing them to think I want to go to bed with them.

Both you and Sue have mentioned to me that maybe I was being "used" when I thought I was in control. I'm afraid that I am pretty naive here, even though this may be hard to believe. I guess that I wanted to feel needed, valuable, strong and warm. I wanted to feel those things enough so that it didn't occur to me to question the girl's motives. It is easy for me to see the possibility of covert hostility once you point it out, but it never occurred to me at the time. I trust that being warned will be enough to help avoid being used another time. There is also, apparently a tendency to overlook my own motives. When I hired Joan, for instance, I already had some inkling that she might be receptive to my advances. I submerged this motive quite successfully and justified her hiring to others and to myself on the basis of her very real talents for the job. Again, having identified the tendency, perhaps I can handle it.

A couple of questions are related to the next to last paragraph on the previous page. Tess had a penchant for "putting down" others, including me. What influence does the accumulation of put downs, even from someone you do not respect, have on ones image of himself. Would this be related to the need to prove one's self. Sue has just the opposite effect. She makes me feel about ten feet tall. But then I haven't really had any trouble in her presence. We have talked (Sue and I) about developing the skill of living in the "presence" of the other.

The other related question relates to times when I am feeling sorry for myself. Generally, I know that I am an extremely privileged member of a privileged class in the most privileged nation. Even so there are times when I feel as though I were working my ass off and nobody appreciates me! I really try and all I get is guff. I face a nearly impossible task and others are not even aware of it. A recurrent daydream (occurring usually in the evening) as I walk through the city alone is that everyone behind those shaded windows is happily screwing and "here I am alone, disadvantaged, forlorn." It is as unrealistic a daydream as I can imagine, yet there it is. It is no less real at the time for being indefensible in any longer perspective. The question really is whether this sort of self-indulgent mood has anything to do with a self-centered view of sex. It might be used as a kind of emotional screen to hide from the emotional impact of my behavior on others close to me.

One friend suggested once that some of my behavior might be related to the inability to have natural children in my marriage to Tess. I have little perspective on this suggestion. It seems unreal to me, but plausible enough so that I don't forget it. In the environment-heredity argument, I tend to be an environmentalist. Rationally, at least, I tend to put more weight on my contribution in setting an example than in fertilizing an egg.

I have forgotten whether it was you or someone else who asked about when this strong commitment to professional success developed. I am told that as a youngster I was sweet and gentle and easy-going. I didn't study hard in high school nor in my first year and a half in college. It wasn't until I was married during my sophomore year in college that I began to "pour it on." Suddenly I had something outside myself to work for. As long as goofing off only disadvantaged me there was no problem. The altruism of working for "us" was quite strong.

Then as a conscientious objector during the war I developed something of a minority complex. It became terribly important to me to demonstrate that one could be true to his pacifist principles and still be a success in life. It was touch and go for a while during the reaction right after World War II and during the McCarthy era. The drive endures. I don't think of it as unhealthy, I think Tess did, for she saw it taking me away from the home. Perhaps I should rethink my division of time between work and family, but my estimate is that it is a good healthy drive toward success and toward making a contribution.

There was one other identifiable event in the development of the strong drive. That was the death of my oldest brother, Stephen. He and I had been very close during childhood. He was four years older than I. I was almost always aligned with him in any fights with the second child in the family, Peter who was two years older than I. My sister, two years younger, was often excluded. If not she often sided with Peter.

All four of us were sharp, but Stephen was near genius and a "natural" athlete too. He was struck down by Polio at 17 and only saved by experimental doses of the anti-toxin in use at that time (1931). He never regained use of his legs, graduated with honors from Harvard, having gone thru in a wheelchair. He worked for the National Resources Planning Board for several years, but a malfunction of the liver (?) caused severe hypertension and he died in 1942. His death was a powerful event in my life. I felt that his chance to contribute had been cut short arbitrarily. I resolved to try to make my life count for him as well as for me. I didn't really expect to live two lives, though that was the phraseology I used at the time. I did take myself very seriously, feeling somehow that I must make good for him as well as for myself.

Periods of relaxation have been short since then. Recreation has tended to be of high intensity. I would categorize seduction as one of the exciting forms of recreation. My relationship with Deborah had a constant tension in it. So did the earlier stage of my relationship with Sue. One of the things which helped me decide to choose Sue over Deborah was the sense of relaxedness with Sue, a feeling of being at ease with her, of not having to live up to any artificial expectation.

Well, I have written myself out. I'm not sure how much of this is relevant. I hope it is best to err on the side of completeness. I'll get a copy in the mail Monday morning early. I'll bring another along with me Tuesday. Looking forward to being with you then.

Nick Helburn

We must have patched things up quickly, because in a letter post-marked June 21 Nick tells me of going to see *A Man and a Woman*, "a beautiful love story of a widow with a daughter and a widower with a son. I love you very much. Did you see the crescent moon?"

And June 22,

Sue Darling, Sunday afternoon—at home—doing a bunch of little things. Don't know why I can't settle down to something significant. I wanted to send off one last note to 250 Stanford [my Berkeley home] and let you know how much I love you and miss you…. It was beautifully fresh and quiet on Green Mountain this morning early. I felt good climbing—took an hour and 15 minutes up. Didn't see anyone bigger than a squirrel until I was almost back at the car. Thank you for calling this morning and for being a good mamma to Pete.

And again,

Sue love: Talking to you is so wonderful—refreshing and reassuring and sweet dream producing. Enclosed is a pressed pasque flower, I made a mistake in pressing the pasque flower I picked on my Saturday hike. It shows the grain of the paper towels.

And maybe a day later,

Just a line to tell you that I do love you and always will. Cool morning but threatening almost 90 today. On my hike this morning all the trees were ticking. I finally tracked the sound to a longish bug with glassy wings, prob-ably some sort of cricket. I even found a pair screwing. It doesn't seem so long now and you'll be able to share all of this with me.

In sharing our correspondence with Nick's niece Kathryn Legan, Kathryn accepted as fact that Nick overcame his habit of seduction and considers it a great achievement for him. She suggested a powerful explanation. She was curious about an important, probably relevant event in Nick's childhood that he had told her about but did not mention in the Vercio letter. This was coming home from school with older brother Peter when he was about seven to find his mother's bedroom door locked with her inside with a lover. I think this occurred more than one time. Kathryn noted that sexual encounters for Nick seemed to be super-charged, that they may have been fueled by an unconscious desire/need to not be excluded from his mother. If sex held such intense value for him, it would be hard to be faithful to one woman. Furthermore, his parents gave overt approval to promiscuity so that it makes a lot of sense that he would funnel his considerable life force into casual and not so casual love affairs, particularly so given his charm and gentle, loving nature.

Kathryn suspects that he was ready to grow beyond these habits when he met me, "he glimpsed an entirely new way of being and he responded with profound interest even though the old way still lured him." But each time he got lured he felt how these encounters paled in comparison with genuine intimacy. His motivation was only partly that he didn't want to cause me pain. Kathryn thinks "Nick was able to stop the seductions because he understood what they cost him in soul substance. He was growing accustomed to real love…. Will power is insufficient when deep unconscious forces are activated, as they were when Nick saw an attractive, available woman. Freud called the return to old patterns, the Repetition Compulsion—and the word compulsion really nails it…. What he did in committing to you was transcend these powerful old patterns by permitting authentic love to grow inside him…. By choosing you, he was choosing his own true interest, his own profound well being."

We were married August 2, 1969 in a simple meeting for worship at the Boulder Friends' Meeting House on a beautiful day. The children— Peter, Sherry, Lesli (Sherry's friend from Berkeley)—organized the reception at our apartment. Nick gave me a double mummy bag for a wedding present that served us well on many camping trips and adventures. (I particularly remember using it on our trip to Mongolia in 1995, also sleeping on our deck at the farm moonlit nights that eventually we had to discontinue because I couldn't get to sleep because the moon was so bright. Nick could sleep through anything!)

Nick did get lured one more time that I know of, actually at our wedding reception. Towards the end of the evening, after considerable drinking and good spirits, Lesli caught Nick dancing with a very pretty Quaker woman who he was also kissing, I think to console her because she was having marital problems. (I barely knew her; traditionally, Quakers Meeting Friends are all invited to weddings, regardless of how close they are to the couple.) This brought the reception to an abrupt close (most people had already left), some anger from me while we talked it out on the balcony, and a trip to Dr. Vercio the next day where I explained again what I needed in marriage—emotional security, to live in a loving relationship.

To my knowledge, in our marriage Nick remained committed to me, a constant companion and a great well of loving support. He created the security that allowed me to flourish and mature. Literally, he was "the forest in which [my] flowering endures." He was a very romantic man, but also a calming, steadying influence on me. In all our years together I never had a single inkling, well, only one inkling, of a possible seduction. And he had little time or energy for more serious affairs.

I wish we had talked about our life together before Nick died. I don't know whether it would have been possible to rekindle those earlier talks in old age (although I am certainly reprocessing them now). I would have liked to have had his assessment. I think we had a deeply satisfying marriage despite the twists and turns in family life.

What was it about me that so captivated Nick? Part of the answer, as Kathryn suggests, was his need for deep, authentic love. "If we have 'minds akin', can we have friendship as well as love. Is there anything mutually exclusive about 'love by the senses' and 'love as education.'" Nick was outgoing and loving from childhood as his mother remarked to me when she sent me the photo of him as a three-year-old. He sought intimacy and affection as an adolescent in his two-year relationship with Nat Pearce. But displays of affection were absent and apparently not valued by his father. About halfway into what seems to have been a fulfilling marriage with Tess, things fell apart for some reason and Nick sought emotional reassurance outside his marriage that resulted in a long term relation with a family friend. Initiating divorce proceedings was a difficult decision for Nick for whom marriage meant a permanent commitment. In his letter to Dr. Vercio, Nick refers to the effect on him of the accumulation of "putdowns" from Tess on his image of himself and his need to seek reassurance outside the marriage. He told me in one letter that he got little assurance in his marriage. In a letter to the University Friends Meeting in Seattle informing them of his divorce from Tess, he asks, "How did it happen that we never learned to talk about the really fundamental aspects of our relationship? ...we never mentioned some parts of our lives and we went so far in not hurting the other's feelings that we bottled up how we really felt."

I came into Nick's life at that moment with no baggage, fresh from four years of insight-producing therapy with the General, having success-fully redirected my life to career and family (Sherry). I understood my emotional needs and their basis, but had pretty much given up on remarriage. Still, I was mindful of Stillwell's advice. Then I met Nick and we clicked! I was younger than he, open to new experiences, fun, spirited, emotionally wise, not particularly phased by his history of playing around. He was gentle, modest, manly (fatherly?), romantic, affectionate, a grown-up, a bit mysterious. He had a big heart and good brain. We could both love and learn from each other.

However! We both had a tendency to fill our lives over full. After a brief lull both Nick and I took up life again at a fevered pace. I don't think I slowed him down much. (Possibly, our tendency to work at full throttle represented a kind of complementarity.) Our work responsibilities meant frequent separations, but nights when we were separated we almost always talked on the phone. I think these separations were actually good for us; we were so happy to get back together again. Maybe they further cemented our relationship as it moved from ecstatic love to secure togetherness. Maggie had a term for it, watching us she would remark, "Isn't this companionable?" a comment we often repeated to one another as we relaxed outside in the sun.

Of course, Nick never lost his desire to express affection toward women. The young women in our community were very aware of this! But he did a reasonable job of controlling whatever impulses he felt. And we had lots of outlets, the sauna during the community days and our hot tub in the later years gave ample opportunity for nudism, back rubs, foot massages—I was mostly the grateful recipient. However, in the legacy section of his memoir to the question, "If you were forty again and could do anything you want for a day, what would you do?" Nick replied, "There are women that I would like to know better, or would like to have known better."

Kalamazoo and Our First Year of Marriage

Nick doesn't say much about our life in Kalamazoo except that it was a terribly depressing year. He comments on the problems of going back in to the classroom and on the gloomy weather. Nick loved gazing at the moon and stars, bright sunny western skies, and looking out over the plains to the long vista. It's interesting that place and weather take such an important place in his memory. I remember the year as engrossing and fun.

Sherry's friend Lesli came with us from Berkeley to smooth the transition. I got an appointment in the Business School Management Department where I was the token female, feminist, Marxist, much to my colleagues' enjoyment. Peter went off to school in Majorca, came home for Christmas, broke his leg skiing during our Aspen trip, went back to school only to come home to join the family at the end of January. Steve was discharged from the Navy in April, and he and his wife Mary enrolled at Oregon State. Maggie visited us in March; Sherry went off with her friends to the big demonstration in DC against the war. Hal Casteel, one of Sherry's friends, came to live with us off and on, I think in the spring, as he started breaking away from his own family. Although Nick doesn't mention much of this in his memoir, he did write about our life to his mother in pretty upbeat letters.

9/25/69 In the air to Chicago and Denver

Dear Mother:
...I'm on my way to Boulder for the 1st consulting this fall. Back tomorrow evening. Peter's off tomorrow to Palma to school. We probably have a better understanding now than any time in the last 4 years. Hope it keeps on improving. Sue is worried about the way things are drifting with Peter. But I've felt that this is the best we can do.

The house in Kazoo continues to develop nicely. Both our jobs have some adjustment which still remains. Sue finds some opposition in hers. I find teaching a little strange after 5 years out of the classroom. The students seem so naïve, it is hard to stay at their pace. But I have some planning responsibilities toward next summer and the future which impinge on any time left over from preparation, even on preparation. Sue is still working on the curriculum project she's been doing for the past several years.

So we don't get as much time to ourselves as we should.

Off now to my Denver plane.

Love, Nick

1/18/70

Dear Mother:

It hardly seems right that a whole week could have slipped by so fast. When I realize how much I have done in that week, I begin to be pleased with myself, until I realize how much I have not done. Until this noon I've hardly paid any attention to the family and none to the house. But the teaching goes well with students generally caught off guard by informality, and sincerity and novel procedures in the classroom. This weekend has been fully devoted to planning for next summer's institutes. A fresh snow last night prompted me to dust off the cross-country skis before anyone else was up and get a good run on them this morning. Wish you could have been along.

What news from Tucson? [Maggie was going there for the sun.] Keep us posted and many thanks for a pleasant weekend with you and Peg and Pete.

Love, Nick

2/9/70

Dear Mother:

Just as I was beginning to wonder if you had fallen into a cactus, two cards and a letter arrive. Ever so glad that the sun and the temperature agree with you. How about the dryness? Any interesting people?

Pete seems to be making the adjustment. He likes a couple of his teachers very much. Many of the kids are provincial and naive—but that is to be expected and one gets used to it. Hopes to have the cast off Friday.

Did I ever write you about our new acquaintances here, the Todds? They knew one of the Votaws in Washington, D.C. They invited us to dinner on the strength of a postcard saying the Helburns and the Votows have known each other for 50 years. The Todds are very interesting—good people. His family goes back several generations here. He was in Congress briefly, now commutes to NYC where he leads Planned Parenthood.

We do have a room for you. Really, the house is quite spacious. Coordination of the two bathrooms will be our only problem. We are counting on you, though it seems chilly here now. Snowed all morning—but near 32 degrees.

Love, Nick

3/27/70

Dear Maggie:

It hardly seems real that this is the end of the week already, the week at the beginning of which you left. Your presence is still very real.

Your note arrived today—glad to know the trip was easy and that you made better time than expected. Hope that means that you will feel you can come again.

Hal is still with us, but will be returning to his own home tomorrow. We've been able to give him some respite from the stress with his father. Peter is off tomorrow to Montana and Colorado for the Easter recess. Sheri will be going to Urbana, Illinois to visit her father and step-mother.

Preparations are under way for Africa—though it still seems unreal to me. Summer institute is developing well. 100% of responses have been acceptances. 1st nibbles from Colorado. Who knows what tomorrow brings.
Much love,
Nick

4/4/70

Dear Mother:

Beautiful crisp morning and springy by the middle of the day. 8 inches of snow on everything but the streets and sidewalks.

Peter just home this morning after flying all night—too groggy to give any news.

There is a card from Steve saying they have found an apartment, still looking for a house. He will enroll part time for spring quarter and then full time in the summer for both of them.

I'm glad to hear that you are keeping active. Stay with it. There is a principle about low energy activities taking over from high energy activities unless consciously reversed. "Entropy" I think it is called.
Much Love
Nick

April 17 I wrote to Maggi to try to talk her into coming with us to Tassajara Hot Springs in August, and to give other news, "Hal is back staying with us again and Nita Nickerson was here for two days this week. She was very pleased to see us in such good spirits. The children are having a dinner party tonight—very gay and sophisticated. But Nick and I went out to dinner; we are home now, upstairs, subtle chaperons.... It's pretty certain that we will be returning to Boulder and Nick received a 100% vote for a job in the geography department at Colorado. So he will have an appointment there as well as the ERIC Directorship. We'll probably rent a house in town, but we've taken the Tall Timbers house off the market. Eventually we'll move back into it. [We never did!] Off to Uganda April 27 til June 1. We'll be traveling around most of the time, but will come back to Kampala between trips for the first two weeks. May 27 we fly to London to visit friends of mine in England. Sherry and Peter will go to Switzerland and Paris by themselves while we're in England, so they'll have fun on their own."

6/16/70

Dear Mamita:

On our way home from a full week of meetings. Wednesday in Washington D.C. with the directors of ERIC Clearinghouses. Thursday through Sunday with the Social Science Education Consortium. Monday and today with the H.S.G.P Steering Committee.

One wonders how busy he has to get before he knows he is wanted.

And we go back to K'zoo to 3 weeks of one institute and 6 weeks of another. Actually the summer program has enough staff so that it should not be too bad.

This last week has been fun too and more fun because Sue has been with me most of the time.

Much love,
Nick

6/17/70

Dear Mamita:

I just this evening remembered that I forgot the 10th. Horrors! I guess I was involved enough both at the time and when I should have been preparing for the time to drive such extraneous circumstances out of my psyche.

Anyway I feel badly about it now. If I weren't so buoyed up by the events of the last couple of weeks, I'd feel even worse.

The meetings in Denver included a wide variety of social scientists and social studies education. I wasn't elected President, but I held my own as a member of the Board and chaired a meeting that could have been bad for the new ERIC Clearinghouse. It turned out very well and I had the warm feeling at the end that my potential enemies really were friends.

The other occasion contributing to my euphoria was the final meeting of the High School Geography Project. Gilbert White ran it well as usual, avoiding both sentimental recollection and wild forecasts of the future. The group concentrated on the kinds of recommendations to make to future projects and other efforts based upon our experience.

The success already experienced and that expected gave me a lot of satisfaction. Many others there who shared the credit are close friends.

Sue was in on the SSEC meetings in Denver, went house hunting in Boulder. The retirement home I liked best there is adding a large new wing. I'm writing for an application for you.

So happy birthday and much love,
Nick

7/7/70

Dear Moth:

Nice to have your cheery letter…. All my travel this month is West. 10 days from now I do an institute in Minnesota, go on to Corvallis to see Steve, Mary and Wendy, stop in Boulder for 2 days to get in a few licks on the new job. Then a short hop to Iowa City and another 2 days in Boulder for HSGP early in August.

…All's well here. Peter is just back from visiting Tess over the weekend, reports that she is in pretty good spirits most of the time, but suffering a lot of pain from both ankles and back.

Pete works full time at the Travel Agency, is also screwing up his courage to take driver training. Sheri spends all morning in a summer school biology course. Afternoons she has been helping Sue with finding materials for the ECON 12 course. A new sewing machine as a combination birthday-Christmas present has created a lot of excitement.

My work is more exciting than anything in the past 18 months. Very fine working relationship with George Vuicich and a couple of others. The teachers seem to be good material to work on.

Sue is on the Summer Institute circuit—Boulder and St. Cloud, Minnesota in 1 and 2 day stands—but would send her love if she were here.
Much love from me.
Nick

8/15/70

Dear Maggie:
Greetings from the middle of packing. Almost everything but the desk Is packed and that will go soon. The movers are expected Monday or maybe Tuesday. Terrible decision about whether this or that should be packed today or whether it would be best to wait until tomorrow 'cause it might just get used in between.

A wild party last night put on by Peter and a couple of the neighbors. We met more people than in the 11 months we have been here. The fact that the house was full of moving boxes didn't seem to diminish anyone's enthusiasm.
Much love,
Nick

Back To Boulder (Fall 1970)

We moved back to Boulder the end of August, living on 10th street quite near the "hill" (across from the University where students and the young crowd tended to congregate). The first semester I was flying back and forth to San Jose to avoid paying back my sabbatical salary, leaving Monday night and returning Thursday night. The family had really come together and Hal Casteel had joined us. I think Hal had graduated from high school. Nick was working too hard at ERIC but enjoying it. I resigned the San Jose job in January, was worried about becoming a dependent housewife, but was working on a project at SSEC. Steve and family, Maggie, and Peg had visited. Nick and I were flying off, often together, on various business trips. Peter passed his G.E.D's in the spring and went back to Kalamazoo to work at a travel agency. Sherry was becoming a serious student, she and Hal a couple.

9/20/70 from Boulder

Dear Maggie:
We got her on the plane! It was nip and tuck whether the manuscript would be in shape to take along. You must remember many such deadlines. We worked until we couldn't keep our eyes open the last few weeks and often got up before we were ready. The final corrections, copying, sorting and collating today was particularly tense as we faced the deadline of the plane's departure. But she got there with 2 copies (about 1000 pg) in her suitcase. Wish her luck with the publisher.

She'll usually spend Monday, Tuesday and Wednesday nights there.
More later—
Love, Nick

9/20/70 From Boulder to me in San Jose

Dear Suzie:
I'm tempted to call and find that you arrived safely and tell you I love you and that all's well here. But puritan economy holds me back and also the curiosity of seeing whether mail might get through.

I stopped at Wally and Becky Toev's on the way home from the airport, found them finishing Sunday dinner on the terrace.... Wally asked if I wanted to help in the Regent's campaign. I said sure. They will keep us posted.

Peter had a tuna casserole in the oven, Sheri had made a slaw salad this time with melon balls. It was delicious. Susan's layer cake stuck in the pans even worse than mine. Most of the evening they watched melodramas on T.V. I cleaned up after dinner, though Sheri offered to. 10ish Sheri came up to finish her homework and Pete went off with S. and J saying he'd be back soon.

Gladdy had his usual distractions on his evening walk. An aggressive St. Bernard was following us and I had to put Gladdy on the leash to keep him from attacking the St. Later he went gaga over a couple of puppies.

Talked to Ron Lippitt finally about 7. He was most sympathetic about your travel schedule and congratulatory about the manuscript going to the publisher.

I'll try to do a note to Maggie before I fall asleep—dreaming of and missing you.
Love, Nick
Love to Joan too

10/5/70

Dear Maggie:
No excuses, only distractions. Lots going on and much of it fun. We climbed to tree line Sunday—Suzie and Sheri and I and a young couple from the Meeting. The colors are nothing like New England but the Aspens were gold in the dark green pines and spruces. Sumac and a couple of other low reds add variety.

The boy who was along Tim Tschinkle is helping me with a research project. We are going to try to map the noise levels, then see if the map tells us anything we didn't know already. Everyone we talk to thinks it is most worthwhile, but doubts whether it can be done.

I'll try not to wait so long before I write again.

Much Love,

Nick

10/23/70

Dear Maggie:

Another big day. It's almost bed time. I might be better off with a Scrabble game rather than wondering if I can edit another piece or write a few more paragraphs on the column for *Social Education*.

The rhythm of the San Jose commute influences our weeks profoundly. Tuesday, Wednesday, and Thursday the children and I tend to business and move quietly thru our chores. I get a lot of work done, often have lunch with someone I need to see.

Thursday night I go in to Denver to pick up Sue—and often we are up until 1 a.m. reviewing the week. Friday starts late and often the office work spills over until Sat. or Sunday. The week-end we often take longer hikes—2 hours or more before breakfast. The children often have errands on Saturday and maybe we have people in. I usually try to go to meeting on Sunday but usually alone.

Monday Sue's bag is out to be packed, my office week starts promptly but is cut off at 3:30 when I take Sue to the plane.

Geography Department faculty meetings destroy Friday afternoons once a month. Yesterday we were trying to pick a new chairman. 8 months ago, five of the old guard had decided on one of their number, a not very good choice.

When the subject came up a month ago they thought they would make the nomination and push it through, in spite of a strong schism in the Dept. and a bitter antagonism against this particular person.

Gilbert White saved the day by securing approval of a committee to survey the situation. The committee found a couple of candidates. The best was a member of the old guard, but a respected scholar. Gilbert nominated him. He withdrew his name. He nominated the earlier candidate. All of us were shocked. For an hour and a half opposing sides jockeyed for advantage with all the parliamentary tricks, finally quit at 5 more disgusted than exhausted.

It all seems very petty and unnecessary—but it is part of the growing pains of the Dept. coming out of a simpler phase into a new one. Nothing that strenuous in the ERIC Clearinghouse.

I do have a trip to Washington coming up and could stop in Boston on the way if it's convenient with you.... More later.

Love, Nick

11/16/70

Dear Mother:

Glad to have your cheery note. I'll have a chance to introduce Sue to Peg and Eric at Thanksgiving. Also we'll see David and Helen Loth. And a jillion people at the National Council for the Social Studies.

Sue off to San Jose this evening. The job prospects seem a little brighter. It looks as if I may be drafted into the chairmanship of the Geography Depart.

Peter is looking for a part-time job. Off soon to Montana for Thanksgiving. Reports from Tess sound as though she is doing very well.

Love Nick

P.S. our 1st newsletter enclosed.

I wrote Maggi December 3 on my flight back home telling her about the New York trip, "We had Thanksgiving dinner with the Kochers and it turned out to be great fun. Mrs. Kocher, Eric's mother, broke the ice (not really ice, but formality) by insulting everyone about the length of their hair, skirt, beards. After that, we were all great friends and comrades. Glen and Debra were very warm, Chris less so. The wonderful surprise was the picture of Nick at three. Thank you so much. It's a treasure."

I told her that I was going to quit at the end of the semester, because I couldn't do justice to home, or get organized to start a career in Boulder. But the job situation in Colorado was grim, so I was worried by having to resign my professorship "but I suppose I'm just going through a difficult transition—from independent single female to financially dependent wife. I never thought it would be such a trauma. Nick is suffering too, because I talk about it with him constantly...."

I encouraged Maggie to come visit in the spring, "We can start a women's lib cadre! And you can teach us things and entertain us and be with us."

1/4/71 after a big crowd visiting over Christmas

Dear Maggie:

It's all over now, even the shouting. Steve and Mary have taken their bright and good tempered Wendy home to Corvallis. Hal Casteel has caught his ride back to Kalamazoo. The three from Berkeley caught their plane.

Tonight I even took Sue in to the airport. She will stay for 3 weeks and save some money and will finish teaching and try to finish her text. We think we can survive until then but we're not sure.

Now I buckle down to the bills. I may even get to the Xmas cards. My desk at the office is a mess too.

Much love, Nick

3/7/71 Sunday

Dear Mother:

I don't have your last letter with me here at the office—but I want to get this off right away as I have been too slow already responding.

I've just made a reservation for you at the Boulderado Hotel starting March 16th. We will meet you at the airport—let us know your flight number. The clerk said it was a nice room and it has a tub. I enclose the hotel's brochure.

Our big news is that Peter has passed his High School Equivalency exams and so is thru with his required education. He thinks he will work part time and study part-time for a year or so while he gets a better lead on what more he wants to study.

More later. Love,

Nick

4/26/71

Dear Maggie:

I can't believe how long it has been since I wrote. I haven't even sat down at this desk for several days.

Got Peter off to Kalamazoo this Sunday. He'll be working full time for Campus Travel Service. It was a little hard to break away with no temporariness about it. Hope he won't be too lonely.

I feel as though I had been working very hard, but I don't have much to show for it. At times I have felt as if I were doing everything for everybody else, nothing for me. Some of this comes from planning for grants for next winter, some from family errands.

Our conversations about intentional community seem to have got nowhere—then suddenly there seems to be something going again.

Sue made presentations to the Economics Department at the University. No word yet about their decision.

We have started a discipline called Transcendental Meditation. It is not clear to me what it transcends but it does seem to be a useful discipline.

I'm off the end of the week to Ohio for a speech, two workshops and hopefully a visit with Ann. Meanwhile we are pushing our publications with the fiscal year this month.

Your asparagus cooker has been doing valiant service these last few weeks. Soon we should find wild asparagus.

For now all the trails are muddy. No sun for 10 days and almost 5 inches of rainfall.

Hope all goes well with you.

Much love,

Nick

5/24/71

Dear Maggie:

It's 10pm and I'm just settling down to the desk work after a full day—a couple of hours on a research proposal for summer '72, an hour looking at land for the intentional community, another hour proposal writing, 3 hours on general desk work, an interview with a Harvard Graduate School of Education student looking for a summer job. Home to barbecue a chicken for supper. Good communication with one guest and the family. A few chores, a couple of phone calls and here it is—late.

Much excitement this weekend as the "street people" took over a portion of the city—not a very big portion.

Don't know what happened but I never got back to it. [Continued 6/7/71.]

I was just starting to describe the "riot" when I was interrupted. The Friends meeting was concerned about the violence and spent a couple of long meetings ending in a mild statement in support of moderates on the City Council who have successfully avoided repressive measures. The discussions reminded me of how conservative many of the members of the Meeting are.

But much of our effort has been expended on our new—and still name-less—community. It is a rectangle of land ½ mile by 3/8th of a mile stretching back from the road on a high flat ground across two swales of irrigated hay meadow.

It is also 6-7 families mostly in their twenties ready to live simply and take personal risks in order to create a new living group.

We will move some people onto it this month—but Suzie and I won't move out until early August. We will probably live in the chicken coop. The first year or so the level of living will be low—crowded and inconvenient.

Everyone is committed to the value of several generations living together and both the Rosenbergs and the Seebaums have urged us to bring you into the community.

Since we will have room for you here during July, Suzie and I would like to have you come visit for a week or so to meet the people and see the land. We would like to have your wisdom on a number of topics.

May we give you the plane fare for that visit as a birthday present in addition to what Peg has included us in? We'll write soon what our schedule for the late June and July is.

Meanwhile HAPPY BIRTHDAY!

Love in large measure

Nick and Sue

The Community about 1972

Farm community potluck dinner 2005

THE COMMUNITY AND
LIVING ON NELSON ROAD

In a January 1971 letter to Maggie I report, "we continue to be a very happy family, Nick is very pleased with his job and with the prospect of heading the geography department in the fall although he is, as usual, overworking." I was focused on finding a job and getting nowhere. I tell Maggie, "I've been toying with the idea of starting a school, so as time allows, there is reading and visiting of schools to do.... Both Nick and I are worried about a job for me—this is a bad time for a forty-year-old married woman to be looking for an academic job. I am toying with the school idea as a substitute, but am a bit timid about starting such an all consuming venture which I know has a high chance of financial failure."

At the time Nick and I were learning about the many alternative schools being formed in the U.S. and England. After Quaker Meeting one Sunday at the Bouldings, Elise expressed her interest in creating a learning community. She captured our imagination and we joined a group she started to explore the idea. I thought that this might be something I could put my energy and imagination into. However, by the time we launched the community I had landed a job at the Denver Extension Center of the University of Colorado, but it wasn't secure because the university was thinking of shutting down that campus, and I was hired initially as an untenured faculty member. The campus did survive, and I was promoted to full professor the next year, so that I had the responsibilities of the job, the community and finishing ECON 12. Both Nick and I entered the community experiment way overcommitted!

It's hard for me, forty years later to know with any certainty what effect the community had on us personally and on our marriage. It took a lot out of us. But our marriage survived, our love and care for each other grew. Eventually, we built a beautiful home and helped create a lovely little hamlet at the farm where we lived happily for another thirty years. Nick adored the farm and living on it, so, in this sense, the community decision helped us find our place, our home. I just wish now that we had taken more time at the beginning of our marriage savoring that early emotional bliss and enjoyment of our new family.

Nick provided three kinds of records describing the community experience in addition to the account he gives in his memoir in Part I.

Below are his letters at the time (and some of mine) that describe our daily lives and struggles. Second, the Appendix on Community includes the introduction to a book Nick intended to write that gives a brief chronology of the first 30 years. It also includes short essays written at the time, later more reflective pieces, and an illustrative description of the consensus process that was so much a part of our decision making. It also includes Nick's initial announcement/invitation to a twentieth reunion that we held in June 1991. Third, and most interesting, is the DVD Nick produced of the weekend celebration of our twentieth anniversary at the farm. The videographer captured twenty-seven hours of the weekend activities, much of it as organized discussions about our experience and "what it all meant," some of it capturing the fun. Nick and the videographer edited the tapes down to two hours that achieve much of what Nick had hoped to accomplish in the book. It is clear that Nick never gave up on the ideal of community building.

Here is the continuation of Nick's letters after the beginning of the community plus a little commentary by me.

9/23/71

Dear Mother

Sure we got your letter and read it happily and have wanted to answer it ever since. But...somehow all the exciting immediate pressures get in the way.

We still have not moved out to the farm. The coop is not ready yet — may not be for a month or 6 weeks. When we do the address will be: Route 3, Box 330, Longmont, Colo. I'll look up the zip. There are a couple of phones now 449-3663 and 443-2408. We have applied for a party line but have no idea how long it will take.

We did get Judy's house finished, except for plumbing, a couple of weeks ago. Tom's end of the garage got closed in last week-end and is almost ready for painting.

Lots of work has been done on the chicken coop — wasps out, insulation in, window sills, partitions — but lots more remains. The big problems now are sewage and water. Sewage plan has been submitted to the county Bd of Health, well driller due tomorrow.

Of course there are still plenty of personal and social problems. But they will always be with us.... Meanwhile lots of other excitement. I have taken up my new duties as chairman of the Geography Dept. They seem leisurely by comparison with ERIC. I trust I'll be able to help breath new fire into the group. The students seem eager and ready to work. Some of the faculty are first rate. The Dean's, etc., are so pressed for money at the moment that they seem paralyzed.

ERIC and its sister institution SSEC have moved into a new building, just across the street from the University. Even after 3 weeks, the place has not settled down. Some stresses, which probably were there all the time, show up under the new conditions. But it is relatively spacious and under our own control....

Suzie is well under way in her teaching at the Denver Center, never doing as well as she would like but always doing. She continues her editing of ECON 12 and is working on a small Environmental Education curriculum project [that Sherry participated in]. Together we have been meeting with several others about a proposal we want to put in for a new project on Social Science skills.

Sheri is enjoying school: chemistry, college math, Russian Lit, etc. Pete works as a janitor for the new SSEC-ERIC Building. Hal is back, working on the farm.

Big snow storm this week which broke many limbs on trees and finished our tomato season.

Much love, Nick

[No date]

Dear Maggie:

Not so busy I can't plan ahead for professional reasons. I hope we can see something of Betsy [his cousin in Philadelphia] and then come up to Cambridge for a couple days at New Years.

All's well here except the continuation of the over-commitment. I have a sort of built in anesthetic which keeps me from getting too involved or wound up. But Suzy was so nervous last night she couldn't sleep. She's off to Vail today to a conference on teacher education.

The big news this week was the approval of the sewage system for the farm by the County Board of Health. Now we are starting a well and ready to put in plumbing, electricity. Who knows we might be living out there in another month.

Pete' toe is recovering. He'll be back janitoring next week. Meanwhile he's been filling in as receptionist while one of the girls was sick. Sheri enjoys her Environmental Curriculum Development job—off and on. She's wondering about colleges and has mentioned Radcliffe and Wellesley. I told her you'd love that.

Much love, Nick

Sometime that fall the SSEC building was invaded by antiwar activists. This was the time of the Cambodian war and press coverage revealed that the U.S. had been spraying millions of tons of defoliant in Vietnam to expose the Vietcong. June of 1971 *The New York Times* had started to publish *The Pentagon Papers*; the Administration got a restraining order that the Supreme Court overturned by the end of the month. These revelations brought about the end of public support for the war.

Boulder was preparing for a big demonstration down Broadway. Youngsters had snuck into the building during the day and took it over after hours. Irving Morrissett, SSEC's Executive Director, was out of town so Nick was called that night to deal with the "invasion." Nick's immediate response when he arrived was, "How can I help you?" Negotiations proceeded quickly. The protestors were allowed to fly a huge banner on the wall of the building facing Broadway and Regent Hall and they agreed not to destroy documents or anything else in the building. Out of this we gained a lifelong friend, Steve Hodes, who joined us at the community from time to time. Not the least of the benefits of this new friendship was access to the vegetarian garbage for our pig from the Carnival Café where Steve worked.

10/25/71

Dear Mother:
Your check made a great hit. It is posted on the bulletin board waiting for the trip to town to buy the bulbs. Patti, chairman of the gardening committee, is two weeks overdue for delivery of the baby—but I trust that won't keep us from getting the bulbs in.

We irrigated all the trees last week. Well driller and sewer installation due in the next couple of weeks. Weather continues beautifully open, minimum near 32 and max in the 60s.

Suzie making good progress on her manuscript, but Pete is in a severe depression and I don't know how to pull him out.
Much love,
Nick

These references to well drilling remind me of the reason for delay: finding water! We had permission to drill three holes, and Nick, the geographer/geologist, was sure he could use his scientific acumen to find where to drill. Most of us were in to having a diviner come, but Nick wouldn't stand for it. After several tries, however, we finally won out. I can't remember who the old guy was, but he quickly found us three places to drill; one in the East pasture provided the water we needed; the other outside the chicken coop where we lived, gave enough water to help with the irrigation. Nick took it all quite gracefully!

January 17, 1972

Dear Peg:
This is the first of what I hope may be a number of semi-diaries. I'll try to share them with Mother and maybe with others and will try to keep a carbon here at the community. It is inspired by the *NY Times* article which you sent a month or so ago and which I meant to share with Mike, one of our group who was writing a piece on communities for a curriculum project in Indiana. It never got delivered to Mike yet and it is yellowed from the sun which streams in on my desk on bright days. Too much of what David Fremont says in that Oct. 3, 1971 issue is familiar for comfort. But enough is different so I can comfortably say "but we are different," but not without a haunting sense of potential failure. The feeling that we are trying to escape/get away from/find an alternative to/build something different from the dominant way of life in America without knowing what we are building toward is very similar. Whether we have enough constructiveness to overcome the negativism is the big doubt.

Of course tonight is not the best night to start such a diary. I just finished two hours of cleanup after supper and pickup of the living room of stuff that had been left around—boots, books, magazines, toys, a ball of twine, a hammer, a parka, it sounds worse than it was. But we had run out of dishwashing soap so the cleanup wasn't as efficient as it should be. And it is bitter outside so no one wants to make an extra trip to a nearby house. And I have been running on short rations of sleep for two weeks and that not only changes my disposition, but also changes my digestion. And last night I spent paying bills from the last 6 weeks and got to the bottom of this month's income before I got to the bottom of the bills. And today I had my first good run-in with the bete-noire of the department. And Suzie has been in California for 2 weeks and I miss her muchly. So in the family vernacular I am feeling "woofy," a condition I don't know how to get out of consciously.

Actually any part of the setup has good and bad points. We had a terrible wind storm this week. Millions of dollars of damages. We lost the roof of our old barn. It is a serious loss as this was a storage area in which we had a lot of sort of useful stuff. And it was a beautiful old weathered barn which might have made a place for square dances and community meetings and whatnot. But we hadn't started to remodel it as a residence as had been suggested, and no one was hurt as the roof blew off. Some of it ended 300 yards away, across a major draw on the place, and the roofs of the two attached sheds which were being used as carpentry shop and building materials storage stayed intact so these areas are still usable. And the walls of the barn didn't fall in so nothing was crushed and we have a chance to recover the weathered wood siding, several hundred dollars worth.

So it goes. One of the number borrowed Judy's fragile Austin American to go into town and then loaned it to a friend to take a business associate to the airport. On the way back the transmission went out, destroying the engine in the process. What is the responsibility of the friend, of the borrower? What to do about providing Judy with a car? Should we reduce the number of cars and use them all communally? Can we find a way to maintain cars which do not "belong" to one individual or family? Are we ready yet to give up some of our precious mobility? How do we handle genuinely contradictory experience in matters of brands of cars? (One thinks VW's are the most dependable machine available while another finds them completely unreliable and unsafe.) What to do with differing expectations and styles: "I've got to have a car available to me because of my special and different schedule" vs. "I can get along with any old piece of junk, so why can't you?"

On the one hand it seems ridiculous to try to get 14 adults to give up their individual trips and learn to pool resources, share joys and sorrows, plan together. On the other hand, the individual family in the ticky-tacky box on the hillside seems even more ridiculous. I guess the big question is whether we have the motive and the wisdom, patience and forbearance, insight and energy, flexibility and persistence to find what we want, not just get away from what we don't want.

January 25, 1972

Another chapter. I can't begin to fill in all the gaps, just give flashes of what is going on and a past highlight or two. Things are kind of smooth right now. Everyone (but one who was spending the night in town) ate together curried vegetables, cauliflower salad, corn bread, rice, and apple sauce. The children were a little noisy but mostly well behaved. Everyone was getting caught up with everyone else's concerns. Some rehash of an experimental seminar on free and open schools which we started last Sunday. It had started as a moneymaking and educational idea combined. Serve an exotic, but inexpensive dinner and ask one of our friends who was an expert in the field to lead the seminar and charge all the guests $3.00 for the combination. Mike and Anne Moore who helped get a public open school going in a neighboring county brought two of the school's teachers and the four of them were leading the seminar. Bobbi and Sheri took the brunt of the preparations and most of the rest of us helped around the edges. The meal was not an unqualified success. Russian Stew may be too far out for the piece de resistance. But the experiment was successful enough to make us want to go ahead with a series of four more with modifications from what we learned and what we will learn.

Just got interrupted by a visit from a couple of young people working on a grant from the Johnson Foundation trying to find ways of helping people find alternative life styles and to tie communities together in useful networks. It's midnight now and I have to quit if I'm going to be any good tomorrow.

Many thanks to MH for the suggestions about the automobiles. I'll try them on the next meeting. Clearly the communality of automobiles is a major issue. Off tomorrow evening for a three and a half day workshop on teaching Earth Sciences at the college level.

2/29/72 from Hotel Presidential, Washington, D.C.

Dear Mother
    Moth
    Maggie
It's 12:30p.m., the end of another full day — getting the family off, morning in the geography department including fellowships for minority students and a sack lunch planning for a grant to improve graduate training of college teachers, then over to ERIC to sign checks the end of the month, do some phone calls about the ERIC system as a whole and catch a 3:45 plane here.

The end of the day includes meeting a delightful Zambian on assignment to the International Bank and planning our presentation to the central ERIC staff tomorrow — our annual review. If all goes well, we will have our assurance of next year's funding by noon. But the whole system is in turmoil caused by budget constraints and the threat of consolidating 19 clearinghouses to 10 or 12. I don't feel personally threatened since I have asked to be replaced as ERIC/ChESS director to work full time in Geography. But I do feel compelled to try to protect the system.

The family is upset about our over-commitment. Suzie, Sheri and I are all too busy, too little time for contemplation, rest and intimacy. We will get a weekend of skiing this next weekend, but that won't be enough. We will work at cutting down our tendency to respond to every request.

Peg writes well of her weekend with you too. Wish I could fit one in.
Love Nick

Clearly, as a family we were getting out of control! On May 19, 1972, I wrote a plea to the community that I was moving into the Harvest

House in Boulder, hoping to come home after the weekend, to catch up on the pileup of work. I state that the impulse to move came that morning at 8 a.m. I had gotten home at 11:30 p.m. the night before—the whole farmstead was dark. I took a scotch to bed and spent an hour and a half writing to Nick. The letter had been brewing for days as I began to detect a gradual drifting apart—possibly a natural effect of three years of marriage unless deliberately checked. Another sore point with Nick was his involvement in the community—or rather lack of involvement, a basic conflict over job and community. I had put myself on the line emotionally and time wise so that I had pushed aside my work on ECON 12, and I was increasingly resentful of people's lack of understanding of my needs, "Just this week it came to me that while people at the community—me in particular—have been concerned about younger people's growing pains, problems of finding themselves, of disciplining themselves into a life work, I have not felt support for ending my work.... When Nick and I were first married, one of our major kinds of working together intellectually was in his really valuable help on ECON 12. This year he has been too busy...and I have not been upset, I just miss the collaboration. He did agree to help this spring and I think that this is at the base of some resentment about his trips. Three of them have consumed 2 ½ weeks of time, ample time to help me or to do some organizing work here which would also relieve me.... I hope that while I'm away community members assess the plusses and minuses of living in this community, their contributions to it, their willingness to take initiative and to be concerned.... I will not be here this summer as the straw boss.... I must complete ECON 12 this summer, and if necessary, will move off the farm to do so."

Nick responded to this memo. I have no record of my letter to him; I hope we took some time to reconnect. In an undated memo from Nick to me he outlines his university and geography contributions, and justifies them: they provide a steady income that he shares, personal satisfaction, an opportunity to attempt social change, a respectable label that has some protective value. Within the community he said he wanted to take an active role, not just to satisfy his need for physical work. But he felt constraints as the oldest and richest community member in not exerting undue influence in decisions, and a hesitation in committing all our resources to the community. He admits to being negligent in exerting leadership, doesn't know how much of this had been due to the fact that it is "hard" to do and how much it was because of external commitments, but he resolved to make a bigger effort.

As the ECON 12 project (renamed Economics in Society) was nearing publication I wrote another desperate plea in March 1973 and announced that I was moving into an apartment in Denver until June to finish the project (home weekends). Evidently I had become enmeshed in the community's problems when I simply couldn't afford the emotional outlay. I was working fifteen to seventeen hour days for six to seven days a week and had to meet a June 1 deadline. But I pledged myself to providing real creative effort starting in the summer and to begin scheduling real leisure for Nick and me.

That memo also touched on some important issues, "We are back again reconsidering whether we want to be pioneers in building something really commanding of our talents or are we willing to settle for being just a living community." I end the memo rather dramatically: either way "we are recreating a culture for America, hopefully a socialist one. It may be insignificant in terms of its effect on the whole world, but it's not as far as our own sanity is concerned. Maybe we will even do something good beyond ourselves. It seems to me that it takes a lifetime of effort to save oneself, to die with distinction, and that's what it's all about. From that point of view, Nicki and Barbara are two of the really distinguished people I know."

The pressure on us continued. For the month of July 1973 I kept track of my use of time. Rarely was there any slack time at all. Days ended at midnight at the earliest, mostly I stayed up for an hour and a half until 1 or 1:30 a.m. talking to someone, often Nick, sometimes our children. The most frightening entry was staying up late one Friday talking to Nick related to "his outburst about things closing in." In a community discussion December of that year we each did an exercise on why we came to the community, why we are staying, and why we are thinking of leaving. Nick's response to the last question: "I only think of leaving when I get so tired and hassled that: (a) all the joy goes out of life; (b) I start neglecting my health—exercise, teeth, diet, stress. Then leaving seems the only way to get enough release—other than resigning from the university."

More letters during the community period:

7/23/73

Dear Maggie:
We hear about you indirectly from Peg and Dorothy and are glad as I'm sure you are of your progress. Trust it will continue.

In spite of planning only a 1/3d time job for the summer, this one seems more hectic than ever. I serve as chairman of the Dept but do no teaching at the University. But it seems as though there is a lot of advising, thesis reading, paper work and the like. I don't get to the office until 10 or 11 and leave at 4 or 4:30.

Suzie is working hard on her curriculum project which is now partly at the printer, partly in the last stages of editing and one book still in the writing stage. I'm not able to do much to help except to provide emotional support when she gets discouraged. I have been able to provide her with good working conditions—office, typewriter, etc.

The community continues to soak up time, energy and initiative. If it didn't seem so promising as an experiment in alternatives to the general mode of the society, we would abandon it, to simplify our lives. But it is hard to visualize going back to a nuclear family whose principle goal is capital accumulation.

Steve tells us he is being transferred to Grand Coulee Dam. The Oregon project is stalled by a strike. He had thought that he would be transferred to Denver where the company is expanding an oil refinery but was shifted to Washington the last minute.

Peter has finally decided to go to England (London) to attend Shiller College. He is dubious about its vocational value but by the same token, he feels as though he is marking time as pantry chef for the Boulder Country Club. He was very upset by Tess' accident. She fell off her desk after hanging a picture and broke her shoulder and leg. The bones are finally beginning to heal but what to do about the excessive drinking and the sense of not being needed? Not such a new problem.

This letter is finally being finished almost a week after it was started. Sorry! A reflection on how poorly I manage my time.

Welcome to Merion. [Philadelphia suburb and home of Nick's cousin Betsy Swope]

Love, Nick

8/9/73

Dear Maggie:

I just kissed Suzie off to California for a week with her publishers and friends. Gam—her first husband's mother is just out of the hospital from a cancer operation so Suzie will spend a few days with her.

Peter leaves for 10 days in Montana with Tess before coming back to pack for England. Sheri off this weekend to visit her father in Oregon. Maybe I can do a little catching up.

But this noon we entertained a plant geographer from Texas. Tomorrow an educational geographer from Hong Kong. Then a doctoral exam: He wrote a 450 page dissertation.

Weather bright and hot again after a spell with clouds and showers in the afternoons.

Let us know how you are fitting in in Merion. Love to Betsy and all her family.

Lots for you too

Nick

8/12/73

Dear Maggie

Things were very quiet when I got the paper and pen. Suzie is in California. Several members of the community are away—and there was no group meal in the chicken coop.

But by the time I got things together there were 6 of us sitting around the table. But people have left now. Sheri is cleaning up from the experiment in drying apples and Bob Dylan is wailing on the stereo.

Sheri and Peter and Hal will take the Ghia to Montana tomorrow a.m. I may feel even more alone then. It seems strange when I live in a community and usually complain of over-stimulus—that I should feel alone.

I had a very satisfying session yesterday with a school geography inspector from Hong Kong. He already knew about H.S.G.P. We went on from there into Open Education and Theory of Curriculum.

How's by you?

Love

Nick

8/20/73

Dear Maggie:

Hope that Philadelphia is not as hot as Boulder this week. We make it to 95 every afternoon, but fortunately the humidity is low and the geography Dept. is in a big old brick building that does not respond to the extreme. Even now at 9p.m. the coop seems hot though it is very comfortable, fresh and soft outside. I wish we had followed your advice and planted nicotinia. The fragrance would be a perfect addition. The coop does look nice with cosmos and salvia, pansies and green peppers, zinnias and snapdragons all in full growth. Only three out of six junipers survived, but they add a lot. The forsythia and flowering plum seem in good health. The herb garden will soon be completely a strawberry patch unless we can be courageous in controlling the strawberries. Meanwhile dill, shallots, curly cress, eggplant, rhubarb, garlic and lots more share the space.

We're selling beans, squash, turnips, bunching onions, cucumbers, garlic and a few tomatoes from the big garden, and still getting lettuce, peas and snow peas for our own use. It will still be a while before the sweet corn comes in. We harvested an enormous crop of yellow transparent apples from the orchard. They are making into apple sauce and butter. We tried drying some but that seems an awful lot of work. You don't have an old cider press in the attic do you? I remember taking the apples from the Coolidge farm in Pittsfield to the press and bringing back the fresh cider the year they had the polio epidemic in Boston and you kept several families in Pittsfield until late in the fall. The only commercial press we have been able to find here wants to charge us more than it seems worth.

All well with the family. Suzie back from Calif in good spirits, working hard on her books. Peter visiting Tess who seems to be recovering ahead of schedule. Sheri and Hal drove up with him, have been climbing, will visit Barbara Cole before returning here in a week.

Steve excited by the challenge of installing enormous pieces of the tubes carrying water to Grand Coulee turbines—like a giant 3-D picture puzzle.

How are you adjusting to Betsy's?

Much love

Nick

9/3/73

Dear Maggie:

Classes for the fall term start tomorrow and I could hardly be less well prepared. Hope my students are forgiving. I have not really got things put away after last year.

Physically the farm is on an even keel. We irrigated today—all the animals are well. Bessie dropped a fine black calf. We were given 3 full grown ducks this morning. The first danger of frost has passed and warm weather is forecast. (We understand you've had a terrible hot spell.)

But psychologically we aren't all that well off. One couple and their 2 children—Pat and Carolyn—left last week after 4 months trial with us.

Bobby and Lyle are both in therapy and agree that it is very important but that doesn't make it any less painful.

Meanwhile we are all trying to understand how we can get the unenthusiastic to live up to the expectations of some of us who work dawn to midnight—or how we should change those expectations.

We have added another family to replace the one that left. And have reassigned space. Suzie and I will move into the little house where you stayed when you were here. The new family will move into the coop. Off to bed now. We think of you often in your transition. [Maggie was in Merion waiting to move to the Kendall retirement complex.]

Much love,

Nick

Undated letter to me spring, 1974 on the way to Washington and to help Maggie move to Kendall.

Dear Suzi.

Ready to board the plane—all on time. I tried to reach you by phone, but the line was busy. I was just going to tell you I love you and say good bye.

I love you.

Good bye.

See you as soon as I can.

I'm due back on United 719 arriving 11:35, but I have not been in touch with Betsy or anyone at Kendall.

We had a pleasant visit with Tom and Kris. We went over the jobs to be done in a drizzle. We had had ½ an inch of rain during the night. That should help the hayfield get started as well as keep the garden and trees.

I got a lot done with Bonnie during the a.m. The exams did not get graded, but Steve Thompson came in and agreed to finish them up.

I'll be at the Sherry Tower South this evening (202) 861-8200. I'll try to phone after I get in.

I missed you last night. Got up about 5 and went thru 2 piles on the desk. Also did a little pruning on the apple tree in the small pasture but some buds had started to leaf out.

Much love, Nick

The last surviving letter from the Community period, dated July 1, 1974, is from me written to Maggie. (Sadly, it's the last surviving letter from the correspondence between Nick and me and his mother. She was moving to the retirement home at Kendall and must have stopped keeping our letters.) I tell Maggie that we're on our summer schedule. Our life sounds relaxed and pleasant with Nick enjoying the farming. He gets up at six o'clock every morning to start the water in the vegetable garden and the flower beds, then he weeds and works in the garden for another two or three hours. I join him or do some food preserving. We eat breakfast, shower and get to the office around noon. I tell Maggie that I will be taking off a week in August to recuperate from a hysterectomy. I report on the kids: Sheri back East having visited Maggie; Peter in great shape loving his job as cold chef. He had just served us and two visiting friends a terrific lunch, commenting, "If we have to live poor on the farm, he should provide some class to our existence."

Community life was not just hard work and emotional strain. Most of the time we had a very good time, particularly for those of us who liked building things and learning new skills. Few of us knew anything about construction, gardening, farming, preserving food. And we learned from each others' passions. The initial group all became initiated into Transcendental Meditation; my only annoyance with it was the commercial aspect, having to pay for my mantra. So I initiated John Sperling for free. Our seemingly endless meetings were often captivating. And we learned how to run meetings, make consensus decisions, work on conflict resolution. We were all great cooks and we could throw a pretty good party!

We also indulged some. Both Nick and I thought the group to be a little up tight. At some point, I can't remember when, after Jay and Harriet moved out, we decided to convert the geodesic dome that had served as the billy goat Sweet William's barn into a sauna. Quite an operation to eliminate the smell! But I think that Sherry and Hal took on the major responsibility for laying the foundation and sides on which to place the dome. And we had an old wood burning stove that supplied the heat. The sauna was a great success! It could fit ten of us comfortably at different heights on the shelves we built. We cooled off by rolling in the snow before going back for more heat. We could walk all the way back to our houses virtually nude, still warm.

The children were a constant source of fun and joy; differences in child rearing beliefs interesting, if sometimes frustrating. Two stories from the period became part of family lore. Nick's favorite involved his woofing at Andrea, Bobbie and Lyle's two-year-old. He was digging a hole near her house and Andrea kept throwing the dirt back in the hole even after repeated requests to stop. Finally, he barked at her and told her to stop. She dissolved into tears and ran back to her mother to say, "Nicky told me to stop helping him!!! ALL DAY!!!" My story involved a funeral. I was sick in bed watching out the window at the children playing with our whippet, Gladstone, when I noticed that James opened the gate to the rabbits we were raising. Of course, Gladstone whipped in and quickly killed one of the rabbits. The children picked up the dead rabbit, found a box to put it in, marched to a location under the trees with a shovel, dug a hole and buried the rabbit with much ceremony. They told the story at dinner, leaving out the first part about how Gladstone got into the rabbit hutch until I let the cat out of the bag!

We were learning a lot about other experiments in community living. Nick and I took a trip back east to Philadelphia, my original home town, to visit the folks at the Movement for a New Society (MNS). Their big house was located just fifteen blocks from where I grew up in West Philadelphia. We were very impressed with what they were doing as a living unit but also in publicizing communitarian politics. An MNS group moved to Colorado, I think, near Durango. Chris Moore from MNS settled in Boulder to start CDR and helped us work through the final stages of dissolving the community in 1975.

And Boulder was learning some about our experiment. An article about us appeared in the *Rocky Mountain News*, Sunday May 12, 1974, "Farm commune still thriving north of Boulder." It reported on a national survey in 1970 that identified 2,000 communes throughout the U.S., but reckoned there must be thousands more that live in obscurity. The author, Beth Gaeddert, described the Community on Nelson Road as one of six Boulder-area communities and summarized interviews of members, commenting that the "group is held together by its members' desire to live cooperatively, rather than competitively, in a way which will enhance the individuality of each." Sounds very much like Nick! "What really 'carries the thing through,' says Barbara Cole, 72, the group's oldest member, is a 'very genuine affection' toward each other. 'It's rocky at times, but so is all life.'" Gaeddert reports on our history and the then current Commune II phase organized around the goat and cooperative construction enterprises.

The Appendix on the community describes the dissolution of the community in early winter 1975 -76. The community focus and norms gradually changed as Jay and Harriet Lynch became the new elders and social center. Nick and I didn't fit in. Our decision to leave brought about the end of the community when we moved out and the group decided not to purchase the land.

I'm not sure what moved us in the first place to embark on such a quixotic venture not quite two years into our marriage! We subjected our marriage, ourselves and our children to enormous stress. Nick and I took on even more responsibilities and more overwork than usual. As we took on the community responsibility, we both needed and wanted to continue our academic careers, compounding the pressure on us and the contradictions. As the affluent seniors we had ultimate power, but we couldn't exercise it because of the time and creative demands required by our outside jobs. Eventually, the community evolved in ways that were not compatible with our goals.

One thought, maybe we created the community together in place of a child! Was it our love child? For sure, we were creating an extended family. (Missing Nicki as I do today, I wish we had been able to have a child.) Did our new sense of inner fulfillment nourish our idealism? We were living our ideals. But what a life, particularly for me. I got caught in the emotional entanglements of group living which were exhausting, if not permanently damaging. Nick suggests in one of the essays in the Appendix that a stable community needs a core of stable people who can be supportive of individuals at different stages of development during the stress of their moving from one stage to another.

How was our marriage affected? A lot! But possibly the intensity of group living enhanced the intensity of our marriage. We were forced to talk about values in a deep way that most couples might be able to avoid. My records of time usage show Nick and I staying up late at night, many nights, talking (no record of what about). The experience enlivened us, creating a habit of serious open conversation delving into the core of who we are.

Our exhaustion turned out to be fleeting. We finally caught up on our sleep! I remember the overwhelming luxury of those nights of twelve hours of sleep after we moved in to the Shady Creek Apartment in September 1975. However, we still had a lot of temporary trauma getting the farm and buildings in good enough shape to be closer to our standards.

Glenn Browning stayed with us after the dissolution of the community. He was a fine carpenter and a devotee of community life; he took on the job of managing and rebuilding the place. There must have been a lot decisions to make and work to complete before we could move back. This letter from Nick to me indicates the tensions, that the wounds of community living were still open, and that I was still capable of flying off the handle. How sweet a man was Nicki!

2/14/76

Dear Suzie:
This may not be worth the try but why am I feeling so close to tears, a kind of desperation feeling in the relationship with you. Having missed you so much. Specifically having realized how different my life is without you even when you are gone only a few days. And then when we do make contact Saturday night you go off on a rampage about Glenn's and my indecisiveness and how this will preclude any successful move back to the farm.

It seemed very wrong at that distance and interval to be arguing indecisiveness. I, of course, had not briefed you on Debbie's horse or Buckie's pig which I had dealt with in what I hoped was an even-handed but firm way. And maybe you had no way of knowing how vulnerable I feel in missing you so much. But the end result is me feeling like you have come down on me with both feet shod in hobnailed boots because I think that Glenn is lining up work in Denver. (No hint as to whether this is one week or one month or one years work. I really don't know.) And neither you nor I have ever said out loud: "Glenn, before you do anything else I think you should make the estimates on the Coop, the W. Garage and the E Garage. For unless we program those carefully we may find ourselves hopelessly behind. And all it will take is one more time…." In fact, my memory, fuzzy as it is, establishes that the spring should be a mix of Glenn finding jobs for himself and Glenn working on the bldgs in the Lykens Gulch farmstead. So why didn't I say that on the phone and tell you to reconsider—because I didn't remember it until later clearly enough to state it. Meanwhile I feel as though I had been tromped on.

Putting the emotions of the moment aside and looking forward to the future, if the farm is a threat or an anathema or something, say so! If you have been so burned by the communal experience that you don't want to even think about it let us know. We love you and don't want to put you thru unnecessary trauma. We want to find a way which is mutually satisfying. It will be a lot easier if you can alert us to the fact that X hours a week on the farm is the maximum you can stand and that you feel we must have a return of Y% interest on $Z invested, otherwise we should sell the farm and carry out the A-B-C alternative.

The rent isn't in. The horse is in the pasture. The gate for the sauna fence is broken and unhung. The seeds are not inventoried, sprouted or ordered. Only half the evergreens have been watered. The units haven't been written and the quizzes haven't even been started. And I am obviously feeling sorry for myself. But it is after 11 and I couldn't do better if I started over. Maybe I'll tear it up in the morning. I really do love you and that's why I have to tell you how much it hurt tonight.
Goodnight. NH

A postscript the next morning. After a good nights sleep and a first cup of coffee spent reading the rest of the second chapter of the monograph on values while the sun streamed in the bedroom window so that the colors in the bed-spread seemed to shine themselves. I haven't reread the above and I suspect it does accurately reflect my mood of the time, but this morning I feel very lucky. Luv NH

Unfortunately, Nick had to adapt to my outbursts. Although I got less volatile over time, I still have a tendency to erupt over something that gets me angry, blow off steam and then immediately forget it all. Meanwhile, Nick could be affected by my outbursts for half a day.

We moved into the chicken coop sometime that summer (we were away much of it in Russia and Europe) where we fixed up the bathroom a bit and installed a bidet—the plumber was amused—and improved the kitchen. Glen lived in the East garage that he made beautiful. From the interim period before we moved back, the only renter we've kept close to was Debbie Taylor. Debbie and some other lesbians had rented the big farm house. One amusing story was about their dog that didn't like men and nipped at them. I didn't believe this until I was following Nick into the pump house and witnessed an attack! Evidently, Nick asked the women to leave at some point. But by that summer of 1976 we made friends with Bob Adams who stayed at the coop while it was under construction. Sadly, we've lost track of Bob.

We rented the other houses and tried to maintain some semblance of community. We made news again in The *Sunday Camera*'s *FOCUS*, "Comfortable living in…a chicken coop" by Barbara Jameson (February 10, 1977) that includes several pretty good shots of the coop as of 1977. Jameson begins, "Would you cluck if I told you that at this very moment two University of Colorado professors are living in a chicken coop?" She summarizes the evolution of the coop as a dwelling from commune days to the then present emphasis on a subsistence life style. She gives a thorough and approving description of the house, except for the bathroom, "The bathroom which seems to suffer a stylistic identity crisis, could be described as Sophisticated Neo-Primitive."

I can barely outline the following seven years. As I remember it the first five years or so went along quite pleasantly. Summers brought young people to live at the farm; we made good friends with our renters—Ivan Getting, Steve Thompson and Lynn Fuller, Natalie and Paul Gellatt, Anne Widerstrom, Carl Formosa, Kathy Partridge and Jim Glasscock and others. Particularly adorable was a little elf-like family of parents and two children. The parents made beautiful soft leather moccasins and boots, and, to entertain the children in the old farm house, they fed the mice on little plates every night! The family left at some point, but not the mice!

We played together. For several years we organized a Memorial Day weekend overnight in the valley of the farm. I can't remember why, but I think we all realized we had a beautiful piece of land and we wanted to make use of it. I can't remember what we did other than eat and sleep out, but we must have explored the property and enjoyed it. We used it in winter to cross-country ski, and I think this is where Nicki taught me to use my new, beautiful Norwegian wooden skis.

We also worked. Glen, in particular and his friend Carol (they eventually married at the farm), really worked at maintaining the community spirit. We maintained the extensive grounds, gardened together, processed apples together into cider, planted a shelter belt to protect the west side of the houses, generally spent time together. Saturday mornings each fall we took breakfast and drove up Left Hand Canyon and other mountain roads to find, fell, and cut fire wood. Most of the houses were heated by wood burning stoves, and Nick loved this whole process. In fact, we left the farm permanently only after Nick was no longer able to maintain our wood supply.

We even educated some visiting parents. One summer, we decided to grow pot in the garden. I was put in a difficult situation when a mother of one of our visitors asked me what that row of plants was. I answered, "tomatoes." She said, no, in back of the tomatoes. I said, "corn." She said, no, in front of the corn. I gave up and left it to Nick to tell her the truth. She was distressed, but by the end of the week she had Nick take her picture by the row of pot!

That same summer, the grasshoppers really invaded and it turns out grasshoppers love grass. They destroyed several plants. One of us, not an avid gardener but keen about this crop, built screened enclosures for each of the remaining plants. The grasshopper pruning encouraged the plants to sprout out into mammoth plants. But finally we had to cut them down and dry them in the barn after a pot farm had been identified near us up Left Hand Canyon in Jamestown. We all enjoyed an enormous supply that lasted us a long time.

Grasshoppers supplied lots of work and entertainment. The next year, I think, was the big siege. Since we didn't at that time believe in chemical killers we learned that they don't fly for long distances, so we formed a human line with blankets and literally shooed them down into the gulch.

We also opened up the farm to political workshops and overnights. The Geography Department held its retreats in the "barn" once we rebuilt it. I invited the Econ Department from UCD to some workshops. After 1983 the Rocky Mountain Peace and Justice Center used the farm and park, as did other political groups. We were involved in supporting the development of other communities and, with Dave Bramhall and Bonnie Mapes (who was living in our yurt) founded Colorado Connections to try to develop and maintain a directory of such organizations and people. And we maintained some connections with MNS. We were following through on Nick's desire to make the place available for like-minded groups.

Then there were the weddings. Sherry got married twice at the farm! The first was to Hal, a gala, somewhat hippy, event down in the middle hayfield in an opening near the gulch. We spent the day of the wedding gathering choke cherries, but then we all dressed up and marched down to the site with Nick at the head of the group playing his recorder. Peter organized terrific food. I think I remember that we forgot to buy the alcohol and it was a Sunday back in the days when the liquor stores were closed. Somehow we rounded up the booze. The second marriage to Jim was more sedate, but lovely, and took place in front of the coop. Ronnie and Len married at the farm, as did Carol and Glen, and many of our friends and students. Throughout our time at the farm, we continued to have weddings. Most memorable were those of Carolyn Kastner and Rick Counahan in the 1980s and our granddaughter Wendy Helburn to Brent Mather in 1989.

Around 1980 we made the mistake of renting to a few really serious lefties interested in turning our cooperative ventures (the garden, chicken, cattle, bees) into real worker-controlled "collectives" that they thought had to be separated organizationally from the landlord/tenant relationship.

This exposed the elephant that had been in the room for the previous nine years! Our records show back and forth documents. After exhausting me, Nick took over the interactions and things smoothed out. But our daughter Sherry and her husband Jim, observing the unpleasant bickering and us working so hard on the place, suggested that we end it all by subdividing and selling the lots. Jim's logic was that if we subdivided and created an HOA that owned the outlot that included the old farm buildings, the garden, and a park area, we'd finally have our community. With Sherry's and Jim's help that's what we did, and this new set of legal and economic relationships led to us living at the farm happily for another twenty-two years in the beautiful house Jim built for us.

We used some of the proceeds from selling the lots to make improvements to the potential HOA property. Most important was a barn to replace the one that had blown down the first year of the community. In September 1983 we organized an old-fashioned barn raising among our friends that Jim supervised. We had the foundations poured along with a trombe wall to provide solar heat to the building, and we ordered the roof trusses. He, Glenn and two or three other experienced carpenters supervised teams of inexperienced friends and in one weekend the building was raised. We must have had about forty people to feed and keep happy while they worked. Uncle David was in charge of making the ice cream. The following weekend a smaller group came out to do the roofing, and then Paul Gellatt, one of the home owners, finished the refined carpentry. The first floor became the carpentry shop with equipment supplied by Jim, and the second floor became our community center.

Midge MacIlroy wrote a charming article in the November 13, 1983 *Sunday Daily Camera FOCUS* section, "The People Barn: Nick and Suzi Helburn want to raise more than a roof" that describes the barn raising and our hopes for community at the time. She captured some of our spirit: promoting community by creating a cooperative village and making the barn available as a center for community outreach through hosting retreats and workshops and offering resources for non-violence training. She reports on a lunch meeting to clarify goals for a statewide organization we were creating, Colorado Connections, a clearinghouse for progressive projects (we were a bit ahead of our time, before the IT revolution; the project never really got off the ground). In "condominiumizing" the farm we made it available to families who couldn't otherwise own such a property in the country. The HOA created a structure where, as Thea Tenenbaum described it, "You have the isolation when you need it and the community when you need it. Separate yet together." And that separate but equal part appealed most to Nick. "This is a way to share the farm...because it is a privilege to have it. Life is too short to be niggardly... This is our pragmatic phase. We're trying to find a lifestyle involved in profound change even as we're functioning as contributing members of a society we don't always believe in. This is our way of searching, of helping others understand the contradictions they get caught up in."

Above left, Steve and Porn; *above right,* Peter and Sherry;
below, Jim's and Sherry's family

FAMILY

U nfortunately, I don't have much of Nick's accounts to go on to write this section, only the Part III annual letters and the letters to his mother included above. His energy gave out before he got to write much about our family in his memoir. In filling in this hole I will briefly describe our coming together as a family at the beginning of our marriage, and say a bit about the people in our nuclear and extended families and, when possible, their relations with Nick.

What to say about our family over the last forty-three years? Family life and family ties were a crucial part of that balance that Nick sought to achieve in his life. When I met Nick my family was me and Sherry in addition to a small extended family of aunts and cousins. Although family ties were very important to me, enlarging our immediate family beyond the two of us seemed a remote dream. Early on Nick must have tapped into my submerged emotional needs, and they may even have attracted him to me, for he was a great caregiver. We were both ripe for deep commitment to each other and to our children although Nick's attachment to the children may not have been that obvious. Nick wrote me from Leysin, Switzerland, "let's go ahead and make the 'love-in' so deep that it lasts a lifetime and infects all those around us with its warmth."

Weaving together our immediate family worked out quite well, even before we were married. It started when Peter came home from boarding school in Switzerland in December 1968 and Nick and I were seriously "dating." Peter and I really hit it off and he was my ally. At this time Peter's wellbeing was an ongoing concern. I think that for Nick, marriage created the prospect for creating a happy family. In his letters to me Nick continually brought up the children, their welfare, and the prospects of building family. In one of his earliest letters after jumping off the fence he asked how Sherry felt about the possibility of moving from Berkeley to Kalamazoo, and later he suggested that Lesli might want to come with Sherry to ease the transition. Similarly, he was hoping that Peter would want to live with us and suggested that he too could bring a friend.

Nick and Peter came to California to help me move, and we all attended goodbye parties. We spent a lovely pre-marriage honeymoon at Tassajara Hot Springs, but only Sherry came along with some other friends. The children organized our wedding reception. Right after the wedding we had to get to Kalamazoo; it involved moving two households, two cars, two dogs and two unfriendly cats along with three teens and Nick and me. We moved into a big house built in 1910; the three kids each had a bedroom; Peter's cat lived upstairs, ours lived downstairs; the dogs roamed all over, but Lance, the older dog never adjusted and finally had to be put down. Peter decided to retreat and went back to school in Europe, this time to Majorca.

Lesli and Sherry were dismissive of the Michigan kids until forced to integrate by a mom I met in the neighborhood. The girls fixed up the basement room as a pool room, painted it bright red and furnished it with 1920s cast offs. Our trip to Aspen at Christmas to ski further cemented things. I predicted that Peter would break a leg or something that would end up with him moving back to Kalamazoo, and that's exactly what happened. The family really came together when Peter came back from Majorca in January, enrolled in high school, and actually seemed to like it. Lesli had gone back to Berkeley and we were becoming a jolly family. I remember trying to buy liquor with Peter unsuccessfully because the liquor store clerk thought I was underage too. A big compliment! We took turns cooking dinner, turning it into a kind of competition so that everyone became accomplished chefs. Sherry and I got to meet Nick's older son Steve when he came to visit after he got out of the Navy that spring. The trip to Africa with the kids provided another bonding experience; we spent a lot of time together, and Nick and I thought we had knit together our little family.

Moving to Boulder might have been a mistake for Peter. In Kalamazoo he had gotten a job at a travel agency and seemed pretty content. The year in Boulder on 10th Street was somewhat problematic because of my commute to San Jose for the fall semester. The kids and Nick made the most of it, but my coming and going was disruptive. Peter enrolled in a new private school that Nick and I were wary about; it didn't work out for Peter, but we all became friends with Len Barron and a couple of the teachers—Jay Jennings and Jimmy Buener. Peter went on to pass his G.E.D. Hal, Sherry's boyfriend, graduated from high school and came to live with us in the spring.

Peter started a pattern of coming, going, and coming back into family life. He was eighteen, and I guess we thought it was normal behavior. We were not aware of, or not adequately attentive to, a pattern of disquietude in Peter. He was always such fun when he was around, and he stayed close by through the five-year commune experience and rented one of the houses when the commune disbanded. He was very attentive to his mother when she became ill and was with her when she died (a few years after we married). In Part I Nick tells about the trauma surrounding the Blue Note jazz club Peter started. The incident weakened Nick's relationship with Peter, but not his love and enjoyment of being with Peter. He took pride in Peter's accomplishments as an adult and his success in the hospitality business. He joked that it was impossible to have dinner with Peter at a restaurant in Aspen without allowing for the twenty minutes it would take Peter to get through the crowd of other diners to our table. He often repeated a comment made by his Uncle Hugo, "It's amazing what fine young men they grow up to be despite everything we do to them!"

Steve had already left the nest, was in the Navy, married and a new father when Nick and I married. He's a very different guy than Peter, although both sons share Nick's tendency toward workaholism. We have pictures with Nick and his granddaughter Wendy when Steve and Mary were at Oregon State. Steve started out his career at Chicago Bridge and Iron; he and Mary and children (Wendy and Nathan) moved around the country quite a lot. We saw them more when Steve moved to Oceaneering where he worked most of his career, ending high up in management before retiring at a fairly early age. Until the end of his life Nick loved talking endlessly on the phone to Steve about Steve's work. Steve's work required that he travel a lot to oversee projects. He ended his career in Singapore and after retirement settled on his ranch in Wyoming with his second wife Benjaporn—Porn for short, a name that causes a few raised eyebrows. Porn is from Thailand and theirs is a marriage made in heaven. Only an angel could settle so happily in a foreign country on a ranch fifteen miles from the nearest tiny village. Porn and Steve were very attentive to Nick in his last year, as was Peter.

We've been pretty close to Wendy since she moved from Houston to Denver after she finished her architecture degree and apprenticed with our son-in-law Jim Logan. She loved hanging out at the farm, often with her friends. She married another architect, Brent Mather, at the farm, and we became very fond of Brent (despite his libertarian leanings) and his parents—George and Karen. The Mather clan spends every Christmas Eve with us, and Nick enjoyed George's low-key attention to him.

Nate spent some time with us while growing up. We have a lovely picture of Nick showing Nate how to play the baritone recorder. One summer Nate stayed with us and attended a Peace camp in the foothills behind Boulder. Nick thought he was making a convert when Nate got very interested in the peace movement that summer.

I think Sherry was relieved to see me happily married and fairly quickly accepted Nick into the family. Over the years he became her father (her own father always remained remote). However, Nick wasn't that easy to get to know. Possibly his tendency to overwork and his drive created some emotional distance, and, as a generally quiet man, he could be pretty self-contained. Occasionally, he could also erupt. The kids referred to his deep baritone explosions as woofing, unpleasant because they were unexpected from such a taciturn person. Sherry's and Nick's love and respect for each other showed up mostly in deeds rather than in overt shows of affection. But Sherry comments that she appreciated and loved him more and more as an older man as he slowed down and his sweet, gentle disposition, enjoyment of life, and wit predominated.

Sherry and Jim and their children have been the core of our family. We have lived near, sometimes right next door, to each other their whole marriage. We depended on them and they on us. After Jim and Sherry married they included us in their family life which was probably helpful to them, terrific for Nick and me, but also a burden for them. They took responsibility for the transformation of the farm into the present HOA structure. They shepherded the process through the HOA, and Jim took charge of building the barn. We gifted Jim and Sherry their lot on the farm and eventually the hundred outlying acres when we moved in to town.

Over the years, Jim and Nick formed a special bond. They shared a love of the land; Jim helped maintain the acreage, and took over responsibility for it after we left the farm. Towards the end of our life there, he dropped in to see us almost every day; the two truly enjoyed each other's company, although I often bristled at Jim's lectures to us about the perils of aging, specifically about driving. In Nick's last year after the accident Jim kept tabs on Nick almost daily and sat by his side much of the last couple days while Nick was dying.

Jim and Sherry's crew includes four grandchildren: Michael and Joseph, Jim's twins from his previous marriage; Brian, Sherry's and Hal's son; and Dana, Sherry and Jim's daughter. Sherry thinks Nick might have been a better grandfather than father. That's because by the time the grandchildren came along Nicki hardly ever got woofy. And he was free to openly show his affection.

I think we knew Michael and Joseph before we met Jim. They and their mother, Jan, moved in to the old farmhouse about the time the community was breaking up and lived there for a few months. The twins were a big part of the extended family while they were growing up, but they had gone off to college by the time Jim and Sherry moved next to us at the farm. We followed their careers, and Nick was particularly pleased when Michael, influenced by A. O. Forbes (a teacher Nick had mentored), became a teacher himself.

We spent a lot of time with Brian and Dana. Brian said his first sentence at our house after I warned him about picking up bees, repeating "A bumble bee will ting u." Our cat Esmeralda trained him to be properly respectful of cats. He became great friends with our St. Bernard, Didi. He loved the farm tractor. He spent a good deal of time with us, partly because of what we learned from Lelle's Italian parents. We visited Thea Tenenbaum and Lelle Malferrari right after Brian and their son Emiliano were born. Lelle's parents had outfitted a whole room in their apartment in

Bologna for grandchildren to make it easy for their children to leave the grandchildren with them. We set up the same arrangement for Brian, and later, Dana.

We also took the kids to Europe when they got old enough to enjoy it, just before puberty. Brian chose England and we spent a month there when he was thirteen. He visited girls in Scotland he had met earlier during a family summer in Italy and we spent time in London. The most fun was on a canal boat trip with our friends Lou and Pat where Brian got to work the locks and grumble about hiking to pubs at night, also a weekend with my friends, the Skidelski's, who lived in John Maynard Keynes' former country house and introduced Brian to champagne. Robert was trying to make up for Keynes' complaint that the only thing he regretted was that he hadn't drunk enough champagne. Dana chose Italy and as it was a hurried decision to go over spring break. Marjorie Shaw (Insider's Italy) organized a terrific trip starting in Venice, then Florence, Assisi, Rome, and Milan. Dana had just had a year of Greek history so knew all the gods and her parents coached her on what art to see. She was a delight; enjoyed all the restaurants and the attention she attracted as a preadolescent charmer.

Before Dana came along, Sherry miscarried twins, a real blow to us all. Wisely, she got pregnant again, and we promised to take Brian and the baby every other weekend. The kids had their own bedroom in our new house and a swimming pool! Over time, we taught them to eat soft-boiled eggs out of the shell (Sherry didn't like eggs). We introduced them to ballet in Denver. They learned to swim at our house. Probably most important for Nicki, he got to read stories to them, sing them songs at bedtime, and kiss them goodnight. Brian, who lives in Boulder, spent a lot of time with us in Nick's last year. About three nights before Nick died he brought the words to one of Nick's favorite songs, "The fox went out on a snowy night" for us to sing around Nick's bed; that elicited a big smile but there were too many words sung too fast for him to chime in. The next night we sang another favorite and this time Nick sang along with us, "I saw a ship a-sailing, a-sailing on the sea."

In addition to Nick's mother, the elders who were so much a part of our family were David and Helen Loth, Tess's uncle and his wife. They moved to Boulder in their retirement to be close to Peter and us. We saw them constantly, and for a few years before we got our own swimming pool, I swam a couple days a week with David in the pool at Shady Hill Apartments and joined them for breakfast before going off to school in Denver. They became family, and they showed us how to grow old gracefully. The trick, of course, is to live interesting and full lives to begin with. We shared so many parties and dinners, and scintillating conversations. Helen had good eyes and so could drive; David had good legs and could walk, so between them they managed very well and remained totally independent. A couple weeks before Helen died, she joyfully soaked up the late afternoon sun and ambience sitting on our patio at the farm bundled up in a blanket before coming in the house for cocktails and dinner. We were with her when she died from an unfortunate accident. By mistake, starting the car to go shopping, she put it in forward gear instead of reverse and slammed into the wall, and the steering wheel rammed into her frail ribs. When I got to the hospital she was conscious, but told us to take care of David and then told the nurse to "let 'er rip," the painkiller, that is. The next day we were all there while she peacefully passed away. David lived another three years and wrote a wonderful memoir of their life together. In the Part III annual letters (December, 1988) Nick tells of his quiet death. We saw him his last night as he wished us well at the party we were going to.

Nick was very attached to his siblings, Peter and Peg. Peter a bit less so, but they had some common interests—the wilderness, experimental/innovative schools, and female companionship. They were both charmers in their different ways. Pete's wilderness was the ocean. When I knew him he lived part time in Maine in a shack at the end of a dock where he kept his boat and part time in Puerto Rico where he owned another modest dwelling. We visited him both places. Every year he sailed back and forth between Maine and Puerto Rico. Often, sister Peg would sail with him part way. I had my first taste of sailing with Pete and Nick in Puerto Rico and loved it. When we (and Jim, Sherry, Dana, and Brian) were in St Croix one January, staying in the lovely home of parents of a couple who got married at the farm that summer, Peter sailed over to join us; the brothers really enjoyed each other. That was our last visit. At eighty-five Pete, who had always depended on his hands and physical strength for sailing and working, found that arthritis had so crippled him that he could hardly use his hands at all. After some family discussion, one snowy morning he had a couple stiff drinks, took some muscle relaxants, and lay down next to his car to take his final sleep. Nick was deeply moved and admiring of this last act of his older brother.

Peg and Nick became very close in their later years as she settled down in Dougleston after her husband, Eric, retired from the Foreign Service. We visited her frequently in Dougleston, often on our way somewhere else. She visited us almost every summer at the farm. Like Nick, Peg was a worker; unlike Nick, she had a hard time relaxing. Coming to us provided lots of opportunities to do—to garden, to preserve, to mend—and to revel in our affection for each other and for her. She joined us on our trip to Turkey, and I was able to enjoy the carefree Peg. It was a wonderful holiday for us all. Nick joined her in Seattle where she was helping her son Terry recuperate from a brain operation to alleviate seizures. That period was pretty hard on her and Nick came home worried about her. Just after this Pete died. Nick flew back to Vermont for the memorial, met

Peg to drive her to the event and continued to notice a decline in spirit. Soon after she suffered a series of strokes (pretty much the same time that Nick had his stroke). They left her seriously paralyzed on one side of her body. We tried to visit her twice a year in Atlanta where she was moved to be close to her children. She continued to enjoy our visits even as we saw her decline. On our last visit, we all teared up because Peg thought she was going to come home with us, and we had to witness her profound disappointment when she realized that we were leaving without her.

Peg's three children and their children and spouses are the last ring in the immediate family circle: Eric and Kathryn (now divorced), Chris and Kacy, and Debra. Particularly Eric, Kathryn, and Debra have visited us on and off over the years, and we've shared vacations as well. Deb spent a couple summers with us at the farm as a teen and experienced a pretty different life style! They all, I think, became part of the "love-in" that Nick described, that indeed became so deep that it infected those around us. I expect to keep in their family circle.

I haven't described my own family, the most important, my cousins Bette Ann and Rich. Bette Ann and her family lived in Littleton, Colorado, until several years ago, so we visited them and enjoyed the holidays and summer evenings together. The Christmas we moved into the Chicken Coop in 1971 at the beginning of the community, before the bathroom had been installed, Gene, Bette Anne's husband, gave us a gold painted toilet! Bette Ann visited us when we were on sabbatical in England and had to share our living room with Reggie and Bernie (from the commune) on their honeymoon, who were also visiting! And she stayed with us in a wreck of a little hotel in Paris where her room was under the eaves on the sixth floor of a walk up. She was relieved that her husband wasn't there!

Nick really enjoyed my Uncle Coop who was married to my Dad's younger sister Mary. Coop was a great storyteller, humorist, and Democrat, and another gentle, idealistic guy who loved working with his hands building things. He and Nick hit it off as did Nick and his son Rich who shares many of his Dad's endearing masculine traits. Nick fit right into their world view, but we never had enough opportunity to be together, since they live on a farm on the Chesapeake Bay (that Coop bought after he got out of the Navy). Susan Tapper is another first cousin who Nick and I got acquainted with when we were traveling to San Francisco and she and her husband were living in the Bay area.

The other part of my "family" are my in-laws from my first marriage—Jerry's mother and his sister Patty and her four children. Patty and Gam were charmed by Nick and relieved; they had given up hope for me. We visited back and forth over the years; Gam had become part of our family and Nick welcomed her warmly. One amusing incident involving Nick occurred at Gam's eightieth birthday party in L.A., quite an extravaganza of the sort Patty loved organizing. Nick, probably a little bored at the fancy dress dinner, drank quite a bit and gallantly wandered around the room giving selected women gentle backrubs, many of whom were gay and decidedly not interested in Nick's attention! He got a dressing down the next day! We remained closest to Patty's oldest child, Georgia, who spent a summer with us at the farm while she was interning after completing her law degree. Nick gave her away at her wedding, a great treat for him! Debby, her sister, spent a summer in Estes Park when we saw her some, and I keep up with her family.

So much for family. It turns out to be quite crew.

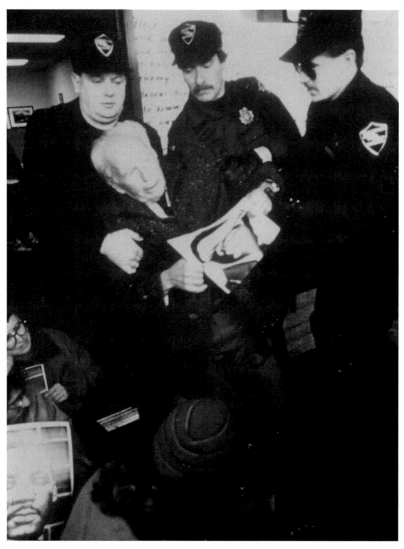

Just before the U.S. invaded Iraq, Nick was one of thirteen demonstrators arrested January 13, 1991, outside the Army Recruiting Center in Boulder.

Beliefs in Action

Nick's Quaker Connection

Although Nick considered himself a nonbeliever, throughout his adult life he maintained a loyalty to the Quaker tradition. In Bozeman, Tess and he hosted the allowed meeting in their living room most Sundays. We were married under the care of the Boulder Meeting. Many of our friends in our early years were members of the Boulder Meeting, and some still are. I am the product of Quaker charity — Ellis College, School for Fatherless Girls, a boarding school I attended from age ten to seventeen, was founded by a Philadelphia Quaker, so I have always had a sentimental attachment to things Quaker, loved marrying a Friend. Nevertheless, after our marriage I didn't always accompany Nick to Meeting and never joined the Meeting.

Even as we were planning our marriage, I was not wholly won over to the Quaker way. I had written to Maggie in May 1969 when we were planning our Quaker marriage that I was happy to agree and become part of it "to a certain extent; I am really not very impressed with most churches, Friends included; there always seems to be too much outward manifestation of goodness which makes me think they think they're good people when I think that most of us are just people." In later years I often preferred using my Sunday morning some other way. Looking back now, I hope I didn't discourage Nick from pursuing his spiritual needs. With the help of Mary Hey we did have a last meeting for worship in our bedroom about three days before Nick died.

One event early in our marriage may have reduced somewhat Nick's long time attachment to the Friend's Meeting. In 1971 when Hal was living with us, he had to register for the draft and was trying to decide whether or not to become a conscientious objector. In Nick's letter to Maggie dated May 24, 1971, he describes Hal's participation in the confrontation/riot between the "Street People" and the police on the "Hill" in Boulder May 21 and 22. Hal went out to join the demonstration and came back, having thrown a mace can back at the police, shouting, "The streets are for the people!"

Nick was asked by the Friend's Meeting to write a statement for the meeting to be presented to the City Council. The Meeting rejected his statement, reproduced below, for a much milder one. This experience may have dampened his loyalty to the Meeting, for he was deeply disappointed. In Nick's 5/25 - 6/7 letter to his mother he comments that the incident reminded him of the conservatism of many members. Here's Nick rejected draft.

Sunday, 5/30/71

Boulder Friends Meeting, Religious Society of Friends, Draft of Statement to the Boulder City Council

With reference to the confrontation of May 21st and 22nd between the "Street People" and the Boulder Police, we express our deep concern and regret at the increase in bad feeling, the destruction of property, and the violence. We appeal for wisdom, for policies which will lead to long term solutions.

We understand the feelings and financial losses of the vocal minority who speak for the so-called business community, but these losses, real and painful as they are, cannot justify rash and repressive measures. The road to totalitarianism is paved with decisions to punish non-conformity, to drive out unpopular minorities. We are not calling anyone a communist or a fascist. We only point the direction repressive policies will lead us.

The problem must not be approached as a WE/THEY antagonism. It is a problem because it exists within our community and in the connections between our community and the rest of the country. The street people are a part of us.

The street people are our children. Some literally are members or former members of our families. The rest are the children of our equivalents in other towns and cities across the land. They are a part of us.

Their condition is not well understood but partly it comes from the meaninglessness of our schools and the emptiness of our homes; partly it comes from the absence of satisfying work opportunities; results from a rapidly changing culture, and partly it is a stage of life they are growing through. We need to know much more about them if we are to solve our problem wisely and we urge the opening of communication and serious study and discussion. The hearings of the Human Relations Commission might be directed to that end.

Why the street people choose to congregate in Boulder is not clear, though some of the reasons they like Boulder are the same as the reasons we like it: Beauty and friendliness and freedom. We cannot make Boulder unpleasant for them without making it unpleasant for us. They are a part of us.

Why they choose to congregate on the Hill is also unclear. There is nothing so attractive about the south side of College between 13th & 14th until it becomes a game between the street people and the police. Ten days ago we learned that the tensions of the game could increase to explosive force. We must learn to relax the tensions, or better yet to call off the game, possibly by providing some uncontested turf for the street people.

We too believe in law and order and justice administered equally to all members of the community. Even Quakers use obscene language occasionally. If street people are to be arrested for swearing, so should we. There is no legal way to drive out the "uninvited transients." If we distort the legal system with special laws and discriminatory enforcement to carry out the mandate "They must go," we brutalize ourselves and them. We who were on the hill the 22nd and 23rd are very much aware of how little violence it takes to get a large increase in hatred. We would be driving our own sons and daughters from their homes and into the repression of other intolerant cities, and thence to revolution.

We support the city council and Judge Hansen in using what discretion they have toward cooling the tensions. We know how difficult it is for the police to restrain themselves in the face of abuse and provocation. But a policeman's lot was never a happy one. Keeping the peace does require restraint by those in power. We urge the council to avoid the kind of rigid legislation which cannot take into account all cases, and which so often prevents purposes of government being served.

We appeal for more information about the street people, more widely shared.

We appeal for equal treatment under just laws for everyone.

Finally we urge the Mayor and all others who can support him to call for a national conference on the subject of homeless and alienated young adults. Part of what has paralyzed Boulder and kept it from allocating good public facilities to the street people is the fear that 100,000 more would congregate here. Such fears can only be allayed when we have a better picture of the problem nationally and when we have the assistance of federal experimental legal funds.

To borrow the phrase from the spokesmen for the business community, remember that on this earth, we are all "uninvited transients."

Aesthetics and the Wildness Continuum

It should be clear by now how much Nick adored the outdoor experience, how little patience he had with Harvard Square/Ivy League snobbishness, with urban living at all. His father never succeeded in convincing him about the delights of intellectual sparring, although we remember Nick's habit of inserting unexpected, amusing, often sobering comments into "serious" conversation; and he did follow his father's advice in adopting courtly good manners (for me, one of his endearing qualities).

Nick moved West and never looked back. The further removed he was from the constructed environment, the happier he was. No wonder he chose geography as a profession. Often he would say to me that geography allowed him to keep his feet on the ground and his head in the skies. Beauty, particularly natural beauty, was a core value. His eye for beauty extended to the arts, crafts, architecture. I suspect that his love of women had something of an aesthetic base.

The three houses he built and lived in are more-or-less permanent monuments to his aesthetic imagination. In his memoir he describes the Neutra Montana house and Tall Timbers outside Boulder. Equally significant is the house our son-in-law Jim Logan designed for us at the farm on Nelson Road. They all fit into and take advantage of a specific, handsome place in the country. Interiors are lit by sun in the day and stars at night. They are simple and elegant. They made use of natural light and heat and cooling as much as possible. Our house at the farm used the indoor swimming pool (a gift to me to compensate for my commute to

Denver to work) and solar panels to heat the house. Even our last home together, our apartment at 1140 Portland Place, chosen by Nick, is surrounded on three sides by floor to ceiling windows and patios so that sun flows in all day.

Nick wrote about the wildness continuum that he thought an essential part of city and land use planning. In the Appendix is his paper, "The Wildness Continuum," from the November 1977 issue of *The Professional Geographer*. He begins, "There appears to be a profound need among human beings for things natural, that is, nonhuman. This paper asserts that…this human tendency can best be understood as a continuum in which the Bronx petunia and the ski wilderness are extremes." He argues that one component of the outdoor recreational experience is an increment of wildness. And there are different demands by different folks. Some are content with the urban park, others want to get out of town, some need to experience true wilderness areas. He argues that "recognizing a variety of resources and a variety of users provides the recreational planner with the conceptual framework for taking advantage of opportunities available to offer areas of different degrees of naturalness." And "The wildness continuum raises serious doubt about the further extensions of motorized access to wild lands. It points rather to the 'wildening' of attractive sites close to population centers."

> Our conclusion is manifest in truths that seem familiar, that the good life is balanced with some civilization, some wildness, some downtown and some Walden. We all need a change of scene, but some of our frantic escape from the city derives from the one-sidedness of the city. Recognizing the universal need for naturalness in our lives, we can build and care for more harmonious landscapes across the whole continuum.

AAG Presidency and Retirement from the Profession

Nick touches only briefly on his involvement with the AAG, the Association of American Geographers, and he is very modest in describing his accomplishments as a geographer. In fact, he was well thought of in the profession although he did not make his reputation through the usual publication route, but rather as a leader who could mediate among diverse groups of individuals. (Perhaps Willard correctly forecast Nick's talents in that 1940 letter to Tess.) As the Director of the High School Geography Project he managed a highly complex initiative that is still recognized as a model of educational reform. During the five years with HSGP he worked with illustrious and imaginative colleagues who participated in developing the curriculum materials. The project had an important impact on college teaching of geography. Also, he successfully led the Geography Department in Colorado to become one of the distinguished departments in the country. Within the profession he helped female geographers break through the traditional male hierarchy.

In 1981-82, Nick served as President of the AAG. Dave Hill notes that his election was unprecedented because he was a write-in candidate and the successful write-in campaign was conducted by an informal women's caucus who were struggling for recognition in the AAG. The women thought it was important to have Nick in this important position in order to balance the otherwise more conservative people running the Association. Since Nick's presidency, the AAG has had at least six women presidents. In the seventy-five years prior to his presidency, only one woman was elected president. It was also the first time a member of the University of Colorado Department was elected to this prestigious position.

His Presidential Address, "Geography and the Quality of Life," was delivered In San Antonio, Texas April 27, 1982 (*Annals of the Association of American Geographers*, 72(4), 1982, pp. 445-456). As a kind of swan song to his professional colleagues he reminds them of their responsibility to promote "the quality of life," both in their personal lives and as policy makers. The speech resonates with me because he uses illustrations from our personal life together and because it is such a clear expression of his world view. Typical of Nicki he wrote on my copy, "Trusting we can work together to improve the quality of our lives. Love Nick."

Nick starts the essay:

> Geography has had a lot to do with the quality of my life. Geographers can and should have a lot to do with the quality of life in America—indeed in the world. I choose the subject because it gives me a double opportunity. First, I make explicit the joy of understanding our surroundings...a joy that enriches our lives and those of our students. Second, I demonstrate the importance of quality of life as a primary public policy goal and express my concern about the current framework which evaluates policy narrowly in terms of economic costs and benefits.

He points out that quality of life has two meanings: "one personal, the other environmental; one internal, the other external; one quite subjective, the other more objective." The first meaning refers to the quality of an individual's life and this starts with our own "experience—whether it be conscious awareness, perceiving, remembering, imagining, thinking, feeling..." The second and broader meaning refers to life in a certain society or place, "the extent to which the necessary conditions exist for a good quality of life in the region or state." The two meanings interact; one uses one's personality and abilities to achieve satisfaction within a milieu created by the second meaning, but he emphasizes that part of a person's satisfaction is based on his or her contribution to the shared environment.

For Nick, the major contribution geography makes to our personal lives is aesthetic—from understanding and appreciating what goes on around us. It widens our horizons and also provides vicarious experience. This is not just a matter of our personal satisfaction.

… insofar as we share these understandings with others—our families, our clients, our students—we empower them to share the joys of geography. In our teaching, both formal and informal, we spread the knowledge of process and its connection to place, we share an ecological way of thinking, heightening the relational view of events and things; we contribute a model of the world into which our students can fit data and generalizations. From all of this they derive deeper understanding and thereby lead richer lives. This is part of a liberating education.

As a policy goal, Nick identifies and then discredits the criticisms that have been leveled at using "quality of life" as a public policy goal, ending with an amusing jibe at those who discredit the goal because it runs counter the goal of "progress" which he defines as "that which, in retrospect, we observe to have occurred." The force of his disdain, however, for what he rightly considers an ideological objection, relates to the close connection of the discipline to economics when operating in the public policy arena. He states, "For when the improvement of the quality of life is proposed as the ultimate goal of public policy, economic efficiency, productivity and growth are reduced to instrumental goals: they are useful only insofar as the contribute to the quality of life." The connection with economics is strengthened by the division of the social sciences into separate disciplines and the tendency of many geographers to adopt the "homoeconomicus" model and its underlying ideology. Nick considers the disciplinary approach a barrier to studying public policy problems and illustrates the superiority of a complex holistic view over narrower (often "quantifiable") economic goals using the case of the struggle over rural electrification.

In policy applications of the quality of life goal it is the geographer's role to "speak up for space" to "defend and promote the livability of places." Cities, in particular, because of their scale and disorganization, have lost their sense of neighborhood and foster a sense of powerlessness. We should redesign cities to recreate a sense of neighborliness to share activities and skills and help each other when needed, so that the people feel a sense of participation. He proposes the following directions geographers should take:

To reduce alienation and fear;
To increase the number and quality of social interactions and the cohesiveness of social groups;
To improve the aesthetics of all places but especially public places;
To optimize variety and stimuli in the landscape;
To provide for the activities that increase a person's sense of competence, that encourage active participation as against passive reception;
To protect the public interest in private land;
To delay life-threatening, nonreversible decisions as long as possible, for we may find a better way;
To foster the ecological health of the wider community—that includes humankind as well as other living things.

Nick concludes on geographers' political responsibilities.

> When the industrial complex teams up with the military establishment in a way that threatens all life on the planet, geographers who have a global perspective and who are sensitive to the ecology of human life, have some extra obligation to speak out. You may not be ready to grant that centralized corporate power dominates our political and economic system, but if you are, the remainder of the argument follows logically. Corporate profit drives a system that cannot care for the natural environment nor for equity among the peoples of the world. A transformation must take place to preserve life. Indeed it is already taking place.
>
> In the next decade we need much more geography that overtly recognizes the ideology of the present political economy. We need study and debate:
> - On the processes that bring about the deterioration of the environment,.
> - On the processes that widen the inequities,
> - On the processes that decrease the concern for the public interest.
>
> ...In both our applied research and our theoretical work, geographers who want to make a difference must take into account the profound power relations in the world. Then our own lives are enriched as we facilitate the fundamental changes that can improve the quality of all human life.

Nick retired from the Geography Department in May 1989. At the time of retirement David Greenland, the Department chair, summarized his influence in the Department. Elected department chair in 1971, he served until 1975, "a period of great change: rapidly rising enrollments and a large number of new faculty. During this time of instability, and subsequently as Director of Graduate Studies, Nick's leadership in the department set a much-needed tone, that is, that we should actually listen to one another! Then, and to this day, Nick keeps dialog going and he makes our decision-making more democratic. But he does not withhold his own strong convictions. He speaks forcefully to us on matters of principle: Teaching and students are important to him and when he thinks we have let other things get in the way, he tells us so. He reminds us of our responsibilities to pursue affirmative action. Social justice and the quality of life are important to him."

David summarized Nick's contribution to geographic education over and above directing the High School Geography Program. (Earlier, in 1975, Nick was honored at Montana State University for the growth and success of the Department of Earth Sciences that he chaired from 1946-1964.) These included: developing and teaching a graduate seminar in geographic education, participating in the NSF funded Teaching and Learning in Graduate Geography Project, developing a very successful self-paced course in introductory physical geography that used undergraduate tutors in a Personalized System of Instruction that encouraged mastery learning of the course content, teaching for his last four years in the summer institutes for secondary school teachers applying his earlier experience from HSGP. One teacher from the last summer institute wrote a letter of appreciation of Nick saying he was the "soul" of the institute. The final tribute: "Now, tonight, we would like to say to Nick. Thanks Nick. We appreciate you. You are the soul of our department."

Nick's Activism

Except for the last few years of his life Nick participated actively in the peace movement—through writing, speaking in public forums or on KGNU, demonstrating, getting arrested, working for the Rocky Mountain Peace and Justice Center. His seventeen years at Montana State were also marked by activism and controversy. He was investigated during the McCarthy era. Nevertheless, he successfully defended the right of pacifist Hutterites in Montana to vote (there was a move in the state legislature to deprive them of the right on grounds of their lack of patriotism). And he successfully confronted the American Legion when they opposed his invitation to Bayard Rustin, a politically leftist openly gay black man, to speak on the Bozeman campus and the University of Montana in Missoula.

In 1977 Nick was involved in Boulder in the nationwide campaign, The Mobilization for Survival. Delegations of more than one hundred non-aligned nations had called a Special Session on Disarmament to be held at the U.N. in New York in May-June 1978. The Mobilization was a multi-issue coalition that grew out of a gathering of peace activists from all over the world in Hiroshima in August that year to plan a year of internationally coordinated popular actions to put pressure on governments to work for disarmament.

Nick channeled most of his activism in Boulder and Colorado through the Boulder Friends Meeting and, after its formation in 1983, the Rocky Mountain Peace and Justice Center where he joined causes with LeRoy Moore, his best friend during his later years. One of the first actions was a protest march from Boulder to close Rocky Flats in October 1983. In preparation we organized an "affinity group" and helped surround the Rocky Flats installation. Ours was the Rosa Luxemburg group.

Nick had been alert to the horrendous environmental impact of Rocky Flats on the Denver metropolitan area. As early as May 1978 he had testified at a public hearing on a Draft Environmental Impact Statement about the diffusion of plutonium and its impact on the nearby populations, wildlife, drainage and other technical matters. He continued to appear at public hearings on Rocky Flats in 1990 through 1992, testifying as a geographer about the problems of risk assessments. In 1992, as part of the Rocky Flats Alliance he worked to prevent the resumption of production at the site. In testimony delivered January 16, 1992:

> I have testified before as a geographer that toxic chemicals are impossible to contain absolutely and indefinitely, that they diffuse along predictable vectors leaving the northern part of the Denver metropolis at greatest risk from Rocky Flats. In safety considerations there is no such thing as absolute safety and

therefore risk must be balanced against need. Since there is no demonstrable need we should take no risk whatsoever....

At best the Denver metropolis is at risk from the nuclear waste already in, under, and around the Rocky Flats plant. All of us concerned for safety should be sure that no more waste is generated. For every gram of plutonium increases the danger. The intractable waste problem is reason enough in itself to prevent the opening of the laboratory in question and to preclude any further plutonium testing or production.

Thank you for your attention. We value your sincere devotion to the protection of the workers at the plant and the public in general.

Meanwhile Nick continued to take an active role promoting peaceful responses to international tensions. In April 1985 he took part in a two week long series of events organized by the Community in Action to Resist the CIA, (events concurrent, I think with the World Affairs Conference) highlighting the CIA illegal activities in Central America—mining of Nicaragua's harbors, arming and training the "contra" forces, creating the Death Squads in El Salvador and Guatemala. In response to the CIA recruiting at CU, they formed a committee to carry out a Citizen's arrest of the CIA recruiters when they arrived on campus April 9 and organized picketing and a support rally. All participants were required to attend non-violence training before hand.

Nick was one of 172 people (mostly students) arrested the first day of the three-day nonviolent protest. At the rally protestors trying to make a citizens' arrest of the CIA recruiters deliberately crossed police lines to force police to arrest them. The day before Nick spoke:

I want to tie tomorrow's citizen arrest to the evolution of our legal system, the law and order that permits our peaceful existence.

There is something wrong now when Union Carbide kills thousands and cannot be tried for murder, not even manslaughter.

There is something wrong when Johns-Manville in their asbestos operation kills and maims hundreds and there is no death penalty or life imprisonment for the corporation.

There is something wrong when the CIA kills and maims hundreds, does it in violation of international and national law—and does not get prosecuted.

Instead it is protected in its conspiracy by the Police and by C.U.

We need to invent the legal mechanisms to hold the corporations and the agencies responsible.

The first page of the April 10 *Denver Post* shows Nick with three of the organizers crossing campus police lines to be arrested. The *Post* reported that "CU officials, protestors, and police praised each other for maintaining the peace. Police and protesters acted so friendly that officers did not use handcuffs." By the end of the three days the rally had grown significantly with singing and speeches and joining of hands around an enormous peace sign. In all, 477 people were arrested and Community in

Action called on the University to create a panel of enquiry into allegations of wrong-doing by the CIA.

Nick made headlines again in March 1987, this time in the *Daily Camera* and the *Longmont Times Call,* as one of four participants in a well attended Peace Panel sponsored by the Boulder Meeting of Friends and RMPJC. The *Camera* featured Nick the day before the panel, interviewing him about his experience as a conscientious objector. Nick told the staff writer that he realized he made a mistake "soon after he entered the CO camp. My doubts were that I registered at all.... I had a sense that I had compromised." Given another chance he would refuse to register for the draft. He would "make a public declaration of draft resistance and risk criminal charges and a five-year jail sentence."

Here is a short essay Nick wrote March 1, 1987, that he may have used at the Peace Panel.

> I am a conscientious objector to war, all war, and consider myself a pacifist. I have avoided violence against persons and hope to continue to do so. Further, I hope that I can live my life so as to reduce the occasions for war and for violence.
>
> War and violence do not solve problems. They resolve power relations between competing states. The states themselves are built on violence or the threat thereof.
>
> Only the refusal to participate in the organized, state-violence and by generating a society held together by familiarity and love and trust can we live in a good society.
>
> Thus, I not only refuse to serve in the military forces and all those institutions that support the military, I try to find and develop those institutions and ways of living which encourage face-to-face relations and mutual trust. I find the draft, the intelligence agencies and the "military industrial" complex all to be institutions supportive of and supported by warfare and organized violence.
>
> I have been exploring and developing a life that is less dependent on the market economy and more dependent on close personal interactions with other families. I have diverted symbolic amounts of taxes, and am interested in exploring the tax protest further.
>
> Most of these beliefs were not developed from formal religious institutions. Their foundation must have been the valuing of truth and sincerity, intelligence and personal integrity in my parental family. They were intensified by experience and by discussions in student movements as an undergraduate while the United States was preparing for its entry to World War II. Contact with the Society of Friends, worship in Quaker Meeting and Service with the American Friends Service Committee further developed the convictions and their application to social, economic and political problems....
>
> I have been a member of the Society of Friends since late 1943 and have been active from time to time in the work of the American Friends Service Committee.
>
> In the last 15 years I have been experimenting with communal or cooperative life styles where several families can live in close association

with one another sharing in subsistence production and processing and supporting one another emotionally and spiritually. I hope to continue such experiments and the diffusion of such ideas in my personal, civic and professional life.

Recorded here in Boulder County at 3743 Nelson Road, March 1st, 1987. Nicholas Helburn

Fast forward to the First Gulf War. November 12, 1990, Nick wrote a guest opinion in the *Longmont Daily Times-Call* that prompted an angry letter to the paper, "Helburn's Marxist Analysis." In Nick's statement he recognizes the complex situation in the Persian Gulf/Middle East, but comments that the media oversimplifies with thirty-second sound bites. He comments, "Not since the Spanish-American War, when yellow journalism pushed Teddy Roosevelt up San Juan Hill, has the American press been so one-sidedly warlike." He suggests chipping away at the euphemisms used to justify the use of force, in this case "stability" is one of the words, since everyone is in favor of stability. He points out the inherent instability of the region with the tiny countries with their artificial boundaries and with the oppression of Palestine Arabs. "Maybe Americans are ready to go to war to protect the price of gasoline. But let's not be deluded that we do it for the sake of stability in the Middle East."

Just before the U.S. invaded Iraq, Nick was one of thirteen demonstrators arrested January 13, 1991, outside the Army Recruiting Center at 30th and Walnut Streets in Boulder. Partly in celebration of Martin Luther King, "Protesters carried pictures of King and recited a litany about him before the 13 people sat down in front of the recruiting center's doors." Other protesters were somewhat more rowdy, blocking the intersection and throwing red paint at the recruiting center. The January 15, 1991, headline of the *Daily Camera* read: "COUNTDOWN FOR WAR Police arrest 13 at Boulder protest." Our friend, Mayor Leslie Durgin watched the arrests, listened to complaints and remarked, "It's typical Boulder. There are strong feelings on all sides of an issue." Nick is in two pictures, one being carried off very delicately by three police officers (including an ex-student of Nick's) and another with his hands cuffed behind his back waiting in the police wagon. Nick explained that with the heavy coat and a recent injury to his left shoulder he was in quite a bit of pain and the police officers were trying to remove him without doing more damage.

January 26 Nick spoke at the Longmont Peace Vigil about the arrest and the need to build a peace movement. He recounts,

We felt pretty good about the civil disobedience action. It was fully in the spirit that King would have approved of. The next afternoon we got the news that the bombing had started.

Like so many others, I was deeply depressed. My wife was away. I spent the whole day at home alone. Then the invitation came to participate in this vigil and I accepted. For the die was cast. The protests had been in vain. Now it was senseless death and destruction. By evening I had recovered. I knew what I had to say.

We must continue to show our opposition to mass murder.

We must continue to show our empathy for all the brothers and sisters, sons and daughters doing the fighting. They are a source of our concern.

We must build an enduring peace movement. It's not enough to have an anti-war movement. We need to learn to live in peace.

We must try to keep the system open. The first casualty of war is truth. We don't get news from the gulf, we just get military public relations....

The second casualty of war is freedom. Military personnel and reservists have already lost theirs....

There is another group of who is hurting worst and especially need our support. They are the men and women in the military who disagree with the ambitions of the generals and the power elite....

And all the time we need to build peace...

And we must build peace in our own lives,

Lives built on cooperation and community along with competition and individual fulfillment.

Lives of trust and truth, not deception.

Lives of understanding and consensus, not orders from above.

Lives that radiate love. There is no room for hate.

This was Martin Luther King's Dream. We can learn to live that dream.

In 2003 we were again embroiled in a war in Iraq. July 3, 2008, Pamela White interviewed Nick for an article in the *Boulder Weekly*, "From World War II to Iraq: Elders compare the patriotism of the 'greatest generation' to that of today." Nick responded that although one might assume that refusing to kill Nazis would be seriously frowned on, that he didn't find that.

> I really expected more discrimination, more semi-violent reactions, and on the whole I had a fairly easy time of it.... There was certainly some prejudice against us, some feeling against us, but not much. Even among the veterans and active members of the armed services, why, the attitude was "Well, this is what we're fighting for—the acceptance of differences of opinion."

Comparing the social climate of the 1940's with today:

> I think that the educated public is probably more skeptical in the sense [of believing] that patriotism is "that last refuge of scoundrels" [quoting Samuel Johnson]....
>
> Among the less educated part of the public, I'm not sure that's the case, but it seems to be in the more educated part.... The less educated are more of the flag waving type, and those who are educated are too skeptical to do that...We can sing "The Star Spangled Banner," but the reality doesn't measure up to it.... That's probably the greatest thing. Within the memory of a lot of us, we've seen too many wars that ended with no tangible improvement.

The appendices include two essays Nick wrote that show his pene-
trating insights on two subjects he had thought a lot about. First is a 1993
essay raising questions about what position peace activists should take on
the use of military personnel on humanitarian missions, and about the mil-
itarization of the United Nations. The second is a 2001 essay, "A Primer
on Islam." Both essays still seem relevant.

Nick devoted himself to the work of the Rocky Mountain Peace and
Justice Center (RMPJC). In 2002 RMPJC honored him by naming him the
Elise Boulding Peacemaker of the Year, an honor RMPJC bestows on one
or more people every year. For Nick's award the News Alert from RMPJC
read, "Nick Helburn has been a positive presence in Boulder for decades.
A revered teacher to several generations of students and a professor
respected by his colleagues at the university, he is known by some as a
voice of wisdom on the radio, by others as a pioneer of sustainable living,
by yet others as a leader of the community movement. The Helburn farm
on Nelson Road north of Boulder has been a setting for experiments on
how to live well with people and the planet."

"Nick will be 84 years old in December," remarked LeRoy Moore, one
of the founders of the Peace and Justice Center, "but in spirit he's as
refreshing as a spring breeze. He's a man of parts.... His vision of peace
encompasses natural ecology, right livelihood, community-building,
respect for the individual, politics of consent and consensus rather than
war, and an economics of need not greed."

In his introductory remarks at the Peacemaker award LeRoy had this
to say about Nick:

> The work of peacemaking can be difficult. There are things with which one
> must deal. In the case of Nick Helburn, women find him irresistible and men
> regard him as a role model. What impediments! It's enough to drive one to
> drink, in moderation of course....
>
> In face-to-face situations peace can be elusive, and Nick was at times put
> to the test. But I've noticed his ability to be surprised at nothing and, when
> human relations break down, to put feelings aside and to go on, with an
> almost stubborn resolve that you can't stop living and that the suspended con-
> versation will resume in time.
>
> It's been my privilege to observe Nick in varied settings. In the many meet-
> ings we've attended together I've seen him fade and go to sleep right in the
> middle of what to everyone else is a lively exchange. Then, just when I thought,
> he's gone, he'd stir, smile, get that wondering look on his face, and begin to speak
> right on cue with a pointed story or a poignant observation, maybe to explain
> the origin of the peace sign or of the dove with the olive branch on its beak.
>
> Ah Nick, charm us, woo us, win us to peace. May your tribe increase.

Nick's own opening and closing remarks at the event are revealing:

> Thank you! Thank you from the half of me that still works, that is able to walk
> and build a fire and do the shopping, etc. And thank you from the other half

of me that has trouble writing a sentence, that gets messily distracted, that forgets the end of a thought half way through. I am grateful for the 83 years I was whole. I am deeply gratified by this recognition tonight, noting that I have not been alone. All of you here, and many who are not, have supported and worked in common cause with me. You too deserved to share the credit. Thank you....

Two more thoughts:

When I began to work with LeRoy Moore here at the Peace Center I read an essay in which he made the distinction between "power over" and "power with." That simple substitution of one preposition for another seemed to clarify a whole bunch of things:

The egalitarian community,

The need for consensus decision-making,

The horizontal rather than vertical (hierarchical) organization,

The inquiry style of teaching,

The way one uses consultants,

The dangers of over-specialization,

The respect for all human beings.

With this in mind, we remember that

Security is neither in your possession, nor in mine.

It lies forever between us.

If each of us could restrain the childish desire to snatch for ourselves,

We could live forever in mutual trust.

Thank you.

On lake crossing from Chile to Argentina 2006

End of Life

The last several years of his life Nick and LeRoy Moore celebrated their birthdays, December 20 and 7 respectively, together in a big party where they also raised money for RMPJC. It was always fun and a chance to get our many local friends together. In Nick's files I found a tribute to him on his eighty-fifth birthday written by one of our special friends, Philip Gordon, with whom we had gone to Cuba in 1978.

> When I think of Nick Helburn I think of geography. And when I think of geography, I think of integration. So it's no surprise then that I think of Nick as an integrator—of places, of people, of times and ideas. Of soil and seasons and crops and diet. Of traditions and aspirations, of principles and practice.
>
> Like many of us here, I have known Nick for many years, in fact, about half of my lifetime. And for all of us here, it would be very difficult to imagine how different it would have been for us not to have had Nick as friend, mentor, companion, comrade, teacher, confidante, and role-model.
>
> Above all, Nick bridges the militarized zones so prevalent between the individual and community. I sensed that first in Cuba, where on a beach one day a group of us (mostly from Boulder) ran into a group of Russians. It was 1978, and while the 2 groups may have shared a profound appreciation of Cuban beaches and rum (and perhaps even that country's apparent nobility), we had no common language. But Nick proceeded to draw a world map in the sand to help us all explain where we had come from. It was one thing to point out the Rocky Mountains on the map, but Nick also traced the Volga.
>
> Many of us have the ability to identify where we've come from, or even where we individually would like to go. But Nick has helped so many to understand where we are in a context that doesn't seem to polarize the individual or community. In so doing he illustrates how community does not have to mean what the term is used for nowadays—as in the "intelligence community" or the "gay community" or the "downtown business community" or the "peace community." A community is, after all, not a special interest, but a place of integrated interests.
>
> And Nick has helped me integrate matters of disparate size—as in being interested in big things and happy in small ways.
>
> In short, Nick is a *mensh*, wise even beyond HIS years. And, if wisdom is really just good judgment in hard times, consider the definition of *mensh*, then, as character; rectitude; dignity; and a clear sense of what is ethically imperative.

Perhaps you know this exemplary definition of *mensh* (which would certainly have prompted our friend Larry Senesh to have said, "Don't make me drool"). Anyway, does or doesn't this definition of *mensh* fit Nick? The mensh is the guy who opened the door to the bathroom and there—completely naked—stood a beautiful woman. He gulped, cleared his throat, eyes downward, then backing out said, "Excuse ME sir..."

Nick had trouble adjusting to the disabilities of aging. He was such a vigorous outdoor kind of guy. Nick often claimed that when the time came he would like to walk off in to the snow and peacefully die. In July 1989 LeRoy undertook a twenty-four-day fast on the state capitol grounds, the "Fast in Solidarity with all Victims of Rocky Flats," after an unsuccessful attempt to get Governor Romer to call on the Department of Energy to halt production until it could be demonstrated that it could be done safely. Nick joined him to fast for three days. While there he thought a lot about end of life and wrote me this letter on June 26, transcribed on July 30, 1989.

Dear Suzi:

During the meditation this morning on the capitol lawn I spent some time on the cooperation I will need when I decide to end my life. I know this is a distasteful subject and I assure you that I have not immediate plans. But it seems to me that there are several reasons to consider not just letting nature take its course. It might be OK if it was "nature" but it is badly complicated by high tech medicine.

One reason has to do with economics or perhaps efficiency is a better word. Most of one's life one hopes to contribute to the general welfare more than one consumes. Toward the end, in retirement, it's OK to coast, to use up some of that accumulated surplus, to enjoy the "fruits of ones labor." But at some point it seems immoral to keep on drawing down the general account, especially as the satisfactions decline.

Another aspect of the efficiency consideration has to do with the time it takes to take care of oneself. We all depend on others to some extent for our personal care. But when one cannot reach his toe nails, someone else has to trim them. And when one cannot button the shirt or change the bed or drive oneself to the doctor's appointment or—or—, one becomes a drain on other people's lives.

A hospice nurse here on the lawn asserts that there is a positive aspect to being dependent, that people learn and gain in taking care of others, that being dependent is in some sense a gift that one can give in old age. It will take me a while to think this one thru.

Another dimension is the pain/gratification ratio. At some point the pain of living must exceed the pleasure. At that point it would seem that keeping someone alive would be a form of torture. The courage of those who continue to bear the pain is an admirable example—but when it is not temporary, it seems an unnecessary form of martyrdom.

Perhaps the most important dimension is the degradation. I don't know quite how to phrase it. If maturity and capability are ideals, then senility and infirmity are departures from the ideal. What value is there in the decline? As long as humor and wisdom and service to others survive, one accepts the decline of powers graciously.

The usual phrase is "I don't want to be remembered as—," but that seems rather vain. It seems rather that having strived to be competent (and continent), one shouldn't have to suffer incompetence and incontinence.

But what I started out to think thru was not the justification for cutting off the final stage or stages of decline, but various scenarios, various forms of decline and the clues of when it would be appropriate to let go.

A sudden stroke, heart attack, or accident resulting in irreversible loss of function or of consciousness seems like the simplest case. If it is a coma, I trust that as soon as it is clearly a case where the chances of resuming a full life are negligible, all life support systems will be withdrawn. Then indeed nature can take its course.

If after the accident, stroke or heart attack, I am conscious but somehow unable to act for myself, then presumably I'd need some help in bringing what would then be a "half-life" or less, to a graceful end. Actually the three day fast which did not involve any pain, points to not eating as a perfectly appropriate way of moving nature along.

The very gradual loss of functions and competence with the accompanying very gradual increments of pain and dissatisfaction seems like the most difficult scenario. When to call it quits? When one can no longer drive? When one cannot live alone with the traditional partner and has to move into a nursing home? Both of these seem like places where there is a marked loss of control, making suicide more difficult. But both are times when others are involved in the decision. In making the decision, which then would be followed by the suicide, they would tend to hold themselves responsible for the suicide, which of course they are not? What to do about that?

Between these two extremes, the sudden heart attack and the long slow decline there must be an infinite and depressing combination of sequences. In general, loss of physical abilities seems less troublesome than mental competence, though continence does seem especially important.

And that's as far as I got. I've added a little in the process of transcribing. Basically all I need from others is honesty about their feelings and their non-interference when I feel that the time has come for me to quit. But maybe I need more than this and don't realize what I will need at this time.

Love,

Although Nick could be very expressive of his inner thoughts and feelings on paper, he didn't tend to verbalize them. He kept his own counsel. I often commented to friends that Nick was one of the few people I knew who was not neurotic; he seemed quite comfortable in his own skin, although it took some time and work to manage this kind of equanimity. In our long marriage, although I loved him deeply, I can't say that I really "knew" him. He remained a mystery, a reassuring, wonderful presence that I didn't quite comprehend even though I was pretty good at predicting his behavior.

Nick lived another twenty-two years and during that time he successfully recovered from quintuple bypass surgery that strengthened his heart and a small stroke that weakened his balance and almost put an end to skiing, and weakened his voice some, but I thought he recovered beautifully. He never complained to me (our wonderful family therapist, Joan Block, who we used occasionally, provided a confidential presence when he needed it). He did struggle sometimes with depression for a couple years after the stroke as he learned to cope with his aging. It was hard for him to give up his active physical life and his own sense of being useful. But we knew we had to move into town when he could no longer chop wood or use the chain saw regularly! When we did relocate, he really succeeded in relaxing into old age.

His pain/gratification ratio must have stayed well below one into the last month of his life. I think he learned the wisdom of that hospice nurse that being dependent is a gift to the caregiver. After coming home from the hospital having recovered from another congestive heart failure three weeks before he died, I asked him if he wanted to go back to the hospital if he has another attack; his reply: "Why not?" But the next day he wasn't so sure.

Of the different scenarios he mentioned in the letter he ended up valiantly trying and almost succeeding in healing broken bones in his leg and hip from a freak accident the year before he died on our way to Tassajara Hot Springs in June 2010 to celebrate my eightieth birthday. He still enjoyed living. He was mentally competent, and mostly continent, to the end. He died peacefully surrounded by love, at home June 11, 2011.

The afternoon of July 8, 2010, our friend Kathleen Kellaher visited Nick in the cardiovascular wing of Boulder Community Hospital where Nick was recovering from a massive, almost fatal bout with congestive heart failure after his second operation to stabilize his right leg. I had been spending most nights with him in the hospital. Kathleen recalls that Nick was cold and she pulled covers up over his shoulders. "But then, after a late afternoon thunderstorm, the sun came out and it shone through the window and across Nick as he lay there looking out the big window at the foothills. As Nick warmed up, he asked me to take off one layer after another until his whole upper body was bared and taking in the sun. There he lay, quite peacefully, with his chest all wired up, his freshly cut beard… soaking in the sunshine.

> I asked Nick several questions….I wanted to have—I needed to have—one more conversation with Nick before I headed down the road and before he passed on to a better life. I asked him to delve into his past, and he brightened and energized as he gave me his responses. Here is what he told me when, first, I asked him to tell me who's the most important person in your life. Without a second thought, he responded, "Suzie."
>
> "What was your first impression of her?" I asked Nick. "I first saw Suzie at a conference. She was giving a talk about pedagogy. I remember looking at her… she was really cute…and curvaceous! I wanted to meet her to see if the

reality matched her reputation. She was young, but already she was very respected in the profession. I called up to her room that evening at about 11:00 to see if she'd like to join me in a drink. She laughed and said she would... another time."

"Then what happened?" I asked him. "Then I had to get back to Boulder... and see about my divorce."

"What did you most like doing with Suzie?" I asked. "What I loved doing the most with Suzie was exploring. One of my favorite memories is our trip to the Nile. We travelled up the Nile on a steamship to Luxor and there we explored the Temple of Luxor that goes back 4,000 years. It's hard to imagine something being so old. We stayed at an old hotel that went back to the time of the British. It was in pretty good shape, just a bit worse for the wear. It was a very romantic trip."

"What was so romantic about it?" I asked him.

"Suzie," he said, and a smile lit up his face. "She's the light of my life."

In 1965 as the national director of the High School Geography Project

Nick and Suzie at their wedding in Boulder on August 4, 1969

Above, on a family hike to the tree line in October 1970;
below, Nick ties Sherry's bootlaces.

The farm as seen from above in 1984

Nick in the community pump house after gardening

Community farming basics: ditch digging and ditch cleaning

From *Lykins Gulch News* with the caption,
"Toes are for kissing, not for kicking."

Hal and Sherry with Peter at their wedding, August 1975

Community kids summer 1973

Community folk about to reroof the horse barn, around 1977

Barn raising led by Jim Logan, in 1983

Jim Logan and Sherry's wedding in 1981

Tanya and Nick about 1978

Nick helps his grandson Nate play
the bass recorder.

Above and middle, the community gardens north of the new "people barn"; *lower,* the new house Jim Logan designed in 1983

David Loth, on left, and his wife Helen, seated on right, were colleagues, mentors, and beloved friends of Nick's family.

In 1977, Steve, Suzie, Sherry, and Nick on their way to The Blue Note opening, Peter's local jazz club and night spot

Nick with grandsons Brian, Joseph, Michael and son-in-law Jim Logan

Nick's granddaughter Wendy married
Brent Mather at the farm, June 2000.

Nick and Suzie, always celebrating

Nick and Suzie in Italy with grandchildren Michael, Brian, Joseph, and Dana

Dancing and romancing at Wendy's and Brent's wedding

Rowing on Lake Como at Bellagio, Italy in 1998

Visiting Telc, Czech Republic in June 2006

Nick with his dear friend and fellow activist, Leroy Moore

Nick, Suzie, Bill Hinton at the gorgeous Yellow Cliff Canyon, site of the 8th Route Army munitions factory and barracks, destroyed by the Japanese in 1940-41

Still protesting in Boulder in 2009

Grandson Brian's graduation June 2009

On a trip to Uzbekistan in 2008, Nick paid homage to his folk hero, Nasreddin Khodja, the Cosmic Joker of Sufi legend.

"The legend says that there is the mausoleum to Khodja Nasreddin somewhere in Turkey. It is the summer house without the roof supported by four poles. The wind is freely blowing through it but there is a strong wooden door there with the big iron lock… It, certainly is a joke.…In reality you can see Nasreddin in the broiling sun of holy Bukhara where he is solemnly sitting on his favorite donkey near Lyabi-hous. And cunningly smiling and looking forward to meeting us."
—from *Khodja Nasreddin: A Great Smile of the East*, San'at Publishing House, 2007

PART III

LETTERS

The SHOREHAM

Hotel and Motor Inn
CONNECTICUT AVENUE AT CALVERT STREET
Washington 8, D. C.

1 Am
5/21

Suzanne love:

Let me repeat - I feel so
loving and warm and happy
and rich living in your
presence I can hardly believe
it's real.   Good night again.

Nick.

Letters

Starting in 1970 Nick's annual letters to friends and family give another glimpse of his life and our life together. They provide some chronology of Nick's last forty-two years although they by no means cover every year. We loved traveling together, and it is a special treat to explore new places with a geographer! Several of these letters give Nick's impressions of some of our more memorable trips abroad. Some of the letters are a bit stream-of-consciousness and no attempt has been made to clean up the grammar.

May 1, 1970

We've been here three days already and until this minute I haven't taken pen to paper. Somehow it seems selfish enough to engage in such an adventure personally. Not to share it in words seems even more selfish.

In one sense I'm writing from the deepest darkest kind of corner of Africa. We are in Kidepo National Park in the very northeastern-most part of Uganda, only 15 miles from the border with Sudan and 10 miles from Kenya.

We are a long day and a half drive from Kampala and much further from Nairobi or Khartoum or Addis Ababa. Mbale is the closest central place which could be called a city. It's 200 miles away, only 20 of which was paved. We forded 4 streams in the last 2 hours, one of which was very scary without 4-wheel drive.

The scenery is reminiscent of the semi-spiritual descriptions of the dark continent. Wide almost flat plains connect irregular mountain and hill masses—some of which are very steep. This is the height, or almost the height, of the wet season in a decidedly wet and dry climate bordering on semi-arid. The thorn trees, usually white and skeletal, are a young green of almost full leaf. The grass is already shoulder high. The mountains are dark, blue-green and misty in the dusk. They could be drawn on the diorama at the Museum of Natural History until you get almost into them. The rock of the mountains seems volcanic and shows boldly in the steeper areas.

The park itself is not inhabited, but the people we saw on the way from Kampala were fascinating. Kampala itself is Buganda country. Then north of Lake Victoria with plenty of precipitation they subsist in a planting culture heavily dependent on bananas. As you drive through, it's some-times hard to tell the cultivated from the wild for both have so much vegetation on them. The cassava growing under the bananas looks like underbrush as does the coffee bushes. Old hands must know immediately, but a greenhorn from the middle latitudes knows he is out of his element.

The only fully "domesticated" landscape are the tea and sugar plan-tations, clear cases of commercial monoculture.

The road—two lane asphalt—leads north and east, past Tinja where the Nile flows out of Lake Victoria. The old falls are now generating a steady supply of kilowatts. The road to Kenya continues East, but we turn north after tea at a beautifully landscaped hotel to Mbale. Our party of 10 splits up to spend the night with friends—or friends of friends. Gil Thorn-ton and wife and daughter stay with Peace Corps contacts. He is deputy director of the P.S. in Uganda. We stay at a teacher education school 5 miles out of the town.

Our hosts are Americans and Canadians: A taciturn black whose wife died unnecessarily in childbirth several months ago, the other two gregar-ious and pleased to get the sterling and be hospitable, eager to get the flavor of what is going on in North America. They live in spacious homes with almost every convenience of suburban domestic life in the household. The frustrations of mail, shopping, etc., wear differently on the different personalities, some hoping they can stay on; others counting the months until they can go back home.

The school takes youngsters 15-18 who have finished 7 years of ele-mentary school, prepares them as elementary school teachers in 4 years. But the staff is discouraged by the low salaries elementary teachers get and the lackadaisical attitude in the schools. Teacher absenteeism is chronic and serious. Moonlighting is widespread. Practice teachers find themselves in complete charge of the class with no supervision. New teachers sometimes face classes of 80 students. There is little evidence of revolutionary or altruistic zeal.

As we pushed north the next day, we left the pavement behind after 20 miles. Fresh rains supplied plenty of puddles, but the traction on the graded and granulled road was generally good. We were soon out of forest and in "savanna" of one sort or another. Grass, shrubs and trees mix in varying proportions. Bananas drop out of the agriculture. Maize, millet and soybean become more obvious. Different tribes occupy the huts—less and less rectangular wattle or brick with tin roofs—more and more round wattle with thatched roofs.

There was an unusual amount of bus, taxi, bicycle and foot traffic on an early stretch of road, all of it going north at first until we came to a market place—a field beside the road with some frames thatched to provide shade—but otherwise an undistinguished piece if ground. There was no permanent settlement at the location. Quite a crowd was present already by the time when we passed. Then we met the people coming from the other direction.

Somewhere in the middle of the morning, we passed into Karamajong territory. The tribe occupied much of this marginal almost semi-arid northeastern corner of Uganda. They are active cultivators, herdsmen and warriors, primitive enough to be a real embarrassment to the more advanced majority of Ugandies (?) and a strong attraction to tourists who goggle at men, stark naked, or who are thrilled to be able to photograph bare breasted women.

Problems of corruption of a dignified but different people occupied a good chunk of our conversation for awhile, as later we talked with the ranger about the impact of tourists on game habitat and upon the game.

Enough for now. We'll try to do something similar again—as we move to Marchison (?) Falls, Nairobi, Mombasa and who knows where.

1971

Greetings from the Helburn-Wiggins clan from the chicken coop in the community on Nelson Road—just off the Foothills Highway, ten miles north of Boulder. We moved December first and our new address is:

Route 3, Box 330
Longmont, Colorado 80501
Phone: 303 442-0372

It's been both hectic and inspiring, exhausting and exhilarating. We started talking "intentional communities" about a year ago with others of like mind and differing backgrounds. By May a group of six families had decided we'd do it. By mid-June we'd bought 118 acres of slightly rundown farm. One family moved in July first and ever since and still we apply most of our spare time and energy to making the buildings liveable: two houses, two garages and a chicken coop have been transformed.

But community isn't built with lumber and nails alone. Clarifying our purpose, building trust, tolerating idiosyncrasies, discovering underlying motivation, learning cooperation, unsnarling communication—all these have occupied us evening after evening. We are learning. God willing, we'll soon be able to share our learning more widely, be ready to learn from others who can be with us a day or a week or a year or a lifetime. Come and learn with us. Meanwhile our love to all. May peace and happiness and satisfaction be a large part of your lives as it is in ours.

P.S. Peter is living in Boulder and expects to find an apartment soon. Meanwhile he gets his mail at our address.

1972

This has been another hectic, complicated and eventful year for us; in fact, our preoccupation with living it makes it impossible to write a thoughtful review of events. This is the briefest summary of our news to let you know that the Helburns—Nick and Suzie—are alive and well in Colorado.

Sherry is spending her first year in college (University of Colorado) in Kyoto, Japan learning Japanese culture and ways. Peter completes a year living in his own apartment in Boulder, now a salaried employee of SSEC. Steve and Mary have completed their B.A.'s at Oregon State and Steve is pursuing (we mean that literally, they move to another location every three months) a promising job with Chicago Bridge and Iron. At this moment they are en route to southern California. Suzie continues to enjoy teaching at the Denver Center of the University and uses every spare minute to finish *Economics in Society*, now a six volume paperback series from Addison Wesley late summer. Nick resigned his ERIC directorship to spend full time in the Geography Department being chairman and teaching. Life is a little simpler with fewer people and procedures to take care of.

The community continues to be an absorbing experiment—plenty of rewards and potentials to balance the frustrations and problems. The garden and cow contribute to our table. The dozen of us who came through the turnover of spring and summer have grown together. Basic improvements to provide housing and simple amenities have been made. Next year we hope to get the farm into production and to do the planning and building which will allow us to start reaching outside ourselves. One such outreach is a community newspaper—Lykins Gulch News—chronicling our growth and change. Let us know if you want to be on the mailing list.

All good wishes for the holiday season and the new year.

October 18, 1975

Apologies for the impersonality of a group letter, but it may be better than no letter at all. Enough has been going on here so that we would like to keep you up to date. We say it over and over again to friends who inquire solicitously, "How is it going? What's new on the farm?" I'm never sure but that they are reveling in the failure, glad to welcome us back into the ranks of the sane.

At present it seems clear that "the community," the residual group now on the farm do not want to buy the farm. When faced with something like a $90,000 second mortgage along with a $60,000 first mortgage, only Jay out of the six has any sense of wanting to try it. (There were ten of us at the beginning of the summer but Suzie and I asked for the leave of absence in June and Ronnie and Len indicated they felt that they must leave in September.)

It is not clear how many of the six will actually do it, but the thought is that the residual group will take their assets including the breeding herd of goats to another site which has more productive soil and where the price is not inflated by being so close to Boulder and Denver. We have offered the group something in the neighborhood of $13,000 to cover the

"Community's" share of the equity in the farm and the capital gain. We did have the farm appraised and it came out about $185,000. How they will divide up or keep together the $13,000 is not clear, but is basically not Suzie's and my problem.

There are a couple of lesser problems still to be worked out. One is the timing and mode of transfer of responsibility for the farm back to us. We don't want to move back right away. We have enjoyed catching up on our sleep here in the apartment and are not about to go thru another move immediately. Peter has suggested that he might be willing to take on the resident managership for a while. We probably will have responsibility soon after the new year and may move back to the farm itself either early or late summer. We have been planning to attend the International Geographical Union meetings in the USSR during July and August, '76.

Given the uncertainties on the farm and the investments we would like to make in order to bring it up to our "bourgeois" standards of comfort, neatness and efficiency, we are uncertain as to whether we really should spend the time and money to go to the USSR.

Another variable not yet worked out is the disposal of the communal property including livestock, farm machinery, etc. We assume that will be divided somehow among the 10 of us, but that still has to be worked out. We have been going out to work on the place on weekends and find ourselves concentrating on long-range aspects such as watering the trees so that they will come through the winter better, and weeding and composting the garden. It has been a glorious fall, still warm enough to work in shorts without a shirt most of the day.

Meanwhile Suzie and I are trying to sort out what we want to do in the long run. Are we content to play country gentleman and gentlewoman on a $200,000 acreage? Can the Nelson Road farm become a coming home place for children and grandchildren scattered from Houston to Vancouver as well as nieces and nephews? Is there a way to use the farm with our students and with social scientists with similar concerns, a rural outlier for the University? What politically self-conscious movement promises significant change in a humane mode and needs a rural Colorado node in its network. These are the kind of alternatives that go back and forth across our breakfast table.

As for the moment, we both take our teaching seriously, actively searching for ways to involve students in their own learning, ways to get students to participate while legislative and administrative pressures force us to work with impersonal numbers (ca 200). We are careful to get almost daily exercise—the pool in the apartment house is a big help in this. Three or four nights a week we read a few paragraphs of Magister Ludi aloud to each other before we fall asleep.

Give us your news. We think of you all so often and wish we were closer.

January 18, 1976

After two years of boycotting the Christmas card biz and relieving the seasonal crisis of the Post Office, maybe it's time to catch up with those of you who are still on reading terms with us.

I'm writing from the beautifully appointed town house of David and Helen Loth in Greenwich, Connecticut. My jeans and western informality feel incongruous—though warmly welcomed—here. But then, much of the last couple of years has felt incongruous. The day before the day before yesterday we were visiting a Libyan farm a few kilometers outside of Tripoli owned by a man about my age, in part as a place to exercise his constructive interests and fulfill his desire to help things grow. But in part he owns it as a hedge against inflation and the possibility that the economy will fall to bits—and then at least the family will have something to eat. It seemed incongruous to find such parallel reasons a third of the way around the world in such a different culture.

He has been a cloth merchant as long as I have been an academic. His English is better than my Arabic which is all but nil. His olives and oranges are a long way from our apples and cherries. He could stand some of our clay in his sand and vice versa. We didn't talk community with him, but with a wife, eleven children and four hired Egyptian farm hands, they counted almost as many as ever occupied the Nelson Road farm.

We were in Libya at the invitation of the University of Tripoli to lecture about Geographic and Economic Education. Our host assured us that the student demonstrations which started four days after we arrived were not a result of our visit—in fact, they represented a protest against the Khadafi government. But we didn't get a chance to talk as much as we expected. We were very well received both at the university and informally by faculty and students. Impressive were: large, loving families; many women still veiled in public; almost everyone with a new automobile; farms with irrigation pipe, new wells, tractors, pickups, new orange trees planted between the older olives, and chick peas growing between the trees; signs in Arabic only; great pride in language; no alcohol; no beggars or shoe shine boys; lots of foreigners in the labor force; enormous numbers of construction projects; good roads, ships waiting at anchor because harbor facilities are still being built; miles and miles of bloody desert.

We kept making comparisons—with Turkey in 1953, with Cuba in 1968, with Uganda in 1970. Nowhere had we seen as much capital available for so few people on such a thin resource base, such competition for materials, labor and managerial skills.

What reservations we had about the Puritanism, Arabism and xenophobia of the Khadafi regime disappeared as we spent two days in Tunis. Tourism does tend to degrade a society.

During the last twelve months the Community on Nelson Road came unglued, or maybe it just went through mitosis. We took a leave of absence in September, moved to Boulder, and almost immediately realized that we would not rejoin that group. Structures and procedures we had worked so hard to build among us were being allowed to dissolve. Those on the farm could not afford to buy it. They located another in southwestern Colorado (near Durango) for almost half the price and are in the process of moving.

Glenn Browning who was part of the group will stay with us. Son Peter has rented one of the houses and is looking forward to learning some of the rural skills and living closer to us both physically and emotionally. We will move back onto the farm this spring, probably about June 1. Meanwhile we are carefully considering the alternatives for the future. Should we try to make the farm a hospitable focus for Helburns and related families? Should we use the space to gather like minded social scientists and practice different learning/teaching situations? Should we concentrate on political and social change? Whatever choice, we'll make it carefully. The last year has been rougher than we like to admit: the pain and strain of separation along with the final shattering of a Utopian dream.

There were plenty of satisfactions along the way—don't get us wrong. Sherry's and Hal's wedding in our alfalfa field was a high high. An increasing interest is our involvement with MNS—the Movement for a New Society. It is a network of groups dedicated to profound social change and as concerned about the people as they are about the institutions. They recognize that means and ends are one, that the processes of change and of living are outcomes we want to achieve. Another ongoing involvement, especially for Suzie, has been a deepening understanding of Marxism, both theory and praxis. The variety of contemporary experiments is part of her academic responsibility. The application to social change in the U.S. and in the world as a whole involves both of us.

Our own teaching grows each year in satisfaction as we develop more fully both the theory and the practice of involving students in more active participation in their own learning. The revolutionary implications become clearer to us. Perhaps that is part of the explanation of why the University is so resistant to change.

Let us hear what is going on with you and within you. Stop by in your travels west; there will be plenty of room at the farm.

Moscow, Thursday, July 15, 1976

[This trip started in Florence, preceded to Rumania to meet our friends the Senesh's in Suceava Rumania to visit the famous medieval monasteries in the countryside and travel on to Hungary, ending in the Soviet Union to attend the IGU (International Geographic Union) conference. Of special interest was the pre-Congress Symposium of the Commission on Man and Environment which took place on a river boat going from Rostov on the Don through the Don Volga canal on to the Volga to Kazan. The main conference was in Moscow and we ended the trip by taking the overnight train to Leningrad where we stayed for a few days on our own. Nick didn't do much of a diary of this trip, except for the following entry.]

Before we really launch into the next chapter of this journey it would be fun to record impressions of the last few days more systematically than the collage of post cards we have sent. The arrival in Moscow was a surprise for the airport guard inspecting passports and visas turned us back and called a chubby superior who pointed out to us that our visas were dated for entry the 24th instead of the 14th. Obviously a typo but not so easily corrected. They must be sent into the foreign office. Without visas we could do nothing but stay in the Aeroflot Hostel.

Our worries about joining the group in time to fly to Rostov and get on the boat were heard sympathetically but no one in the airport could do anything about it. The hostel was a single floor of a gray building across the street with two beds, a closet and a table in each of 15 or 20 rooms. But the woman in charge took a real interest, shouted into the phone for half an hour until finally tracking down Gilbert White at the Hotel Russia. Gilbert assured us that he would apply what leverage he could.

Sure that we had done what we could, we relaxed and prepared ourselves to fly home right away if we could not get onto the boat. No meals in the hostel and a largish group due so the matron took us to the departure lounge restaurant and left us there. A couple of vodkas and a bottle of wine and a good Stroganoff and we had struck up a conversation with two young Brits headed for "peace corps" type work in Bangladesh. Finally the Aeroflot people found us again—our visas had been corrected—a limousine would take us to the Hotel Russia—and by midnight we were happily in a proper room in downtown Moskva.

Except for this one incident and a couple of minor items everyone has been kind and helpful within the limits of language, and the trip has gone very smoothly. The most pervasive impression is of prosperity— general economic well being. Bodies vary from well fed to obese. Clothes are bright and appropriate if not very stylish. We've only seen a couple of beggars the whole trip. The few gypsies we've seen stand out in contrast to the rest.

[Suzie: Since I had no responsibilities at the Symposium I took charge of the ditto machine Gilbert had brought for distributing information. Gilbert teased me about being so competitive in running the equipment; I replied that I was involved in "socialist emulation," not competition, with the others manning the machine. But the highlight of the river trip was the final night when Nick and I participated in an opera that had been written by the Russian graduate students on the trip. Nick, playing God, died in the first scene. But I was Environment and, of course, survived. Nick and Bob Kates wrote the English lyrics to the Hymn Of Man and Environment, an Ode to the Commission. A couple stanzas give the flavor:

We met in Godollo
And then in Calgary
What a fine meeting we had
There in Calgary
Hazard Reports, an Olympic Race
Where Ian Burton took first place
Oh the Commission
Oh the Commission
Glorious Commission on
Man and environment.

Now we are K – 10
Rostov to Kazan
Statzvidya friend
We inspected Rostov-on-Don
And were told how the fishes ran
Oh the Commission
Oh the Commission
Long discussions on
Man and Environment

Section one can show
To make the rivers flow
Arctic to desert
Only Geographers know
Crazy people in the early morn
Greet Tsilmanekoye before the dawn
Oh the Commission
Oh the Commission

…
Must Moscow be the end
Or can we recommend
Some new activity
Environment and Men?
Yes, we stubbornly will still survive
A new name will keep our group alive
A new Commission
Great new Commission
Glorious new Commission
Women and Environment

That last night was also memorable for vast quantities of caviar and
Vodka, finally ending at 5 a.m. In Moscow we celebrated our seventh
wedding anniversary with the Kates and a very jolly Russian—another

memorable night of over eating drinking, dancing until the wee hours. Russian hospitality is balshoi!]

November 9, 1978

Greetings from Merry Old London and it was that today. Brilliant clear morning and mild breezes across the oak and maple and plane and horse chestnut trees. Everyone was enjoying the fine weather in Kensington Gardens: Mums and pups (what do the English call fathers?), light skinned and dark, babies and children, terriers and hounds. It was the last day of a magnificent exhibit of Henry Moore's recent sculptures in honor of his 84th or some such birthday. Monumental and mostly abstract pieces. Several of the reclining figures and arched pieces were powerfully attractive visually. Children found them even better for climbing. We were particularly moved by a blind man in among the playing children, feeling his way around one mammoth piece. One smaller torso we agreed would look good in the coop. We were glad to have the underground to rest our feet on the way home.

Exploring the variety which is London, of course, is a continuing pleasure. And contrary to nasty gossip (pronounced nahsty) England does have good (but expensive) food. Our second night here Nancy Hirshberg (Nancy is the second Mrs. Wiggins) and her husband took us out to fine Pakistani fare, spicy but not too hot, unfamiliar enough so I cannot begin to describe what we ate. We shared with cousin Bette Ann Hindes one of the best meals we've ever had in a tiny country pub-hotel in Northern Wales. The English generally take their food seriously; it's just that it tends to be the rib sticking variety, good, honest food as our English friend Pat Braddell describes it. We even get good cheap curry at the University cafeteria at the School of Oriental and African Studies. Pub snacks can be terrific and good value—we've found a couple superb ones.

The music available here is mind boggling: contemporary and classical, vocal and instrumental, full orchestral and 500 voices or quartets and recitals—many of them free right in our neighborhood at lovely old Anglican churches. Perhaps its part of the survival of aristocratic traditions, but they do take their music (and other arts) seriously. The Greater London Council, which is the major unit in the Metropolitan government, makes significant grants to all sorts of musical groups, theatres, ballet, opera. Some are the old standbys with large, posh audiences. We saw a gripping Royal Ballet Company new production called Meyerling last night—about the dissolute life of Prince Rudolf of Austro-Hungarian fame who killed himself and his mistress—and found the Royal Opera House as grand as the Palace scenes in the ballet. Others are experimental groups whose paid audience hardly equals the cast.

Early in December we'll join hundreds of other enthusiastic amateurs in a performance of the "Messiah from Scratch." Soloists and non-string instrumentalists are screened, but everyone else just pays their admission in advance, about £2.50, and shows up with their copy of the score.

We've hiked some in the outer suburbs, paid homage to Marx's grave, listened to the organ in St. Paul's, but we've only begun. We haven't been to the Zoo (which is just a few blocks away), nor gone to the Lord's Cricket grounds which are equally close by, nor listened to the speeches in Hyde Park, nor made the pilgrimage to the Royal Observatory at Greenwich. Plenty to look forward to.

We have seen quite a bit of Lou and Pat Braddell. Lou was Suzie's roommate in college. They live in a lovely 17th century limestone Cottswold cottage in a village about half way between Banbury and Stratford-on-Avon, not far from Shipston-on-Stour, or Moreton-in-Marsh or Stow-in-Wold. In fact, we took many bushels of apples to Sutton-under-Brailles where the blacksmith has an ancient cider press. The juice was put by in a 35 gallon barrel under the yew tree with sugar and raisins, not to be disturbed until February. We indulge our needs by pretending to earn our keep through working in the garden, picking wild blackberries from the nearby hedgerows, making apple and mint jelly and apple sauce.

We've done some work too. Suzie has made one consulting trip back to the States: Washington, Phoenix and Salt Lake City. Now she's digging into the preparation of a couple of papers she has agreed to write as well as the reading program she laid out for herself before she came; in addition, she is helping out in the teacher preparation program at the Institute to get some idea about economics education in England.

Since early October Nick has been teaching in the Institute of Education of the University of London. (We haven't mentioned it before but we're both on sabbatical and attached to the Institute for the year, Nick in a formal sense as a lecturer/tutor, Suzie as a visiting scholar). Nick has occasional responsibilities in three other graduate courses but his major role is as one of four faculty, team teaching a group of 40 recent geography graduates through a year-long preparation for their Post Graduate Certificate in Education. It is similar to a MAT program in the U.S. He is "tutor" to a dozen of them, working very closely with them as they begin to get their classroom experience. It draws upon all of his knowledge of the subject and how it is learned and the nature of schools and the way teachers fit into the mix. He's especially able to coach them on how to prepare materials which will get the children really involved. We trust this makes up for his relative ignorance of British educational institutions, ways through the red tape, and the like.

We've both been out in the schools—at the secondary level, comprehensive schools mainly, which are an amalgamation of the former secondary modern and grammar schools, the two types of publicly supported high schools. This reform was an attempt to democratize the schools by putting all students together in one school whether or not they are Uni-

versity bound. There has also been some movement toward more heterogeneous grouping by dropping the streaming of students from 12 or 13
streams to a mere four to six. With discipline so much an obvious part of
the curriculum, with the quite substantial streaming according to school
success, with the use of national tests to place students into the comprehensive schools and then into or out of further university training, with
the necessity of teachers to teach to the national testing program, with the
dullness of didactic teaching geared to the testing program and the con-
sequent choices to opt out for many students — with all this and probably
more, one cannot but see the schools as a major instrument for reproducing class relations. Many educators at the Institute think that is as it should
be. In our small circle of friends the Americans and Australians seem to be
the exceptions to this point of view.

By Christmas we'll be even farther away. Lesotho seems almost the
end of the earth. But we'll be with Sherry and Hal who are there to help
manage a weaving operation developing handicraft products for export
trade. We hope to share the responsibilities and the joys surrounding the
birth of a new Wiggins-Casteel. They have changed assignments since
arriving in Africa (they started working in the Peace Corps but are now
working for a private Danish outfit), but seem to be getting plenty of satisfactions to more than balance out the frustrations of introducing efficiency to the native women weavers who are not used to capitalist
discipline.

David and Helen Loth will be sharing Christmas with Steve and Mary
and Wendy and Nathan in their new house in Houston. Steve continues to
progress in Chicago, Bridge and Iron as they expand their marine operations.

We've had a very unhappy and sad conflict with Peter over finances
and the Blue Note. The situation still is not resolved ten months after we
thought we had it worked out. The estrangement is severe. We trust it will
all be history in another year.

It's been delightful to share London with several people from home
this fall, hopefully there will be more in the spring. But we do miss friends
and relations, as well as familiar surroundings and responsibilities. Letters
from home are always a reminder, but we still feel far away from home and
a little out of touch. Still we look forward to the next six months here. Meanwhile, our warmest wishes to you all for the holidays and the new year.

January 20, 1979

I don't know whether I can make this worth reading, but I'll try. I'm
just back a week. What a shock to come from mid-summer to mid-winter
and from mid-Lesotho to mid-London. I was on the train from Heathrow
to downtown London in time to see the sun rise in a crisp sky over the
suburbs. The Piccadilly line stops at Russel Square, just two blocks from
the Institute so I struggled my bags to the surface: a big suitcase, two back-

packs, a couple of bottles from the tax free shop and two woven straw hats, the distinctive item in the Lesotho costume. I left it all with the porters on the ground floor and spent an hour sorting thru the mail. What a wonderful feeling, all those greetings and good wishes, especially after being so out of touch for three weeks.

Hence this letter, to try to share with you some of my reactions and to give you some of our news, Actually I caught a cab back to the flat and found another pile of mail there, so I spent the whole weekend wallowing in Christmasy New Yearsy good feelings. Suzie is still in Lesotho, but I called her Sunday to share my good feelings and to pass along news and greetings. She reports that all is well there.

In case our cards did not get thru, Sherry delivered Brian Bruce Casteel, weighing in at 3.3 kilos, at 2:50 AM on December 30th. Friday evening they had intended to go to the movie at the Teyateyaneng Club, but when she identified regular pains they decided to drive to the hospital at Ficksburg, for the international border closes at 8 PM. Everything went smoothly, though Hal was disappointed not to be able to stay in the delivery room as he had been promised. The nurses were a little stand-offish perhaps because with both Wiggins & Casteel being used they may have questioned whether the couple were really married. Sherry had some insecurity about whether Brian was going to nurse, but after a couple of days it was clear that he liked it and there was plenty of nourishment. How do you bring a new baby home across an international boundary when he doesn't have a passport? They worked that out. Brian looks a lot like Hal: prominent nose and slightly olive complexion. His relaxed, good natured disposition and his penchent for long sleep periods make him easy to take care of.

Lesotho reminded us a lot of Arizona or New Mexico: a treeless landscape with wide horizons, bright sun, sharp escarpments, flat topped mesas. The circular "rondavels" with conical thatched roofs have a higher silhouette than do hogans and there are a great many more of them. There are villages everywhere! The population pressure is enormous. A million and a half people try to scrape an agricultural living off an area the size of Maryland but mountainous. The range land is cropped short by sheep, goats, horses, donkeys and most of all, cattle. Fields of maize, wheat and sorghum look ragged, not because of environmental conditions. The rainfall is normally about 30 inches. Rather the tenure and labor institutions make it important to plant one's fields but not necessarily to tend them. Most families get most of their income from some male member working in the gold mines in the Republic. Crop land is not "owned." Rather one is awarded the right to use a parcel or two or three. This right usually continues thruout one's lifetime, but only if it is continuously used.

A most dramatic part of the landscape are the enormous gullies reaching up from the valley bottoms through the crop and pasture lands to the base of the sandstone cliffs. Overgrazing and lack of maintenance of terracing established in the '30's contribute to the gullying, but one school maintains that the gullying is mostly a natural consequence of torrential rains occurring after a series of dry years.

Maseru, the capitol, is full of AID missions, both from governments and from private sources. Many of the handicrafts derive from Europeans trying to help the Basutu to develop other sources of income. Tourism has a little potential. South Africans take advantage of the availability of gambling and prostitution in Maseru. It takes on something of the Aura of a black Las Vegas. We only spent part of one afternoon in the Casino (owned by Holiday Inns) but my impression was that there were more blacks gambling than whites. I suspect that the gambling takes money out of the country rather than bringing it in. We did not get a chance to study the prostitution in person.

We did visit an irrigation project and get to know the director, an impressive young black educated in Lesotho and Swaziland with a Masters in Irrigation Engineering from Southampton. A dam in the mountains will hold back flood crests to be let out later for village water supplies and for irrigation of crops. The land to be irrigated, about 5,000 hectares, will be collectivized into about 5 large blocks and managed by experts with the labor being performed by the villagers who had control of it before. They will get all or most of the income from the sale of the crops. Though the dam will not be completed for another five years, they had a small (70 Ha.) demonstration area in operation making good incomes from garden truck and hay.

We were very warmly received in the European community in Ty, short for Teyateyaneng. They put on a dizzying round of parties from Christmas past New Years. Lovely women, handsome men, warm and friendly and hospitable, cultured and widely travelled, mostly making their living as traders. They seem undisturbed by the enormous gap between their level of living and that of the Basuto who are their customers, their employees and their servants.

We visited parents of a friend right in the middle of the Republic not far from Kimberly the last couple of days before I returned to London. He is a very successful businessman and rancher. He was not a bit shy about talking about race relations. Apartheid was his solution. The black homelands should not be given self-government for blacks could only make a mess of things. The blacks need the kind of leadership and organizational skill which he was giving, apparently not only now but indefinitely into the future.

Perhaps most disturbing of all to me as a romantic idealist, was the effect of the caste system on the children. Growing up with subservient maids, even six year olds learn to give orders in a snotty tone of voice. A soft and flabby 15 year old white boy drives around the ranch in his own pickup with a 10 year old black boy riding in back to open the gates. The reality of the gulf is so powerful that it would be nearly impossible to grow up there without accepting it as the "natural" situation.

I am reminded of the story which is sometimes ascribed to me, sometimes to my brother Peter, as we were growing up in an affluent New England family. "When I grow up I'm going to have four children, two white and two black. That way there will always be someone to do the washing." Maybe we are not so different after all?

April 29, 1979

I don't quite know where to begin, so much has happened since I was last at this typewriter and got the first part of my last letter to you started. Within a week and without too much travelling we have been in Belgium and have been all over Holland. Kendrick Vlaanderen was our host and guide. Three or four years ago he had come thru Boulder and we were able to make facilities available to him on campus. He does the same type of thing for the U. of Amsterdam as I am doing here this year for the Univ. of London. He came to London for the GA meetings at which I spoke 10 days ago. He had his car so we picked up Suzie in Canterbury where she was giving a talk to the Economics Association. On to nearby Dover to catch the Hovercraft ferry. It would have been very fast, but one broke down so we waited for the next and we still had 5 hours driving to Bruges where we had a reservation, at the Duc de Boulogne, a very famous hotel right on one of the canals. It is where Churchill used to stay and sketch when he was in that part of the world. We were late enough so that they had sold the room out from under us. That was the only disappointment of the week. They found us another and we were in no discomfort.

I can't put my finger on what it is that makes Bruges so breathtakingly beautiful. I felt almost like a voyeur: privileged to look in on the city 500 years ago. There is a quality of restfulness about a city that has been asleep that long. But it must have been a beautiful town to begin with. Certainly the canal helps to give it a harmonious variety. We finished our walking tour with a stop at the medieval "hospital" which is now the museum housing the works of Memling. His pre-renaissance paintings were new to me, worth the trip by themselves.

On soon after noon with bread and cheeze and sausage to cross by viaduct, bridge and ferry the several mouths of the Maa, Meuse and Rhine (whose upper courses we had traversed three weeks before between Paris and Munich. This is the Dutch "Delta scheme" to control the estuaries so as to create some fresh water lakes as reservoirs & recreation sites, to keep one large bay brackish for the production of oysters and other shellfish, and to provide flood protection for the whole region to the highest flood in 10,000 years (on the average), at the same time permitting navigation of the whole area and disposing of the water which flows in from upstream.

The Vlaanderens live in Zeist a smaller city suburban to Utrecht, at one end of a horseshoe shaped megalopolis including Amsterdam, Haarlem, Leyden, The Hague, Rotterdam and several other cities. Keeping the "green heart" of the horseshoe green, preventing urban sprawl or even creep, from displacing agriculture, is one of the great planning problems of the Netherlands. One of their girls is married and living in Jordan, another lives at the Univ. of Utrect, so their two boys could squeeze a little to free the two little rooms on the third floor for us. It was lovely to feel the warmth and the humor of the family.

In the next three days we traversed and studied the riverine landscape between the two major branches of the Rhine including the dykes designed so that areas could be flooded against invading armies; pumping technology from windmills restored and in working order thru to modern diesel stations; the bulb growing areas close to the dunes, fields of brilliant reds and oranges and yellows with an occasional patch of purple-blue hyacinths; the manicured park where growers lease beds to show off their prize varieties; (it has been a slow spring all over N. Europe. Normally this would be late for the tulips). The wholesale flower market, acres of floor space filled with cut flowers and potted plants moving steadily thru four auction halls being bought for shipment all over the world; (Amsterdam airport is adjacent.) the Van Gogh museum—a whole floor of paintings, another of his sketches; (Suzi was so absorbed she didn't say a word for an hour and a half.) The Zuider Zee project with its enormous polders; (by this time our eyes were getting attuned to watching for topography measured in centimeters) a maritime museum set up by volunteers who have a special sense of beauty and good taste. Hank and Adinda had to drag us away.

Suzi left for London Thursday AM and I worked on a presentation to be given the next day at the Univ. of Utrecht to specialists in geographic education. The program there developing geography information specialist for planning problems & environmental concerns and for international flow of information about Holland is another whole page in itself. It was a great climax to our spring break.

November 24, 1980

Such poor correspondents we are but we'd really like to stay in touch and are pleased to keep our long-distance bill below $20/month.

We do feel the reduced purchasing power and wonder how others less fortunate than we manage. We do continue to make improvements in the farmstead which soak up income now but pay off in satisfactions and possibly more income later. Glenn's house (the East garage) is finished beautifully now with a bay window designed for passive solar collection and growing plants. We renovated the old farm house so that it now sports a new kitchen, tiled bath and some closets and looks lovely with Ann Widerstrom's charming furnishings. (Ann works with Suzy at UCD and is a fellow traveler.) Two more houses were repainted this spring/summer, so we are mostly a white farmstead.

We took the leap this summer and bought a two wheeled Gravely tractor with a 30" lawn mower attachment as well as plow and sprayer. It was the sprayer which triggered the decision—the grasshopper infestations demanded something more than swatting (so we gave up some of our principles re organic gardening in favor of saving our trees). Judicious spraying with "sevin" brought the plague under control with minimum impact on other species (we hope). In the end the garden was very productive with all we could eat, pickle, freeze, can and dry. The root cellar is well stocked with winter squash, pumpkins, apples and even green tomatoes, wrapped and ripening slowly. The apple harvest was unusual. There are 20 gallons in carboy and barrel bubbling quietly and gallons of sweet cider in the freezer.

Our major extravagance this year was a three week trip to England with Janet Moone. A week-long conference on Social and Political Education was our excuse. Suzie gave a major paper there which was well received in spite of (because of) its truly radical analysis. We saw friends and colleagues in London, stayed a week with Pat and Lou Braddell in the Cotswolds, toured Cornwall all the way to Penzance and Lands End. A sampling of excellent theatre (including the new Hamlet at Stratford-on-Avon), and the Royal Agricultural Show (where Suzy actually ran into Prince Philip)—a "state fair" on the national level—widened the experience.

We continue to put most of our time into our university careers and to get most of our satisfactions from them. But this year Nick is also President of the A.A.G. which is a nice thank you from the profession, somewhat of a challenge and good fun, since it involves going around the country talking to geographers about the future of the profession. Nick serves as coordinator of the graduate program for the Geography Department at CU. The orientation retreat for new graduate students this year was "one of the best ever" and deeply gratifying. He treats teaching as a very personal interaction and students seem to appreciate it.

What time he takes for research right now goes to trying to understand people's response to severe winter storms. He also plays a small part in the administration of the Natural Hazards Information Center.

Suzy describes her position as "being on administrative strike." After being chair of the economics department last year at UCD she saves all her time now for teaching and thinking about what her next project will be. With mainly women and third world students in her classes she too gets an appreciative response in introducing them to non mainstream economic analysis.

A long standing interest in transferring some of the educational effort to the farm came off this summer and fall with the Committee for Popular Economics, a group Suzy is part of, which held a series of weekend workshops at the farm. Up to twenty-five participants—mostly activists in ecology, feminism, anti-nuclear, labor, community organization—gathered to learn both traditional and alternative economic analysis and to share problems and solutions, to start building networks. Various camping out arrangements for housing and a rotation of kp for meals kept the costs low and the camaraderie high.

We see quite a bit of Sherry and little Brian as they are happily settled in Boulder for the next few months (they were living at the farm for about six months which was really super). Peter lives in Boulder, works in Denver at the Fairmont Hotel, but we have little interaction. Helen and David Loth, Nick's aunt and uncle through his first marriage, live in Boulder and make up part of our local family. Steve and Mary and their youngsters, Wendy and Nathan, are settled in New Iberia, Louisiana, where Steve is engineer and executive in marine construction. We'll be with them for Thanksgiving and hope to re-gather in Montana for a week of skiing after.

Our love and good wishes for next year. The political and economic scene should be interesting—a great time to teach economics! As always, our home is open for visits. As of now we're not planning any big trip for next summer, and we hope to see some of you in 1981.

January 10, 1983
A chill wind is rattling the stove pipe—maybe 35 or 40 mph. It seems as though the wind has been blowing all year. Considering how badly Denver was hit by the Christmas Eve blizzard and how easily we got off (8 inches) we have little to complain about. Nothing grows in this weather, while the wood pile shrinks. But we're grateful for the storm windows and the glow of the wood stove.

Suzie's daughter Sherry and her husband Jim and grandson Brian braved the storm to get here Christmas Eve. Peter joined us Christmas day. We had a traditional celebration—both too many presents and too much food. We hardly recovered when Suzie and Sherry put on a classic birthday party (well not quite, Brian ordered turkey) as Brian turned 4 December 30th. All that had been preceded by my celebration of my 64th right before Christmas. By now we've dried out and are on our diets, trying to repair the damage to our waists.

Teaching takes most of our time. My Natural Hazards class enrolled 60 students again this fall—gratifying but tiring. The second time through I felt much better about it. Last spring I had a light load—just a seminar in recreational geography while I focused on the preparation of the presidential address delivered at the Association of American Geographers at the annual meeting in San Antonio in April. It felt good to concentrate that hard and the response was very gratifying. (Copies available on request.)

Suzie still suffers the commute to Denver, and is going through a bit of a life crisis, trying to figure out what direction the last stretch of her career should take. She enjoys the teaching, but is looking for a good project to capture her attention for the next several years. And she is restless about the long distance between the farm and job. She increasingly accepts invitations to speak on economic policy issues, feeling that it is important to develop these skills. Her work with the Committee on Popular Economics grew into our involvement with Colorado Connections, an attempt at networking and building an infrastructure for progressive causes: calendar, newsletter, skills bank, forum. But it's hard to redirect time, energy, imagination from ongoing commitments. At the moment the network is "on hold" until we find more energy to keep it going.

Georgia Lynn, a niece on the Wiggins side of the family, shared the farm work and farm space this summer while doing a legal internship in Denver. We hope she decides to locate around here after she completes her degree.

LeRoy Moore joined us during the fall. He and I worked together many mornings. Suzie found that it was pretty nice having two considerate men around the house; two husbands might just do the trick if one lives on a farm! Unfortunately for us, he left us and we are back to making do on our own.

There is no immediate slow-down in the offing. I have responsibilities in two geographic gatherings: April in Denver and October in Boulder. Suzie is planning a major conference on economic thought just before the AAG in April. Celebrating the 100th anniversary of Marx's death and Keynes' and Schumpeter's birth, they will review the three sets of contributions, both to economic thought and to economic policy. She hopes to edit a book from the proceedings.

During the fall we have been talking with Sherry and Jim about doing a "planned unit development" here on the farm. By this time we are serious about it. It will allow us to sell the five existing houses individually and to build two more—one for us, better adapted to our old age and one for Sherry and Jim. It will put us in a better financial position, possibly allowing us to buy an apartment in Denver, and it will reduce the responsibility of the farm considerably. And it will eventually get us out of the uncomfortable social relations of being a landlord and living with our tenants. Finally, it will give Jim a chance to practice his profession; he will build and design the houses, using the latest solar technology. We might even build an indoor swimming pool, which should make it much more important for you to come visit.

Re children. Steve and his family will be moving to Rio de Janeiro soon. He has been made manager of Latin American operations for his firm, Oceaneering. Sherry is pregnant and is supposed to deliver the end of June. We just found out that there are twins. Quite a shock, and she's having a difficult pregnancy; one of the fetuses is low in the uterus and she is confined to bed, hopefully not for five months. Brian has informed

Suzie that he'll keep one of the babies and that he'll give her the other since she's too old to have babies and he can't "beeteck" (protect) more than one. Peter is doing a good job of running a local restaurant which has some of the best food in Boulder; but he wants to get on with his career plans, which is to get into the hotel business. Now is not a good time, so he hasn't made a move yet. Hopefully he can sometime in 1983.

That's it for last year. Hope to see some of you this year, and that you have a good 1983.

December 23, 1983

The quiet is extraordinary. Moonlight filtering through shallow clouds that left another inch of light white snow last night. It's the pre-dawn silence when you think of so many things that you can get done before everyone else wakes up. The silence when you can feel close to those far away who have shared your life. That's why this letter now, in spite of all those other things to do that helped to keep me from going back to sleep.

Of course the Christmas cards and presents, wrapped and unwrapped, the tree that grandson Brian helped to decorate with his special five year old enthusiasm and perspective, the boughs and elves and candles, all help to close the distance. But also birthday cards add to the clutter that must be an external expression of the internal fullness as well as the unwillingness to let go of warm connections and worthwhile roles and functions.

There is a suddenness to ones eligibility for Medicare—a change in trend, almost like a discontinuity in the sedimentary rocks. The current of ongoing projects leaves little time to speculate on the change of trend, a change that has been going on, of course. It is only the legalism that is sudden.

Sometime in the next three years I'll pull away from most of the formal teaching. I am clearly less patient with the careless students, but I wonder what life will be like without a new cohort each semester—without the challenge, without the admirers, without that hidden sense of inadequacy at the beginning of every new class.

Very soon—within weeks, we should have finished changing the property relations on the farm so that each dwelling will be owned by the resident and the barns and garden will be owned collectively. Immediately we'll start designing, along with son-in-law Jim Logan, a new house for ourselves, one that includes a lap pool and that loses so little heat it can get by on what energy it catches from the sun.

And maybe—even in the next few months—I can get to some of the writing I keep postponing. Right now I'm wondering if I should try to make a case study out of the enormous cold wave of December 1983.

Meanwhile Suzi's deep into the chancy and lonely process of editing the spring conference papers—a dozen or more—into a coherent book while carrying on her other roles, both academic—senior colleague, graduate advisor, teacher, co-founder of a center for the study of children and public policy—and domestic—mother, grandmother, wife, organizer, counselor. We both continue to struggle with the question of how to be effective in countering the brutalizing of the world and the hierocracies that obscure it.

We hope you struggle too, that you do so from the warmth and support of a closely knit intimate circle, and that Christmas has intensified both the intimacy and the struggle.

December 26, 1988

The echoes of "Merry Christmas" have faded. A sliver of pecan brittle caught in the removable bridge hints of the delectables prepared and consumed the last few days. A stiff forearm remembers chilly woodcutting with the bow saw while the chain saw is in the shop. The windows are black for the pastfull moon isn't up yet to reflect the snowscape newly fallen and blown.

And I'm not a week yet into my eighth decade. The warmth of family gathered from nearby and from East and Gulf coasts still glows actively like the coals in our stove. We rather enjoy the incongruity of our very modern house with no central heating system. But the design is such that the sun heats it by day and the insulation and thermal mass (including and indoor lap pool) keep it comfortable with only a modest fire in the evening and early mornings.

I have wanted to write to each of you who have sent cards and letters but three years ago I wrote a "Christmas Letter" and then only got 10 or 12 copies mailed. This year Suzy has abandoned me for most a week to attend the meetings of the Am. Economic Assoc. in New York so with a little luck and some self-discipline I should be able get this off to you. Further the Compac with Word Perfect 5.0 has increased my speed and accuracy marvelously.

I did go with her to the AEA meetings a couple of years ago when they were held in New Orleans and we sampled the tourist delights. I was able to help with the interviewing, serving as sort of receptionist and messenger boy. I attended a few of the sessions and enjoyed them, but on the whole I feel as out of place at the AEA as she does at the Geographers' meetings.

She did go with me to the International Geographical Union meetings this summer (our summer, their winter) in Australia. Even there, I enjoyed the month more than she did. We both enjoyed visits with friends in several of the cities and in a village in Tasmania. But understandably the field trips organized by geographers for geographers were more my cup of tea (I should say "pot of billy"). It turned out to be more expensive than we had expected—another good reason for me to stay home this week.

We would be even further behind if we hadn't been able to rent the house to a wonderfully appreciative couple from Tulsa who have children & grandchildren in Boulder.

We had managed to fill the spring and early summer so full that we hadn't done the preparation for the trip we should have to get the most out of it. I had even forgotten to get visas so we almost missed our first field trip. But an anxious 12 hours in Los Angeles provided the visas followed by a restful afternoon with friends in the Hollywood hills. We were able to catch the next flight to Sydney and to meet our field trip with 45 min. to spare.

I had taught an intensive week of summer school, a part of a workshop organized by my colleague, Dave Hill, for Geography teachers. I have enjoyed immensely working with in-service teachers these last three summers and wonder how it will feel to give that up as I retire this summer. The teachers seem to enjoy the participative activities, many of which they can adapt easily to their own classrooms. It has been a special joy to see them go on to improve, elaborate, and invent new activities as we turn them loose after a little stimulus. There was no question about how I felt about retiring from my big beginning Physical Geography class. I felt a great release as I finished my last lecture Dec. 13th.

Suzi gave two papers between the end of classes and our Australian adventure, one to the Socal Science Education Consortium on the need for a wider vision of Economics in History and in the Social Studies — straight neoclassical theory doesn't explain, much in the real world, present or past — and the other on the early papers of John Maynard Keynes to the History of Economics Society. This latter area is her true love, but she keeps being distracted by other opportunities and responsibilities. Her socially significant research on cost of living for single mothers has been very well received and leads her into an economic study of the child care industry.

I have done precious little research myself, though I have one study going on "Farming in the Shadow of the Metropolis" which I am excited about. There is an important time geography study to be done related to Suzi's work with single mothers: what are the time and travel demands on single mothers of small children as they have to deal with the several welfare bureaucracies. This is not my area of expertise, but maybe I can interest a graduate student in taking it on.

One important 1988 preoccupation of mine was helping Uncle David Loth with the denouement of his life. Aunt Helen had died three years before. Increased blindness had not interfered with his enjoyment of memories of their 55 years together, but it did reduce the stimuli in his life. Just a year ago a dose of the wrong medicine set him back severely. He only partially recovered, moved into a group home and then into a nursing home. The old fire had gone out of him. There were still sparks of warmth and brilliance, but he was ready to go. The very end of May his heart just stopped. I wrote in a letter to his friends that I think he would agree that his luck stayed with him to the end. Friends and family gathered here early in October to celebrate Helen's and David's lives and the joy they shared with so many others.

May the new year bring you as much happiness as David had on the average over his 88 years, or as I have had over my 70.

June 2, 1992

I'm back from an African trip and want to share it, but June being what it is on the farm, I want to get something off pronto, lest it all go stale. The University of Botswana paid my way so I could be External Examiner for the Dept. of Environmental Sciences. There was a long layover in London so I got in a good visit with niece Deborah Kocher and her husband, Dewey Johnson, and their newborn daughter, Jordan. But I had left my address book at home. I remembered how to get to Sterndale Road but I didn't remember the number. At 7:30 AM several search strategies did not work. Finally I thought I remembered 57. A sleepy young man came to the door. "Oh yes, they live next door in 59."

I earned my ticket by grading papers from 10 or 12 courses plus 3 Masters Theses—solid grading for 4 and a half days. Then a session reporting back to the faculty, impressions from reading their students' papers. I made a strong pitch against straight didactics and rote memorization, for inquiry and problem solving. Some were ready to hear what I had to say, some not.

Saturday we all had luncheon together on the shady lawn of the Professor's house. Early Sunday morning Sandy Cooper drove me to the airport for the flight north a couple hours to Maun. I don't know enough to make much sense out of the landscape from the air. It looks very empty of people, a sort of random alternation of shrub, trees and grass. Maun is a metropolis of a couple of thousand people that serves as the gateway city to the Okavango Delta. See National Geographic, Dec. 1990, for a good description and much better visuals than I can produce. From here I'd like to transcribe notes I wrote. If I get a chance I'll add something on the end.

I don't know whether I'll ever send this. It is probably more of a journal than a letter. I guess I feel the need to communicate and writing it down will be almost half of a communication.

It's Sunday afternoon—2:45— the latter part of a siesta time here at Shindi Camp, 45 miles N of Maun which is 3 or 4 hundred miles N of Gabarone. We're on the NE edge of the Okavango Delta and not very far S of the Caprivi Strip that separated Portuguese Angola from British Bechuanaland and is now a panhandle of Namibia.

It's the heat of the day which is hot, maybe 85 degrees F, but dry and occasionally a little breeze. Sitting outside the tent on a little porch or stoop, shaded by several trees, I'm not perspiring but it would not take much exertion to get my hand sticking to the paper.

Camp is very quiet and restful feeling with a moderate chatter of birds high above. The concrete platform can't be more than 6 or 8 feet above the present water level in the swamp. But that must be enough so that very permanent installations can be made. Seven apparently identical tent platforms are spaced south of the Lodge/dining area, each with its spacious green canvas tent with zippable netting, twin beds, a couple of clothes racks with shelves, a tiny table with a water thermos and a bowl of fruit, and two lamps, one that is on whenever the generator is on, the other hooked to a 12 volt battery.

Tightly-tied bamboo makes a tall fence around a toilet, wash basin and shower in back of the tent. Insect spray, repellant, flashlight and stationery are all supplied. The firm—Ker Downey—runs several camps, some for photo people, some for gun people. Apparently those are the only two kinds of people. Time to get ready for the afternoon "expotition" to quote Pooh. What adventure lies ahead in this luxurious wilderness?

Continued Monday, same time of day, same weather, same birds, same routine. This morning I chose the canoe trip. There was room for a second passenger in the plastic version of the "makuro," the local dugout. A few of the real dugouts have been preserved to decorate the grounds. I tried to get a paddle but no go. I was to sit on the cushion and relax. The name of the game here seems to be sloth accompanied by unlimited food, drink and service.

The silence and peacefulness was powerful as we slid thru the bay into the channels and ponds. One of the guests described the silence as deafening. Mostly pond lilies and papyrus at first, alternating with a tall grass called "riz." That may be what I pronounce as "rice." It did have a shaggy seed head not unlike rice. The boatman used a paddle in the open water, a pole in the reeds. He identified half a dozen birds, letting the smaller ones go unnamed. Then we found the trail of a hippopotamus. He or she leaves quite a swath in the swamp reeds. We must have followed it for an hour—no tracks, just crushed weeds and mud—got close enough to hear it grunting and groveling but never did see it. The noise was enough to start my adrenalin going.

We did spot the rare swamp antelope, but not close enough to photograph. Big round ears. It is reputed to have splayed hooves with extra hair that help it stay up in the mud. Elevenish, we'd been out 3 hours, we headed back to camp—up-wind thru mostly open water. No landmarks I could discern but he had no trouble. Sherry, spaghetti Bolognese, corn fritters, green salad, cole slaw, and cut-up fruit. Plenty of choice.

Good conversation at the luncheon table: A young couple from Los Angeles on their honeymoon, Two Australian women who do consulting and training related to old people's homes, A travel consultant from Seattle and her recently widowed friend. She specializes in African safaris and was combining vacation with further inspections and explorations. The camp is being managed by a young English woman, Clair, who has her cute two year old on her hip a fraction of the time. She is only filling in while Jeannie and Philip, the long-time managers are on holiday.

Continued Tuesday, same time: At this rate this document will be all mornings and no late afternoons & evenings. This morning was quite chilly, took an extra resolve to get out from under the covers. After all it is the beginning of winter here. Coffee (or tea) delivered to the tent @ 6:30. Great red glow across the eastern sky with the birds starting their cacophony. This I remember from the central Kalahari last year. Breakfast of cereal and fruit and toast and this morning off on a walk. Brian in the lead with a rifle, the newlyweds and I following quietly. He would point out an unusual bird. Lots of letchwe, sesebe and impala. After a while a couple of giraffe browsing 25 feet above the ground. (The doves around the tent are making unusual and distracting noises.) Very few insects, no rodents in evidence. Mostly a variety of birds and antelope. Broad flat meadows of tall grass, grazed down in places to within a couple of inches of the sandy soil. Clumps of trees on mounds in the meadows, often with a termite "stack" on the mound. And the meadows, maybe half a mile across, ringed by trees along continuous ridges, only a few feet above the meadows. The water is rising now. In another month it will flood the meadows. 360 degrees of horizontal horizon. Geologically this is a delta.

At the appointed time and place the Toyota was waiting for us, a half ton 4 wheel drive pick-up with padded seats in the back, high enough to see over the tall grass. Brian asked if we wanted to go back to camp directly. No hurry! So we went on in search of LION. More antelope, baboon—dozens scattered near one of the ridges. Frequently Brian or the driver or both would hang out over the side of the vehicle looking for lion track. "Mostly yesterday's." Then they spotted vultures circling. Using clues I could only guess at: tracks, matted grass, ? ?, they got closer, spotted one on a mound 200 yards away. It turned out to be two males. They sauntered out into the tall grass. They would have been impossible for us to see but for the height of the vehicle which they brought up to within 30 or 40 feet. After many shutter clicks they moved on, found a recent kill, a roebuck. Skull and horns, most of the backbone, one leg with the hoof, that's all that was left. Not enough meat left on it to make a vulture landing worthwhile. The mother and cubs must be somewhere nearby, but it was time to head back to camp.

We arrived at 11:30 just as the boat was bringing back a planeload from the airstrip. Greetings, introductions, and pre-lunch sherry. The arriving party included Jeannie and Philip, the regular managers of Shindi camp, Clair's husband, the pilot and a new guest from Florida. The conversation had all the cordiality of a very temporary in-group (as on shipboard), hosts and guests more or less indistinguishable, upper-class English manners and mannerisms and a mix of accents. Bream, a delicious local fish that had been caught by one of the Australian women, was served as the hors d'oeuvre.

I should fill in some of the afternoons before the post-siesta interruptions begin. One was a drive on the Toyota Land Cruiser thru the same landscape as this morning but without lion. Sunday, just at dusk Brian spotted something dark far across the Meadow. Buffalo. He drove us over. Maybe 200 of the fearsome looking beasts and their calves. They were not scared of the machine, moving away from it but not very far.

A powerful red sunset across the wide horizon and a chilly ride back to the welcome diesel powered lights of camp, a hot shower and gathering around the campfire for drinks before dinner at 8. More fire and drinks after dinner and off to bed.

That's the end of my longhand notes. It has taken several days to get this far so I'll try to wind up quickly. There was one more afternoon outing—a boatride to an area where the cormorants, thousands of them, nest along with another species. We saw another of the rare sitatunga, the splay-hoofed swamp antelope, the eyes and a couple of inches of the back of a crocodile, a beautiful fish eagle among other things.

Three of us flew out Wednesday morning after a chilly boat ride to the airstrip. Eight giraffe sauntered slowly out of the way as the Cessna roared into takeoff. A lone elephant and a herd of zebra enlivened the flight. We met our Seattle friends at the Maun airport and flew together to Victoria Falls. They convinced me to take a chance on a flight the next day to Harare, and to stay over with them at the classic Victoria Falls Hotel, rather similar to the big Canadian Pacific Hotels at Banff or Lake Louise, and the Stanley Hotel here in Estes Park. Except at Victoria Falls there are still hundreds of people around to serve you.

The falls themselves are impressive. The water flow was lower than normal but even so!! Parts have heavy flow like Niagara, but it goes on and on. You walk half a mile or more along the edge of the gorge with the water pounding down across from you. The gorge is so steep and deep you cannot see the bottom most of the time. The pounding vibrates through the soil so you can feel it with your feet. The mist rolls up through the gorge to soak you. (They rent raincoats at the gate.) A great rainbow was there whenever you looked down, away from the sun.

We browsed the souvenir shops. Prices are even lower in Zimbabwe than in Botswana. The "Dance Spectacular" didn't seem authentic to me, but that's out of my field. The next morning we crossed the bridge into Zambia, got a cab to take us around the town of Livingston, much less tourist oriented, though looking in that direction. My Seattle friends were impressed with the lack of military presence compared to previous experience. Prices are still lower in Zambia, but my bags were already overloaded.

So then the flight home: 36 hours from boarding the plane at Victoria Falls to meeting Suzi at Stapleton field in Denver. Modest layovers in Harare, London and Washington, D.C. Everything shipshape at home and happy to be there. A week of rainy weather had everything green. Suzi took off the next day for meetings in Fairfax, VA. She brought her uncle, Cooper Bright back from Baltimore for a few days. Soon she's off again to Atlanta for different meetings where she will stay with nephew Eric Kocher and family.

We're looking forward to six weeks here with several visitors including Bill Hinton and a group of Chinese agriculturalists interested in dry land farming and maybe 30+ disarmament activists organized by the Nevada test site protesters. Then we're off to Scotland and England for most of August with grandson Brian. Except for a damaging hail storm requiring much replanting in the garden, no catastrophes.

We hope that all's as well with you and yours. And Suzie just heard that her big grant was financed — at least half way!!

New Years Day 1993

I resist writing an "annual" letter lest it sound trite and stale. But as the holiday season draws to a close it seems clear that if we don't stay in touch at this season we don't stay in touch at all. (A little touch is better than no touch at all, that's what I always say.)

As I try to make sense of the year's events, continuity stands out rather than change. While the political change abroad seems unfathomable, here in the US continuity seems more likely than profound change though Clinton's rhetorical readiness to face the problems is very welcome.

The farm continues to be a deep satisfaction both in its physical-biological nature and in its social functions. The home-owning community stays together. Many outside groups from preschoolers to adults use the loft, enjoy and learn from the grounds.

Among us we've added a high quality sand volleyball court, two additions and two houses. One of them Sherry and Jim are building so we will have children and grandchildren next door. Other children continue in familiar patterns. Peter is in business for himself now in Aspen, though he's considering a change of venue. Steve & family have built a new house in Houston where he is Senior Vice-President of Oceaneering.

I continue to make very slow progress on the reunion video footage shot a year and a half ago. I hope to have a version for circulation by Spring. We continue to enjoy superior music: season tickets to the Colorado Music festival and the Colorado Opera and uneven amounts of Colorado Symphony and Ballet with the children, Gilbert & Sullivan, etc. I don't do much with professional Geography, though I did lead a couple of good field trips this summer for the International Geographical Union. I did my second consultancy with the University of Botswana followed by a luxurious 4 days game watching in the Okavango Delta and a day at Victoria Falls. Wow!!

Suzie continues to work as hard as ever, maybe even harder, for after working on it for four years, the big research grant finally came through. Four foundations have chipped in $915,000 to support a 2-year study of the child care industry. Much of the effort will be in gathering the data. Teams in 4 states will visit 100 sites each.

The statistical analysis will focus on the relationship between cost and quality. They expect to demonstrate how expensive really good child care is and how mediocre most of the present care is, unless it is subsidized by the low wages and volunteering of the care givers themselves. Nevertheless there is some hope that they will find ways that children's learning could be much increased at many sites with relatively little increase in cost.

Another change was getting reacquainted with Bill Hinton, my closest friend in grade and junior high school. Ellen Matteson Knox had arranged a winter class reunion when Bill was back in the US from China where he has lived much of the last 45 years. It must have been as much of a shock to him to find me looking 73 as it was for me to encounter this broad shouldered six-footer whom I remembered as a skinny 15 year old. It was fascinating to find how much we had in common in spite of having lived very different lives for almost 60 years. Then this summer he brought 2 groups of Chinese agriculturalists to the western US including stops at the Nelson Road farm: one group bureaucrats who were quite disinterested, the other village leaders with voracious curiosity and learning capacity.

Our big travel this year was a month in Britain with grandson Brian. London, Edinburgh, the Cotswolds, Cornwall, Devon, Surrey visiting friends and seeing sights, and a week on a "narrow boat" put-putting restfully thru the quiet countryside. It is a do-it-yourself vacation with the 50 ft long, 7 ft wide boat outfitted like a camper. There are pubs along the canal for the meals you choose not to fix yourself. You take turns steering, opening and closing the late 18th century locks. We recommend it for a change of pace. You get so under-stimulated that even a couple of ducks in the reeds hold your attention, a welcome change for us.

We hope that your year has had enough continuity to hold together, enough change to be challenging and that the new year will be more so.

October 28, 1993

Rather then wait until Christmas or after New Years, it seems better to write while the images are vivid, the odors still in the nostrils, the flavors still stimulating saliva. I started this letter longhand at 9448 meters over clouds covering Hungary in the slightly smoky cabin of Turkish Airlines flight 581 Istanbul-Brussels-Newark, close to noon depending upon whose time you choose.

What to include? Exclude? The skeleton itinerary wouldn't mean much though it can easily be supplied on request. We left Boulder mid-September for 2+ weeks touring the dry interior of Anatolia and then had 3 weeks along the shores of the Mediterranean and Aegean seas and the Bosporus.

I had spent most of a year in Central Anatolia in 1952-53. This was my first chance to revisit. We were joined by longtime friends Bella and Leonard Feldman. Our camper, rented in Istanbul, was not really big enough to sleep 4 adults but it gave some security lest we get stranded without a hotel and it was convenient again and again for picnic lunches. Further it easily carried our increasing volume of purchased carpets.

Rugs were sold everywhere. We found them beautiful and the shop owners accomplished in their techniques, each in a slightly different way. Suzie really enjoyed the bargaining process once she got accustomed to it. Bella speculated that one could carpet a six lane highway around the world with the inventory of rugs in Turkey.

The first few days included: a hot springs resort; the ruined cathedral where the Council of Nicea was held; a major center of ceramic handicraft; a well preserved Roman temple dedicated to Zeus and Cybele, aka Artemis; a village where I had been a guest at a wedding 40 years before; and the capitol, Ankara. Similar sequences followed: museums; familiar landscapes; ruins of ancient (like 4,000 years ago) cities; overgrown present cities 5 to 10 times what I remembered.

Perhaps the high point for me was finding the very house where I had spent the night in Ispili Kőy, a small stone mountainside village. A missionary doctor had taken me there on horseback as he made his monthly rounds. The structures in the immediate neighborhood had hardly changed, but the village had grown into a town. The meadow across which the women had carried their jars to get water from the stream was now completely covered with houses and a few stores. The trail up which our horses picked their way was now a paved road.

Finding the very spot in the town of Develi where I took a 1952 photo looking up the cobblestone main street at the snow-covered volcano, Ercias Dağ was a similar thrill: cobbles now smoothly paved; trucks, busses, taxis, cars and tractors in lieu of the single truck and donkeys; no chickens picking over the street debris; a handsome new mosque and three story buildings completely obscuring Ercias Dag. In both cases friendly people went out of their way to help. Polaroid pictures were a small token of our appreciation.

For Bella the highpoint seemed to be the "Cappadocian" landscape. Like a cross between the South Dakota Badlands and the spires of Bryce Canyon, this area of lightly consolidated, deeply eroded volcanic tuff was a refuge for early Christians (6th to 10th century) who carved homes, churches, warehouses, stables, whole refuge cities, into the soft tuff. Many of the church frescoes survive though marred by iconoclasts. Our hotel rooms were so carved. The fantastic natural landscape was as much an attraction as the human use thereof. We stayed a day longer than planned.

Konya came towards the end of our tour of the interior. It had been an important area of settlement since Hittite times. It was the biblical city, Iconium. Early in this millennium it was the capitol of the Selcuk Turkish Sultanate of Rum and it was where the great poet and mystic, Mevlana, lived and died. He was the founder of the Whirling Dervish order. His tomb is a marvel of tiling.

As we were getting out of our van at our hotel, a woman on the sidewalk said: "I recognize you. Aren't you an artist?" The woman was travelling with a tour organized by the San Francisco Art Museum. It turned out that Bella knew several of the group including the leader. He invited us to join them that evening at a special performance of the Whirling Dervish music and dancing. This Dervish order was so powerful in the Ottoman Empire that when Ataturk was secularizing Turkey after the revolution in the 1920's he had to outlaw the order. The music and dance is preserved as a "cultural heritage." It was an unexpected privilege, even though I felt something of a voyeur watching someone else's worship.

We all had some stomach trouble and Konya was my turn, delaying us a little. From Konya we spent a day and a half up and down, more down than up, through the rugged Taurus Mountains to the Mediterranean coast. We gave up our camper, and stayed in the luxury of the Tutav Turk Evi Otel. It had been recommended by a friend of my sister, Peg and it lived up to its recommendation. They had taken 3 or 4 classic Ottoman houses nestled against the city wall and renovated them beautifully and equipped them with appropriate antiques. Bar and terrace restaurant looked out over the harbor and the mountains beyond. It was a welcome change from the accommodations in the interior: utilitarian at best and sometimes shabby. We paid $15.00 for two doubles in Beyshehir.

We gawked at stupendous Greek/Roman ruins at Side, Aspendos and Perge, were joined by eight others including Peg, were minibussed along the steep coast highway to Fethiye where we boarded our boat. The Turan XX was a sturdy 60 ft. ketch with 6 cabins. Adequate but nothing fancy. It had a friendly crew of three with limited English but wonderful nautical and culinary skills.

January 1995

I thought to myself at lunch today how lucky I (we) am (are). We enjoy civic peace and services, the material blessings of home and nourishment, and can watch a bald eagle roost for a few minutes in the tall cottonwood only a hundred yards away. I wonder that there are enough rabbits and prairie dogs out in this snowy landscape to make it worth the eagle's time and effort. There could well be more small rodents available in this somewhat protected ecosystem than in the overgrazed horse pastures nearby.

We certainly are fortunate to have landed on our feet in this lovely dwelling in its beautiful setting. We're grateful too for the many greeting cards and letters in spite of the infrequency of our correspondence.

Suzie is in the last semester of her appointment at the University of Colorado at Denver and looking forward to her formal retirement as of the end of May. She had a better semester teaching last spring than in the previous couple of years, is looking forward to this last semester with mixed feelings.

She is in the climactic stage of the Cost and Quality of Child Care research. The final reports are in draft form and their executive summary is being printed. They will release it in a press conference at the National Press Club early in February. There are very interesting findings about how the "market" contributes to the generally poor quality of care delivered by centers. This applies especially to the younger children: infants and toddlers. (It's even worse in the informal "aunts and grandmothers sector.") The unfriendly turn of political events makes the reporting all the more delicate, for anything negative about the child care situation could be twisted to justify cutting rather than increasing subsidies.

I continue to enjoy the lack of pressure associated with retirement. Puttering around the garden, the orchard, the raspberries and strawberries, harvesting wild asparagus and chokecherries and processing all of the above could happily take all of every day until winter when there is always wood to saw and split and occasionally snow to shovel.

The farmstead continues to be an attractive venue for visitors. Only one wedding here this year. Visits from family, friends and children of friends from both east and west coast cities and from England have helped us to stay in touch. Both Peter from Aspen and Steve from Houston came to help during my surgery and recovery. The Wiggins-Logan children and grandchildren live next door. The Helburn grandchildren from Houston were with us, Wendy for the summer while she interned in Jim Logan's architecture office and Nathan for his Christmas break from High School.

Some pleasures derive from continuity in place. We attended Emily Hey's Boulder High graduation exercises this year. Her mother spent the last few months of the pregnancy here on the farm. Sherry and Hal helped with the preparation and birthing. A poster-portrait of chubby one-year-old Emily with the caption *What About Emily?* was a prominent part of our 1st Rocky Flats protest march dramatizing the continuing nuclear hazard. Mary and Emily have been part of the extended family for over 18 years.

The rural idyll is intruded upon by a variety of more or less worthwhile activities. I joined the 25th Venceremos Brigade for two weeks in Cuba this Spring. One hundred and fifty of us worked in tobacco sheds for a week and had another week of orientation to the way in which Cubans are adjusting to the cruel and senseless US blockade. With practically no petroleum, bicycles provide most personal transportation supplemented by a few terribly overcrowded buses and trucks. Oxen drawn plows, harrows, and seed drills are more common than tractors. Compost replaces chemical fertilizers. Integrated pest management reduces the need for pesticides. Nationalism and loyalty to the more equitable political economy maintains most people's spirit in spite of grinding shortages and hardships.

Quintuple by-pass surgery restricted me from mid-August thru October. It seems like a miracle to have the heart stronger now than a year ago. Peace and justice work with the Rocky Mountain Peace Center is a major focus. The need continues as the national security complex has found minor wars, drugs and deficits to replace the communist threat and derail most efforts create a more humane society.

It has been gratifying and fun to be drawn back into geographic education. I've done a little consulting for a project putting the High School Geography Project books along with the materials from 7 other projects onto CD ROM so that they can be easily retrieved by teachers and curriculum developers.

Opera, ballet, symphonic and chamber music, and a few plays spice up the pervasive naturalist aesthetic of our environment. We added the Santa Fe Opera for the first time this year, but missed the Aspen Music Festival for the first time in years.

We look forward to a little more leisure with Suzie's retirement. Both Austria and Mongolia are in the travel plans for the coming year. We will try to do a better job of staying in touch. (We always say that.)

All the best to you and yours for the new year.

December 1995

Merry Christmas to you. Enclosed is a book, *Ninth Heaven, Ninth Hell* which I, Suzie, read on our recent trip to Mongolia and China. It's edited and was brought to press in the U.S. by Bill Hinton, our host in Mongolia, and the author of *Fanshen*, and *Shenfan*, two books about the course of land reform and then the cultural revolution in Long Bow, a town further south in Shanxi Province than is Dazhai, the subject of this book.

Bill is a long-time worker in China although he spent most of his years in the U.S. since 1953. He is dedicated to the pursuit of a rational agriculture in China and to the need for collective self-reliance in the countryside. i.e., he does consider the socialist part of the Chinese revolution a noble experiment and its success crucial for the wellbeing of China's peasants.

Anyhow, I read this book on the way to Ulaanbaator and was captivated by it, even though it is too long and I couldn't keep track of the cast. We want to share some of our enthusiasm for our 8 days in China with Bill including two days in Dazhai (it is the famous village, "Learn from Dazhai" of the 1960's), some of you may even have posters. This we think is a way to do it. Two days hardly makes us experts but it was enough to generate the enthusiasm we want to share.

When the present leadership took over from Mao and Deng and started the privatization rush, they felt they had to destroy the reputation of Dazhai and its most prominent leader Chen Yongui, the symbols of successful socialism in the countryside under Mao's chairmanship. This book is a careful refutation of the propaganda issued to discredit Dazhai and Chen. In the process it details an amazing story.

After our three weeks in Mongolia we had stayed with Bill's sister, Joan, and her husband Sid. They have lived in China helping with agricultural innovation since the late 1940's. They help to run a big dairy farm near Beijing. Shanxi province sent a car for us and Joan came along as far as Dazhai.

We arrived at the enormous "guest house" (Photo #1, which is one of 3 wings) in the late afternoon of Sept. 22. It had to be that big to accommodate all the visitors who came to "learn from Dazhai" before the sharp political changes.

The following morning, as we walked toward the center of the village, a car stopped. It was Guo Fenglian, former "Iron Girl", recently returned to Dazhai as party secretary at the insistent request of the villagers. A warm reunion as she greeted Bill and Joan. (Gua and Joan are at the left in photo #6.) We visited the village offices and the knitting factory upstairs (#10). Chen Yonggui is no longer alive, but his son, Chen Mingzhu, joined us at the village offices. He was obviously delighted in #2 to receive a copy of the American version. A Chinese version has only recently been published.

The village itself is very compact and no thoroughfare goes thru it, but you can look down on it (#3) from the road that leads up to the grave of and monument to Chen. The museum, at the foot of the long stairs in #4, is still under construction. Just beyond it in the picture one can pick out the village by the parallel rows of houses. These are the cave dwellings which are common in this part of Shanxi province. The book tells of the move from actual caves to stone-lined caves which provided better protection from the rains.

The terraces with stone risers shown in #5, 6, 7, & 8 were built by the villagers during the winter months when the farm work was slack. Straight terrace walls in the bottom of the small valley were washed out by flash floods so they learned to arch the terrace wall up-stream (#7). Pictures #7 and #8 show what the villagers did to end the gullying in Wolf Den Ravine. Irrigation works, like the aqueduct in #5 with the assistant party secretary, Song Liying (who figures in the book quite a bit) also demonstrate the skill, ingenuity, and determination of the villagers.

Pictures # 4, 5, 6 were all taken from the burial memorial for Chen on Tiger Head Mountain. We climbed another 1/2 hour to get to the top, a spot where Chen used to say that from here one can see to Tienamon, that is, one feels the connection of the little village of 90 families to the Chinese Republic as a whole.

The annual recognition lunch for retired villagers, was being served in the shelter near the museum (#9). We were invited: happy toasts, many stories and some criticism of the current emphasis on industry at the expense of agriculture.

Qin Huailu, the book's author, joined us briefly that evening. He too was pleased to receive a copy of the English version of the book. He gave Bill another manuscript, hand copied, he hoped could be published abroad.

The following day we drove what seemed like a long way to "West Water, East," a trans-mountain diversion project carried out by several villages working together to provide more irrigation water. We are standing at the east end of the 20 km tunnel in #11. #12 shows the reservoir. Everything was completed except the diversion structures which would have put the water into the west end of the tunnel, when the national government stopped the project, part of the campaign to discredit Dazhai, Chen and Mao.

Finally we were entertained at lunch by Zhang Huaiying, the former county party secretary (#13), who "discovered" and empowered Chen Yonggui and other village leaders. The conversation was formal, the food was good and generous, and his personal library was enormous including the complete works of Mao, Marx and Lenin, and the histories of all the Chinese dynasties that have been recorded.

A compulsory inspection of a new cement factory finished our Dazhai visit and we headed south over the terraced mountains toward Long Bow, which is another story! We hope that you can find some of the excitement in the heroic story of Dazhai, its discouraging period and possible revival.

We wish you happiness during these holidays and all the new year.

January 1998

We're in the second day of a classic Chinook. But for the wind it would be tennis weather. In town many are wearing shorts. Convertibles have their tops down enjoying the sun. All but the most shaded drifts have melted/evaporated. The wood box is full. The big chuck hole at the top of the driveway is filled and smoothed over. The bills are paid. I have no excuse. It is time to acknowledge your cards and greetings, to try to maintain contact even as tenuously as this kind of correspondence does.

We hope your Christmas-Hanukah-Kwanza was pleasant, that your new year will be happy and that it will not be too difficult to get back on your diet. Since the 19th of December with two luxurious parties in Phoenix and then Christmas and New Years here with children and 5 of 6 grandchildren, we've been off our extremely low fat diet as many days as we've been on it. But we've been quite good about the exercise routine and faithful with our combined yoga/stretches. While over-commitment does create stress in our lives, it is mostly intermittent. We resent the aches, pains and weakenings of aging but we are in good shape considering our chronological age. We look forward to a vigorous year ahead, grateful for everything that works.

Much of our life continues to revolve around growing and preserving vegetables and fruits, tending our immediate landscape, sharing the home-owner's association chores. The beauty of the house, lawns, shrubs and flowers are deeply satisfying. There's a bonus when we can provide the venue for a summer wedding. Equally important is the close friendship with six other families here in our cooperative village. It is no surprise to me that I get homesick when we are away for long periods.

Suzie still keeps an office at the Denver Campus of the University but is glad to be free of teaching and committee responsibilities. The spinoffs from the *Cost and Quality of Child Care* study keep her busier than she'd like to be. St. Martin's Press has contracted for the public policy book she and Barbara Bergman are writing. The manuscript is to be completed in August. I continue to volunteer a bit with the Rocky Mountain Peace and Justice Center.

Theater and music spice up our bucolic idyll with season tickets for the plays at the Denver Center for the Performing Arts and the summer performances of Boulder's Colorado Music Festival. A weekend at the Aspen Music Festival seems to have become an annual event.

Our expectation that we would do more traveling once Suzie was retired too, has been fulfilled. 1997 included Chicago and its great Art Institute, San Francisco and Santa Cruz and Washington, D.C. The paper Suzie read at the Santa Cruz meeting will be published soon in Capitalism, Nature and Socialism. The major trip, however, was six weeks in France, most of it in the same house we had rented the previous summer/fall. It was a special pleasure to have son Peter and daughter Sherry with us for our last week there. While there, Suzie got a chapter of her book written. I wrote an article, a retrospective of the High School Geography Project which had been invited several years ago.

Inshallah, 1998 promises: Bozeman, Montana for a celebration of the Department of Earth Sciences I helped to get started 50 years ago; Anguilla in the Leeward Islands where Suzie and Barbara will write most of the time; New Orleans where son Steve will receive a major industrial award; Santa Fe for a friend's 50th birthday; Boston for the Association of American Geographers annual meeting and a cardiac checkup; Bellagio on Lake Como in the Italian Alps for most of April as guests of the Rockefeller Foundation where Suzie and Barbara will be chained to their respective computers but I will be free to roam; most of June in the Netherlands and Norway at two different meetings; and several days in nearby Fraser, Colo. to gather family for my 80th birthday. The gardening will just have to suffer! Maybe I can stay home in 1999.

January 1999

The problem is how to stay connected when we are so scattered across the globe. One description of a proper commune from years ago was that everyone in the group knew where everyone else's head was every day. They touched base with each other every day. Can we do that every year?

I'll let Suzie add her share, but my major concern seems to be staying healthy enough to enjoy our current vigorous nature-connected life style. Having started into my 80th year, I am grateful for every week that I can saw and split the wood, shovel the walks, patrol the irrigation ditches, plant and weed the garden, prune the hedge and shrubs. Every new ache or pain, every new forgetfulness revives the commitment to exercise and diet. Arteries, prostate, cataract, sciatica and arthritis are the obvious threats but all are thankfully in abeyance.

So the daily routine includes sharing the household chores with Suzie, doing or supervising most of the outside chores including those we share with the other six households in our cooperative village. Gardening, hiking and skiing double as health maintenance and recreation. A modest volunteer effort with the Rocky Mountain Peace and Justice center much of it concerning non-violence training adds a sense of contribution. This year I wrote a radio editorial on U.S. policy toward Iraq, a retrospective article on the High School Geography Project, and paper on the short half-life of curriculum reform. The year was spiced by a month in Italy with a side-trip to Slovenia, Austria and Switzerland, and almost a month in England, Sweden and Norway. What more could one ask for a 79th year.

Now it's my turn (Suzie). I hope that 1999 will be a transition year for me. I'm finishing research and writing related to my work on child care that has preoccupied me for the last ten years. I've just edited an issue of the Annals of the American Academy of Political and Social Sciences on child care, am finishing up some research with a colleague that grew out of our big study on the cost and quality of center child care, and am finishing a book on child care public policy with my friend and colleague, Barbara Bergmann. Hopefully the book will be out this year, published by St. Martins. It makes what we think is a convincing argument for large increases in federal spending to enable any family who needs it to be able to purchase reasonably good quality services. For too long the public debate has been controlled by the conservative think tanks who argue that the only thing wrong with the current system is too much government interference and that moms (except poor ones) should actually be paid to stay home with their kids. We hope our book will counterbalance this view and encourage a more open public debate and more public spending on early care and education. If the book is well received Barbara and I will, hopefully, hit the road talking up our ideas, but in any event, I will wind down my more academic activities and really retire. That's the transition part, an interesting but an unknown prospect.

The Italy trip came about because Barbara and I were invited to spend April at the Villa Serbelloni at Bellagio, Italy — a magnificent villa overlooking the north leg of Lake Como. The Rockefeller Foundation hosts small conferences (usually on international concerns, while we were there they involved international agriculture and fishing concerns) and scholar/artist residencies. Barbara and I wrote during the day (I had a charming studio tucked away in the woods) and socialized in the evenings after bocci ball. The experience of being totally cared for in a luxurious and intellectually stimulating environment has had a permanent impact on my world view. I know I should be thinking of retirement as an opportunity to do important volunteer work, but now I'm also thinking of ways to reproduce, on an admittedly less grand scale, the Bellagio experience. There is a lovely small retirement community that has just opened in Boulder that I think will fit the bill. But Nick is not quite ready, as you can tell, to give up the rugged life and I have to make sure that I can get cappuccino on demand, and have access to a bocce ball court.

September 13, 2000
Drs. Ewing, Jenkins, Doucet and Fulton:
I am writing in the aft cabin of a canal boat moving slowly westward on the Canal de Midi parallel to the north shore of the Mediterranean. (Just so that you have the context.) But we will be home by the 6th of next month and I would hope that we can be better prepared for a couple of decisions by my alerting you now to my concerns. I think I had expressed to each of you my felt need for better coordination in matters related to my health.

Just before I caught the plane from DIA to Paris I underwent a nuclear stress test. I had expected to call Dr. Doucet from the airport to get the results, but there was no time there so we asked our daughter Sherry Wiggins to inquire if there was anything serious. Since she did not call us, we assume that I had no serious blockage. I will make an appointment with Dr. Doucet to get the detailed report soon after our return. It might be helpful if he would have a copy of the written report sent to Dr. Peter Ewing at Dakota Ridge Family Medicine in Boulder.

During the preparation for the test Dr. Doucet noticed that I had a small hernia at my navel. (I had noticed a slight change in the navel but did not realize that it was a hernia.) I assume that I should have that operated on soon after we return to Boulder.

The urgency for the stress test derived from a set of vague symptoms including: lack of energy and ambition, getting tired easily, slight shortness of breath when I started to exert myself, very mild sense of indigestion (no nausea but what I called a "queasy stomach"), and difficulty passing a stool which sometimes led to constipation. Urination has been getting slower and my PSA was up to 4.0 the last test.

Our best guess was that some of these symptoms were associated with stopping the administration of the human growth hormone which had happened 5 or 6 days before. But Dr. Doucet and I were both concerned enough to go ahead with the stress test.

I would like Dr. Ewing's receptionist to reserve an appointment for a general annual physical exam as soon after the 6th of October as convenient. Confirmation could be sent by postal mail or fax, but I will check in by phone soon after arrival.

As you may surmise, this is written with profound confidence in your medical knowledge and experience, but also with the sense of the importance of the involvement of the patient. We had an adage back in the 70's that good health was too important to be left entirely to doctors.

Thank you for your attention. Sincerely

December 21, 2001

It's not a Christmas letter. We're always too busy between Thanksgiving and Christmas. It's not an annual letter for we didn't do one at all last year. Hannukah and Ramadan are not major celebrations in this household. This year I guess it is a biennial letter.

The big news is that Suzie's book is done: researched, written, proofread, sent to the publisher (Palgrave, a division of St. Martins Press) and printed. *America's Childcare Problem: The Way Out* by Suzanne Helburn and Barbara Bergman will be released January 7th. We have taken a deep breath and started helping get the word out not only to the early care and education community but also to people who may be influential in the national debate concerning welfare in general and child care in particular. By midyear most of that will be done. Suzie will have time to think about what she wants to do "when she grows up" while she sorts the drafts and sources and correspondence that clutter the home-office.

Other than the child care policy book, the dominant characteristic of our life is stability and the enjoyment of home and gardens, community, and environment. We have lived at the same address for over 31 years and have every reason to want to stay put until we get crippled up so that we cannot enjoy the work: the maintenance both inside and out, along with the chores we share with the other six families here on "the farm." There is profound satisfaction in the subsistence lifestyle: growing and preserving most of our fruits and vegetables. We do live with most of the maladies of old age but none of them are severe enough to keep us from enjoying the garden and grounds. Every day we are grateful for our good health and sympathetic with our contemporaries who are not so lucky. We'll let you know when we have a change of address.

The children are well set too. Sherry has shifted from sculpture to painting while her husband Jim is a successful "green" architect with a developing institutional practice. Peter has his own hospitality business in Aspen, organizing other people's vacations, weddings and parties. Steve has started to retire from the underwater construction business, devoting some of his time to a ranch he owns in northwestern Wyoming.

Grandchildren, of course, are less settled. One, Wendy Helburn married Brent Mather in a lovely ceremony here on the farm. Another, Michael Logan, is planning a marriage on a Greek island next summer. A third, Dana Logan, is in high school in Izmir, Turkey with the American Field Service, completing her junior year. Brian Logan is living and working in Boulder, Joseph in New York City, and Nathan Helburn in Houston, TX.

We hope that you are well and if not that your problems will soon pass. With the world in its present state, it seems incongruous to say "Happy New Year." Let us rededicate ourselves to making the world a better place for all.

July 26, 2002

It may seem foolhardy to start a Christmas letter when I have only half an hour to write but then, whoever suggested that I was sensible. Let's start with the most recent events and work backwards. Right now Suzie is in San Diego at a Family Day Care convention. She is taking every opportunity to speak on behalf of a 30 billion dollar increase in Federal appropriations with suitable safeguards for expanded early care and education.

She took 20 copies of her book: America's Child Care Problem: The Way Out with her just in case someone wanted to buy one at the "Resource Sharing" session. She and Barbara Bergmann finished it in September of last year and it appeared in bookstores in January. The first printing is sold out and we understand a paper back edition is planned.

We were hardly back from France a week when she left. We had been on our annual sojourn to Suzon adjacent to Provence and St. George des Agouts near Bordeaux. We spent a quiet week in each. In Suzon we were joined by Eric Kocher and family. It was fun showing them our familiar haunts. In Bordeaux we were joined by Lou and Pat Braddell, our friends from England. We took it easy in both places doing very little "sightseeing" and enjoying catching up and going to market and fixing and eating good meals and drinking good wine.

Before France we spent a week in Turkey. Granddaughter Dana had spent her junior year in high school with a family in Izmir, arranged by the American Field Service (AFS). A couple of fortuitous circumstances combined to make it possible for us to visit her and her host family just before she returned. It was a great visit. The husband worked for a very large corporation, was not macho in the least, was sweet and thoughtful in the extreme. His English was minimal. The wife worked for a bank but was semi-retired. She had interests in painting, philosophy, and comparative religion. She was learning English so not only did she and Dana have common interests, but they could teach each other their native tongue. The daughter was fluent in English but was away much of the time, attending university in Ankara.

Dana had a very hard time at first because of the language but after a couple of months of submersion she began to master it and start on the road to fluency. And the AFS arranged trips to the Black Sea, the Mediterranean coast, Istanbul, etc. so she saw many of the Turkish landscapes.

We were hosted royally but relaxedly. We did spend a whole day visiting Pergamon, now called Bergama, accompanied by a neighbor who was a professional tour guide. They practiced aroma therapy and used dreams to guide therapy 2300 years ago!

I was (and still am) recovering from a stroke the middle of March. Suddenly I couldn't use the computer without making the same mistake over and over again. My handwriting, never very legible, deteriorated to the point where I couldn't even read it myself. My speech was slow and very soft. I had some cognitive, coordination and balance losses, but mostly one could not notice it from the outside. A brain scan discovered the clot in the left basal ganglia.

Compared to my sister, I got off easy. She had a stroke or a combination of strokes just before we left for Turkey which left her paralyzed on one side and unable to talk. She is undergoing rehabilitation in Atlanta where she has a son and a daughter and their families. She is recovering some abilities and control but it is too soon to forecast how much. Based on my experience patience, determination, and rehabilitation exercises are all helpful, but the greatest of these is patience.

Reaching back before the stroke seems like a long time ago. The big event was the completion of the book and it finally appearing in hard copy in January. I had hoped to plan a major celebration, but travel to push the recommendations has kept Suzie almost as pressed as she was when she was writing and I haven't been able to help as much.

We did two trips to Europe last year. One was our usual venture to southern France but the other in early summer took us to Norway and England. The International Assoc. of Feminist Economists met in Oslo. We added the train trip across the highlands, a couple of days in Sognefjord where we retraced some of the trip that Tess and I did in 1960, and Bergen. Then to Britain for the annual meeting of the Social Science Education Consortium in Oxford. It included a memorable field trip to London, led by geographers from the Institute of Education where I taught on a sabbatical many years ago.

Another break in the routine here at the farm was a few days in Seattle. Our nephew, Terry Kocher underwent a brain operation there. Sister Peg was there helping with the recovery and I joined her for a couple of days. Also I accompanied Suzie to Atlanta between Christmas and New Years where she attended the Am. Economics Assoc. annual meetings. We stayed with the Eric Kocher family and visited the Debra Kocher family and got reacquainted with the ever changing children.

Steve, semi-retired from Oceaneering, divides his time between SE Asia, consulting, and ranching in northwestern Wyoming. Peter continues his successful hospitality business in Aspen. Sherry continues her art career here. We venture in to the city for music, drama and cinema. Otherwise we follow the march of the seasons here on the farm.

May the rest of 02 and the following years shower you with good health, happiness, and Security.

December 2003

We are still here, alive and well, in case we haven't written in a couple of years. We are still on the "farm," enjoying life in our semi-rural setting. Nick still cuts the wood for our heating stove since the sun doesn't shine all the time contrary to some Colorado boosters (or boasters). He still works in the garden and does a variety of chores around the farm but he has definitely slowed.

Suzie's economics of child care has done quite well and is now available in paper back but she has finished going around the country, promoting the ideas in it. She still keeps a shared office at the University of Colorado, Denver where she works about once a week with another retired economist, John Morris. At present they work closely with John Sperling, doing much of the statistics for a political book. Her other major commitment is to the YWCA where she is on a national committee and serves on the local Board of Directors. She asserts that these commitments will be finished by spring so she can practice being retired and be more leisurely gardening.

We started the year in Mexico on a consulting trip with John Sperling which included time for swimming near Cancun. March and April included visits with Bella Feldman and Beth and Jim Eckenrod. It also saw son Peter's 50th Birthday party in Aspen. We finished a long tradition: the final Easter Party. Suzie has done it for the children at the farm since Brian was two. He'll be 25 the end of this month. Several of the other children here at the farm turned 18 this year and have gone off to the college of their choice. This includes granddaughter, Dana, who is at Reed College in Portland, Oregon, reveling in the challenging studies and unsupervised social life.

Our yearly trip to France included: the two families we usually stay with, three friends from Boulder, two who split their time between visiting in the U. S. and cruising the canals and rivers of western Europe, one from the Netherlands, and two from England. We were happy to forego formal sightseeing in favor informal socializing.

Knowing that we could not keep up the labor intensive farm life style for ever, we started looking for a condominium in the spring. Gradually the allowable target price kept inching up. Finally, we settled on a very well located, two bedroom place just 5 blocks north of "old downtown" in Boulder, and adjacent to an older community shopping center, two blocks south of the hospital. Sherry commented, "You can walk to the emergency room!" Within two days of our purchase it was rented. We hope to be at the farm for another two or three years, but we'll decide each year that the lease comes up for renewal.

The Quaker meeting asked me to present my "spiritual journey" early in November. I was a little taken-a-back for I thought I had never had a spiritual journey, but it turned out that what they wanted was an ethical or moral or religious autobiography. Its composition, 7 pages, was quite a satisfying discipline. If you would like a copy I can mail or email it to you (if you provide your email—a good thing in any event since we've learned to keep in touch via this quite wonderful technology).

December brings a happy round of holiday parties including some friends we miss throughout the year, not the least of which was my 85th birthday (that yielded two parties!) Jim Logan was waiting to see if I could blow out all 85 candles!

We trust this finds you well, happy, looking forward to a constructive and prosperous New Year, and, if you are one of us in the U.S., ready to help bring about regime change here at home.

November 26, 2005

We're breaking tradition this year by sending Seasons Greetings Cards. This is because all other news pales compared to our change of location! As of August 10 this year we moved from our Nelson Road Farm-Community that we helped start 34 years ago.

We enjoyed the privilege of the same address for a long time. But Nick's failing eyesight and lagging energy made the farm a less hospitable place and almost a prison since he hasn't been able to drive since this spring. We're now half a block from a convenient bus stop, and two blocks from the grocery, hospital, and other convenience shopping (Sherry points out that we can walk to Emergency!). And we're five blocks from the downtown Boulder mall. Nick's learning the public transport system and his morning walks are acquainting him with the neighborhood.

Suzie has been in charge of the move — readying our house for sale, selling it, readying our apartment for our needs, divesting books, papers and all sorts of belongings so we could fit into 1400 sq. feet, and moving in. This is one of our last errands — letting you all know that we are alive and well, shed of much unnecessary impedimenta. We now know why Sherry and Jim were so insistent on our moving and we have advice for elderly friends—let the children deal with the downsizing after you are no longer with it! It's a lot of work, although I guess I'll be pleased with myself when I get a chance to put my feet up and read a novel!

Other news, if you haven't seen it already, check out Suzie's latest writing project, *The Great Divide: Retro vs. Metro America*, written with John Sperling, John Morris and Carl Hunt (Polipoint Press, 2004). It's on the net as well as in print. It's meant to push Democrats to get their act together!

On the lighter side, we continue to go to France most Septembers and this year we're taking a trip to Chile to experience the glacial landscapes of the southern coast. Once a geographer...!

Our kids and grandkids are all well and constructively occupied. Please look us up if you come this way. We have access to the guest apartment in our very pleasant building.

All the best for the holidays and the New Year. Let's all do our bit for regime change next November.

Christmas 2007

Just a short note to wish you well in 2008 and to tell you we will be active in promoting regime change in the U.S. in the coming year. Can we finally get real leadership to bring U.S. actions back into sanity?

Nick's pre-Christmas has been clouded by complications from an ablation to stop atrial flutter. The procedure went very well, but was complicated by internal bleeding which is very slow in going away. However, the docs promise that his energy will surge!

We've actually had a pretty good year. We had a lovely time in the North West, including Seattle, Victoria, and Vancouver where Suzie got an award from the Social Science Education Consortium for her long time commitment to econ ed. We also got to Portland to participate in our granddaughter Dana's graduation from Reed College and Suzie visited her this fall in Cambridge where she's at the Harvard Divinity School studying American religion. Seems like we might have another academic in the family. Then, of course, we took our annual trip to France, this time spending some time in Burgundy with good friends, the Eckenrods, who took us under their wings, important now that Nick is nearing 90. We also visited friends in England before coming home. So there's still a bit of traveling in our lives.

Sherry, Suzie's daughter, has been having a very productive year, working with a women's art collective that has been developing ties with Palestinian women artists. Her husband, Jim, an architect, is very involved developing policies to minimize the carbon footprint for residential housing. Steve and Peter are prospering, as are our grandchildren. Suzie involves herself in various volunteer projects, but will be searching for something more personally rewarding in the new year. Meanwhile, we've adapted to town life in Boulder, while retaining gardening rights at the farm.

Again, have a good 2008 and help turn the country around!

November, 2008: Impressions of Uzbekistan/Tajikistan September 2008

[This was our last big trip and it was to the semi-arid, mountainous landscape that Nick loved so much. We traveled with the Boulder Dushanbe Sister City group organized by our friend Mary Axe to inaugurate the cyber café given to Dushanbe by Boulder.]

We were so close to Afghanistan, yet there was no hint of warfare/ violence. Suzie's reaction was disappointment that we didn't get to see the Oxus River separating Tajikistan and Uzbekistan from Afghanistan [if we had perhaps Nick's impression might have been different!]

Suzie's favorite part was the trip by car (we were in a caravan of 6 cars) from Samarkand to Dushanbe up and over the mountains with an enforced stop at a lovely mountain village (to arrange for a new car for our caravan because one of them had broken down), the spectacular mountain scenery, the evening and overnight in the small mountain town of Aini with all of its inconveniences that nevertheless provided some direct experience of life in Tajikistan, the drive over the pass the next morning into Dushanbe with our very skilled driver driving as fast as possible around the myriad of pot holes (Suzie pretended it was like a disorganized roller coaster ride), ending with an enforced car wash by a lovely 10 year-old boy (using a garden hose) before entering Dushanbe in order to avoid a fine!

My most vivid impression was the barrenness of the mountains, hardly a speck of vegetation overgrazed by the herds of sheep and goats that we met occasionally on the roads. We loved meeting the Tajik people, particularly in Khujand where we had more opportunity to visit, but also in Dushanbe at the Parenting Center.

We haven't mentioned all the gorgeous relics of the past. Our favorites where in Bukhara where one could actually imagine the bustling Silk Road trade. You could almost hear and see the traders exchanging silks and spices. And Sasha and Sons was our favorite hotel, an old residence turned into a small hotel.

As an economist and geographer we were impressed by the miles and miles of bloody cotton fields, mainly in Uzbekistan. We wonder what positive and negative consequences have devolved from the 19th century Russian decision to impose cotton growing in much of Uzbekistan and some of Tajikistan.

We were sick the day that the Cyber café was turned over to the city of Dushanbe, but when we got to see the café we were very impressed with the structure and particularly with the use of solar technology. We hope this inspires imitating in the country.

Finally, there is the impression of the presence of graft as a way of life! But we are social scientists and don't often get to live in countries where the major function of government seems to be control over resources for personal gain.

December 15, 2010 (by Suzie)

We've had a busy fall and so I'm combining holiday greetings with an update on Nick's health.

Despite the sorry state of national and international politics and economic performance we do wish you a happy holiday season and a good 2011. Even with the recent action by the Senate, Nick and I are distressed over the stalemate in national politics that I, at least, am sure will prolong the current weakness in the U.S. and world economy. At the end of 2008 I was heartened to see a resurgence of interest in Keynes and Hyman Minsky who years ago explained the tendency in advanced capitalism of financial crises and continuing financial instability. Unfortunately our President chose to listen to mainstream economists and to protect the financial sector. Now we will have to wait out Republican posturing claiming that their policies will reduce uncertainty and create a resurgence in investment spending. What brings about investment spending? Dreams or actual increases in demand? Oh well! Too bad we dissident economists are ignored. So I don't expect a big expansion in the economy to reduce unemployment to 8% by 2012! But Marx's predictions about financial crises—increased concentration and centralization of capital—certainly occurred in the financial sector. I'm not quite sure how the power of the financial sector can be reined in. Luckily, I'm old enough to divert my attention to more pleasant things, like the holidays. So again, we both hope you all have some fun and that 2011 is good for you.

Remarkably, Nick is very slowly and very surely recovering from the June accident. He's been home 5 weeks from Frasier Meadows nursing facility where he lived for four months, got very good physical and occupational therapy but not so good food, also benefitted from his own caregivers who hastened his recovery and spoiled him. Coming home started a real spurt in recovery so that he now can walk 100 feet without stopping using a walker, and he can go down and up a flight of stairs to the garage where our car resides. Mostly, he's in his wheelchair but navigates with it quite well. His brain has cleared up remarkably so that intellectually he is almost back to where he was before the two operations and near death congestive heart failure episode at the end of July. I feel free to leave him alone in the apartment for an hour in order to run an errand, but for a while he'll need more-or-less constant surveillance to make sure he doesn't fall and to provide support if he has a temporary loss of confidence. We still have wonderful help from two caregivers who are here five days a week from 7:30a.m. til noon and all day Wednesday, and two nights a week so I can be sure to get a couple good nights of sleep. I don't know what the future holds, but bone-wise, Nick is definitely going to be knitted back together. He may get the two pins out of his hip in the spring if they give him any trouble.

As far as the accident has affected me, it's interesting. As I said to a friend, it has tested my goodness!! I've been in remarkably good spirits, rolling with the events. Today Nick conjectured that he thought he'd still be around the apartment for another Christmas and I think he's right. I've maintained my exercise program, continued to do my volunteer consulting in state level and county level early care and education. I've been named to the Governor's Early Childhood Leadership Commission and this should keep me involved.

The family seems fine. Sherry, Jim, and Brian have been very supportive, as have Nick's sons who come for visits and to help out frequently. We have much to be thankful for.

Again, best wishes for the new year.

APPENDICES

Twentieth anniversary reunion of the Community on Nelson Road in June 1991

Appendix A: Community

Nick always wanted to write a book about our community experience at the farm on Nelson road. I suggested a title, *From Commune to Condo*, which pretty much described the evolution of the place that we loved and where we lived for thirty-four years, most of our married life. He changed the title to *From Commune to Cooperative Hamlet, or 30 Years on the Nelson Road Farm*, and wrote an introduction and some notes. The revised title better suited Nick's hopes for creating a community structure that could support individuals and families living.

Here is Nick's introduction and notes for the book, slightly edited, and expanded. They are followed by some articles Nick wrote for the community newsletter, *Lykins Gulch News*, the invitation Nick wrote to contribute to the twentieth anniversary, excerpts from minutes of meetings concerning the disposition of the one-hundred-acre outlot owned by us, and two short essays on community. I've included the outlot discussions to illustrate the community commitment to "Getting to Yes" by managing conflict, and our process of reaching consensus. The last short piece, written around 1992 just after Nick returned from Botswana, shows how profound and permanent a hold "community" had on him despite the toll living community had on us in the early years.

From Commune to Cooperative Hamlet
or Thirty Years on Nelson Road

Our Community is a sort of a rural condominium in Boulder County, Colorado, about six miles north of the city of Boulder, about forty miles from Denver, a very cooperative and much admired hamlet. In sixteen years (1984-2000) there has only been a turnover of one family. If we kept a list of the individuals and families who have expressed an interest in joining us, it would be very long indeed. Unfortunately county land use regulations prevent us from expanding.

- The physical space is 120 acres at the foot of the Rocky Mountains.
- The constructed space is 7 dwellings, a pottery, a carpentry shop with a meeting room upstairs, an artist's studio, a chicken coop, a barn and out-buildings used for storage.
- The population is 7 families with a total of 9 children living at home.

- The property is 7 lots owned individually by the 7 families, an outlot owned by the Homeowners Association which includes the outbuildings, the driveways and a large playground, and a second outlot of 100 acres owned by us.
- The legal institution is a non-profit corporation with articles of incorporation similar to other condominiums.
- The process consists of uncounted personal ties among the 7 families, shared chores and maintenance, a monthly meeting operated by consensus with a rotating facilitator, and various shared celebrations.

It started in 1970 with discussions over a period of several months among a dozen or fifteen idealistic adults interested in forming an egalitarian commune. We met weekly and talked and talked. We recounted our biographies in detail. We listed our hopes, our reasons for wanting to live close to others. We were not well off and thought that group living would be less expensive. We wanted the efficiency of shared work, and the resulting freedom for political activism, we wanted the power of numbers in that political work. We wanted to raise our children in close association with other adults. We wanted less dependence on the commercial economy and greater self-sufficiency. We recognized that the nuclear family was unstable in this culture and we yearned for mutual support. We disliked the competitiveness surrounding us and wanted to be cooperative. We wanted to show the world that it could be done.

By the time we had been talking for five months we began to feel that we had to "do it" or quit talking about "it." Where? Boulder was mostly one-family homes and zoned that way. A 120 acre farm six miles north had just been offered for sale at what seemed like a reasonable price. In addition to two small houses it had two garages and a large chicken coop that seemed suitable to be made into dwellings. Suzie and I, both university professors, had some capital. We bought it.

The first members moved into the two houses in June of 1971. Many have asked how the commune evolved into the existing cooperative hamlet. The evolution can be divided into four rather distinct stages:

I.   Commune One, 1971-73
II. Commune Two, 1974-76
III. Tenants village, 1976-1983
IV. Cooperative village 1983 to the present.

Commune I

Although we read a lot of what little had been written about communes, we were feeling our way with little knowledge. We had not visited The Farm in Tennessee or Twin Oaks in Virginia, and we really did not want to tie ourselves into the seemingly rigid structure of Twin Oaks based on Skinner's novel. Of course, we knew of the kibbutz in Israel and the agricultural communes in the Soviet Union, but no model resembled our dream. We were seeking an egalitarian group life style based on voluntary cooperation with the service drive, not a profit drive, as the primary motivation. We understood that it would take discipline to make it work and we thought we had the self-discipline to carry it off. If Mao and Castro could create "socialist men and women" after their short violent revolutions, why couldn't we do it within the loose restraints of affluent capitalism.

Perhaps we should start with a brief chronology:

Elise Boulding called a group together in November 1970, not once but at least twice. Nothing happened right away, but after the holidays I remember getting together with Bobby & Lyle Seebaum, Hans and Gayle, Tom Smith and maybe Judy Hurley. We agreed to meet again the next week. It developed into a weekly potluck. Joel and Patti Rosenberg were in and Mike Haldeman, too. Mostly Elise was not there. It had become clear that Kenneth Boulding would not consider living in a commune.

We included autobiographies in the discussions. At first they were very brief, 5 or 10 minutes. But each one got longer and longer until one biography took the whole discussion time. [That was Judy's amazing story.]

I don't remember Matt and Andrea at the meetings [Bobby and Lyle's children]. I do remember Patti suckling Adam during the meetings, and my feeling very warm about that.

March or April 1971, Elise brought an Austrian friend, Ernst Winter, who had a commune in Austria, to our weekly meeting. He described the castle they lived in and the division of labor and the income from research, and it all seemed feasible. Maybe it was on a second visit that he asked us how much we each could contribute. We went around the room and surprisingly it seemed enough to support the group, not generously, but adequately.

May 1971, we decided to go ahead and do it. Our search for a site in town was frustrating. Anything attractive was zoned for one-family dwelling only, including the magnificent Mapleton Mansion that was within our means and had quite a bit of room. The one apartment house we looked at was depressing, dilapidated and run down. It smelled bad. So we started looking in the country. The first place we were shown was the farm on Nelson Road. It had just come on the market, not yet even printed in the multiple listing. Dick Blumenheim, who was showing it to us, asked us to make up our minds quickly, for it seemed such a good buy to him that he wanted to form a small group to buy it and hold it for a year or two and make a big profit on it. We walked out over it. In the middle of May all the wild flowers were in bloom on the rather-overgrazed pastures, also the lilac tree in the front yard of the old farmhouse. I could see no alkali. I visited Andy Steele our neighbor to the West and he agreed the only hazard was the wind. There were two small houses on the place already being lived in. Further there were two sturdy garages and a very well-built chicken coop, two rather old and rickety barns and several sheds. Without any thought about zoning we calculated that we could make residences out of the two garages and the chicken coop. We agreed to buy it for occupancy the 15th of June, 1971. My "How We Began" from #4 *Lykins Gulch News* gives my June 1973 description.

June 15, 1971, Hans and Gail and Leslie Ford moved in to the little farmhouse. A few days later after some hard feelings and hard words, the tenant in the big farmhouse had moved out, and Bobby and Lyle and children (and who else?) moved into it.

June/July/Aug 1971, we converted the smaller East garage into a dwelling for Judy and James and Katie, including a concrete floor for the back area that had been the blacksmith shop, plumbing the bathroom with advice from Jerry Crawford our neighbor to the West, as none of us had done any plumbing before, a hardwood floor for the living room, and a tokonoma. By this time Len Mogno had joined the group.

Aug/Sept 1971, we reroofed the west garage, closing it in, flooring it and adding a kitchenette & bathroom.

Hans and Gail decide to leave. We were not pure enough for them.

Fall 1971, Ronnie Rosenbaum who had been in Vista in Detroit and had known Len there came out to visit and decided to stay.

Dec. 1, 1971, the chicken coop remodel was far enough along for Nick & Suzi and Sherry and Hal to move into, even though the plumbing in the bathroom had not been installed. Kitchen plumbing in the coop allowed cooking for the collective evening meal to move to the coop. Christmas 1971 the toilet was finally installed.

January 1972, the roof blew off the big barn. My letters to sister Peg and Mother in Part II describe some of my state of mind at the time.

Spring 1972, we plowed up almost half an acre of the young orchard and started converting it into a garden. See my description below from #5 *Lykins Gulch News*, "From the Clod Patch," describing our efforts.

June 1972, Tom Smith was asked to leave the commune, the only time a member was asked to leave. [Suzie: we continue our long friendship with Tom, including time in Prague in 2006.] Sometime near this time Joel and Patti left. They bought an apple orchard on Colorado's Western Slope, near Paonia. We were all surprised since they had seemed to have a difficult time summoning the energy to do the physical labor expected of them in our rather modest garden. Taking on a commercial orchard seemed like a heavy physical commitment. I remember that there was a financial aspect to their leaving also. When they had moved onto the farm they had sold their house in Boulder and had around $15,000 from that sale that we all expected them to contribute to the commune. We speculated later that this might have been too much of a commitment for them.

July or August 1972, Judy took a group of CU students (including Sherry who was a freshman) to Japan for a year. Reggie Gray, who had been observing closely with the expectation that she might join, moved in to the East Garage with son Ethan.

When did Barbara Cole join us? She was our oldest member (70+), very steady, and energetic, and an assistant editor of *Lykins Gulch News* first published February 18, 1973.

June 1973, Bernie Mayer and Matt (?) came out from NY to "work on a farm for the summer." Lesli Dalaba, Sherry's good friend from Berkeley must have been visiting for the summer.

July 1973, Bernie paired with Reggie, Lesli with Matt.

End of summer 1973, Matt left to the west coast. Lesli went on to music school.

August 3, 1973, #5 *Lykins Gulch News*, I wrote an article, "Small Children Incompatible with Young Garden."

> As we started the garden this spring we had group work every Saturday and Sunday morning. Everybody turned out and worked for an hour at least. The children came along with mothers and fathers. After the peas started to come up and the little trees which will be the shelter belt were planted, group work was punctuated by "be careful of the little peas" and "watch your step!" It soon was clear that the young garden and the young children were incompatible. One person took the children elsewhere during group work, so mothers and fathers could work in the garden. Was this the beginning of the community child care program? The older children have begun to take some responsibility for garden work. It turns out that James is an industrious irrigator, Katie a meticulous weeder, Beth does well in the lettuce and carrot harvest, and Matt has a garden all his own.

September 25, 1973, *Lykins Gulch News* reported that we "stirred."

> On Saturday, September 15, Sherry moved into the yurt, (which Judy, James, and Katie had vacated). Bernie moved into the Seebaum's back bedroom (which Sherry had vacated). Judy, James, and Katie moved into Bernie's room. Nick and Suzie moved into the little green house (which Pat and Caroline had vacated) and Jay and Harriet Lynch moved into the chicken coop. Rainy day in September: we crawl into one another's shells.

Fall 1973, we entered into serious discussion about creating a youth collective. In #2 of *Lykins Gulch News* Bernie recounts the hard time adolescents have growing up in America, some of which stems from her/his role as a member of a nuclear family while struggling with conflicting needs for dependence and independence. When conflicts are the product of the family situation, it is often impossible to resolve them within the family.

> To provide a better alternative than the parental home, foster and group homes, as a community of individuals and families, we can accept a number

of teenagers into the structure of the community and the special sub-structure of a youth collective within the community. As youth collective members, they will neither be expected to play the role of children nor bear full responsibilities of adult membership. They will take part in a peer group structure that fits naturally into an adult community rather than being divorced from and in opposition to such a structure.

Winter 1973, spring 1974, serious problems develop with Bobi and Lyle and Mike and they leave, a major blow since they were so central to the community, working full time there. Also the youth collective comes up against the financial and zoning constraints despite overall positive responses from Melba Sheppard of the Youth Services Bureau, Don Reed of the Mental Health Center, and Bob Hamm, Placement Officer for the courts.

Commune 2

Late Spring/Early summer 1974, Bernie and Reggie leave to form a new commune with his brother, Tom Mayer and family and a few others—the Juniper Street Collective. Disappointment at the inability to form the youth collective may have contributed to their leaving. Teddy Tripp, Jimmy Buener and John Schell moved in. Was it earlier or later that Marty and Ellen Hines and John Winans joined us? And after a few months a woman friend of John's. This was the turning point in the community. We moved from creating a youth collective to starting a goat dairy and Co-op Construction under Jay's leadership. The construction company would provide employment for most of the men. Harriet would manage the dairy.

Early summer of 1975, Glenn Browning joined the group. We were unhappy at the direction the group was drifting. The group started discussions about the community taking ownership of the farm. In June we took a long weekend in the mountains at Janet Moone's and came back with a written description of the direction we saw the community moving and expressing our concerns. We outlined the current drift of creating small enterprises that provide employment and adequate financing to take over the mortgage by 1979, also six alternative directions that had been discussed: creating an exemplary farm as a model for others, developing a self-sufficient diversified farm—a Noah's Ark—in preparation for a societal breakdown, focusing on extended family living, living simply/poor, focusing on self development, being part of an alternatives network. Only the last two appealed to us and we also expressed skepticism about the success of the current direction and our lack of interest in it. We took an apartment in Boulder where we would be close enough to attend meetings and participate in some of the work. By the September community meeting it was clear that the community had little desire to modify the drift, and we asked for and took a "leave of absence." There were profound divisions within the group. Who would stay together, who would go, and where? These discussions took place during the fall of 1975.

Winter 1975-1976, dissolution arrangements were made during the winter as the group decided not to buy the farm. Len and Ronnie bought a house in Longmont in September. The "big green house" was rented to Debbie Taylor and friends. Jimmy Buener and Jay Jennings left for Idaho to work on a guest ranch at the edge of the wilderness. Jay and Harriet bought a farm near Bayfield in southwest Colorado.

April and early May 1976, Teddy, John, Jay and Harriet moved to Bayfield with tools, machinery and goats. Jimmy Buener, writing on the occasion of the 1981 reunion: "I still think that a community on a farm is the best way to incorporate rural life and thoughtful persons. How this gets implemented is another question. Intentional community *is* intense. The balance lies in our humor and our love for each other. At Lykins Gulch in what I might call the "cooperative construction period" our objectives were very similar. Where we failed—? Shall I venture setting limits? Realistic Goals?

February 1976, We hired Glenn Browning to add a greenhouse onto the chicken coop.

June 1976, we moved back into the chicken coop. Gradually Glenn took over the day-to-day management as well as the maintenance of the farm. Glenn remodeled the east garage with beautiful craftsmanship and added a solar component, to it. Carol Young was a frequent visitor, and Suzie and Nick stayed with her in Denver during the week to reduce Suzie's commuting.

The Tenants Village

Summer 1976-1983, we rented the four other buildings. We remodeled the west garage. Peter moved into the little green house. Renters included Jan Logan and the twins, Sherry and Natalie, Steve Thompson and Natalie (who changed partners as Natalie and Paul Gelatt and Steve Thompson and Lynn Fuller), Ivan Getting, the leather boot people and the mice they fed in the big farmhouse, Nina Wolf and children who rented the coop while we were away in 1976, Kathy Partridge and Jay Jury (changing to Kathy Partridge and Jim Glasscock), Jo and Tomoko (Bulletin of Concerned Asian Scholars editor), Carl Formosa, Anne Widerstrom, others? In the early years of this phase we enjoyed a good deal of community living including fall trips to the mountains to cut down dead trees and haul them back for fire wood, gardening, pressing apples for cider.

September 1981, with a change in tenants, the landlord/tenant relations created problems in sharing. One couple distributed a long Open Letter to residents; the main objection was mandatory renter participation in the garden, but voluntary participation in other group activities such as the egg and chickens operation. They maintained that all of the cooperative activities should be organized as "worker collectives" independent from control by the landlords, us. They concluded, "our wish is, through workers' control, to strengthen commitment and involvement in democratic collectivism." So much for renting to Marxists! Suzie countered in a long response,

> ...at this point it is inaccurate to think of the activities here ... in terms of collectives....You did not move out here with that in mind. Nick and I are very shy about committing ourselves to community living after our experience... [we] have had a real need to gain some degree of control over our home life, some need to fix up the place ... at the same time making the farm available for others to use.... We are willing to let others do their thing as long as it doesn't hit one of the areas that we care about. This is not democratic but it is real....we want to do what we can to make the situation pleasant and fair.... We realize that this place is more like a feudal fiefdom than a socialist commune....but the farm is almost the only property we own, so we must be wise in planning for the end of our lives. Furthermore, we must be fair in managing our property in terms of our own kin. While there is certainly a lot to be said against inheritance by ones children, it seems to me that there is even less to said in favor of leaving one's worldly goods to someone else's children.... Let me end with your quote, "From each according to their ability, to each according to their need." Lenin points out that this is the ultimate goal of communist society, but that it cannot be achieved without socialist man and woman. We're far from that. Probably what we can hope for is the socialist goal of to each according to his contribution. But it's really tricky to figure out one's own and everyone else's contribution.

Cooperative Village

1983, the non-urban Planned Unit Development and conversion to a condominium association. The PUD idea was suggested by our daughter and son-in-law who saw us working too hard for an ideal that was not panning out. They suggested subdividing, so that people living at the farm would own their own lot and collectively own an outlot. This arrangement could encourage the development of a true community. Sherry and Jim helped us through the PUD process, and we succeeded in selling the lots to renters or people we liked. We made improvements to the property that we wanted, and we created bi-laws that made sense based on our twelve years of community living. Initial buyers of the lots were Kathy Partridge and Jim Glasscock, Natalie and Paul Gellatte, Thea Tenenbaum and Lelle Malferrere, Mike Zimmerman and Kathy Widmer, and Tom Stermitz. Tom sold the east garage to John and Judith Davis a few years later, the only turnover in the sixteen years.

November 1983, the barn raising. As part of that plan to sell the house lots and reorganize into a home owners association, we decided to use some of the proceeds to reconstruct the hay barn that had blown away our first year on the farm. It would become the community center, carpentry shop. We organized a barn raising over two weekends. Jim Logan and Glen Browning were expert carpenters and Jim organized the whole thing.

Over the summer we made all the preparations—doing the foundation, raising a trombe wall on the south side for solar heat, ordering the roof trusses. Then we contacted everyone we knew to come help. We supplied the food and drink, and we offered the finished barn to anyone to use if they helped. There was an article about it printed in *The Sunday Camera*'s FOCUS November 13, 1983, "The People Barn: Nick and Suzi Helburn want to raise more than a roof."

Friday to Sunday June 7-9, 1991, we held the community's twentieth anniversary. I wrote in the invitation,

> Present planning focuses on two big parties Friday and Saturday (food and drink, music, singing and dancing). During the day we can share what the period at Lykins Gulch meant to you and how it has affected your life since. We will structure some time each morning and afternoon to encourage the sharing of experiences. But we'll leave plenty of time for games (volley ball, softball, swimming, etc.), informal conversation and maybe even an optional work project. I'd like to commission someone to record some of the reunion with a video camera. Maybe it's the academic in me, but I think we learned a great deal thru the 5 years of commune, the years of renting and now in the rural home owners association.

The videographer shot 27 hours of tape and we edited it down to two hours. [The DVD is included with the memoir.] I also asked folks to write me their vivid reflections to possibly collect in the *From Commune to Condo* book.

1992, demolition of the original farm house, replatting of subdivision lots to provide a new lot for Thea and Lelle, and expanding the acreage of the two adjacent lots. This came about as Thea and Lelle decided to enlarge the farm house. Sherry and Jim advised against sinking money into the poorly designed structure. So we tore down the house to replace it. As soon as it was down, it became obvious that the space looked terrific without a house and Sherry suggested moving their lot to the north of the vegetable garden. This created serious dissension among homeowners requiring Reggie Gray and Bernie Mayer to mediate a solution. After all person's concerns and fears were aired we quickly came to a solution—an Olympic sized volley ball court in the park.

1994-99, consensus decision making about transferring ownership of the out lot and water rights.

1983-2005, mostly wonderful years, see my annual "Christmas" letters for proof.

1971-2005, lots of events. How many weddings? Of the original group Sherry and Hal, Sherry and Jim, Len and Ronnie, Carol and Glen, but also granddaughter Wendy, and many, many friends. Weekend workshops, political events, parties—

June 11, 2005, Farm Reunion and goodbye. A lovely time was had by all! We sang this: For Suzi and Nick on moving from the farm to Boulder:

Thanks for the memory and many more
(Lyrics: Nick Helburn?)

Thanks for the memory
Of candlelight and wine,
Dinners oh so fine,
With family and comrades who were friends,
Of yours and mine.
So thank you so much.

Thanks for the memory
Of sunny afternoons,
Hot tubs by the moon,
And lovely walks and earnest talks
Of times that're coming soon. (We wish)
And thank you so much

Thanks for the memory
Our daughter came to wed,
Amidst the flower beds,
Down on our knees to pick those peas
And lettuce by the head.
And thank you so much.

Thanks for the memory
Of kids all running free,
Of camaraderie,
Of building barns and spinning yarns and apples from the tree.

We thank you so much.
There are many worlds to make.
Ways to give and ways to take
Each other joy and love another cake to bake.

Thanks for the memory
A truly giant sum,
Of all the things we've done,
But nothing yet, we wanna bet, to match the ones to come.

Thank you so much.

*   *   *

Articles from The Lykins Gulch News by Nick

"How We Began," *Lykins Gulch News*, #4

When I opened the door of the Boulding cabin and we picked our way across the legs of people sitting on the floor, I thought—what a motley crew. What could Elise have in mind to bring such a mixture together? Every shade of the counterculture and a few straights were crowded into the tiny room. We each talked about our dreams of community and a little about where we had come from to have those dreams.

A gifted cabinetmaker on probation from a drug bust looked toward a workshop where street people could learn job skills. An ethereal young woman hoped for a simple life where meditation and spiritual purity could be achieved. A lean fellow with a scraggly beard wanted a life full of self-awareness. Foam domes, social revolution, harmony with nature, alternative technology and on and on.

That first meeting was in late December 1970. Several of us felt together enough that we met again a few weeks later. A weekly discussion group formed. Sometimes it was potluck, sometimes after the children were abed. Between times we got together in small groups to get to know each other better. We talked about music and art and pottery. We talked about children and family and marriage, about jobs and capitalism and socialism, about experience and learning and school. We talked and talked and talked.

We took advantage of some help. Ron Lippitt and Emily Girault helped us clarify our alternative futures. Ernst Winter shared his ten years of communal life in Austria, and his insight on leadership.

Each of us invited friends into the group. A few stayed. The less committed missed a meeting or two, lost track and dropped out. We felt closer and closer to one another. We began to believe it would work. We added up our incomes and tried to estimate the money costs. In May, after three months of talking, we agreed we had gone as far as we could go talking—we had to do it!

Then came the search for a place to do it. Could we move into adjacent houses? We looked at a rundown apartment house for sale. We cased the mansion on Mapleton. We found the farm on Nelson Road, walked over it in the Spring in the early-morning light. We did it!

"Our Community Structure Described," *Lykins Gulch News*, June 15, 1973

We live in five dwellings, all part of a single farmstead on a 118-acre farm about 10 miles north of Boulder, Colorado. We bought the farm in June of 1971 and began to move in July 1st. All of the dwellings were occupied by December 1971. Much of our effort has gone into improving the two houses that were here and into converting two garages and a chicken coop into dwellings. By now we all have reasonably comfortable and convenient quarters with room for several more people. Thus far when more than one family have shared a dwelling there has been stress, sometimes friction. We hope to add one or two more dwellings and a community center to the farmstead.

We live as distinct families but keep trying to share the childcare more widely. We have widows, divorcees, married and unmarried couples, and single people. Some of us consider the community a sort of 20th-century equivalent of the extended family, it being supportive of the nuclear families and individuals within it. There has been no interest in group sex and the relationships have been monogamous. But a number of the group object to marriage, at least at this point.

Most of our sharing has been of food, work, learning, and discussion, with a little sharing of transportation, clothing, and recreation.

We eat evening meals together. All food is purchased on a single weekly shopping trip. We have a large garden, which provides most of our summer vegetables and some extra for the winter, and our milk cow provides our dairy products. We hope to produce more fruits, vegetables, and animal products, but have no expectations of becoming completely self-sufficient.

We hope to develop a school or a non-school educational facility here. We are actively exploring the possibility of establishing a living situation for teenagers who need an alternative to their parental homes.

All major decisions are reached in weekly whole-group meetings, almost always by consensus. Smaller groups meet irregularly to organize food, finances, and work.

We seek to diminish egotism, competition, dominance and subservience, and invidious comparison. We are consciously trying to substitute socialist for capitalist modes.

Simplicity of life is a value widely held. But a number of our younger friends in the counter-culture feel we are bourgeois if not opulent. We certainly are a long way from asceticism. This is an area where our explicit values and our behavior don't match.

Our economic relationships are a long way from what we would like primarily because we are land poor, and one family brings much larger economic resources to the community than the others. Members contract with the community to make a certain monthly contribution of money and work. Community funds pay for housing, land, utilities, food, tools, building and gardening materials, car repairs, and some tuition.

"From the Clod Patch: Tough Soil in Garden Yields Good Food and Good Karma, " *Lykins Gulch News*, August 2, 1973

The garden plays a very large part in our lives this summer, much larger than last summer. In '71, since we didn't move onto the place until the middle of June, all efforts were devoted to making the buildings livable and we didn't have a garden.

Since we started talking together, the idea of good food has been part of our dream; organic food that we had helped to grow. We have held the ideal of a harmonious relationship with the land — an interaction of people with nature, each giving, each receiving, neither misused.

Healthy, productive physical exercise is a constant need of mine. The garden work includes a lot of "unskilled" hours. Unskilled work is one of those common denominators that remind us of our oneness. And as for learning — WOW! Some of us had never transplanted a geranium, much less planted 600 feet of peas. "Why those tarpaper collars around the tomato plants?" "No, that's an earthworm, not a cutworm." "Will the Guinea hens eat seed as well as bugs?"

We've had lots of help. The garden encyclopedia rarely spends a day unused, neighbors, friends, nurserymen, parents all contribute advice. The Soil Conservation men have been out several times. They made a soil survey and found only two acres of really good soil, almost half a mile from the farmstead. So we picked the site for the garden for convenience — near the farmstead and easy to irrigate both from the ditch and from the well. The soil was heavy clay loam.

The soil was so tough we had to rent a larger tractor for the first breaking. When it was wet it stuck to everything: boots, hoes, hands. When it was dry it hardened so that a hoe wouldn't cut into it. It seemed as though there were only a few hours between when it was too wet and when it was too dry. Now we have begun to modify the soil texture by adding tons of manure and compost. We haven't found a cheap source of sand yet and we still have to try "Clodbuster," a mineral humate which is reputed to do wonders. Ten years from now we will have built a deep rich loam. It will be hard to remember the intractable clay we started with.

"From the Clod Patch: The Sun and the West Winds," *Lykins Gulch News,* September 25, 1973

It's easy to forget the importance of timing in the garden. The rhythm of the seasons is so slow that we forget we are in a dance with the sun and the west wind. There are so many other partners too, each responding to one another. Rain and frost, insects and molds, and all the different plants whose tempo is locked into those tiny seeds.

The instructions are deceivingly simple: "plant as early as the ground can be worked in the spring" or "after all danger of frost is past." But we have much to do in the fall to make the ground easily worked in the spring. Cultivation, leaving the ground rough with the litter of the summer crops on the surface, and manuring are most important. Fences for peas and tomatoes have to be stored where they are easy to get at in the spring. Bulbs and perennials need to be planted, or pruned and mulched for their long rest.

Bobi brought from her family's experiences the urgency of early planting — especially of peas. This year we caught the few days in late February and early March when the ground was dry enough to work down into a fine seed bed. The peas got in promptly. Something about their slow germination and early growth gave them strength and a headstart over weeds and insects, which resulted in a bountiful crop.

While many farmers were badly disadvantaged by the wet spring we were able to catch those few spells of dry weather to get in the other early crops—chard, beets, lettuce, turnips, onions, garlic. We were too slow when the warm weather finally came. Only a few of the beans got in soon enough. Corn, squash, cucumbers, pumpkins all missed the optimum planting time, mostly because we couldn't assemble the labor force to get the seed bed ready. They suffered excess drought, insect damage, and weed competition as a result.

On the other side, we started our cauliflower too early in the indoor flats. They were so far along in their maturation as they were set out that they made tiny bitter flowers.

With more skill, experience, equipment, and planning we'll be able to do better next year. But only if we feel the rhythms and do the work at the right time.

"From the Clod Patch: Death is Half the Cycle of Growth," *Lykins Gulch News,* November 16, 1973

Working in the garden all summer, we are very conscious of growth, flowering, ripening. What we see is only half the life cycle. The other half starts with the death of the plant. Plant tissues become the food for millions of tiny insects, worms, bacteria, and fungi. They convert the plant tissue into microscopic bits of humus, which helps the soil texture, and soluble nutrients, which can be absorbed by plant roots.

This decay process goes on all year. The winter months are not wasted time. This is the time when the decay process can catch up.

When all the vegetables have been harvested and the really coarse residues like corn stalk removed to the compost pile, the garden plot should be prepared for winter. Under most conditions deep plowing should be avoided. Organic matter can be added from the top of the soil. No need to worry about a coarse cloddy surface in the fall. Freezing and thawing breaks down the clods. Spring is the time to cultivate for a fine-textured seed bed. The Rodale group recommend sheet composting: A mixture of finer plant tissue and fresh animal manures up to six or eight inches thick spread on the garden plot and stirred into the top few inches of the soil.

By spring this will be thoroughly decayed with the soil enriched and improved in texture. With the right nourishment, winter is really rest and recuperation for the garden soil.

*   *   *

Invitation to Twentieth Anniversary

Dear Friends, former communards, former renters, visitors:

This letter has been put off so many times "until I had the leisure to do it well" it would be normal for me to put it off again for its already after 9 PM. But Suzi's in California and the grandchildren are tucked in and asleep. The tomato sauce has been canned and the green tomatoes are wrapped in the root cellar. Maybe I can get a good start before I start to drowse.

I am anticipating, by 20 months or so, the 20th anniversary of our purchase of the farm on Nelson Rd a.k.a the Lykins Gulch Farm. I'm asking you to plan a visit during the month of June 1991 to celebrate the 20th anniversary. No plans yet as to what form the celebration should take, but it has to be spread over at least a couple of weeks to accommodate enough different schedules. We'd love suggestions about the form, but do save enough time to visit in June 1991.

In preparation for that celebration I want to collect and write, a book about the experiments in group living and cooperation that have gone on here. Suzi came up with the title quite a while ago: *From Commune to Condo.* The book might not be finished by June '91 but it would be important to have a draft that people could react to, comment on and add to.

I've fozzled a good deal about the book. At one time I was thinking of a Michner-type history/narrative. But talking about it with Kathleen Kelleher, who has a good deal of experience writing and editing, she suggested that it be more of a collage, a collection of vivid images in the words of the individuals themselves with just enough interpretation/comment/narrative to make it understandable to the reader who was not part of it. Her suggestion seemed eminently sensible so that's the plan now (until someone comes up with a better suggestion).

But as you think about what images you can provide, we need to think about the readership we are aiming at, who do we think might want to read it. First are the participants, those of us who experienced it. And almost first are those in our immediate and extended families, our intimates who were not part of it but individuals with whom we'd like to share that part of our lives.

Third, perhaps are the individuals and groups who are thinking about starting some sort of group living arrangement, or even planning such. We had a lot of experience others could learn from.

Fourth, would be those interested in the period or in one of the several movements of which we were a part: communal living, back to the land, educational reform, political activism and social responsibility, simple living, cooperative enterprises, egalitarian social structures, and what else? An intimate insight into one of the communes of the early 70's and into its cooperative successor in the 80's will be an important document in itself and any of our contemporary comment and interpretation will be useful too. Who knows we might become required reading for certain sociology classes.

I haven't approached any publishers yet, but I have every reason to believe that we can find a publisher. But no one will nibble until we have a table of contents and at least a couple of chapters done.

The next question is how you should transmit your contribution to me. Basically I'll take it any way I can get it....The important thing is that you think through what remains vivid in your experience at Lykins gulch, what you'd like to share with others. Then let's get it recorded one way or another. Don't be shy. I'll edit it into a compatible whole. If you all respond generously maybe it will be two volumes.

Do let me hear from you, hopefully soon, but anyway within the next 12 months.

Selling the Outlot

When the PUD was approved in 1983, Nick and I retained ownership of Outlot B, the ninety-eight acres surrounding the twenty acres of land that included the seven lots plus roughly ten acres of Outlot A that was to be owned by the HOA. Outlot A included the barns and sheds, the garden area, the park (roughly two acres) and the East pasture (the land buffering the houses from the East). Nick and I also retained ownership of the water rights, a valuable asset in dry Colorado. From the beginning of the community, everyone living at the farm had enjoyed free access to this acreage. By 1994 Nick had retired and I was within a year of retirement, so we were beginning to plan for old age. We asked the community to start thinking about their interests in the future of Outlot B.

Discussions got started at a January 8, 1995, community meeting. Nick summarized the meeting for me:

> Dear Suzie: Just back from the HOA meeting and I want to share with you as much of what went on as possible before it gets lost in my memory.
> The whole meeting which went to 11:30 was devoted to sharing. We took 15 minutes at the beginning to write answers down and then went round the whole group one by one. The questions had been posted:
>
> What is important to you about the farm as a whole?
> What is its best future?
> What places on the farm do you especially care about?
> What places are healthy?   What places are not?
> Collective vision   Individual Vision
> Collective time frame   Individual time frame
>
> Paul: Every inch is precious, it should be maintained in as close to its "natural state" as possible recognizing that this is managed naturalness. Both ecological and social health are important. Strips of native shrubs could be planted and protected from grazing. We have what are becoming traditional pathways

around the place. It would be good to clarify (legitimize) them. It's good to be able to talk about these things.

Natalie sees the place as a giant playground. It's all important. She likes to hike, bike and ski on the place. She'd like easier access to the pond and the creek. Maybe more animals in the future?

Sherry values both the neighborly community and the beauty of both the natural and built environment. We should treat the collective front yard, the farmstead, differently from the collective back yard the Ag outlot. The park, the garden and the outlot seem to work well. The corral and adjacent spaces are not so well. Also the "transition," the area along the road to the pond. In her timing, she has less energy for projects now, we need to be realistic about what we can accomplish but it's good to have the vision of what we'd like to achieve. We should do it in a neighborly way.

Kathy P. especially values the loft, the garden, the park, the openness and a certain route she calls "my walk." Wildlife is good but agriculture is too. Keep the water. We are becoming an oasis among the prairie palaces which will bring suburban impacts: predators including stray dogs and deer. Should we post No Hunting.

Jim L. appreciates the "wholeness" of the community/farm. He sees the outlot as basically healthy but anticipates a huge amount of work to correct problems in areas humans have trashed: several gullies, the pond. In the future he would like agriculture using some water we could save by being more efficient in our farmstead water use. Some areas are very fragile and need to be handled very delicately. He thinks in a time frame of 150 to 200 years.

John: Thinks of the place as a whole interactive system including us. It is a temple, a sanctuary, a playground, a school, a resource, a store. He values the interactions both spontaneous and planned. He wants to keep a mix: wild and tame, near and far. Could we have a tepee, a campground, a designated sacred space? Especially for the children places for roaming, adventure, enchantment, camping, learning. The work itself is a goal. The place will be (is) a model or urban/natural living. A vague survivalist value: could we survive if all else collapses. Three time frames: 1) this summer, this year, 2) 5-15 years, 3) 100-200 years.

Judith: Is feeling a different focus as if entering a new 5 year period wanting to fix up the lofts, appreciating the garden, a shorter time span than those who have spoken. In terms of the outlot, she needs more details. The children are extraordinarily happy here. She's 85% satisfied. Can we get more people involved in the garden? She really likes the MacIntosh tree and the cotton-woods.

Kathy W: Values both the social and the physical aspects of the place. The sim-ilarity of attitudes about development and politics and the creativeness of the children, the general social peace and quiet, the wildlife in the outlot but is glad to have cows too. She hopes our example will make some impact on the surrounding properties.

Mike is impressed with the importance of the place in his life, how long they have been here. It provides a magical childhood for the kids. He loves the wildness and the openness. He finds the park and garden healthy, the corral and pisspond not so good. He added that without the truck the HOA has some savings. We could focus on investments successively: the loft, the corral, more trees.

I came in between Jim L. and John. I had already mentioned my increased awareness of mortality and its effect on our time horizon and our expectation of financial inflexibility with your retirement. I quoted J.B. Jackson on people trying to develop on Earth their image of the landscape of Heaven and added that they do this constrained by the resources they have to work with, that I felt very fortunate to have had the physical resources we have and the social history of the last 24 years. I would like to encourage an optimum landscape for the next few decades. I don't know what it is, but it certainly includes openness. The group's wisdom will certainly help both the intentional effort and the unintended consequences. It will be an example for other land owners and for the county authorities.

I went on with my valuing the subsistence production, the self-reliance, the perpetuation of the simple skills, and the spiritual/aesthetic satisfaction. I would like to see some appropriate agriculture — possibly rotated grazing, and a single cutting of hay. I mentioned my interest in geo-ecological experiments: a wilderness corner, the wetlands, intensive rotated grazing, a ganat on the hillside beyond the sauna. All compete for time with off-the-farm activities.

About 11:10 we had finished the go-round and turned to next steps. Jim gave the Waldorfian trilogy: feeling — thinking — will. We agreed to finish the feelings at the February meeting and then start on the Thinking, the long term plan.

You and I need to think through what we want to do with the land and water. It was asserted "You could do whatever you want to with the outlot and the water." I was going to modify that assertion of absolute freedom with the ethical and emotional constraints of our relationship to the community and the individuals in it.

By August 1997 in a memo to the homeowners Nick wrote that health problems had vividly reminded us that eventually we will want to move to town, hopefully not for a decade or more. We will have to deal with the outlot and he saw three alternatives: give it to Sherry and Jim, sell it to the HOA, keep it and sell it with our house and lot when the time comes. Although we hadn't had an appraisal I though it was probably worth about $50,000, in light of the conservation easement from the county, but Nick thought it was worth more. He asked the community to take up the topic while we were away — August 27 through October 9.

At the September 13 meeting the group decided to use the Getting to Yes strategy of identifying interests, factors, and information without personalizing or taking positions. They agreed they want to use the process to deepen and strengthen the community, that they didn't want to make this decision out of fear. We should give the process the time it needs.

The group agreed that N and S ownership of the outlet created inherent inequities from the beginning of the HOA and selling the outlot with N and S house would reinforce the split between one rich homeowner and the rest of the community. Second, control of the water rights is very important and might be a better use of their money. They agreed that they were not yet ready to make a proposal to N and S.

Minutes from a November 18 meeting indicate that the group identified the plusses and minuses of owning the outlot. They concluded that the community does not need to own the outlot but that they are attached to it, and owning it would complete the equalization of property ownership that started when Nick and Suzie sold the lots. The group came up with several options.

At a November 23 meeting John, Sherry and Thea had organized a meeting for a further discussion of the outlot and proposed an agenda. "Our aim is consensus among all homeowners. We see this entire process as promoting the community and fostering good will rather than as merely a negotiation."

In preparation for the November 23 meeting Nick wrote the following:

November 23, 1997
To the HOA Folks:

Vision. We don't think very much in terms of visions anymore. It's part of our terminal psychology. We spend more and more of our decreasing energy in just staying healthy and completing projects that are important to us. We're both proud of what we as a group have accomplished on this piece of land, but our hope for a more intimate community is past. We certainly would like to use making community here a higher priority for each family, but we don't see it happening, we don't expect it, and it's okay with us. The disposition of the outlot doesn't seem to be a significant variable in facilitating a more intensive social interaction.

We built the house so that we could live here until we died. It's now clearer to us that if either of us looses our driver's license (Nick just got his renewed for 5 years), or is crippled up by something that makes walking painful, or our strength declines so that we can no longer do the work or want to do it—we will want to move into town. We can't imagine that the group can give the support necessary for an old couple that continually needs help.

We hope the community will buy the outlot because we think that your owning it is the best solution for the maintenance of the area and the health of the community. There is some maintenance involved—fences, thistle and weed control are the things that come to mind immediately. There is also some income, though we haven't tried to maximize it. . . .

Preferences. We hope we'll be out here for another five to ten years, but we have no idea about how our own thinking may change with the aging process. We would like to sell the land to the community as soon as possible to tidy up our finances and make it easier to move into town if we have to. As far as the water rights are concerned, we expect to keep them unless we have some financial catastrophe, and therefore the water will be available to the HOA/community, probably until we both die. . . .

Meeting minutes report the groups intent to buy the outlot assuming the price is right, and they made many more decisions, agreeing to meet after we identified the price. January 11, 1998, minutes report that the appraisal came back at several times what was expected, beyond the means of the HOA. Several alternatives were discussed including selling it to the county as part of their open space program. Another alternative was to give the land to Boulder County Nature Association, a land trust active in the area. The HOA pursued these and other alternatives, none of which panned out. In an August 30, 1999, memo to the Homeowners, Nick wrote: "I think you all know that we have decided not to give Outlot A to the County, but rather save it as part of Sherry's inheritance. We are ready to move ahead with selling some of the water shares to the HOA."

Essay: My Own Sense of Community, 5/17/91

For many of us, only after one has secured one's status within the context of a more or less just society, can one easily take the broader perspective and begin to develop the expressive individualism—creating beauty, and the civic (republican) responsibility to try to modify the society as a whole.

Some of us never finish the search for financial success or we allow the drive for power to extend the financial or security drive far beyond the point of diminishing returns. And many, born into the lower levels of an unjust society, never have much of a chance to develop security much less those creative talents and apply them successfully; and never have the satisfaction of a job well done.

A few of us pass up the search for security and job accomplishment and devote ourselves to intellectual and artistic expression early. In the extreme form artistic expression becomes the individual's obsession to the exclusion of security, the starving artist syndrome, but often it is balanced with other drives.

Others get so involved in social justice issues, our civic drive for a good society, that we ignore the other parts of our lives.

I cannot say which is best. In my own case I tried to combine the three almost from the beginning with security from an institutionalized career as an intellectual, but always attentive to environmental and social justice issues in the society around me.

Can community enable/encourage individuals to gain greater satisfaction and fulfillment by being supportive of individuals at different stages and during the stress of moving from one to another?

To be stable, a community must have a core of people who have the security of having come through the utilitarian individualism.

Essay: A Discouraging, Early Morning View of Community, Early 1990s

Awake early, a couple of days returned from two weeks in Botswana, Africa, I had the insight, perhaps revived the insight, that communalism is a protective strategy. I was thinking of poverty, for the thought derived from the contrast between the cluster of rondavels in the traditional South African village which works pretty well under conditions of extreme poverty and the planned city, Gaberone, the new capitol, with fenced lots laid out on cul-du-sacs for modern homes with gardens and porches and gated driveways. With prosperity, you lose community.

And then I was reflecting on the architecture of power (or social purpose). The bank skyscrapers that preside over our central cities. Insurance, retailing and a few other corporate structures may share the domination. The Cathedral that dominated the medieval city. Church supported the divine right of patriarchy as the palace began to rival the cathedral. In Latin America the deputy of the divine king set his mansion across the square from the cathedral, with his supporting barracks on a third side.

In medieval Catholicism, community focused on the worship of the Virgin Mary. The small, tightly clustered settlements were more easily defended in the prevailing anarchy. The amalgamation of power into provincial and national monarchs established law and order and reduced the need for community and translated the need for protection from the local level into the readiness for aggression at the wider scale.

In my own experience, the Turkish village was not walled, but it was clustered as protection from the vagaries of nature and the predation of an unscrupulous government.

The 19th century villages of the Tswana tribes had similar functions: a clustering for efficiency with low technology and protection led to a powerful chief against other somewhat mobile "tribes." The American Indian tribes and pueblos had similar strong communities.

Are we ready to assert that we need community against an unscrupulous government, and to provide efficiency in a technology that is destroying "nature" and us?

Appendix B: Wildness Continuum

As far as I know, the notion of the *wildness continuum* was Nick's invention. At least he talked about it often as a way of describing the preference of people for different degrees of domestication of the landscape or the lack of same. He thought it was an important insight, not only in understanding human needs for some degree of wildness, but also for designing rational public policies related to our public lands. Here is the essay he published in *The Professional Geographer* in 1977.*

The Wildness Continuum by Nicholas Helburn

There appears to be a profound need among human beings for things natural, that is, nonhuman. This paper asserts that this need or urge takes the cross-country skier twenty miles from the plowed road and the sound of an internal combustion engine; that it causes the Bronx housewife to nurture a petunia in the bay window of her apartment; and further, that this human tendency can best be understood as a continuum in which the Bronx petunia and the ski wilderness are extremes.

In its simplest form in the United States the continuum flows from the completely constructed, artificialized landscape with its "single flower" through the atrium, the postage-stamp lawn, and penthouse garden of the inner city, to the one block (or less) downtown park, to the larger lawns of the suburbs and their still larger parks, through the "open space" and scenic value of the agricultural countryside and the densely used county, state and regional parks and campgrounds, to the forest and range lands—uncultivated and sparsely inhabited but still managed primarily for material economic production—to the National Parks and comparable extensive reserves withdrawn from "economic use" and "preserved" for their recreational and scenic value, and finally to those portions of the parks and reserves from which all "works of man" are deliberately excluded—the areas we call "wilderness."

To some extent we can duplicate this plants-vegetation-land-use continuum in the animal world: from the urban Pekinese and parakeet and pigeons to the zoo and on through the suburban setters and shorthairs, robins and chickadees, the exurban horses and fringe chickens and dairy

*Volume XXIX, November 1977, number 4. Copyright Association of American Geographers, reprinted by permission of Taylor & Francis, http://www.tandfonline.com

goats and raccoons and skunks, to the commercial herds of cattle and sheep to the deer in the nearby woods, the ducks and geese nesting on their migrations, the brown bear scavenging in the campground, the semi-domesticated elk of Jackson Hole to the elusive mountain goat in Glacier Park and finally the fearsome predators: grizzly bear, wolf and puma.

A gradational sequence is clear. For those of us who grew up feeding the pigeons in front of the public library,[1] the bantam rooster, guinea hen and peacock on the urban fringe farm may be exciting. And those of us who watch the Canada geese on our pond every spring and fall will go to great lengths to spend a weekend watching and listening to trumpeter swan. And at the extreme a few of us try to protect the lofty eagle from extinction though our chances of seeing one close up are rather small.

The nature of the outdoor "recreational" experience is not well understood,[2] but our assertion here is that one component is an increment of wildness. In downtown Manhattan, a chance to sit in the shade or wheel the baby carriage in Gramercy Park is recreation, and a 50-foot lawn in the backyard seems positively luxurious. Even though at Englewood Cliffs, New Jersey, one can look out on the Palisades, a drive through the farmlands and woods of the Hudson Valley is a lovely way to spend a Sunday afternoon. The enthusiast who jogs daily in the Berkshires uses his two weeks off to get away with a few friends into the wild Adirondacks or the Laurentians.

The incremental character does not mean that the "drive through the countryside" to "suburban living" ratio is identical to the Adirondacks-Berkshires ratio. It does assert that they both are greater than one.

We are dealing here with the "outdoor" recreation experience. We do not in any way deny the recreation which operates in the other direction. The farm boy from Oklahoma finds that "Everything's up to date in Kansas City." In the same way a sophisticate from Waterloo finds delights in Toronto. The existence of this inverse continuum rather tends to corroborate our assertion about incremental wildness.

Along with plants, animals and land surfaces, there is a comparable scale in the wildness of water. Watching the bubbles in the goldfish bowl lies at one extreme; at the other end lies the open ocean and the wild coast, the whitewater of the upper Snake River, the lakes and streams of Quetico. In between lie innumerable fountains, pools, ponds, swamps, springs, streams, rivers, reservoirs and lakes. The edges of these water bodies vary from concrete pavement and sculptured stone through landscaped lawn and protected beach to untouched original vegetation, rocky headlands and sweeps of empty sand.

It would be easy to overstate our case and imply that all outdoor recreation can be explained in terms of incremental wildness. No such claim is made. The enjoyment of physical exertion can take place as well on a paved tennis court as on a mountain trail. The enjoyment of risk taking is as much a part of auto racing as it is of rock climbing. Certainly some skiers choose Aspen or Vail over Loveland and or Winter Park for the snob appeal rather than for the wildness of the slopes.

The assertion is that among the satisfactions of many (most?) outdoor recreation experiences, an increment of wildness and a concurrent decrease in domestication or constructedness is an important factor. Van Burkalow points out "Those resources that nourish our minds and spirits are sometimes described as having spiritual, or recreational, or enjoyment or esthetic, or scientific value. I prefer the more all-inclusive term inspirational, for inspiration is defined as an 'awakening, quickening, creative impulse,' and as such it can affect either the mind or the spirit."[3] Although granting that there are other sources of inspiration, she illustrates inspirational resources with examples from the wilder end of the continuum.

Yi-Fu Tuan traces an evolution of attitudes about wilderness from early times when the familiar garden and village (sacred) was surrounded by the unfamiliar wilderness (profane) through several stages. In the late nineteenth century something approaching our continuum appears with the amorphous city classed as profane and both the "middle landscape" and recreational wilderness having an "edenic" quality.[4]

Aldo Leopold, better than anyone I know, deals with the "natural" in recreation in the essay "Conservation Aesthetic" in Sand County Almanac.[5] The components of the recreational experience, as he analyzes it, are fully compatible with our continuum of increasing wildness. There are satisfactions along the way, and much depends upon the attitudes and experience of the individuals involved.

There are some management implications of the wildness continuum associated with the attributes of the recreational experience. In general the constructed end of the continuum involves:

large numbers of people
in small areas,
close to their other activities,
for short periods,
of frequent occurrence,
very much under the control of the individual,
at very low risk, and
often with much equipment, many things.

The wild end of the continuum involves:

relatively few people
in large areas,
usually remote from their normal daily life,
for longer periods of time,
but infrequently,
with the individual clearly not in control of the environment,
often at considerable risk, and
usually with very little gear.

Quality of the Recreational Experience

Scholarly work on the quality of the recreational experience identifies complex individual differences and interconnected motivations. It is clear that each of us has our own satisfaction curve. Increasing naturalness is associated with increased satisfaction to a point and then drops off.[6]

As long ago as 1964 Robert Lucas was studying the attributes of the wild lands which were attractive to recreationists and their differing perceptions of what was "wilderness."[7] Already it was clear that people with different expectations could be satisfied by different experiences, that there was an identifiable fraction of the public that needed and was prepared for the extreme end of the continuum, paddling canoists in his study. Further, all of the other users could be satisfied by "semiwilderness" at much higher rates of use.

Single-solution thinking might find some modal or median position along the wildness continuum and try to manage the entire recreational resource at that level of wildness. Recognizing a variety of resources and a variety of users provides the recreational planner with the conceptual framework for taking advantage of opportunities available to offer areas of different degrees of naturalness. An optimum distribution of recreational lands should include many small areas close to high-density urban areas. More widely distributed population in suburban and rural areas have less need for small parks. Larger and wilder areas can be more remote from population centers. In part they must be, since it would be impossible to manage a very wild area highly accessible to a large population.

Clawson and Knetsch divide recreational resources into two classes, people-oriented vs. resource-oriented resources, with an intermediate class between.[8] We find the continuum idea more powerful.

Scenic Values. There is an important recreational value inherent in all "open space" lands, whether publicly or privately owned and managed. No present mechanism exists to compensate the private landowner for the public use of the recreational value of his property. Inversely, there are no mechanisms to assure the maintenance of those recreational values. In the present economic arrangement, the scenic value of my farm or your woodlot is an externality for both of us as well as for the highway builder. The public stands to lose if we cannot find ways of recognizing and preserving these commons.

To some extent scenery varies with accessibility. Most of the population of the world is clustered in areas of high accessibility or agricultural productivity. Both accessibility and agriculture are positively correlated with flatness, and negatively correlated with high relief. Thus many wild areas also have mountain scenery. The dramatic scenery enhances the wilderness experience but is not a necessary component.

There is probably little to be gained in arguing whether the public would have been better served if the Going-to-the-Sun Highway had never been built. It is difficult to conceive of a recreational plan which would have left Old Faithful Geyser or Niagara Falls as wilderness experiences.

The wildness continuum raises serious doubt about further extensions of motorized access to wild lands. It points rather to the "wildening" of attractive sites close to population centers, increasing the number of campgrounds near existing highways within commercial forest and range areas.

Wilderness Management

One of the arguments used by wilderness protectionists is that there is no way to increase the supply of wilderness, yet the demand is bound to increase. Sheer intensity of use may destroy the resource (e.g., trampling of vegetation) or the experience (e.g., too many parties on the cross-country trail). One of the solutions calls for buffer zones around wilderness areas. Much of the inordinate pressure on more crowded wilderness areas could be removed if casual tourists were diverted by easier access to semiwilderness and discouraged by more difficult access to true wilderness. The wildness continuum analysis seems to call for a positive and aggressive public program to protect threatened areas such as the Maroon Bells in Colorado or the popular parks in California's Sierra Nevada. Such a program could acquire adjacent land and manage it, providing intervening opportunities for the less-than-extreme wilderness enthusiasts. There is every reason to believe that such a program would increase the satisfaction of both the less and more extreme types. Further, it might avoid some of the tragic accidents which occur when ill-prepared and unskilled tourists venture so easily into areas beyond the reach of mechanized transport.

Economic Justification

A final implication of the continuum concept lies in the area of economic justification. The number of people using an area has long been used in the justification of recreational land use. But there has been no way of measuring the quality of the recreational experience. The continuum proposed here gives at least a conceptual way of inserting the quality of the recreational experience into the justification of wilderness. For those who are ready for it, there is a more profound experience at the wilderness end of the spectrum. If the planner can demonstrate that opportunities do exist for recreators in the middle of the continuum, then he can argue conclusively that the total satisfactions are increased by reserving some areas for low density, simple technology, wilderness use. Other satisfactions aside for the moment, the naturalness component of outdoor recreation must be maximized by many easily accessible nature trails and some inaccessible roadless areas, by many streamside picnic grounds with room enough for frisbee throwing and a few areas where those who are prepared for it can see fresh grizzly bear track.

Our conclusion is manifest in truths that seem familiar, that the good life is balanced with some civilization, some wildness, some downtown and some Walden. We all need a change of scene, but some of our frantic escape from the city derives from the one-sidedness of the city. Recognizing the universal need for naturalness in our lives, we can build and care for more harmonious landscapes across the whole continuum.

1. Tom Lehrer, "An Evening Wasted with Tom Lehrer," Reprise Label 6199.

2. B. L. Driver and S. Ross Tocher, "Toward a Behavioral Interpretation of Recreational Engagements with Implications for Planning," in D. W. Fisher, J, E. Lewis and G. B. Priddle, eds., *Land and Leisure* (Chicago: Maaroufa Press, Inc., 1974), pp. 91-162.

3. A. Van Burkalow, "Neglected Natural Resources: The Inspirational Values of the Earth Environment" in I. P. Gerasimov, ed., *International Geography 1976*, Vol. 10 (1976), pp. 147-150.

4. Yi-Fu Tuan, *Topophilia* (Englewood Cliffs, N.J.: Prentice-Hall, Inc., 1974), pp. 104-105. Those interested in the development of American attitudes toward wilderness are referred to Roderick Nash, *Wilderness in the American Mind* (New Haven: Yale University Press, 1967).

5. Aldo Leopold, *Sand County Almanac* (New York: Oxford University Press, 1949), pp. 165-177.

6. B. Warmerdam, "Wildness and Satisfaction in Outdoor Recreation," University of Colorado, Department of Geography, unpublished seminar paper, 1976.

7. R. C. Lucas, "Wilderness Perception and Use: The Example of the Boundary Waters Canoe Area," *Natural Resources Journal*, Vol. 3 (January 1964), pp. 394-411.

8. Marion Clawson and Jack L. Knetsch, *Economics of Outdoor Recreation* (Baltimore: The Johns Hopkins Press, 1966), pp. 36-38.

Appendix C: Second Thoughts

Here are thirteen of the thirty-five or so "Second Thoughts" Nick read on KGNU, our local FM station in Boulder, from 1989 until 2003. He signed off each, "This is Nick Helburn with Second Thoughts." They are another extension of Nick's desire to educate. They show the range of his social and political beliefs.

Social Pollution, December 28, 1989

Driving into Boulder from the North, you can see far beyond Boulder, past Rocky Flats, past Mount Evans, on a clear day all the way to Pikes Peak. That's 100 miles. One is reminded how precious is the clarity of our almost pristine western atmosphere.

But from the same place on a quiet morning you see the characteristic whitish pollution pall that lies over Boulder. Once in the city you soon forget the view. You don't notice the pollution. You're accustomed to the lower visibility. You adjust to the environment you are in.

Something similar happens to us in our social environment. As we look beyond our own to other societies we notice their departures from what we consider "good." We are very conscious of the poverty in India, of the housing shortage in the Soviet Union, of thought control in China, of hunger in the African Sahel, of infant mortality in Haiti, of racial segregation in South Africa, of the death squads in El Salvador.

But within our own society, we become accustomed to our departures from what we consider good. Whereas we looked over the physical pollution from the highway, we overlook the social pollution in our own system.

To be sure, the Klu Klux Klan is not as active here as the death squads are in El Salvador, but they are the same kind of thing. But we turn away. We overlook it.

Our segregation is not as flagrant as apartheid but it is the same phenomenon. But we've got used to it. We overlook it.

We do OK with maternal care for most Americans. How is it that we do so little about the tragic malnutrition and lack of care for so many young American mothers? We overlook it.

Hunger hurts just as much in rural New Mexico as it does in Ethiopia. But we have learned not to notice. We overlook it.

America's so called free press and media are dominated and constrained by wealthy special interests leaving most of us with inadequate information to modify misguided American policies. But we've learned to live with it. We overlook it.

And how can we justify the presence of hundreds of thousands of homeless in the midst of our affluence? We put the homeless out of mind. We overlook them.

As our rich get richer, more and more families fall into poverty. But they live across town so we can overlook them.

It is more difficult to keep injustice in mind when we are a part of the problem. But must we accept George Bernard Shaw's quip that "custom will reconcile people to any atrocity?"

I prefer to paraphrase our own revolutionary patriot: The price of justice is eternal vigilance.

Process Thinking, April 17, 1990

Language reflects thinking. As we speak and write, so we think. Our language emphasizes the noun over the verb. We stress the thing more than the process of being the thing.

A tree is a thing, but it is also a process of storing energy in a vertical trunk, a process of growing, flowering and making seeds. When a tree dies, the process stops. Only the inert trunk and branches remain. Woodsmen call it a snag. It is a derelict, abandoned by its life force. (Actually a new and very different process has started. We call it decay.)

Similarly a city is a thing, a tangible reality. But it must also be thought of as a process, providing important services to residents who live close together. Our language refers to the thing: the city. We have no word for the process. We'd have to invent one: to municipize.

The buildings and yards, the streets and sewers, the monuments and parks we inherit from decades and generations of people (citizens) concerned enough about living together to invest through taxes and bonds and action, to assemble the material city and organize the social process. We often are unaware of the effort it takes to maintain both the material city and the social processes.

When the residents of a city abandon the civic process, when they stop working at it the city becomes a slum and then a ghost town. It too has been abandoned, a derelict.

Marriage and friendship and family are even less tangible things. There is less concrete to remind one of the noun. Friendships only exist while the people involved continue to be friendly. Marriages are institutionalized and continue as legal conditions even after the husband and/or wife no longer work at being married.

One of the tragic legacies of the fairy tales we inherit from European folk literature is the ending: "And they lived happily ever after." That ending makes it seem as though the bride and groom could relax: for the witches have been overcome, the evil spells broken, the dragons slain.

Hogwash! There was only a short interlude of relaxation (sometimes called a honeymoon). New witches, spells and dragons must be dealt with. We learn that marriage is a process. Again there is no English word for the process of being married. Fortunately all the witches and dragons are paper witches and paper dragons. If we want to make the marriage work, we have to work at it.

If not, it becomes a derelict marriage, abandoned by the husband or wife or both.

The home/house distinction shares something of the same sense. The house is a tangible thing requiring little maintenance. A home, however, is a set of social interactions developed over time and continuously worked at by the home-makers.

These distinctions help clarify the ends-means confusion. Do the ends justify the means? Often the ends are the things while the means are the processes that result in the things. You cannot achieve the end separately from the means. Peace is an end we all desire. It is achieved by living peacefully. Justice is an end achieved by living justly both individually and collectively.

Meditations on the Long Haul, recorded December 12, 1991

Where did they start, our lifetime of activism?

In my case in naiveté, in taking seriously the adage about doing unto others as you would be done by; and

In that strange confidence that I, one person, could make a difference, maybe only a small difference, but still a difference; and

In that gross underestimate of the forces that have created this world as it is. It's a little like having children, in the sense that if you knew all the consequences before you started, you might not have done it.

Gramci speaks of the optimism of the will and the pessimism of the intellect.

In my case, as a teenager in the 1930s, I saw the patent senselessness of the idea that the world could overcome the terrible consequences of one world war by fighting another. There must have been a better way!

But mostly I think it was naiveté:

Believing in the homilies like leaving the world a better place than you found it.

And there were selected commandments: Love thy neighbor and Thou shalt not kill. (There were others that were conveniently ignored.)

And the anarchist ideal that if we all just lived a good life and treated others as we would like to be treated all the problems would melt away.

And Eugene Debs' commitment: As long as there is a man in jail, I am not free. As long as there is a child malnourished, I am not well. As long as there is woman beaten, I am degraded. (He did not go that far, but if he were alive today he would have.)

There was no dearth of saintly role models:

Kahil Gibran who translated moral philosophy into language that touched our hearts;

We read Odd Nansen's *From Day to Day* aloud to each other and we not only understood the oppression of the concentration camp but we also recommitted ourselves to a life that would remove the occasion for concentration camps and jails.

And Dag Hammarskjold's *Markings* reinforced our commitment.

Norman Thomas translated love into policy and demonstrated the effectiveness of the long haul.

Boulding's sonnet dedicated to Vasco de Gama "Cape of Good Hope" says it beautifully:

> Day after day, week after heartsick week
> The ship plunged southward. The appalling sun
> Was north at noon; surely they must soon run
> Over earth's frightful rim! But still the bleak
> Coast blocked the eastward way they came to seek.
> Leftward was pathless land, strait there was none,
> And each day ended as it had begun.
> The unknown stars at night made hope grow weak.
> And then, land's end, the splendid finger of Hope,
> And they sailed eastward into a different dawn.
> So we, in a later voyage, through seas that spawn
> A vast despair, along dark coasts must grope
> Towards destruction. Can we see the shape
> Of our Good Hope, and we, too, round the cape?

There are more role models than we can mention here:

Eleanor Roosevelt inspired us to reach beyond our expectations.

Mahatma Ghandi and Martin Luther King demonstrated the power of love. Their martyrdom deepened our commitment.

Mao Tse-tung and Fidel Castro taught us patience and persistence, and that the whole culture must change through generations, not just the institutions of property, before a good society can really work.

George Jackson's courage against unbelievable cruelty in the Soledad prison made our troubles seem insignificant.

And now we honor the heroes of the struggle against apartheid.

Of course there are many more negative role models, people with whom we would not want to be confused, people whose lives seem to ignore the well-being of the community and the well-being of humanity. When they take power the institutions are corrupted and the culture is brutalized. We feel as though it is three steps back after one step forward. But we are humble in our judgementalism, remembering Bobby Burns', "There's so much bad in the best of us, and so much good in the worst of us..."

All this is tied in to mortality, for idealism is most prevalent among adolescents, and from there on most of us gradually become more conservative and more conforming. Not all of us, but most of us.

There is an insightful line in Boulding's sonnet "For George Fox" describing the influence that crosses several generations: "You speak to me. I cannot speak to you." The saintly heroes keep on speaking to us. Most of us do not listen to the tyrants. We rejoice in our mortality for sooner or later it does away with both the saints and the tyrants. The voice of the saints echoes through generation after generation.

Are we then just retarded adolescents? Or are we the foolish old men (and women) of the Chinese folk tale:

> Two mountains shaded their house and garden so they and their sons took shovels and started digging away the mountains. A wise old man came by and laughed, "How silly of you. It's impossible for you to dig up these two high mountains."
>
> The foolish old man replied, "When I die, my sons will carry on; when they die there will be my grandsons, then their sons and grandsons, and so on until the job is done." So having answered the wise old man, the foolish old man and his sons went on digging.

And we go on digging and digging in the faith that the sun will shine on our houses and gardens. There is a familiar saying:

> Security lies neither in your possession nor in mine. It lies always between us. If each of us could restrain the childish desire to grasp it for our self alone, we could live forever in the joy of mutual trust.

We can rephrase it that:

Well-being lies neither in your possession nor in mine. It is a matrix among us. If each of us could restrain the childish desire to take it all, we could live forever in harmonious well-being.

Reproducing the Environment, February 14, 1992

Most of us are aware that economists make serious assumptions, simplifying reality. The most serious is the idea of "economic woman," the person with full knowledge of everything germane to her decision, a decision made to maximize her own benefit. In so far as this simplification does not fit the real world, it limits the usefulness of economic theory.

Another assumption hurts the environment. It assumes that unowned nature has no value until it has been worked on. To the economist the buffalo and the prairie it grazed on were valueless until the buffalo had been killed and its hide peeled off for a blanket. The prairie was outside the economy until it was fenced and gated to make a pasture. This was a convenient assumption two hundred years ago in a rapidly expanding capitalism where Native Americans, native Africans, and native Australians were not taken into account.

But today we live on a planet with five and a half billion people and no new lands. No mineral can be mined without disturbing the surface. No dam can be built without drowning a valued stream and its valued shores.

Two hundred years ago Adam Smith and Rev. Malthus would not have valued wilderness. Today whole coalitions are formed to protect threatened wilderness, for natural ecosystems and open space are indeed valued.

Early economists began to distinguish between productive labor and unproductive labor. Productive labor contributed to society's well-being, while unproductive labor just rearranged the useful goods and services within society. Most unpaid labor was ignored until recently when feminists created another category, reproductive labor, to account for all the work associated with pregnancy, birthing, child rearing and education for without these activities there would be no labor force to do the productive labor.

Now it becomes clear that we must extend the reproductive concept to the environment. We can no longer take the geoecosystem for granted. Existing economic rules do not maintain the organic matter in our prairie soils nor the rainforest in the tropics. The wondrous natural genetic diversity we have taken for granted requires labor, economic effort, to be maintained.

A simple stream, like Boulder Creek, might seem to go on and on for ever. It is really a complex hydroecosystem. In two hundred years of economic development millions of streams and rivers have been destroyed becoming sewers. Millions more are threatened unless we recognize that nature is not a "free good," that it too must be reproduced. Helping the stream to reproduce itself takes economic effort.

Each of us inhales in oxygen and exhales carbon dioxide. Before the industrial era the world geoecosystem, sometimes called Gaia, could absorb the carbon dioxide and replace the oxygen. Now every factory and chemical plant, every car and truck consumes oxygen and spews carbon dioxide and much more.

Yes, even the breath of life is threatened. Too much ozone here below and too little ozone in the stratosphere threaten life as we know it. We must change the rules of investment and profit so that we can allocate labor to maintain, to reproduce the geoecosystem.

Corporate Responsibility, recorded Feb 1992

The recent attempt by the Denver District Attorney, the Department of Energy and Rockwell to cover up the deadly nuclear carelessness at Rocky Flats reminds me of a not so silly idea I had several years ago. Except now it doesn't seem quite so silly.

It was way back when the Ford Motor Co. was accused, and I think found guilty, of endangering the public by keeping the gas tank at the very back of one of their models, so that in a rear end crash the fuel would explode, possibly killing the occupants of the car. Several fatalities had resulted. In the court proceedings it became clear that the designers within the company knew the danger and reported it, but somewhere up the line the decision was made to ignore the danger, presumably because it would cost a little more to put the gas tank in a safer position.

In my naiveté I felt as though the corporation was guilty of murder. In many states individuals guilty of murder are sentenced to death. Why shouldn't corporations be put to death as well? We think of human life as sacred, but in my theology, at least, there is nothing particularly sacred about the life of a corporation. Theoretically one should be able to hold the individuals within the corporation responsible. But for whatever reason, this doesn't happen in our legal system.

Corporations are considered "legal persons" under the law. In civil law, the corporation is liable for damage to other persons (though it is often hard to collect). But criminal penalties are written for human persons with fines and prison sentences as the usual penalties. But you can't imprison a corporation. The fines are probably considered by the decision makers within the corporations and figured into the cost/benefit ratio. (The scenario might go something like this: We can save X dollars by the more risky procedure. If we do get caught and found guilty, the fine is not likely to be more than Y dollars. As long as X is enough more than Y, it's profitable to take the risk. And if we get caught we'll pretend we did not know of the potential damage.)

In one sense the executives who make the decisions are doing the bidding of the stockholders who want the company to make as much profit as possible. Calculating the risk of injury and death and figuring the penalties from possible conviction in monetary rather than moral terms could easily be mistaken for "good business." (Really good business includes the public relations implications.)

But corporations were set up in the beginning to minimize the risk to stockholders. There is no way that stockholders can be held responsible even for corporate losses, much less corporate crime. So in a way, the executive is caught in a dilemma whether to do what is most profitable or what is morally responsible. The corporation as an institution has no conscience, feels no emotion. Only the human beings within the corporation have consciences. Only the human persons feel compassion, regret or fear.

The cover-ups have been blatant: coal companies with black lung disease, Johns Manville with asbestos, General Electric, Rockwell and E,G & G and others with nuclear radiation, Dow Corning with silicon breast implants. I think corporations found guilty of murder should be sentenced to death. They should be dissolved by order of the court. It doesn't seem like such a silly idea. It would allow executives to act responsibly, to serve the public, as well as the stockholders.

Children, edited February 12, 1994, recorded February 14, 1994

A radio interview not long ago concerning public policy with respect to children ended with the comment, "In this society, children are not valued." What she probably meant was "Other people's children are not valued." (The problem is not that we don't care about children. We love our children. It's other people's children we are careless about.)

There is plenty of evidence that most parents take good care of their children, work hard to clothe, feed, house and educate their kids, often sacrificing their own comfort for their children's opportunity. In spite of this continued prevalence of the child-centered home, the media plays up the powerful stories of neglect and abuse when they find them. Child neglect and abuse have been around for a long, long time.

There probably is more neglect and abuse now than there was twenty years ago. Lots of factors contribute. As urban life gets more and more impersonal and as poverty increases, powerless people including children get abused and neglected. Social service budgets have been severely reduced. In most cities the extended family has all but disappeared. It used to be that when father and mother were in trouble, uncles, aunts or grandparents could take the children and give them loving care. Less and less nowadays.

We used to wash and iron our shirts at home. Increasingly those of us who can afford it, send them out. We used to fix breakfast at home. Now more and more those of us who can afford it, grab an Egg Mcmuffin on the way to work. We used to care for our children at home. Now with both parents working outside the home, we pay others to care for our children. Commercialization means we do less and less at home. The family becomes less and less significant.

Who teaches parenting when families break up so early? Where does a young mother learn about healthy pregnancies, infant care, immunizations, and child nutrition when she herself is not part of a family? Family values are transmitted to the next generation by mechanisms within the family. As that unit breaks down both the knowledge and the values disappear.

As a society we have to establish policies promoting the care of children. Children's well-being is partly a function of individual values within the family and partly a function of the family's social environment. Family coherence is all tied up with welfare policy, with income distribution, with health services and with city structure and housing policy.

If we cared about all children, we would invest in maternity and well-baby clinics accessible to all. We would pay for extended leave for new parents. We would use tax dollars or investment incentives to build low-income housing until there were sufficient decent places to live in neighborhoods where families could thrive. No one would be hungry. Public subsidies would assure affordable child care wherever both parents work outside the home. School budgets would cover health education, sympathetic counseling, and vocational education for all adolescents. There would be jobs at the end of the educational tunnel.

Even measured on a crass dollar for dollar basis, a humane children's policy could do more for the future of the nation than any other investment.

Millet, edited February 4, 1994, broadcast February 9, 1995

Most of us have been baffled by the intractable problems that come out of the breakup of Yugoslavia. What's so special about Serbs and Croats and Muslims living in the same country? Why can't the U.N. or the European community or Mr. Clinton do something about the killing? Perhaps I can make it more understandable.

Let's go back 400 years to the Turkish Empire, often referred to as the Ottoman Empire. By 1600 AD Turks had conquered most of the Arab lands in what we call the "Middle East," and in Europe they ruled the Balkans including what was Yugoslavia and what is now Greece, Bulgaria, Albania, and Rumania.

Their way of governing was quite different from anything Americans are familiar with. There was a great deal of local autonomy. In each community they let each "Millet" run its own domestic affairs. Each religious/language group was a Millet. (When it comes to ethnicity, religion, language and race are all mixed up.) In any city like Sarajevo or Belgrade the Greek patriarch and his advisers took care of all the local problems for the Greek Orthodox Christians, the Greek Millet: marriages, funerals, squabbles between families. The Serbian Patriarch did the same for the Serbian Orthodox Christian Millet. The Croatian Catholic Bishop took care of the problems for the Croatian Millet. The Albanian Mufti or Sharif or whatever did the same for the Albanian Muslims. The Jewish Rabbi and elders took care of internal problems within the Jewish Millet.

The Turkish Sultan appointed officials who controlled taxation, the Army and problems between millets. Foreign affairs were all handled by the Sultan's Court. It was a system that worked quite well from the 13th into the 18th century. Albanians, Shi'a Arabs, Sunni Arabs, Armenians, Bulgars, Croats, Druzes, Greeks, Kurds, Jews, and Turks lived in the same provinces and cities, each managing their own affairs. In a sense, everyone was a minority within the empire. It wasn't always pleasant. The Turkish overlords were often tyrants. Bright children, Christian or Muslim, were drafted at a tender age to be brainwashed and trained as the Sultan's bureaucrats. But it allowed this enormous diversity of cultures to live together in the same region.

Today's extreme nationalism encourages the larger "minority" to oppress the smaller groups and try to eliminate them. We shouldn't be surprised. Modern Spain emerged as Roman Catholics drove out the Moors and the Inquisition scattered the Jews all of whom had been living together under Moorish rule. They didn't call it ethnic cleansing then.

It took a thousand years to meld Angles, Saxons, Normans, Cornish, Welsh, and Scots into a British nation, and the Irish never did come on board.

Modern Turkey went through a revolutionary war of independence. Armenians whose forebears had lived there for generations were slaughtered and starved. Then in 1923 three million Greeks were uprooted from their homes in Anatolia and sent to Greece in exchange for a million uprooted Turks who had been living on the Greek peninsula. Uprooting is more humane than genocide but it is still ethnic cleansing. The Kurds remain as a problem for modern Turkey.

The war in Bosnia can best be understood as nationalism trying to work itself out against the background of the Turkish Millet system. It doesn't make it right. It doesn't excuse the rape, and pillage and killing. But any solution will have to deal with the inheritance of the Millet system. How do you build a modern nation out of a hodge-podge of separate cultural groups living in the same place?

Perspectives on Life (and Death), revised December 6, 1999, recorded February 23, 2000

I was walking along the trail to get the mail and for some reason was thinking about life and death, perhaps because, thankfully, I have already lived longer than most people. Maybe the novel I had just finished had something to do with it for people in France during the Nazi occupation were never far from death. Even under the most severe deprivation, the struggle to stay alive was intense.

I was meditating on several different conceptions of life and death:

The faithful in Christianity, Judaism, and Islam believe that each of us gets a soul which, after proper rituals and blessings, stays with us and survives our physical demise to dwell forever in what must be an increasingly crowded heaven or hell or somewhere in between.

Reincarnation takes a wider view, passing each of us through a variety of physical life forms so that our human existence is but one stage of an almost infinite succession.

I had grown up in an agnostic family with the general scientific view that human life starts with the sperm fertilizing the egg and continues through incubation, birth, youth, maturity, senescence, to death. Finis. Over and done. The end!

These are seemingly irreconcilable belief systems. But there are at least three additional perspectives:

From an ecological perspective each of us humans is but one member of an omnivorous species living in an ecosystem composed of thousands of competing and cooperating species. Each member of each species goes through the cycle of birth, growth, death and decay, returning the nutrients that compose the body to the common organic matter of the soil, a sort of commons from which all life draws its sustenance. Ours is unique in the degree to which we distort the ecosystem, managing other species both for food supply and protection, as well as the fact that we frequently short circuit the normal cycle by cremating instead of decaying the material remains.

We are unique also in the degree to which we change landscapes. Of course ants and termites build mounds. Beavers fell trees and dam streams. However, the disruptive influence of all the other species pales by comparison with the landscape changes we humans bring about. Each of us in our lifetime is responsible, individually or collectively for plowing a field, logging off a forested hillside, paving a highway, building a house or a city, polluting a stream or an ocean. Many of these changes outlast us, leaving our imprint on the landscape.

From a cultural/community point of view each of us grows into a web of interaction and communication that starts as an infant in the family and grows as a child interacts with the neighbors and the classmates and widens into an enormously complex, ever-changing web of friends, mentors, colleagues, customer clients, parishioners, patients, caregivers, students, and correspondents. Some of the strands of the web get lost. New strands are formed. By our behavior and communication each of us influences the others for better or for worse. Death cuts a hole, leaving a gap. It takes some grieving before the web recovers, though memory preserves an image. The other nodes in the web are never the same for they have been changed by the node now disappeared.

While we are still here, we do well to be mindful of our impact on the ecosystem, our modification of the landscape and the messages we send out through the interactive web of personal contact. We probably won't get another chance.

The Fossil Ditch, written December 3, 1999, recorded February 23, 2000

Sand County Almanac, by Aldo Leopold, kick-started the conservation movement and gave us the idea of a land ethic. The first part of the book is twelve essays, one for each month of the year. In the February essay titled "The Good Oak," he has just cut down an oak tree two and a half feet in diameter. He counts the rings, eighty of them and realizes that it sprouted just after the civil war. The rest of the essay reflects on the relation of that tree to the changing ecology and land use for four generations.

I had a similar insight the other afternoon. It was too late to start any major project. The sun had set and I could already feel a hint of the late November nocturnal chill. I shouldered my favorite shovel and hiked down the track to the little dam and reservoir just above the first hay field. I wanted to check on the outlet.

We had built the dam 25 years before, with the help, both technical and financial, of the Department of Agriculture. The pond behind it held the flow from several small springs along the little valley that led down from the farmstead. When we hadn't used the water to irrigate the hay field and the pond was full, a trickle of surplus flowed across the spillway and ran across the hayfield to the intermittent stream known as Lykins Gulch. Over twenty years that trickle had saturated a widening band of soil allowing sedges, reeds and cattails to displace the grasses and alfalfa.

Concerned about the loss of pasture several years ago, I had diverted the overflow into the faint remains of what appeared to be an abandoned ditch that stretched out east along the side hill. Sure enough in the next few months the trickle had made its way two hundred yards across the hill side.

But every summer when the cows are in the pasture they come to drink at that outflow. (The pond itself is fenced off.) In so doing, they trample down my makeshift diversion dam and the outflow goes back across the hayfield. Every fall I rebuild the diversion with muck from the bottom of the side-hill ditch.

That late November afternoon, as I put my shovel back on my shoulder and returned along the old ditch, I was filled with gratitude for that unnamed farmer (and his children) who had had the foresight and persistence to divert the spring water out of the little valley and draw it across the dry hillside at just the right slope to let it soak in rather than erode, to slake the thirst of the pasture grasses. The increased forage was more important to them than it is to me, but I could put their investment to work for me with comparatively little effort.

I was reminded how, in all our accomplishments, we are only marginally adding to the accomplishments of others, some of whom are still with us, but others long forgotten.

Palestine, recorded November 27, 2000

A few weeks ago as the most recent stage of the intifada was under way, an acquaintance commented to me, "It is really getting nasty over there." I paused for a moment before I responded, "It has been nasty over there for a long time." That was not a very good way to start a dialogue. In fact it stopped the conversation.

Maybe this commentary will allow me to open it up.

My unconsidered response was a function of fifty years of familiarity with the Israeli/Palestinian conflict and sixty years of one-sided reporting and interpretation by the U. S. media. Like many of my generation I grew up admiring the young American Zionists who gave up their privileged middle class status to work and live in the kibbutz, the experimental agricultural collectives in the then British "mandate." Their ideal included living peacefully in an Arab land. But in the two generations since, those pioneers are a tiny minority of Israeli citizens. Many of the more recent immigrants are embittered by their earlier violent persecution. Many are profoundly distrustful of their Arab, mostly Muslim, neighbors. Many are religious fundamentalists who believe that their God, Jehovah, "gave" them this piece of the earth's surface. The younger Israelis have grown up in a culture of fear, of violent terrorism and antagonism against Arabs.

Many of the interpretations we are fed presume that the problem started with the 1947-48 war when Israel declared its statehood, fought off the Arab armies, and conquered much of that narrow strip of the eastern shore of the Mediterranean Sea. The war left hundreds of thousands of refugees living in camps in areas controlled by Lebanon and Jordan, displaced from their homes in what immediately became Israel. No one offered them asylum or resettlement. Israel would not take them back. Arab nations closed their doors. Palestinians refugees became expendable pawns on the geopolitical chessboard.

The struggle for control of what we used to call "The Holy Land" goes back long before 1947, through centuries of persecution of Jews and before the seventh-century Arab conquest of the area and the following Christian crusades, before the time of Jesus at least to the time when the little tribe, the children of Abraham, calling themselves "the chosen people" drove out the then inhabitants of this tiny bit of coastal plain and hills, now claimed as Israel.

During most of the last 2000 years Jews and Christian and then Muslims have lived peacefully side by side. But since 1947 it has indeed been vicious and nasty. The present eruption of Palestinian anger comes out of half a century of living impoverished in refugee camps while much of the rest of the world enjoys prosperity. It also comes out of the exaggerated escalation of Israeli military retaliation. Fifty years of ineffective leadership, of broken promises, of faded dreams has created hopelessness among the Palestinians. Hopelessness leads to suicide, including suicide bombings.

A large minority of Israelis understand the Palestinians' need for hope, for tangible progress toward justice and self-rule. The alternative, the end result of present policies, will be the slaughter of the Palestinians, a genocide like what Hitler did to the fathers and mothers and grandfathers and grandmothers of so many Israelis. The United States will be complicit in this genocide by reason of its financial and military aid.

We killed most of the Native Americans, appropriating their resource base and means of livelihood, with a preponderance of power, with an advanced technology, with repeatedly broken treaties and unconscienceable massacres. Are we going to do it to the Palestinians through our client state, Israel? How many genocides do we want on our conscience?

The United States must change its Mid-East policy. We must stop supporting Israeli military oppression of the Palestinians. Without U.S. support, perhaps cooler heads may prevail.

Discouragement, written May 7, 2001, but not recorded

We live in a hamlet of seven dwellings and some outbuildings that has been run quite cooperatively for almost thirty years. From time to time one gets discouraged at the failure of the cooperative spirit. Or is it the inability to harmonize the differing values and priorities, or is it that contemporary American culture encourages everyone to overfill their discretionary time with individual projects leaving too little for collective and mutual activities, or lack of communication?

Yesterday was a good day. With a little organizing we sprayed the blossoming apple trees with agrimycin to inhibit the spread of fire blight. Paul took advantage of the softened driveway gravel to fill several of the chuckholes. All but one of the lawns got mowed the first Sunday after the rainy spell. I was feeling pretty good about the collectivity that we all have been working at these many years.

Today on my way to the garden I noticed that the chickens were loose as they have been for a couple of days. I stopped at one of the houses to inquire about flagstones and in the course of the conversation, one of the children mentioned that the eggs were not being collected. What was wrong with the chore rotation?

I stopped to chat with the other couple who don't commute to jobs in town and therefore are most conscious of the way things are working. Being here more of the time also means that they get called on to help with the emergencies, both those that are accidents and those that devolve from other's neglect. They pointed out that the mowing of the common areas, one of the rotating chores, had not been done last month. I added that the picnic tables I had arranged for a couple of months ago had not been assembled and would be needed next weekend. We reinforced our sense that others were not doing their share. We reinforced each other's self-pity. I came back, started writing a HOA memo but got interrupted.

By the time I got back to the computer this evening I had talked to all but one of the families. One volunteered to assemble the picnic tables. One had completed the thirty inch mowing. The family taking care of the chickens had agreed to trade chores with the family who could most easily do the chicken chore properly.

On the way back to the house this evening the full moon was an over-size orange just above the eastern horizon. Maybe I should not be so discouraged.

Integrity, March 4, 2002

Again and again I am surprised at my own naiveté. This time it was the Enron scandal. I had bought a few shares 50 years ago when it was called Northern Natural Gas and was a small gas distribution company. It grew and I never paid much attention to it until the price started to decline in 2001.

By fall the truth began to be revealed to the public: a few of the top executives had created partnerships between themselves and the company to siphon off millions of dollars for themselves, leaving the company bankrupt at the expense of employees, stockholders and other investors. What treachery! Deception on an enormous scale! Callous disregard for the well-being of thousands! And now gradually we learn that connivance by dozens of others kept most of us from knowing what was going on. Meanwhile the insiders had made millions selling the soon to be worthless stock. Mr. Fastow, Enron's former chief financial officer, is lucky that lynching has gone out of fashion in Texas.

We naïve ones would never have believed this could happen. What happened to integrity? Where is the loyalty to the firm? To the System? Is it OK for them to be dumping their stock while Mr. Lay is reassuring everyone that everything is hunky dory?

I wonder if integrity has been on the decline for some time. My mentor, 50 years ago, would remind me, "A public office is a public trust." Do we still hear in school, "Be true to yourself and you can be false to no man?"

In small tribal societies norms of behavior are learned by example and enforced by traditional methods and social pressure. Conformity is expected. Little variation is tolerated. In more complex societies like ours the immediate personal constraints have broken down. Much of our behavior is constrained by rules, manners, commandments, standards, regulations and laws. But there is still lots of leeway in how mannerly we are, how literally we follow the commandments, how closely we respect the regulations, how consistently we obey the laws.

In the "good old days" strangers would come to town with the carnival or to the county fair. We naïve ones would be tempted to believe the man selling patent medicine. "Snake oil salesman" was the term for an unethical barker. One soon learned not to trust the man with the three walnut shells challenging us to keep track of where he had obscured the pea. Now the snake oil salesman has graduated to promoting over priced stocks on the New York Stock exchange and the shell game has been taken over by the auditors. Guess in which limited partnership the losses had been hidden! The school yard bully is coaching the little league team. The cheater has graduated to the Olympic organization committee taking bribes for choosing Salt Lake City as the site for the 2002 winter games or is colluding in the judging of the figure skating competition.

In big city politics the ward heeler could buy votes for a dollar or a couple of beers. Now he is a lobbyist for a military contractor buying congressional votes with tens of thousands of dollars.

Should I believe the reports of scientific experiments, even in refereed journals? Do I have to count the pills in every prescription bottle at the pharmacy? How can I trust the label on the ketchup bottle? Who's to know what happens to grandpa's body when we take it to the crematorium?

How do I know that the lettuce I pay extra for is really organic? How can I assure my black and Latino friends that they will get equal treatment from the police, the district attorney and the judge?

Obviously we all depend upon everyone else's integrity and they depend on ours and the more complex society, the more impersonal our relationships, the larger the institutions, the more difficult it is.

Security, January 18, 2003

In spite of all John Ashcroft's assurance, I feel less secure now than I did Sept 12, 2001. He has marshaled his forces and is marching off in the wrong direction. Thanks to Bush, Cheney and Co., the threat of terrorism increases every day. The way he is headed we will be strangling ourselves in so called "security measures" and be more frightened than ever.

Either he doesn't understand the contradictions or he refuses to face the obvious. When people are willing to sacrifice their own lives to make us feel less secure, there is no threat severe enough to stop them. We can scare off 49 of them but the 50th will persist. We can jail 60 suspected terrorists but we will miss the 61st. We can build a fence high enough to isolate 75 of them but the 76th is already among us.

The truth is that:

The more wealth we accumulate while the rest of the world remains poor, the greater the danger.
The more arms we stockpile while the rest of the world remains weak, the more they feel threatened.
The more opulent our lifestyle, the more envy we generate.
The more privilege we insist upon, the more resentful they feel.
The more powerful we become, the greater the incentive to bring us down even if it is only down a peg.

We already know this lesson. It is embedded in our history, our literature. Caesar at the height of his power was brought down by Brutus. An old adage says: "Uneasy sleeps the head that wears the crown." Another says: "It only takes one bad apple to ruin the barrel."

Carried to its illogical extreme, in the process of gaining security by suppressing the threat, one is left with the image of a barren earth with two people left alive: Bush and Ashcroft. Every one else was a potential enemy, and then Bush turns on Ashcroft, or vice versa.

What are the alternatives? What can we suggest in place of a police state?

First we have to make our opposition known. We need to raise our voices at every stage: the encroachment on our civil rights, the oppression of immigrants and aliens, actions against people of color, the silencing of dissent, the corporate control of the media, the increasing power of the military, the senseless rush to war.

Meanwhile we need to show our international good will, our willingness to work in concert with other nations. We must abandon our pose as policeman of the world, pretending to know what is good for everyone else. Then we can begin mutually to solve problems, to find win-win solutions. It will take patience and sacrifice.

We cannot continue to consume so much oil and generate so much carbon dioxide.

We cannot continue to rig the world markets weakening other economies.

We cannot insist on our own sovereignty while violating the sovereignty of others.

In short, we must abandon the arrogance of power.

For security lies neither in our possession nor in theirs.

It lies for ever between us.

Appendix D: Two essays

Nick thought and wrote (writing was his discipline for thinking clearly) about international relations. The first of these essays deals with the proper role of the U.S. armed services in peace-making, and with the role of the U.N. in peace keeping. The second essay is one of many Nick wrote about the Middle East, a region he had visited as a researcher, studied and taught about, and about which he maintained a steadfast loyalty.

International Concerns, February 4, 1993
[Draft essay, as far as I know unpublished, but probably shared]

These thoughts do not reach conclusions. They are designed to stimulate discussion.

American peace activists concerned about United States foreign and military policy are pretty clear about a lot of topics: reducing the military budget, stopping nuclear testing and nuclear proliferation, completing treaties, reducing missiles etc., closing bases overseas, no more military assistance to third world countries, stopping the world arms trade, cleaning up the toxic messes on military and nuclear sites, and no more invasions like Grenada, Panama and Iraq whether or not we have the pretense of UN Security Council endorsement.

But there is a lot of confusion on a couple of topics. One is the use of military personnel on humanitarian missions: feeding the starving in Somalia. Another is increasing use of the "Blue Berets," military personnel loaned by national governments to the UN doing peacekeeping work under UN command. This concern brings up the question of whether the UN should intervene without the invitation of the government of the nation in question.

The Humanitarian Pentagon:

There are lots of hungry people in the world and we feel a moral obligation to help to feed, clothe and house them. But what can we do when "law and order" have broken down, there is no government and armed bands steal the food from the non-governmental organizations (NGO's) trying to feed the hungry?

We don't like to admit it, but when you let a problem go too far, there may be no good solution. When the cowboy's horse broke its leg there was no good solution. He could let it lie there and die slowly or he could shoot it. Our fundamental faith in the goodness of humankind and the power of intelligence and outgoing love to solve social problems makes it very difficult for us to admit that we and the rest of the world have painted the people of Somalia into a corner from which there is no graceful escape. It is a problem without a good solution.

Western governments exacerbated the collapse of Somalia. Italian economic development projects, motivated more by profit and graft than by development, were disruptive of Somali economy and society. Military aid to the dictatorial government put plenty of weapons in the hands of Somali people.

It is helpful when considering an intervention, especially a military one to ask at least the following questions:

> Who is the enemy? Do we really seek justice for all? Military intervention is almost always perceived as favoring "the other side." Can we avoid such a perception?

> Does our action de-escalate the conflict?

> Does our action make maximum use of diplomatic and political dialogue, and conflict resolution? Most soldiers are not trained in conflict resolution.

> Have humanitarian needs been addressed no matter what side the civilians are on?

> When all else fails and we call on the military, will it save civilians from violence and save lives? Will refugees be minimized and their rights protected?

> Will the flow of weapons be stopped? Will war profiteering be stopped?

These questions can be asked as appropriately in Bosnia as in Somalia.

We should remember that international conflicts are justified on at least five different bases:

> Legal
> Moral
> National Interest (usually economic)
> Military security
> Traditional friendship (domestic political influence)

There are some who claim that the US is in Somalia because of the strategic value of the "Horn of Africa" adjacent to the Suez-Red Sea shipping route. Others whisper about oil prospects under the desert. After the illegal interventions in Grenada and Panama the US secured Security Council endorsement to legalize the Gulf and Somali expeditions.

The Militarization of the United Nations:

This aspect of the "new world disorder" derives directly from the collapse of the Soviet Union as a great power, for UN action depends upon action in the Security Council. As long as the USA and the USSR were taking opposite sides, either one could veto a plan of the other. Power plays by the US were justified ·as blocking the spread of communism. Now with Russia playing along with the US (and China lying low) the security Council can authorize the UN to act. In Cambodia and Angola the actions seem to be genuine attempts at peacemaking. In the case of Iraq (and possibly in Somalia) the US was co-opting the Security Council for its own purposes. (The irony of the US spending billions to enforce a Security Council resolution, when it hasn't even kept up its own dues, doesn't get much press here.)

Pacifists in the United States have always looked to the UN as a neutral body in contrast to the imperialist tendencies of the United States, a peacemaking institution. Actually it was set up as a security institution by the victorious allies at the end of WW II. Now suddenly we face the possibility of military action by the UN. Where the UN is only the transparent front for US action, the choice is easy. We disapprove of the US using the UN as a legalistic cover. But in Cambodia if the UN is going to carry out its mission it may have to disarm the Khymer Rouge(sp?). In the former Yugoslavia blue helmeted soldiers have been casualties already though no major campaigns have been launched by the UN.

Purists (absolutists) hold fast to the non-violent principle and argue for other strategies. But even purists recognize that many of our supporters are conflicted, unclear, confused. As long as a few blue helmets can keep the peace and allow dialogue to take place it seems OK. But .....

One perspective is to recognize the levels of government and the increasing transfer of power from the lower smaller levels to the higher, larger levels. With urbanization, rapid transportation and communication, regional specialization, high tech and large corporations, uniformity of regulations across larger territories and populations are efficient for production, trade, and profit. The city police and county sheriff are supplemented by the state Patrol and the state militia (National Guard) and they in turn by Federal Marshalls, the U.S. Secret Service, the FBI, the IMNS, the Coast Guard, the Customs Service, and, if needed, the whole military establishment. They "keep the peace." Along with the courts and the jails, they maintain "law and order."

This perspective asks us if we welcome the UN Blue Berets disarming the Somalis and the death squads in El Salvador, are we ready for them to supervise the trial of the LA policemen for the beating of Rodney King or the removal of price supports on sugar in line with a new General Agreement on Trade and Tariffs (GATT)? Is the extension of world government, complete with its own police force, in the interest of the people or the transnational corporations or both?

A different perspective suggests the training of peacekeepers at all levels: local, state, national, regional and UN, in large enough numbers so that they can intervene effectively, so that some can be stationed in areas of tension (including Bedford-Stuyvesant) and developing injustice, to gather the information needed for effective conflict resolution, to identify and call attention to corruption and violation of the public trust and trammeling of individual rights and to report these to the world. Then preventative diplomacy and conflict resolution might start early enough while the problem is still solvable.

Suddenly we are openly considering intruding on (intervening in) the sovereignty of nation states. "Sovereign-ty" dates from the all-powerful king who controlled both the territory and the "subjects" of the realm. Are we finally ready to say that the rest of the world has an interest in what goes on with the citizens and the territory of that realm? Are we ready to assert that preventative diplomacy, peace making, peace building must be tied to disarmament, sustainable development and environmental protection? Are we finally forced to recognize the world as a single system: physical and biological but also economic and political, and that peacemakers must be pro-active within that system?

Nicholas Helburn

I am grateful for several conversations and for material from the United Nations, the Life and Peace Institute (Upsala), the War Resisters League, The Carter Center of Emory University, the Institute for Policy Studies, the Quaker Office at the UN, the American Friends Service Committee, and the Friends Committee on National Legislation in bringing my thinking this far. NH

A PRIMER ON ISLAM
By Nick Helburn, December, 2001

I was asked to say a few words about Islam, and then I was asked for a copy. Here goes!

The Beginnings

Islam is the last of three major religions that start from the same origins. Each was a reform movement reinvigorating what had become corrupt and rigidly bureaucratic. Just as Christianity recognizes the Old Testament and the Old Testament prophets, so Islam incorporates the Old Testament and all the previous prophets and Jesus as a prophet as well. Mohammed is the next and last. Thus Islam shares with Judaism and Christianity the same Old Testament, the same monotheism, the same angels and devils, the same Heaven and Hell, and the same exclusiveness. It is the true faith.

Mohammad was born around 570 AD into a respected family in Mecca, but his father had already died and his mother died soon after. He was brought up by an uncle and for a while was foster homed in a bedouin family in the desert. He was a reasonably successful business man including participating in the caravan trade to the more populated regions to the north. The Arabian Peninsula at that time worshiped a variety of "pagan" gods represented by idols.

He was already in middle age when he began meditating in a cave outside Mecca. The Angel Gabriel appeared to him but he resisted this as an illusion for some time but finally was impelled to take the vision seriously and took down the word of God (Allah) as dictated by Gabriel. The Koran, then, was dictated in Arabic and must not be translated, giving Arabic a special, holy place among languages and creating a "lingua Franca" among educated Muslims throughout the world.

His wife and a few of his close associates were his first converts. The local power structure in Mecca was threatened by this new sect and the group escaped (the Hegira) to a city to the north renamed Medina (the City [of the prophet]).

The sect grew and prospered in Medina and adjacent areas, but unable to convert Mecca peacefully, they conquered the city by force making it the focus of the religion. Mohammed personally destroyed the idols of the pagans making the enormous black stone (the Kaba) the holiest site of Islam and the focus of the pilgrimage (Hajj). The rest of the Arabian peninsula was soon converted and diffusion moved northward. Political and spiritual authority were one. After his death, Mohammed's successor was called Calif.

Expansion

As the empire grew the capitol moved to Damascus and then to Baghdad. Egypt and all of North Africa were conquered and converted quickly. Known as Moors or Saracens they crossed the Straits of Gibraltar and quickly conquered the Iberian peninsula and most of what is now France. Later a separate Caliphate was established in what is now Spain, quite separate from the one in Baghdad. They were not driven out of that part of Europe until the middle of the 15th century.

Persia, occupying the Iranian plateau, was also converted early and the expansion proceeded both east and north into the Mongol area (now Turkmenistan, Uzbekistan, etc. and southern Russia) and on to Mongolia and western China; as well as east and south into what is now Afghanistan, Pakistan, India, Bangladesh, Malaysia and Indonesia, even to Mindinao, the southernmost island of the Philippines. Islam spread southward along the east coast of Africa to Tanzania and all the way across the Sahara desert to the Atlantic.

The spread north and west was delayed by the powerful presence of the Eastern Orthodox branch of Christianity, the Byzantine empire, with headquarters in Constantinople. Only after the invasion of Turks from Central Asia in the 11th century was Anatolia (Asia Minor) gradually converted. The Ottoman dynasty expanded its rule into the Balkans as well as into the Arab lands. Finally in 1450 Constantinople fell. The Turkish Sultan was the most powerful ruler in the western world. He had assumed the title of Calif. He was the spiritual ruler of all of Islam and the civil emperor over most (much?) of it.

Political units have appeared and disappeared, grown and shrunk. The Caliphate disappeared with the Allies' capture of Istanbul in 1919. There is no longer an Islamic Empire. But there remain Muslim majorities or minorities from China's Manchuria to Africa's Ivory Coast, from the Philippines to Algeria from Tanzania to Kosovo.

The Five Pillars

For the ordinary Muslim, Islam is a fairly simple religion requiring five behaviors.

Submission: "There is but one God and Allah is his name and Mohammed is his prophet." This is all you need to say to become a Muslim. In Arabic the word Islam means submission and Muslim one who submits. Pagans conquered by Muslims need only to say this phrase to be spared from execution. Christians and Jews, as "people, of the book" were not to be killed. (They were converted, over time, by taxation.)

Prayer: One should pray 5 times a day facing toward Mecca. Both the words and the body positions are prescribed. Friday noon prayers are especially important and if possible should be performed with others in the Mosque. Hands and feet should be washed before prayer. (The Prophet felt that cleanliness was important and specified that the faithful should be provided with a source of pure water.)

Alms: One should give alms to the poor. At times the amounts have been specified.

Fasting: For the month of Ramadan one must not eat or drink between sunrise and sunset. In Turkey at least the day after Ramadan is a major holiday with feasting and gifts for children.

Pilgrimage: At least once in a lifetime one should make the pilgrimage (Hajj) to Mecca. There is almost a week of ritualized worship there. After one has done it he (she?) has the title Haji.

There are, of course, many other aspects of Islam, but these five behaviors are the core. Abstract theology seems less important than in Christianity. Many traditions derive not from the Koran but from the sayings and behaviors of the Prophet and the first four caliphs: the hadiths and the shariya as interpreted by religious scholars over the centuries. Ali, a cousin of Mohammed, is considered by a large sect, the Shi' a, to be a very special caliph causing a schism between the Shiites and the "orthodox" Sunni.

A variety of customs have been tied in from time to time and from place to place, e.g. fez, turban, etc. The veil and complete covering of the female body is said to have come from India via Persia. Sufi mysticism seems to have come from central Asia. It has become an important element, at least in some areas. The Sufi orders were very powerful in Turkey. When Ataturk modernized Turkey he outlawed them as best he could though some continue to practice illegally and in secret.

People's Names

It is easy to get confused by the terminology used to identify people (and places) in the Middle East: the language they speak, the religion in which they worship, and their nationality or citizenship. An Arab literally is a person who speaks Arabic as her/his mother tongue. She/he may be a citizen of Saudi Arabia, Lebanon, Syria, Yemen, Egypt, or any of several other countries. Most Arabs worship in Islam and are therefore Muslims. Lebanon is mostly populated by Muslim Arabs but it has a large minority of Christian Arabs and a smaller minority worshiping in a religion called Druze. Israel's official language is Hebrew and most of the population worships in the Jewish religion but there is a large minority of Arabic speaking Muslims who are Israeli citizens as well as plenty of Hebrew speaking agnostics.

Iran's population is overwhelmingly Muslim, speaking Farsi, sometimes called Persian. Turkey's population is overwhelmingly Muslim speaking the Turkish language but with a significant minority of Kurdish speaking Muslims and much smaller minorities of Christians speaking Greek and Armenian. Confusing isn't it! Historical changes add another dimension: What is now known as Iran used to be called Persia and the Persian Empire included from time to time territory as far west as what is now Greece and as far east as Pakistan and India. Some of the terms refer to a dynasty: the Ottoman Turks as against the earlier Seljuk Turks. Saudi is such a term.

Of particular importance in the last few of decades has been the growth of fundamentalism, especially Wahhabism. It started in Saudi Arabia, in part at least, as a reaction against the failure of the Saudi royalty to follow the precepts of Islam. It is strongly against modernism and thus against the kind of economy and lifestyles of the middle class and royalty.

In several countries there has been some kind of modus vivendi between the dictatorial civil authorities and the religious clerics (mullahs). It is understood that the mullahs can have control of the mosques and the education and will not mess in politics; that the royal family will have control of the legal system and will not mess with the education of the masses. Civil government allowed the royalty and the upper class to accumulate enormous wealth while the mass of the population stayed poor. The mullahs limited mass education to the bare minimum.

This system worked reasonably well until the demands of a modern economy and polity required changes in daily life that were inimical to the traditional interpretation of the Koran. At the beginning of the 21st century there seems to be an impasse:

> The mullahs resist any reduction in their control of education and threaten civil unrest if the royalty try to change the system
>
> The royalty feels their position is precarious and don't dare to anger the mullahs.

Wahhabism teaches an extreme fundamentalist version of the Koran, the shariya and the hadiths preventing the upper class and the royalty from developing a modern political economy. The Wahhabi will be happy to see the royalty replaced by a theocracy. Similar but not identical tensions exist in Algeria, Egypt, Iran and Pakistan.

Appendix E: Poetry

Of course, Nick was a romantic and an idealist and the great love of my life. Here are some of his poems about the things and people he loved.

"The Earth is Small, " *Lykins Gulch News*, #2 Undated
First presented to a conference on conservation in 1948

We are gathered here, not by chance nor for profit nor by any external compulsion, but by internal forces: knowledge, concerns, beliefs, ideals.
>We know the earth is small
>And the living, fruitful soil but a thin film
>Of weathered rock, decaying humus, uncounted microorganisms, tiny living beings
>A film so thin we've seen it disappear in places,
>So thin that we can walk for miles on dead rock:
>The barren warp and woof from which the spongy nap eroded.
>And yet we know in nature's plan
>No rock showed through save on the mountain top and desert cliff.
>For through unending seasons the water weathered stone,
>The lichen held the tiniest crevice
>Till moss and forb, sedge and grass, shrub and tree
>Succeeding one another patiently
>Built soil and shade and windbreak and water porousness,
>Until there was no ray of sunlight wasted
>Or till water was completely used,
>Till raindrops spent their force on leaves and needles, not upon the soil.
>And animals were sheltered by this growth.
>They fed upon this verdure and themselves,
>Links in an unending chain,
>Rather in a thousand criss-cross chains.
>These things we know.
>We feel the wilderness.
>We suffer the dissonance of maladjusted use.
>We hate the prospect of a half-fed, half-sick people.

We here resolve to stop the waste, to harmonize the dissonance, and where we can, to replace regulation and control with knowledge and belief.

Front Range

Still sweating from the climb
I sat on the tilted outcrop.
In back was mist
And wind and wilderness.

In front the city
A hundred thousand people on the plain
Burning their lights—like candles
For the great God Civilization
A trinity of Order and Reason and Property.

And I a part of both.

Unnamed Poem
October 6, 1975

I wonder at the silence of our meeting, fragile and profound, and wonder
too, how many
　　　other silences.
How different ours from that awkward pause that follows something
gauche:
　　　"I didn't know what to say."
How different from the moment of wondrous awe: "I was speechless."
Different too from the way we use a few moments of silence:
　　　to be grateful
　　　to gather our thoughts
　　　to sense the warmth of love
　　　to rededicate ourselves to noble purpose.
There is a hush in the library, the silence of serious study.
And there are silences of aloneness, both in solitude and in loneliness,
　　　In solo ventures and in solitary confinement.
But all of these are quite distinct from our collective quiet.
　　　Our centering down, so we can hear that still small voice within.

Dusk
August 18th, 1999

It's middle dusk returning westward from the garden.
A last pink cloud is all that's left of the once imperious sun.
The quarter moon will soon dominate the still bright sky.
It's almost cool enough to button up my shirt.

I've almost done my work.
The garden soil is moist,
The newly sprouted lettuce refreshed,
Raspberries still drizzled by the soaker.

Suzie's wrestling with her manuscript
Dawn's just breaking in Tasmania
Lights are flicking out in Queens
And all of you asleep in Europe.

While Western Anatolia weeps in the rubble.

Nick's poem to Suzie
Late June, 1969
[A harebell was enclosed with the poem.]

The solstice with its longest day,
    Its highest sun just passed.

Most forest flowers now have
    Spent their time

Geraniums are wilted and the
    Last surviving daisies look forlorn.

Only the hare bell on its
    Fragile stem decorates the forest floor.

Miraculously, it lasts all summer.
    May I be the forest in which
    Your flowering endures?

Our Wedding Invitation
August 1969

When we join hands
The sacred flame burns a little brighter,
The self-same flame
That lights the re-creation of the race,
That radiates the brotherhood of man.
Join us friends in nourishing the sacred flame.

*   *   *

Mobius Valentine to Suzie

I love you so I hope you love me
Because
I'm all mixed up because my heart
Is all mixed up with yours, so
I want you to be my valentine
Cause I love you and I therefore

Dear Suzie

How to put in words the love I have for you?
I know at times it doesn't show except in purr or mew (wow wow wow)

There are times I think you'd be better off with someone else than me.
You could be gallivanting with a romantic devotee
There are lots of courtly scholars decorated with a goatee.
But as long as you can stand it
Let me play my flute for you
Let us cuddle in the redding dawn
Garden in the early light
Nap together in midsummer heat
Let us fix each other's lunch to take
And sometimes bake a birthday cake
Wherever contradictions, we can find the rising side.
From real tigers we'll learn how to make a paper hide.
And as we plod that zig-zag line
Let me be your Valentine.

About Peg: In Celebration
Summer 1991

With apologies to Grandpa Frank B. Mason
    Who could have done it much more gracefully

Coming fourth after three
    Is not the easiest place to be
As daughter Deborah will affirm
    The boys would often make her squirm

Shady Hill and Buckingham
    Prepared the girl for Radcliffe, so
A summer school, perhaps a scam,
    To spend six weeks in Boulder, CO

Acknowledgements

Finishing Nick's memoir has helped me tremendously—to learn about, remember, and revere this man who has added so much to my life. It's been a mainly solitary journey through Nick's files, my thoughts and feelings, our family photos. However, I also had wonderful help from people I would like to thank. Joan Block initially talked Nick into working on his memoirs, so I thank her for that push. Liz McCutcheon of As Told To helped Nick continue this work in early 2010 and after his accident in 2010-11. Thanks Liz for patiently guiding him to record thoughts about his later life, as well as for your advice, editing, and proofing the manuscript. Bonnie Mettler designed the book and took responsibility for printing. Thank you for your patience and good taste. My daughter, Sherry Wiggins, helped me find and choose family photos to include. Thanks for making the process of selection fun and poignant. My grandson, Joseph Logan, is responsible for the beautiful cover design. Thanks Joseph. Barbara Shark painted the portrait of Nick that appears on the cover. It's been in our living room for ten years and a constant reminder of Nick's vigor and charm in his later years. Thanks Barbara. I also want to thank the following people for permission to use their photographs: Roger Easton, who designed the Tall Timbers house, John Brittingham, Professor of Architecture at Montana State University, for his photos of the Neutra house, and Don Roper for the last photo of Nick and me taken on Don's cell phone two days before Nick died. Finally, Taylor and Francis gave us permission to reproduce Nick's "Wildness Continuum" from *The Professional Geographer*.

June 9, 2011
Goodbye, Nick

Implicit expectations were to steer
    Some odd, adventurous career
Like bouncing eggs to then reward
    An accident reducing (dash)board

Or towing targets to be shot
    By student marksmen, not so hot
Or ferrying east the many planes
    Ready to cross Atlantic lanes

There was a New York stay as well
    (was this heaven or was it hell?)
A year or more with drama filled
    Working for Terry and the Guild

She married now and soon bore
    To Eric children four:
Eric, Terry, Chris and Deborah
    All of these and then no moah!

The state Department moved them 'round
    To Europe, Asia and middle ground
Where she managed ambiguously
    Child rearing and diplomacy

In the first break from peripatetics
    She went to school and learned phonetics
A thesis dealing with black English
    Helped the master's degree to finish

In Douglaston they came to rest
    A gracious mansion was the nest
From which the nestlings, one by one,
    Flew off to school and work and fun.

While she began a new career
    Writing, organizing without fear
To clean the water, and void the trash
    That not so easily turns to ash
An ash that in itself is toxic
    But what to do? You can't just box it.

At Little Neck with less pollution
    Quite early on a summer day
You'll note a minor wet commotion
    She'll be swimming in the bay.